AMERICA'S RANKING AMONG NATIONS

A GLOBAL PERSPECTIVE BY THE NUMBERS IN 2024

MICHAEL D. DULBERGER

Bernan Press

Lanham • Boulder • New York • London

Published by Bernan Press
An imprint of The Rowman & Littlefield Publishing Group, Inc.
4501 Forbes Boulevard, Suite 200, Lanham, Maryland 20706
www.rowman.com

86-90 Paul Street, London EC2A 4NE

British Library Cataloguing in Publication Information available

Library of Congress Cataloging-in-Publication Data available

ISBN 979-8-89205-002-9 (cloth) | ISBN 979-8-89205-003-6 (ebook)

♾™ The paper used in this publication meets the minimum requirements of American National Standard for Information Sciences—Permanence of Paper for Printed Library Materials, ANSI/NISO Z39.48-1992.

Contents

Introduction

In 1960, the U.S. comprised 39 percent of the world's Gross Domestic Product (GDP) compared with 25 percent today and the share lost has been largely replaced by China. Despite this, the economy in the United States continues to be dominant in the world, equal in size to the combined GDP of 177 of the 193 nations that make up the entire world.

Is America's standing as the leader of the free world destined to decline? Has it already begun? It should be easy to know the answers with all the information systems technology that surrounds our daily lives, providing access to information instantaneously with a mouse click or just ask Siri. However, as we have witnessed in the aftermath of the 2020 presidential election and during the COVID-19 pandemic, facts are disputed and are not readily identifiable. What we really mean by facts are truth, and truth derives from sources you trust to be objective. The sources you trust may not be the ones I trust. There is no referee! The media we access including Fox News, Instagram, the *New York Times* . . . are not sources but delivery services. Be careful! Virtually every parcel of information we receive has been filtered by necessity to fit within the columns designated or the time slot allotted. In reality filtering often involves selective omissions of information to better conform to the beliefs of the messenger, whether done intentionally or not. Even more insidious is the deliberate fabrication of disinformation which usually builds upon a kernel of truth allowing the perpetrator to assert proof. The Declaration of Independence uses the phrase*: "We hold these truths to be self-evident"* but who agrees today what is self-evident?

This book endeavors to present the evidence to help you answer these questions and provides insight into America's standing in the world by comparing granular data for the world's nations, compiled by *apolitical* resources, i.e., data collected by government workers that each nation employs to maintain records of births, deaths, taxes, poverty, diseases, exports, etc. . . While skeptics might claim that in some countries the political leaders might "cook the books," and although this might be possible to do for some metrics in some countries it is unlikely that a conspiracy exists among enough countries to significantly distort the overall outcome.

If you are willing to go data mining and bypass distilled results there exists huge caches of information available to virtually anyone with internet access and a computer. Thanks to organizations including the World Bank, World Health Organization, U.S. Census Bureau, and many others, you can readily download their databases providing metrics on most subjects of importance. In other words, these resources do not draw conclusions so you are left to evaluate what you see and formulate your own opinions.

This book spares you the effort of data mining and is the result of compiling, collating, and curating hundreds of datasets that measure attributes of the world's 193 sovereign nations and displays them in graphic format to provide a visual perspective, thereby enabling similarities and differences among nations to become apparent. Comparisons are made not only for the easily identifiable metrics but also for those attributes that are not readily quantifiable.

For example, how do you measure a country's respect for international law? To best answer this we can turn to the United Nations since preserving respect for law has been a fundamental U.N. principle. The preamble to the U.N. charter states that one of its aims is *to establish conditions under which justice and respect for the obligations arising from treaties and other sources of international law can be maintained.*" To that end on February 23, 2023, the eve of the one-year anniversary of Russia's invasion of Ukraine, the U.N. asked members to vote "In Favor" of, or "Against" a resolution requiring Russia to withdraw its forces from Ukraine. The record of that vote provides a litmus test of how each nation considered aggression towards another sovereign nation. Of the 180 nations present for the vote, 141 voted "In Favor" of withdrawal, seven "Against" (including Russia, *of course*), and 32 abstained. Voting "Against" withdrawal or abstaining is indicative of that nation's acceptance of Russia's aggression.

Another important attribute not readily quantifiable is the degree to which the population of a country is "Free." Fortunately, there exists an organization that has been dedicated to assessing freedom throughout the world for the past 82 years. Freedom House is the oldest American organization devoted to the support and defense of democracy around the world. It was formally established in New York in 1941, to promote American involvement in World War II and the fight against fascism. This organization has created a system for "measuring" the degree to which a nation's population has political rights and enjoys civil liberties. The freedom assessment system they created awards a country zero-to-four points for each of ten political rights indicators and 15 civil liberties indicators, which take the form of questions. They aggregate these points and classify nations as "Free," "Partly Free," or "Not Free." The detailed assessment of each nation, including an explanation for how the score was derived, is posted on their website. Nations with a classification other than "Free" are most likely indicative of undemocratic or authoritarian governments.

Finally, and perhaps the most difficult attribute of all to quantify is leadership. We can measure GDP, life expectancy, and nuclear warheads, but the intangibles of leadership and culture among 193 nations is more about influence and a nation's ideals and principles than direct control. These qualities are elusive and difficult to compare. They are what Joseph S. Nye, Jr. referred to as soft power, in his 2005 book: "*Soft Power, The Means to Success in World Politics.*" Soft power lies in the ability to attract and persuade based on the appeal of a nation's culture, political ideals, and policies. Whereas hard power—the ability to coerce—grows out of a country's military or economic might. An important measure of soft power may be the alliances created and their durability.

Since the pinnacle of America's world leadership at the end of World War II, its primary leadership asset today may actually be its proven ability to create long-term durable partnerships with nations that share similar values, who themselves are world-recognized economic and societal leaders.

There are eight nations that exemplify the quality and durability of U.S. relationships. Each of these U.S. partners are among the world's 13 largest economies. In addition to the U.S. they have the highest level of national income per capita of these 13 and therefore can be considered the wealthiest nations on the planet. Each partner shares American principles as evidenced by their U.N. vote for Russia to withdraw from Ukraine and they are all rated "Free" by Freedom House. They have had in place defense treaties with the U.S. for over 60 years and are uniquely qualified to be America's *principal* partners. (*The remaining four of the 13 largest economies are the "BRIC" nations: Brazil, Russia, India, and China—see appendix IX, page 328.*)

Four of these partners—Canada, France, Italy, and the United Kingdom (U.K.)—have been members of the North Atlantic Treaty Organization (NATO) since its founding in 1949; a fifth, Germany joined NATO in 1955. NATO is the cornerstone of America's defensive strength and has expanded from its founding 12 members in 1949, to 32 members in March 2024. This expansion is a significant indicator that America's influence in the world is actually growing. Every nation must choose which nations to align with and as president George W. Bush famously declared following the 9/11 terrorist attacks: "*You are either with us or against us.*" After Russia's invasion of Ukraine the neutral nations, Finland and Sweden, applied for NATO membership. They realized that their best deterrence against Russian aggression was to pick a side.

The remaining three principal U.S. partners are outside the geographic area of responsibility of NATO so in its place each one has a bilateral security agreement with the U.S. They are Australia (since 1951), South Korea (since 1953), and Japan (since 1960).

After more than six decades these eight principal U.S. partners (Australia, Canada, France, Germany, Italy, Japan, South Korea, and the U.K.) continue to be America's staunchest allies and perhaps are the best indicators of the durability of America's leadership in the world. Their combined population of 520 million people account for almost one-fourth of the world's GDP, and when combined with the U.S. control almost half (48 percent) of the world's economy.

Although American leadership status is evidenced by these strong partnerships it remains to actually measure elements of that leadership at the detailed level to compare against recognizable benchmarks and these eight principal U.S. partners—individually and collectively— serve that purpose well. As democracies with advanced economies they have many American values in common. They are used throughout this book for evaluating America's strengths and democratic attributes.

In addition to comparisons with these eight principal U.S. partners and to provide a truly global perspective we also need to compare metrics against other nations as well. Simply aligning any metric in size order for 193 nations, even graphically, becomes unwieldy and in many cases unnecessary if our intent is to focus on the U.S. Instead, for many metrics it is more meaningful to juxtapose the U.S. with the collective memberships of just two organizations.

The first is perhaps the most recognizable organization in the world besides the U.N. The *Group of 20* (G20) includes 19 of the most politically powerful nations plus the European Union (E.U.) In addition to the U.S. and the eight principal U.S. partners, G20 members include India and China with the largest populations in the world and three members with the majority of their population living below poverty level (India, Indonesia, and South Africa). Members include democracies and autocracies; some are U.S. allies and others adversaries. While the G20 provides an excellent cross-section of the planet, comprising 62 percent of the world's population and 85 percent of its economy, it is so diverse it does not provide a very high benchmark for judging the U.S. (*In September 2023, the G20 transformed into the G21 when the African Union (A.U.) joined as a permanent member. The A.U. consists of the 55 member states that make up the nations of the African continent. The G21 accounts for 80 percent of the world's population.*)

The second major organization is the *Organization for Economic Cooperation and Development* (OECD) which has a large concentration of the wealthiest nations. There are 38 members, many of which have modern, advanced economies with highly educated populations. Members include the U.S. and all eight principal U.S. partners. Collectively OECD members comprise 60 percent of the world's GDP, export 60 percent of the world's goods and services, and are home to 17 percent of the world's population. Although the OECD membership includes many of the world's highest income per capita populations the actual size of the economies for some members is relatively small. For example, the combined GDP of Iceland, Luxembourg, and Estonia is less than 1/100th the size of the U.S. economy and although most members have democratic forms of government several lean heavily towards authoritarianism, such as Turkiye and Hungary.

For hundreds of metrics throughout this book you will see the U.S. compared with the G20, OECD, and the eight principal U.S. partners—depending on data availability or relevancy for each metric, and in some instances the world's average is also included.

All metrics in this book are works in process and of course do not portend the future. For example, in 2005, the U.S. depended on imported energy for about one-third of its energy needs, while today the U.S. is technically energy independent. Most would not have predicted such a turn-around. This book illustrates many U.S. shortcomings and may appear to show a nation rife with inefficiency and wantonness, however, the data also show many U.S. strengths and a nation teeming with innovation and munificence.

Here are some examples of what you will learn. Compared with the eight principal U.S. partners the U.S. spends:

- 2.5 times as much per capita on healthcare
- 2.2 times as much per capita on education

In spite of these excess expenditures, the U.S. has a much lower life expectancy of any. It seems incredulous that U.S life expectancy is so much lower. Specifically, life expectancy for male babies born in the U.S. today is lower by:

- 8.3 years than those born in Japan
- 8.1 years than in Australia
- 7.4 years than in Canada, Italy, or South Korea
- 6.1 years than in France
- 5.5 years than in the U.K.
- 5.3 years than in Germany

Female babies born in the U.S. have a similarly reduced life expectancy compared with any of these countries—6.0 years less on average. Life is the most precious human treasure and the average American baby loses up to 11 percent of its potential lifespan on the day of birth.

Compared with these same eight nations the U.S. has:

- the highest infant mortality rate
- the highest under-age-five mortality rate
- the highest maternal mortality rate
- the highest road injury death rate
- the highest total population mortality rate for "all causes"
- the lowest math test scores for 15-year-old students
- the highest income inequality rate

Also, despite all its wealth the U.S. has:

- over 37.9 million people living below the U.S. defined poverty income level
- the world's highest drug overdose rate that killed 106,000 Americans in 2021
- a 36 percent adult obesity rate—higher than any G20 or OECD nation
- a homicide rate six times higher than the E.U.'s
- the largest incarcerated population in the world
- the largest balance of payment trade deficit of any nation

The U.S. helped create a lifesaving vaccine against COVID-19 and distributed it in record time only to have conspiracy theories thwart its use resulting in many thousands of needless deaths. In hindsight we observe the strong inverse correlation that shows the highest death rates occurred in states with the lowest vaccination rates (page 85). Not surprisingly the overall COVID-19 fatality rate in the U.S. was higher than for any G20 nation and ranked 17th in the world. Americans are literally killing themselves!

Nonetheless, America is also a nation of contradictions. While The U.S. economy is often cited as the largest in the world this is correct only when measured by U.S. dollar exchange rates. China's economy is actually 18 percent larger than that of the U.S. measured by international dollars which are based on purchasing power.

Despite many shortcomings the U.S. is the number one destination for international college students and its population has the highest percentage with doctorate degrees of any nation; more patent and trademark applications were filed in the U.S. by nonresidents than with any other nation; the U.S. produces more oil and natural gas, imports more goods and services, and its air transport flies more passengers and freight, than any other nation.

The U.S. grants citizenship by place of birth whereas the principal U.S. partners—except Canada—require that at least one parent be a citizen. In 2022, the U.S. had the largest influx of immigrants—except for Germany—but was host to only 1 percent of the world's 35 million refugees. (Refugees as defined by the U.N. are people who have fled war, violence, conflict or persecution, and have crossed an international border to find safety in another country. In contrast immigrants are people living in a country other than that of one's birth, often doing so to improve their quality of life.)

Between 2003 and 2023, the U.S. funded over $100 billion for global HIV/AIDS treatment and prevention saving an estimated 20 million lives, predominately in Africa. In 2021, the U.S. distributed approximately $50 billion in aid to about three-fourths of the world's nations and then in 2023, paid out $720 billion in interest on federal debt—an amount equivalent to 88 percent of the entire U.S. defense budget.

The U.S. does not raise sufficient revenues to cover expenditures so continues to borrow additional trillions of dollars per year adding to its existing $34 trillion debt, of which 26 percent is held by foreigners—including adversaries. This debt spiral may be unsustainable. U.S. federal debt has now reached a debt-to-GDP ratio of 120 percent, a level not seen since World War II, and that ratio is the sixth largest of any nation in the world. Despite this the U.S. dollar exchange rate index grew in strength by 34 percent between 2008 and 2022.

The most serious issue facing America, however, is the rapid erosion of democracy at home. The U.S.—proudly called *"the land of the free"* by Americans—was rated in 62nd place out of a total of 82 "Free" nations in the world by Freedom House which cites: "*…the rising political polarization and extremism, partisan pressure on the electoral process, bias and dysfunction in the criminal justice system, harmful policies on immigration and asylum seekers, and growing disparities in wealth, economic opportunity, and political influence.*"

Also, the World Bank published national ratings for *"Political Stability and Absence of Violence/Terrorism"* that placed the U.S. below each of the eight principal U.S. partners.

These poor ratings should not be surprising in view of the serious breaches of law and order which have developed surrounding Donald Trump's relentless attempts to overturn the 2020 election. Donald Trump has been able to persuade or coerce many leaders of the Republican party and their supporting media to join his chants falsely asserting that the 2020 presidential election was stolen. Consequently, millions of Americans have embraced these claims and now share in the distrust of the electoral process and American justice system. These views persist despite the fact that none of the stolen election assertions are supported by evidence which is why they failed in more than 60 court cases, and were disproven by multiple ballot recounts across multiple states.

Donald Trump continually spews his disdain for virtually every major pillar of democracy including the electoral process, the judicial system, and the constitution itself. He claimed that not only is the federal government corrupt but also the state governments of the seven states where he lost the election by small margins, including those with Republican governors and Republican controlled legislatures. He has denigrated the institutions of government using a disinformation campaign that would have alarmed George Orwell. Rhetoric turned to action when Trump's supporters attempted to replace the legitimate electoral votes with fake ones in multiple states in order to overturn the election results. Then on January 6, 2021, the vitriol erupted into a violent assault on the U.S. capital. These events have cast a permanent, ugly stain on the fabric of American democracy.

These false assertions are a travesty of free speech and cast an ominous pall looming over the next presidential election in 2024. This highly charged and polarized environment poses an unprecedented stress test for American democracy.

This book provides a factual foundation allowing readers to formulate educated opinions on critical issues. Anyone who wants to hone his/her knowledge of world affairs will benefit.

I welcome your comments. Email me at: RankingAmerica@yahoo.com

Mike Dulberger

Chapter 1

The Organized Planet

Overview of The Organized Planet

All land on our planet is claimed to belong to one or more states. As of March 2024 there were 193 subdivisions of planet earth that were considered sovereign nations, meaning in accordance with international law they have a permanent population, with a defined territory, a government not under another, and the capacity to interact with other sovereign states. All members of the U.N. are sovereign and therefore nations that are not members are either not independent, e.g., *Puerto Rico is a U.S. territory,* or their independence is disputed, *e.g., China does not agree that Taiwan is sovereign.* The data presented in this book refer to the 193 U.N. member nations as described in this chapter and as listed in appendix I (*page 307*).

Seven nations with the largest surface area, including the U.S., comprise 49 percent of the earth's land area. Russia has the world's largest land area and the most natural gas reserves while the U.S. has the largest amount of arable land and most coal reserves. Of course, there exists huge disparities in the distribution of resources and wealth among nations. However, by joining with other nations through organizations and treaties the voices of all nations can be heard and their economies and military defenses can be enhanced.

In addition to the United Nations' world forum there are two international organizations that have become quasi-permanent structures in the geopolitical world order and their members provide convenient yardsticks for evaluating the U.S.

These organizations are the *Group of 20* (G20) and the *Organization for Economic Cooperation and Development* (OECD). In 2021, G20 members accounted for 85 percent of global GDP while the 38 OECD members accounted for 60 percent. The G20 and OECD both provide forums to facilitate discussions on matters that impact many members, including macroeconomic issues, trade, sustainable development, health, agriculture, energy, environment, climate change, and anti-corruption.

In September 2023, the G20 turned into the G21 when the African Union (A.U.) became a permanent member which marked the first expansion of the group since its formation as a group of 20 major economies in 1999. The A.U. is a continental body consisting of the 55 member states that make up the nations of the African continent. The combined population of the G21 membership accounts for approximately 80 percent of the world's population.

Comparing the characteristics and well-being of 193 diverse societies can highlight weaknesses and successes, with the potential to lead nations to adopting best practices. Unfortunately, these comparisons are not universally shared and strict control of information by authoritarian governments deny their populations the benefits that could be derived by learning from others. Government is responsible for creating and enforcing the rules of a society, including its defense, foreign affairs, economy, and public services. However, the manner in which these functions are implemented varies greatly over a wide spectrum of forms of government, from representative democracies to autocracies.

Freedom House is the oldest American organization devoted to the support and defense of democracy around the world and has created a system for measuring the degree to which each nation practices freedom in their society. Freedom House classified the U.S. as a "Free" society, however, in 2023, the level of U.S. freedom ranked in 62nd place out of 82 "Free" nations based on assessing America's shortcomings, including: *"partisan pressure on the electoral process, bias and dysfunction in the criminal justice system, harmful policies on immigration and asylum seekers, and growing disparities in wealth, economic opportunity, and political influence."* Only 42 percent of the world's nations are classified as "Free," with Norway, Finland, and other Nordic nations being among the most free while North Korea, South Sudan, and Syria the least.

There are 11 nations that are members of both the G20 and OECD of which nine are classified as "Free"; Turkiye is classified as "Not Free"; and Mexico is classified as "Partly Free."

The remaining nine "Free" nations are the U.S. plus eight principal U.S. partners: Australia, Canada, France, Germany, Italy, Japan, South Korea, and the United Kingdom (U.K.).

These "Free" democratic nations all have advanced economies and share mutual defense objectives with the U.S. either with North Atlantic Treaty Organization (NATO) membership or through bilateral defense treaties. They have the highest gross national income per capita of the G20 nations with an average GDP per capita of $45,000 which is 4.6 times the average for the remaining G20 nations.

One of the oldest and largest U.S.-led defense groups is NATO, a multilateral organization with 32 members—including Sweden who joined in March 2024—whose primary purpose is to deter and defend against aggression. The U.S. is also party to hundreds of multilateral and bilateral treaties—including defense treaties—as listed in the "Treaties in Force," a document maintained by the U.S. Department of State.

Three of the eight "Free" principal U.S. partners are not members of NATO since they are outside of NATO's geographic purview. For those three, Australia, Japan, and South Korea, the U.S. has entered into separate bilateral defense agreements.

Together with the U.S. these nine nations are principal partners in both commerce and defense. In 2021, their combined GDP accounted for 48 percent of the world's GDP. They are leading trading partners and collectively accounted for 37 percent of the world's trade in goods and services. They all have economies is excess of a trillion dollars and hold the top nine spots among G20 nations measured as gross national income per capita. These principal U.S. partners all supported the U.S. war efforts in Afghanistan and Iraq and have usually been supportive of the U.S. positions at the U.N. General Assembly.

Although the majority of the world has respected the sovereignty of the U.N. member nations some have chosen to challenge the status quo as Russia did by its unprovoked invasion of Ukraine in 2022. Although the U.N. majority has condemned that invasion, the U.N. was powerless to stop it when put to a vote on February 23, 2023. Although 141 nations voted "In Favor" of the resolution that Russia withdraw—including all 38 members of the OECD and all 30 members of NATO—Russia and six others voted "Against," and 32 abstained including three G20 members, India, China, and South Africa. Russia is one of five permanent members of the U.N. Security Council with veto power over resolutions, causing the vote to fail.

All seven nations who voted "Against" the resolution had been classified "Not Free" by Freedom House and of 82 nations classified as "Free" all except for three (Mongolia, Namibia, and South Africa) voted "In Favor" of withdrawal. This U.N. vote appears to have shown that repressive governments find Russia's invasion acceptable, whereas democracies do not.

~

The United Nations

The United Nations (U.N.) is an international organization founded in 1945, made up of 193 sovereign states. The U.N. provides the one place where all the world's nations can gather together, discuss common problems, and (hopefully) find shared solutions.

The Security Council has primary responsibility, under the U.N. Charter, for the maintenance of international peace and security. It has 15 Members (five permanent and ten non-permanent members). Each Member has one vote. Under the Charter, all Member States are obligated to comply with Council decisions.

All U.N. member states are members of the General Assembly. The General Assembly is the main deliberative, policymaking and representative organ of the U.N. All 193 Member States of the U.N. are represented in the General Assembly, making it the only U.N. body with universal representation. States are admitted to membership by a decision of the General Assembly upon the recommendation by the Security Council, of which the United States, Russia, China, United Kingdom, and France are the five permanent members, each with veto power.

On June 26, 1945, the United Nations Charter was signed by 26 signatories: the United States, the United Kingdom of Great Britain and Northern Ireland, the Union of Soviet Socialist Republics, China, Australia, Belgium, Canada, Costa Rica, Cuba, Czechoslovakia, Dominican Republic, El Salvador, Greece, Guatemala, Haiti, Honduras, India, Luxembourg, Netherlands, New Zealand, Nicaragua, Norway, Panama, Poland, Union of South Africa, and Yugoslavia.

In 2023, the U.N. had offices in 193 countries and 37,000 employees, and is the world's largest universal multilateral international organization.

There are 36 countries listed by the U.S. Central Intelligence Agency (CIA) and/or the World Bank that are not "sovereign" since they are not fully independent of their mother country and, therefore, are not eligible to become U.N. members. These regions are typically designated as territories, possessions, or special administrative regions of the sovereign nations. In addition there is the unpopulated continent of Antarctica plus many unpopulated island territories that are nonmembers. Some of these non-sovereign territories actually rank higher than many of the 193 sovereign U.N. members in several significant metrics. For example, Greenland (part of the Kingdom of Denmark) ranked as the world's twelfth-largest land area; Puerto Rico (an unincorporated territory of the U.S.) had a population of 3.2 million in 2021; and Hong Kong (a special administrative region of China), had a GDP of $369 billion in 2021.

In addition, as of March 2024, three countries (Kosovo, Taiwan, and Palestine) were not U.N. members due to disagreement among Security Council members as to their sovereignty.

Nonmembers of the United Nations in March 2024

Country/Territory Name	Mother Sovereign Nation
American Samoa	United States
Anguilla	United Kingdom
Aruba	Netherlands
Bermuda	United Kingdom
British Virgin Islands	United Kingdom
Cayman Islands	United Kingdom
Christmas Island	Australia
Cook Islands	New Zealand
Coral Sea Islands	Australia
Curaçao	Netherlands
Falkland Islands	United Kingdom
Faroe Islands	Denmark
French Polynesia	France
Gibraltar	United Kingdom
Greenland	Denmark
Guam	United States
Guernsey (Channel Island)	United Kingdom
Holy See (Vatican City)	** (observer status)
Hong Kong	China
Isle of Man	United Kingdom
Jersey (Channel Island)	United Kingdom
Kosovo	* (sovereignty disputed)
Macau	China
Montserrat	United Kingdom
New Caledonia	France
Niue	New Zealand
Norfolk Island	Australia
Northern Mariana Islands	United States
Palestine	* (sovereignty disputed)
Pitcairn Islands	United Kingdom
Puerto Rico	United States
Saint Helena	United Kingdom
Saint Pierre and Miquelon	France
Sint Maarten	Netherlands
Svalbard	Norway
Taiwan	* (sovereignty disputed)
Tokelau	New Zealand
Turks and Caicos Islands	United Kingdom
Virgin Islands U.S.	United States
Wallis and Futuna	France

*States that are not U.N. members due to disagreement as to their sovereignty are Kosovo, Taiwan, and Palestine.

**The Holy See (the government of Vatican City) is the only sovereign nation to choose not to apply for U.N. membership, however they have "observer" status.

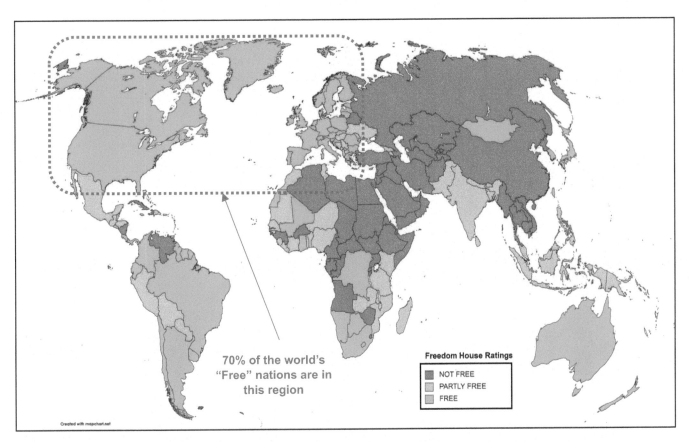

70% of the world's "Free" nations are in this region

Freedom House Ratings

- NOT FREE
- PARTLY FREE
- FREE

Created with mapchart.net

Source: Freedom House, https://freedomhouse.org/countries/freedom-world/scores, accessed on 5-1-23 with permission

World Map Showing Freedom House Classifications in 2023

In 2023, Freedom House had assessed 82 of the world's 193 sovereign nations as being "Free," of which 57 (70 percent) are located in North America plus Europe. Of the remaining sovereign nations 58 were "Not Free," and 53 "Partly Free." (See appendix V, page 315 for freedom assessment listing of all nations.)

Freedom House is the oldest American organization devoted to the support and defense of democracy around the world. It was established in New York in 1941, to promote American involvement in World War II and the fight against fascism. From the beginning, Freedom House was notable for its bipartisan support. Freedom House's founders were prominent and influential leaders from the fields of business and labor, journalism, academia, and government. A central figure among its early leaders was First Lady Eleanor Roosevelt.

This organization has created a system for *"measuring"* the freedom of populations throughout the world. The freedom assessment system they created awards a nation zero-to-four points for each of ten political rights indicators and 15 civil liberties indicators, which take the form of questions. They aggregate these points and based on total score classify nations as "Free," "Partly Free" of "Not Free." The detailed assessment of each nation, including explanation for how the score was derived, is posted on their website. Nations with classifications other than "Free" may indicate undemocratic or authoritarian governments.

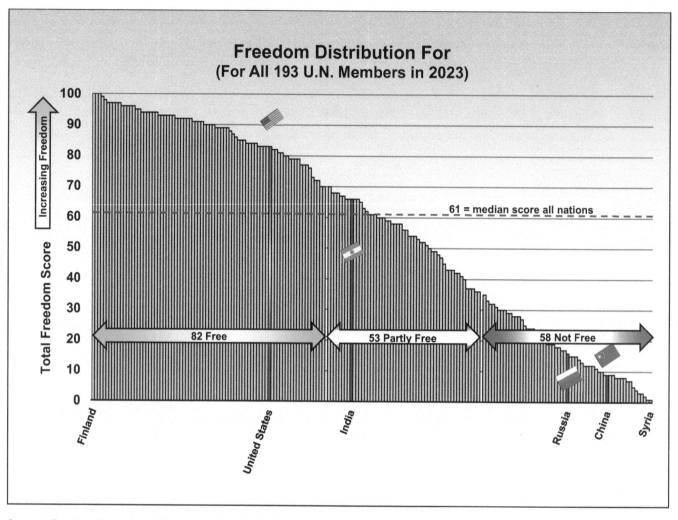

Freedom Distribution For
(For All 193 U.N. Members in 2023)

Increasing Freedom

Total Freedom Score

61 = median score all nations

82 Free — 53 Partly Free — 58 Not Free

Finland — United States — India — Russia — China — Syria

Sources: Freedom House, https://freedomhouse.org/countries/freedom-world/scores, https://freedomhouse.org/reports/freedom-world/freedom-world-research-methodology, accessed on 5-1-23 with permission

In 2023, Freedom House classified the U.S. as "Free," however, the U.S. ranked only 62nd out of a total of 82 nations designated "Free."

The U.S. was rated with only 83 of 100 points for freedom, whereas Finland, Norway and Sweden were each rated 100 points, the highest score possible, while Syria and South Sudan were each rated one point. (See appendix V, page 315 for freedom assessment listing of all nations.)

According to Freedom House: "*In recent years U.S. democratic institutions have suffered erosion, as reflected in rising political polarization and extremism, partisan pressure on the electoral process, bias and dysfunction in the criminal justice system, harmful policies on immigration and asylum seekers, and growing disparities in wealth, economic opportunity, and political influence.*" Consequently, in 2023, Freedom House rated the U.S. with a total score of only 83 of 100 points, due primarily to receiving only 33 of 40 points in the Political Rights category, and only 50 of 60 points in the Civil Liberties category.

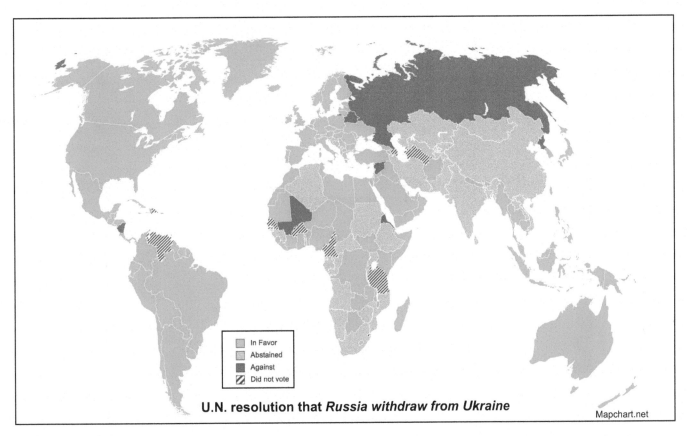

U.N. resolution that *Russia withdraw from Ukraine*

Mapchart.net

Source: The United Nations, https://news.un.org/en/story/2023/02/1133847

World Map Showing U.N. Votes on February 23, 2023

The U.N. General Assembly approved a nonbinding resolution on February 23, 2023, that called for Russia to end hostilities in Ukraine and demanded the withdrawal of its forces.

The vote was 141 "In Favor," seven "Against," with 32 abstentions. (See appendix I, page 308 for listing of voting record for all nations.)

These 13 members did not vote or abstain: Azerbaijan, Burkina Faso, Cameroon, Dominica, Equatorial Guinea, Eswatini, Grenada, Guinea-Bissau, Lebanon, Senegal, Turkmenistan, United Republic of Tanzania, and Venezuela.

Also, on October 7, 2023, the terrorist group "Hamas" invaded Israel resulting in hundreds of civilian deaths. In response Israel implemented a rocket campaign against Hamas in the Gaza Strip and placed a total blockade on all food, water, fuel, etc., from entering the Gaza Strip. Consequently, on October 18, 2023, the U.N. Security Council voted on a resolution that called for "*humanitarian pauses*" to deliver lifesaving aid to millions in Gaza. The U.S. voted "*Against*" the resolution, whereas two of the other five permanent Security Council members—France and China—voted "*In Favor*" while both Russia and the U.K. abstained. This was one of the few times *principal U.S. partners* did not support the U.S. position at the U.N.

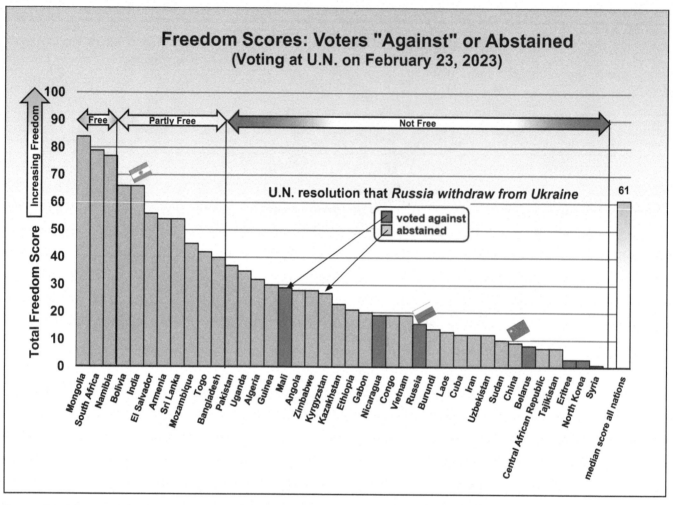

Freedom Scores: Voters "Against" or Abstained
(Voting at U.N. on February 23, 2023)

Source: Freedom House, https://freedomhouse.org/countries/freedom-world/scores, accessed on 5-1-23 with permission

On February 23, 2023, The U.N. voted on a resolution for Russia to withdraw from its invasion of Ukraine. No "Free" nation voted "Against" the resolution, however, three "Free" nations abstained: Mongolia, South Africa and Namibia. The above chart shows all nations that abstained or voted "Against" the resolution. The Freedom scores refer to the ratings by Freedom House.

- All seven nations "Against" the resolution were classified as "Not Free"
- 20 of 32 abstentions were rated "Not Free"
- 9 of 32 abstentions were rated "Partly Free"
- 3 of 32 abstentions were rated "Free" (Mongolia, South Africa, and Namibia)

Also,

- 23 of 141 "In Favor" were rated "Not Free"
- 40 of 141 "In Favor" were rated "Partly Free"
- 78 of 141 "In Favor" were rated "Free"

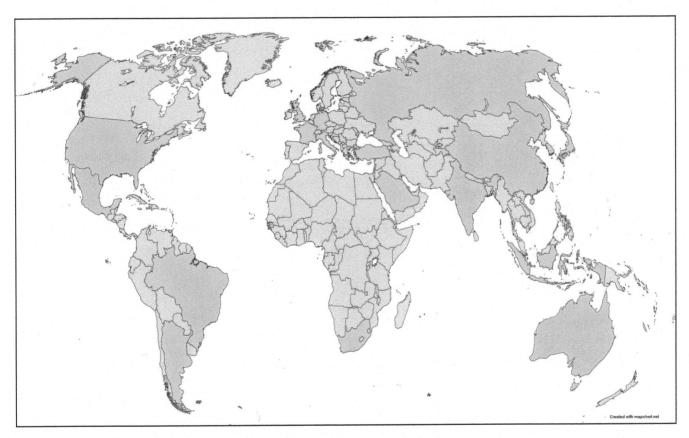

Source: Australian Government, Department of Foreign Affairs, https://www.dfat.gov.au/trade/organisations/g20

World Map Showing G20* Members in 2023

The Group of Twenty (G20) is an informal gathering of many of the world's most politically powerful nations, which provides a forum for discussing economic issues. The group consists of 19 nations plus the European Union (E.U.). The E.U. represents 27 nations (see appendix VI, page 318) including three that also have membership within the G20; France, Germany, and Italy.

In addition to the U.S. and the eight principal U.S. partners, members include India and China with the largest populations. Other members include democracies, autocracies, U.S. allies, and adversaries; some have more than half of their population living below poverty level, including India, South Africa, and Indonesia. Six G20 nations, South Africa, India, Indonesia, Mexico, Brazil, and Turkiye, received U.S. aid.

The G20 was founded in 1999 after the Asian financial crisis as a forum for the finance ministers and central bank governors to discuss global economic and financial issues. The G20 was upgraded to the level of heads of state/government in the wake of the global economic and financial crisis of 2007, and in 2009, was designated the "premier forum for international economic cooperation."

* In September 2023, the G20 turned into the G21 when the African Union (A.U. became a permanent member which marked the first expansion of the group since its formation as a group of 20 major economies in 1999. The A.U. is a continental body consisting of the 55 member states that make up the nations of the African continent. It was officially launched in 2002, as a successor to the Organization of African Unity (OAU, 1963–1999).

G20 Members' Portion of the World in 2021

G20 members account for 86 percent of global GDP, 62 percent of the world's population, and 61 percent of the world's land area. Despite these significant portions three members have poverty levels above the world's average, and five have a GDP per capita below the world's average.

	GDP % of world	Population % of world	Surface Area % of world
Reference page #	*page 137*	*page 29*	*page 21*
Argentina	0.50%	0.58%	2.06%
Australia	1.61%	0.33%	5.75%
Brazil	1.67%	2.72%	6.32%
Canada	2.06%	0.48%	7.34%
China	18.37%	17.90%	7.13%
France	3.06%	0.86%	0.41%
Germany	4.41%	1.05%	0.27%
India	3.29%	17.84%	2.44%
Indonesia	1.23%	3.47%	1.42%
Italy	2.18%	0.75%	0.22%
Japan	5.12%	1.59%	0.28%
Mexico	1.32%	1.61%	1.46%
Russia	1.84%	1.82%	12.70%
Saudi Arabia	0.86%	0.46%	1.60%
South Africa	0.43%	0.75%	0.91%
South Korea	1.88%	0.66%	0.07%
Turkiye	0.85%	1.07%	0.58%
United Kingdom	3.24%	0.85%	0.18%
United States	24.15%	4.21%	7.30%
European Union*	17.80%	5.68%	3.16%
Total Percent*	86.23%	62.02%	60.70%

	GDP per Capita	% Below Poverty Level
Reference page #	*page 147*	*page 227*
Argentina	$10,600	14.1%
Australia	$60,400	1.0%
Brazil	$7,500	18.7%
Canada	$52,000	1.0%
China	$12,600	24.7%
France	$43,700	0.2%
Germany	$51,200	0.2%
India	$2,300	83.8%
Indonesia	$4,300	60.1%
Italy	$35,700	3.1%
Japan	$39,300	1.4%
Mexico	$10,100	32.5%
Russia	$12,200	4.1%
Saudi Arabia	$23,200	?
South Africa	$7,100	61.6%
South Korea	$35,000	1.5%
Turkiye	$9,700	12.4%
United Kingdom	$46,500	0.8%
United States	$70,200	2.0%
European Union average	$38,400	
World average	$12,200	46.9%

* Three members (France, Germany, and Italy) are members of the G20 <u>and</u> the E.U. The total percentages shown have been adjusted to avoid double counting.

Source: (1) The World Bank, https://databank.worldbank.org/source/world-development-indicators, NY.GDP.MKTP.CD, https://data.worldbank.org/summary-terms-of-use

In September 2023, the G20 turned into the **G21** when the African Union (A.U.) became a permanent member.

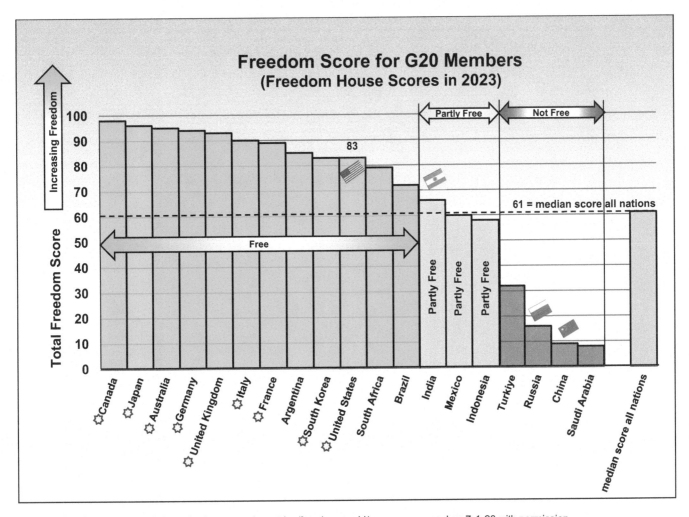

Freedom Score for G20 Members
(Freedom House Scores in 2023)

Source: Freedom House, https://freedomhouse.org/countries/freedom-world/scores, accessed on 7-1-23 with permission

✿ These nine G20 nations are also members of the OECD. In addition, they are prime defense partners with the U.S. either as NATO members or with a bilateral defense treaty. All nine members have the highest income per capita of the G20 nations and are considered principal U.S. partners.

In 2023, Freedom House ranked eight of the G20 member nations higher than the U.S. in total aggregate freedom score. Five G20 members ranked in the bottom half of all 193 U.N. nations as "Not Free." (Indonesia, Turkiye, Russia, China, and Saudi Arabia).

Of the 19 G20 nations, only nine have advanced economies and are "Free" democracies. The remaining ten either have poverty levels above the world's average and/or have a GDP per capita level below world's average—except Saudi Arabia which is economically above average but with an authoritarian government assessed as "Not Free." Saudia Arabia's Freedom House score was at the bottom 6 percent of all nations.

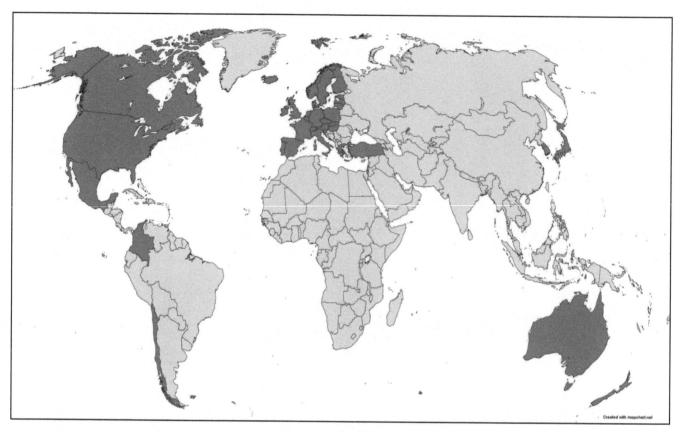

Source: OECD, https://www.oecd.org/about/

World Map Showing OECD Members in March 2024

In March 2024, The Organization for Economic Cooperation and Development (OECD) consisted of 38 member nations working together to promote economic growth, prosperity, and sustainable development. Headquartered in Paris, France, the OECD was established in 1961 as the successor to the Organization for European Economic Cooperation (OEEC), originally created to implement the Marshall Plan in the wake of World War II. The OECD provides a unique forum and knowledge hub for data and analysis, exchange of experiences, best-practice sharing, and advice on public policies and international standard-setting.

All 38 OECD member nations voted "In Favor" of the February 23, 2023 U.N. resolution for Russia to withdraw from Ukraine. (See page 15 for listing of all OECD members.)

OECD Members' Portion of the World's GDP

Organization for Economic Cooperation and Development (OECD)
members' percent of world's GDP in 2021

Australia	1.61%	Japan	5.12%
Austria	0.50%	Latvia	0.04%
Belgium	0.62%	Lithuania	0.07%
Canada	2.06%	Luxembourg	0.09%
Chile	0.33%	Mexico	1.32%
Colombia	0.33%	Netherlands	1.05%
Costa Rica	0.07%	New Zealand	0.26%
Czechia	0.29%	Norway	0.50%
Denmark	0.41%	Poland	0.70%
Estonia	0.04%	Portugal	0.26%
Finland	0.31%	Slovakia	0.12%
France	3.06%	Slovenia	0.06%
Germany	4.41%	South Korea	1.88%
Greece	0.22%	Spain	1.48%
Hungary	0.19%	Sweden	0.66%
Iceland	0.03%	Switzerland	0.83%
Ireland	0.52%	Turkiye	0.85%
Israel	0.51%	United Kingdom	3.24%
Italy	2.18%	United States	24.15%

Source: The World Bank, https://databank.worldbank.org/source/world-development-indicators, NY.GDP.MKTP.CD, https://data.worldbank.org/summary-terms-of-use

In 2021, the 38 OECD members accounted for:

- 60.4% of the world's GDP
- 60.1% of the world's goods and services exported
- 28.0% of the world's surface area
- 17.4% of the world's population

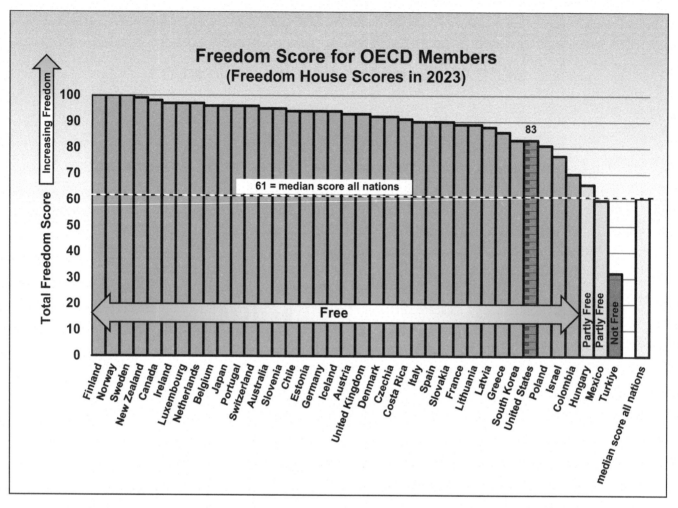

Source: Freedom House, https://freedomhouse.org/countries/freedom-world/scores, accessed on 5-1-23 with permission

Of the 38 members of the Organization for Economic Cooperation and Development (OECD) 35 were designated as "Free" by Freedom House in 2023, whereas Turkiye was designated "Not Free"; Hungary and Mexico were designated "Partly Free."

Freedom House's freedom ranking placed the U.S. in 32nd place among the 35 "Free" OECD member nations.

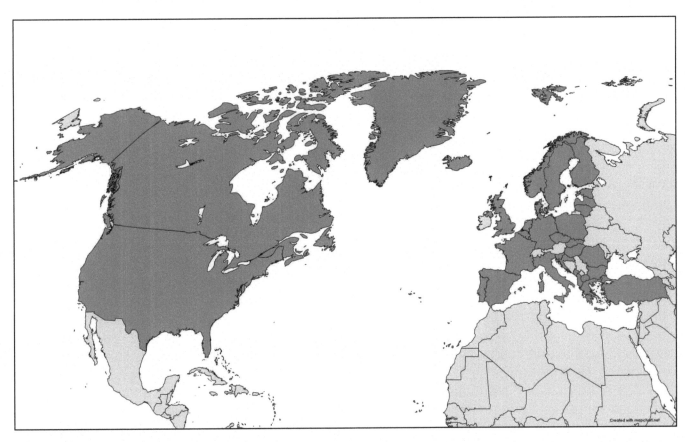

Source: NATO, https://www.nato.int/

World Map Showing NATO Members in January 2024

The North Atlantic Treaty Organization (NATO) was created in 1949, by the U.S., Canada, and ten Western European nations to provide collective security against the Soviet Union.

NATO was the first peacetime military alliance the U.S. entered into outside of the western hemisphere and in 2023, had 31 members after Finland joined that year—then 32 members after Sweden joined in March 2024. Finland and Sweden applied for membership as a direct result of Russian's February 2022, invasion of Ukraine.

NATO has become the United States' best deterrent against aggression due to article five in its founding document that states: any attack on a NATO member in Europe or North America "*shall be considered an attack against them all*." (See page 18 for listing of all NATO members.)

North Atlantic Treaty Organization (NATO)

In 2023, NATO had 31 members after Finland and Sweden applied for membership in 2022. Although Finland's application was approved in April that year Sweden's application was pending Hungary's approval until March 2024, when Sweden became the 32nd member. These nations, called NATO Allies, are sovereign states that come together through NATO to discuss political and security issues and make collective decisions by consensus. NATO's essential and enduring purpose is to safeguard the freedom and security of all its members by political and military means. Collective defense is at the heart of the Alliance and creates a spirit of solidarity and cohesion among its members.

NATO strives to secure a lasting peace in Europe, based on common values of individual liberty, democracy, human rights and the rule of law. Since the outbreak of crises and conflicts beyond Allied borders can jeopardize this objective, the Alliance also contributes to peace and stability through crisis prevention and management, and partnerships. Essentially, NATO not only helps to defend the territory of its members, but also engages where possible and when necessary to project its values further afield, prevent and manage crises, stabilize post-conflict situations and support reconstruction. NATO also embodies the transatlantic link whereby the security of North America is tied to Europe's. It is an intergovernmental organization, which provides a forum where members can consult on any issue they may choose to raise and make decisions on political and military matters affecting their security. No single member nation is forced to rely solely on its national capabilities to meet its essential national security objectives.

32 NATO Members

Member	Military Personnel	Member	Military Personnel
Albania	6,800	Lithuania	21,000
Belgium	26,000	Luxembourg	900
Bulgaria	25,000	Montenegro	1,600
Canada	72,000	Netherlands	41,000
Croatia	15,000	North Macedonia	7,200
Czechia	26,000	Norway	20,000
Denmark	17,000	Poland	123,000
Estonia	6,300	Portugal	30,000
Finland	27,000	Romania	69,000
France	208,000	Slovakia	13,000
Germany	184,000	Slovenia	6,800
Greece	105,000	Spain	121,000
Hungary	20,000	Sweden	24,000
Iceland	0	Turkiye	435,000
Italy	179,000	United Kingdom	144,000
Latvia	6,400	United States	1,338,000

Total Military Personnel = 3,319,000

Source: The World Bank, https://databank.worldbank.org/source/world-development-indicators, NY.GDP.MKTP.CD, https://data.worldbank.org/summary-terms-of-use

Chapter 1: The Organized Planet

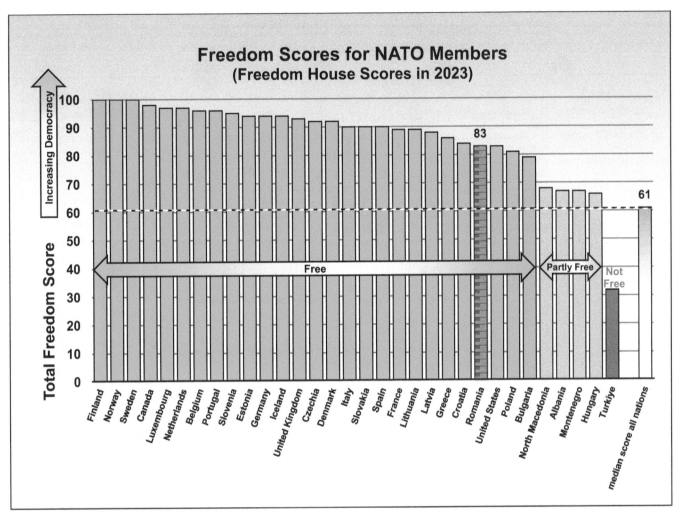

Source: Freedom House, https://freedomhouse.org/countries/freedom-world/scores, accessed on 5-1-23 with permission

Every NATO member voted "In Favor" of the February 23, 2023, U.N. resolution for Russia to withdraw from Ukraine.

Of NATO's 32 members, 26 were designated "Free" by Freedom House in 2023; North Macedonia, Albania, Montenegro, and Hungary were designated "Partly Free"; Turkiye as "Not Free."

The North Atlantic Treaty Organization (NATO, also called the North Atlantic Alliance, is an intergovernmental military alliance between 32 member states—30 European and two North American (Canada and the U.S.

Eight Principal U.S. Partners

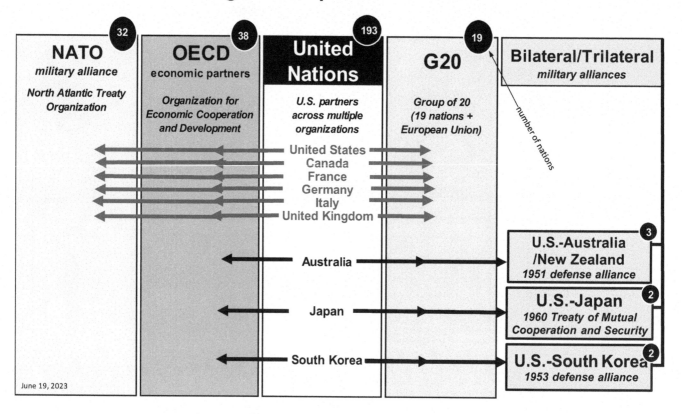

June 19, 2023

In 2023, there were eight nations with a unique relationship with the U.S. They were the only nations, besides the U.S., that met the following five conditions:

1. **Economic partner as OECD members**
2. **Defense partner as member of NATO or with Bilateral agreement**
3. **G20 member**
4. **Voted "In Favor" of the U.N. resolution that Russia withdraw from Ukraine**
5. **Classified as "Free" by Freedom House**

Note that Turkiye satisfied the first four conditions, however, Turkiye was classified as "Not Free" by Freedom House. The remaining eight nations are considered principal U.S. partners. They are:

Australia, Canada, France, Germany, Italy, Japan, South Korea, and the United kingdom.

In 2021, the combined economies of these "Free" nations, including the U.S., was 47.7 percent of the world's GDP while their combined population represented 10.8 percent of the world's population and they all ranked within the highest income per capita of all the G20 members.

Seven of these nine nations were also members of the G7 (group of 7) that was formed in 1975, to coordinate global economic policy and address other transnational issues.

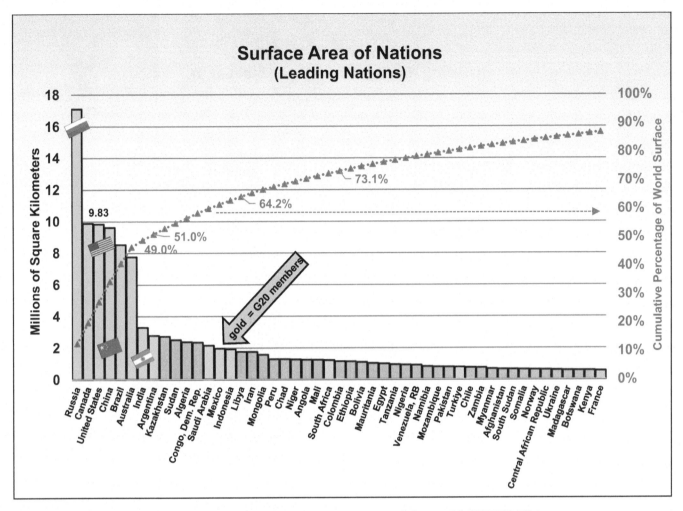

Surface Area of Nations
(Leading Nations)

Source: The World Bank, https://databank.worldbank.org/source/world-development-indicators, AG.SRF.TOTL.K2, https://data.worldbank.org/summary-terms-of-use, accessed 8/23/23

Seven nations with the largest surface area, including the U.S., comprise 49 percent of the earth's land area and are all members of the G20. The U.S. ranks third in area and constitutes 7.3 percent of the world's surface area.

Surface area is a nation's total area, including areas under inland bodies of water and some coastal waterways. Total surface area is particularly important for understanding an economy's agricultural capacity and the environmental effects of human activity. Innovations in satellite mapping and computer databases have resulted in more precise measurements of land and water areas. The data are collected by the Food and Agriculture Organization (FAO) of the United Nations through annual questionnaires.

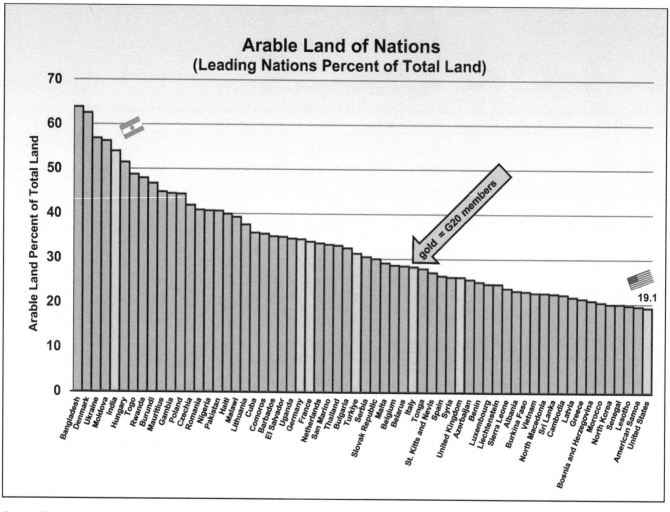

Arable Land of Nations
(Leading Nations Percent of Total Land)

Source: The World Bank, https://databank.worldbank.org/source/world-development-indicators, AG.LND.ARBL.ZS, accessed 8/23/23
https://data.worldbank.org/summary-terms-of-use

The U.S. ranks 63rd out of 193 nations for percentage of land that is arable, however, since the U.S. has the third-largest surface area in the world, the actual square kilometers of arable land of the U.S. ranks as number one in the world (see page 23).

Arable land includes land defined by the Food and Agriculture Organization (FAO) as land under temporary crops (double-cropped areas are counted once), temporary meadows for mowing or for pasture, land under market or kitchen gardens, and land temporarily fallow. Land abandoned as a result of shifting cultivation is excluded. Temporary fallow land refers to land left fallow for less than five years. The abandoned land resulting from shifting cultivation is not included in this category. Data for "Arable land" are not meant to indicate the amount of land that is potentially cultivable. Total land area does not include inland water bodies such as major rivers and lakes.

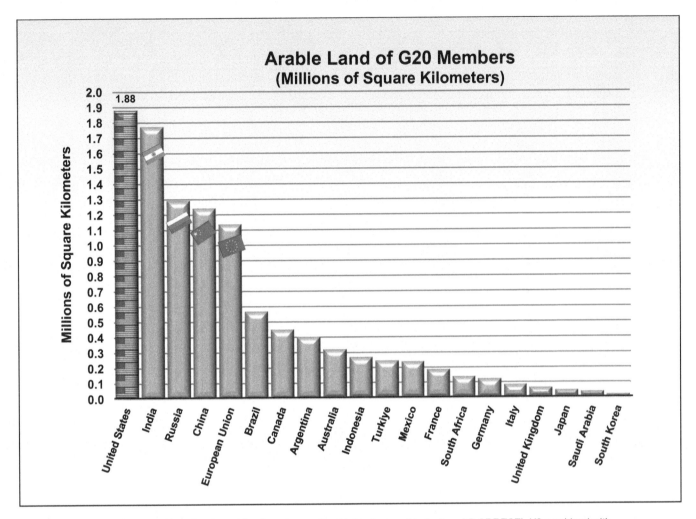

Sources: The World Bank, https://databank.worldbank.org/source/world-development-indicators,AG.SRF.TOTL.K2 combined with AG.LND.ARBL.ZS, https://data.worldbank.org/summary-terms-of-use, accessed 8/23/23, https://data.worldbank.org/summary-terms-of-use

Although only 19.1 percent of U.S. land is arable the U.S. ranks number one in the world for total arable land area due to its large surface area which ranks third in the world.

Data for "Arable land" are not meant to indicate the amount of land that is potentially cultivable. Arable land includes land defined by the Food and Agriculture Organization (FAO) as land under temporary crops (double-cropped areas are counted once), temporary meadows for mowing or for pasture, land under market or kitchen gardens, and land temporarily fallow. Land abandoned as a result of shifting cultivation is excluded. Temporary fallow land refers to land left fallow for less than five years.

Chapter 2

Demographics

Overview of Demographics

In February 2023, through U.N. proxy vote that would require Russia to withdraw from Ukraine, 54 percent of the world's population agreed with or passively accepted (by abstaining) Russia's February 2022 invasion. Both China and India abstained. The combined population of these two behemoths was 35.8 percent of the world's total compared with America's 4.2 percent. Half of the world's population lived in only six nations, including the U.S.—the world's third-most-populated nation after India and China. While America's share is comparatively small note that California alone with a 2023 population of 39 million was home to more people than the combined population of three-fourths (144 out of 193) of the world's nations.

The U.S. population had grown 6.2 percent between 2012 and 2022, fueled by legal immigration. In 2021, 60 percent of the population growth in the U.S. was due to immigration. By contrast, over the same ten-year period, China's population growth had slowed to 4.9 percent due primarily to the one-child policy that ended in 2016. Ending China's birth rate restriction was not timely or sufficient to overcome its death rate. By 2022, China's population growth had slowed to essentially zero and was projected to decrease each year in the future due to death rates exceeding birth rates. Meanwhile, India's grew by 12.3 percent in that same 10-year period. India, in 2022, became the most populated nation in the world, surpassing China by approximately five million people.

Between 1990 and 2021, the birth rate in the U.S. was in decline. By 2021, the U.S. birth rate had declined by one-third, however, it was still 10–25 percent above the rates for China, Russia, and the E.U. In 2021, births in the U.S. exceeded deaths by approximately 420,000. In contrast, China's birth rate had declined to near zero while the natural population growth rate in Russia and Europe was negative, i.e., deaths exceeded births. India's annual growth rate of 0.70 percent translated into 9.8 million more births than deaths each year.

In 2021, the annual population growth rate in the U.S., including net immigration (immigrants minus emigrants), was 0.30 percent. This was 2.3 times greater than the U.S. natural growth rate, the result of a net positive influx of legal immigrants. The birth rates in Russia and Europe including net immigration was not sufficient to overcome their death rates. Net immigration for both China and India were not sufficient to have any significant impact on their population growth, however India's natural growth rate was approximately double the total growth rate of the U.S.

In 2019, the median age for the U.S. population was 38.5 years which was approximately the average age for G20 members' population but 7.1 years older than the world's average. By 2022, the median age in the U.S. had increased to 38.9 years according to the U.S. Census Bureau. Since 1860, the median age in the U.S. has doubled.

In 2019, prior to the COVID-19 pandemic, the U.S. was the primary destination for over one million migrants; only Germany received more. Foreign-born residents in the U.S. made up 13.6 percent of the U.S. population. This was approximately the average proportion for the 34 reporting OECD members but approximately half the level of Australia and Switzerland. Luxembourg had the most foreign-born at 47.2 percent.

It would be reasonable to expect that wealthy nations would have the greatest longevity for their populations due to their high quality healthcare. While this appears to hold true for the majority of nations the U.S. is total outlier with that correlation. Using GDP per capita as a measure of wealth, the U.S. GDP per capita in 2021, of $70,200 was 83 percent above that of the E.U., however, the life expectancy for newborns in the E.U. was four years greater than in the U.S. while newborns in Japan had a life expectancy 8.3 years greater than in the U.S. (84.4 years versus 76.1).

In 2021, Life expectancy for female and male newborns in China exceeded those born in the U.S. by 2.0 years for females and 2.3 years for males. China's life expectancy has been increasing almost steadily over the past 50 years and 2020, was the first time life expectancy in China was greater than in the U.S.

Between 1960 and 1985, life expectancy for newborns in the U.S. was generally greater than for those born in the average of eight principal U.S. partners: Australia, Canada, France, Germany, Italy, Japan, South Korea, and the United Kingdom. Then, beginning in approximately 1985, being born in the U.S. became disadvantageous. Between 1985 and 2019, life expectancy for American newborns continually declined compared to the average of the eight partner nations until 2019, when that disadvantage had grown to approximately four years for both male and female babies. Then in 2020, when the COVID-19 pandemic arrived, the disadvantage accelerated. By 2021, the life expectancy for U.S. males had become 6.6 years lower and for females 5.8 years. U.S. male life expectancy at birth was reduced to 73.2 years.

In 2021, more than one-quarter of the world's refugees applied for asylum in just two countries, Turkiye and Jordan. However, after Russia's February 2022 invasion of Ukraine, approximately six million Ukrainians became asylum seekers (asylees). In 2021, the U.S. was hosting 339,200 asylees. This amounted to approximately 1 percent of the estimated 35 million asylees worldwide reported by the United Nations High Commission for Refugees (UNHCR). In May 2023, the U.S. Department of Homeland Security announced that U.S. government policy changed to presume that individuals who unlawfully enter the U.S. through its southwest land border or adjacent coastal borders are ineligible for asylum, unless they can demonstrate an exception to the rule or rebut the presumption.

Another consequence of Russia's invasion of Ukraine has been an increase in Russian residents leaving Russia. In 2023, the U.S. Department of State reported that an estimated one million Russians have left since the start of the invasion. These emigrants have accelerated the depopulation of Russia which was already experiencing negative population growth before the invasion.

The *old* age dependency ratio is used as indicator of the economic burden on a society with an aging population. In 2021, that ratio for the U.S. was approximately one-half the level of Japan's and approximately 65 percent above the world's average. The *young* age dependency ratio is highest for developing nations, and in 2021, the U.S. ratio was 29 percent below the world's average. Over the period approximately 2010–2021, the *young* age dependency ratio for the U.S. and European Union nations have remained relatively flat. India's has steadily declined by 53 percent over the past 48 years while China's ratio dramatically dropped.

~

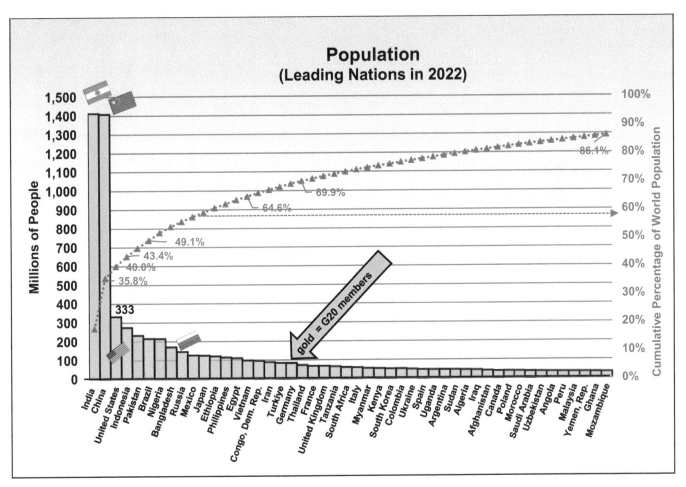

Source: The World Bank, https://databank.worldbank.org/source/world-development-indicators, SP.POP.TOTL, accessed 8/23/23
https://data.worldbank.org/summary-terms-of-use

In 2022, the U.S., the world's third most populous nation, comprised 4.19 percent of the world's population. Together, the top three nations, China, India and the U.S., comprised 40.0 percent of the world's population; collectively, the G20 members comprised 61.7 percent. Half of the world's population lived in only six nations, China, India, the U.S. Indonesia, Pakistan and Brazil. In 2022, India became the most populated nation surpassing China.

Total population is based on the de facto definition of population, which counts all residents regardless of legal status or citizenship. The values shown are midyear estimates. Population estimates are usually based on national population censuses. Errors and undercounting occur even in high-income countries. In developing countries errors may be substantial because of limits in the transport, communications, and other resources required to conduct and analyze a full census. The quality and reliability of official demographic data are also affected by public trust in the government, government commitment to full and accurate enumeration, confidentiality and protection against misuse of census data, and census agencies' independence from political influence. Moreover, comparability of population indicators is limited by differences in the concepts, definitions, collection procedures, and estimation methods used by national statistical agencies and other organizations that collect the data.

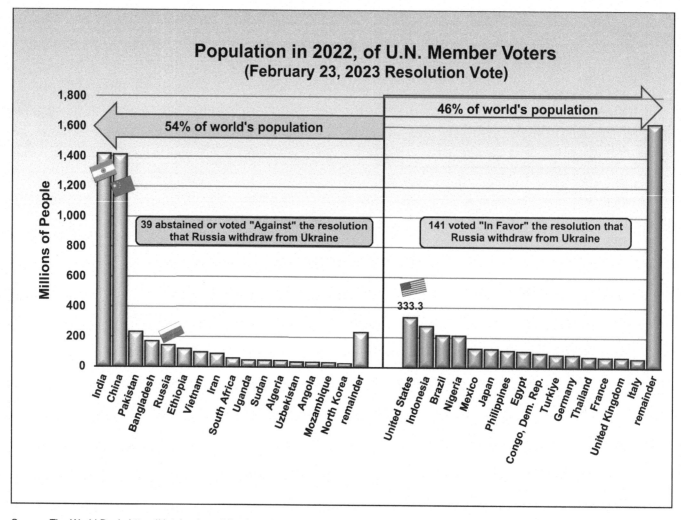

Population in 2022, of U.N. Member Voters
(February 23, 2023 Resolution Vote)

54% of world's population

46% of world's population

39 abstained or voted "Against" the resolution that Russia withdraw from Ukraine

141 voted "In Favor" the resolution that Russia withdraw from Ukraine

333.3

Millions of People

Source: The World Bank, https://databank.worldbank.org/source/world-development-indicators, SP.POP.TOTL, accessed 8/23/23
https://data.worldbank.org/summary-terms-of-use

In 2022, 4.3 billion people lived in the 39 nations who abstained or voted "Against" the U.N. resolution of February 23, 2023, for Russia to withdraw from Ukraine. There were 3.7 billion people living in 141 nations voting "In Favor." (See appendix I, page 308, for the voting record of all nations.)

This U.N resolution vote forced nations to declare their position on the naked aggression by Russia to invade another sovereign nation for the second time, after successfully annexing Crimea in 2014.

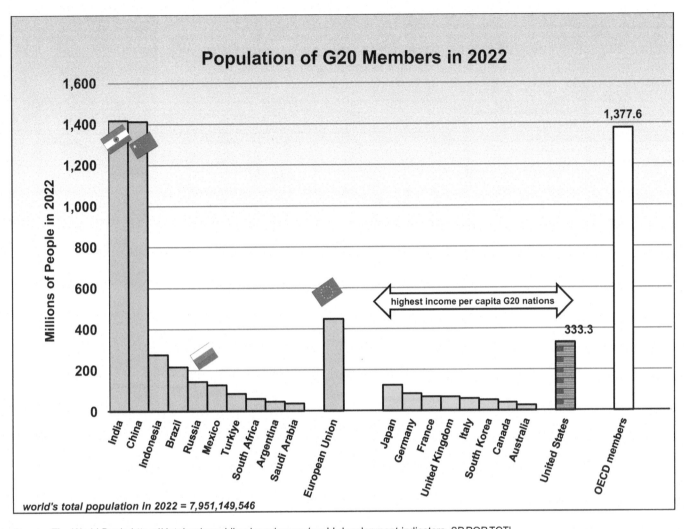

Population of G20 Members in 2022

world's total population in 2022 = 7,951,149,546

Source: The World Bank, https://databank.worldbank.org/source/world-development-indicators, SP.POP.TOTL, https://data.worldbank.org/summary-terms-of-use, accessed 8/23/23

In 2022, India had overtaken China to become the world's most populated nation, with approximately 5 million more people than China. The U.S. count reached the one-third billion level and was the third-largest population in the world, but only one-fourth (23.8 percent) as large as India's or China's.

In 2022, G20 membership accounted for 63 percent of the world's population of 7.95 billion people. In September, 2023, the G20 turned into the G21 when the African Union (A.U.) became a permanent member. The A.U. consists of the nations of the African continent with 1.3 billion people. The G21 represents 79 percent of the world's population.

The U.S. population size is in fourth place among G20 members behind the European Union (E.U.) which has a 35 percent larger population than the U.S. Note that the E.U. is a member of the G20, representing 27 European Nations (see appendix VI, page 318). Those 27 members include France, Germany, and Italy who are also separately members of the G20. The United Kingdom (U.K.) withdrew from E.U. membership in January 2020.

The nine highest income per capita G20 nations, including the U.S. have a combined population of 852 million, and are considered principal U.S. partners.

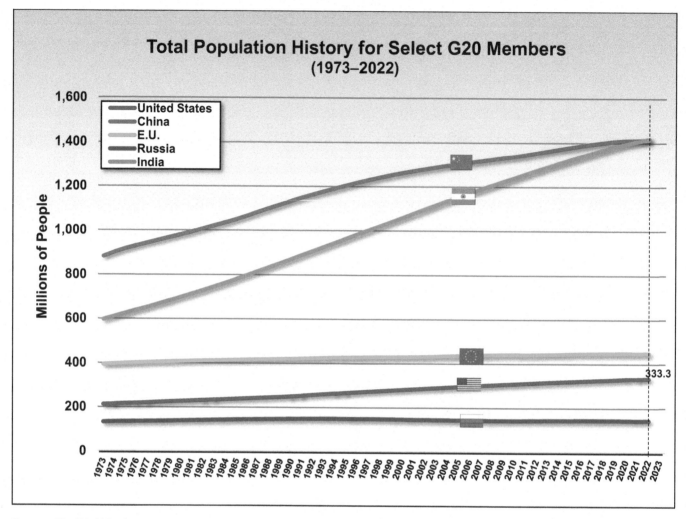

Sources: The World Bank, https://databank.worldbank.org/source/world-development-indicators, SP.POP.TOTL, accessed 8/23/23
https://data.worldbank.org/summary-terms-of-use, CIA World Factbook, https://www.cia.gov/the-world-factbook/countries/china/, accessed 6-6-23

U.S population grew 6.2 percent over the ten-year period ending in 2022, fueled by legal immigration. By contrast, in the same period, China's population growth had slowed to 4.9 percent during those ten years due primarily to their one-child policy. The policy ended in 2016, however, by 2022, China's growth rate had declined to zero. That year India became the most populated nation in the world with five million more people than China.

In October 2015, the Chinese government announced that it would change its rules to allow all couples to have two children, loosening a 1979 mandate that restricted many couples to one child; the new policy was implemented on January 1, 2016, to address China's rapidly aging population and future economic needs.

Over the past 30 years Russia has experienced a decline in total population, due to low birth rates by not replacing their aging population while experiencing essentially no immigration. In 1991, at the time of the collapse of the Soviet Union, Russia's population was approximately 149 million. In 2019, it was at 143 million. Since the invasion of Ukraine, the U.S. Department of State has estimated that one million Russians have emigrated out of Russia.

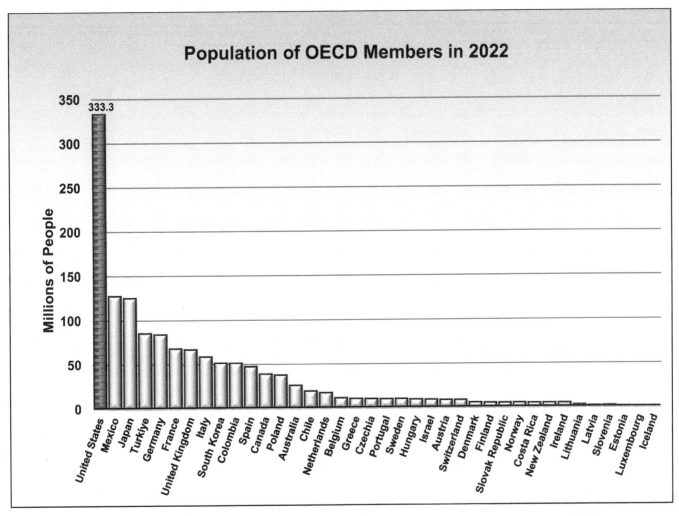

Source: The World Bank, https://databank.worldbank.org/source/world-development-indicators, SP.POP.TOTL, accessed 8/23/23
https://data.worldbank.org/summary-terms-of-use

In 2022, OECD's 38 members accounted for 17.4 percent of the world's 7.95 billion population. All 38 members voted "In Favor" of the February 23, 2023, U.N. resolution for Russia to withdraw from Ukraine. (See appendix III, page 313, for a listing of all OECD members.)

OECD is the Organization for Economic Cooperation and Development

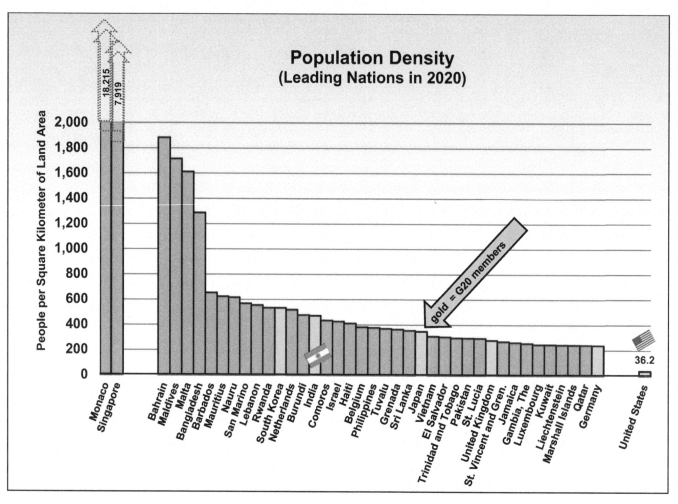

Population Density
(Leading Nations in 2020)

People per Square Kilometer of Land Area

gold = G20 members

36.2

Monaco — 18,215
Singapore — 7,919

Bahrain, Maldives, Malta, Bangladesh, Barbados, Mauritius, Nauru, San Marino, Lebanon, Rwanda, South Korea, Netherlands, Burundi, India, Comoros, Israel, Haiti, Belgium, Philippines, Tuvalu, Grenada, Sri Lanka, Japan, Vietnam, El Salvador, Trinidad and Tobago, Pakistan, St. Lucia, United Kingdom, St. Vincent and Gren., Jamaica, Gambia, The, Luxembourg, Kuwait, Liechtenstein, Marshall Islands, Qatar, Germany, United States

Source: The World Bank, https://databank.worldbank.org/source/world-development-indicators, EN.POP.DNST, accessed 8/23/23
https://data.worldbank.org/summary-terms-of-use

The U.S. has enjoyed low population density due to its large land area, despite being the third-most-populous nation. In contrast, other G20 nations have densities that are approximately ten times greater, including South Korea, India, and Japan. High population density generally means more urban concentration of people with the attendant issues of food supply, health services, pollution and crime.

Population density is midyear population divided by land area in square kilometers. Population is based on the de facto definition of population, which counts all residents regardless of legal status or citizenship—except for refugees not permanently settled in the country of asylum, who are generally considered part of the population of their country of origin. Land area is a country's total area, excluding area under inland water bodies, national claims to continental shelf, and exclusive economic zones. In most cases the definition of inland water bodies includes major rivers and lakes.

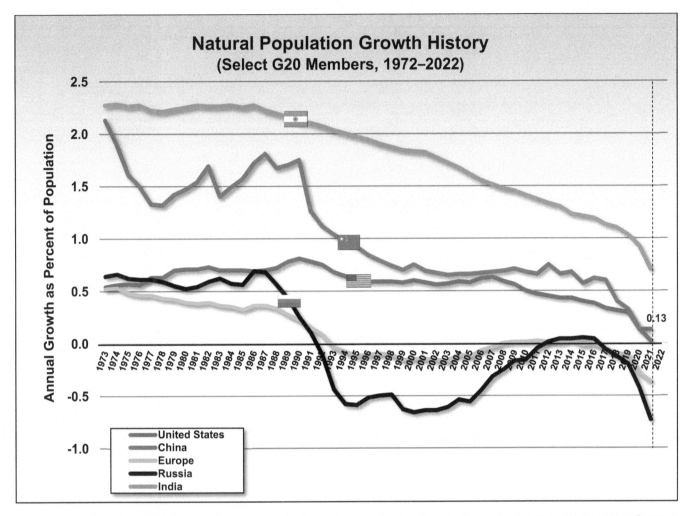

Natural Population Growth History
(Select G20 Members, 1972–2022)

Sources: Our World in Data, https://ourworldindata.org/grapher/population-growth-rate-with-and-without-migration, United Nations World Prospect 2022

The natural, annual population growth rate in the U.S. has declined from .63 percent in 2007, to 0.13 percent in 2021, after 30 years of growth in excess of .5 percent. In 2021, births in the U.S. exceeded deaths by approximately 420,000. In contrast, China's birth rate was near zero while the natural growth rates in Russia and Europe were negative. India's annual growth rate of .70 percent in 2021 translated into 9.8 million more births than deaths in India that year.

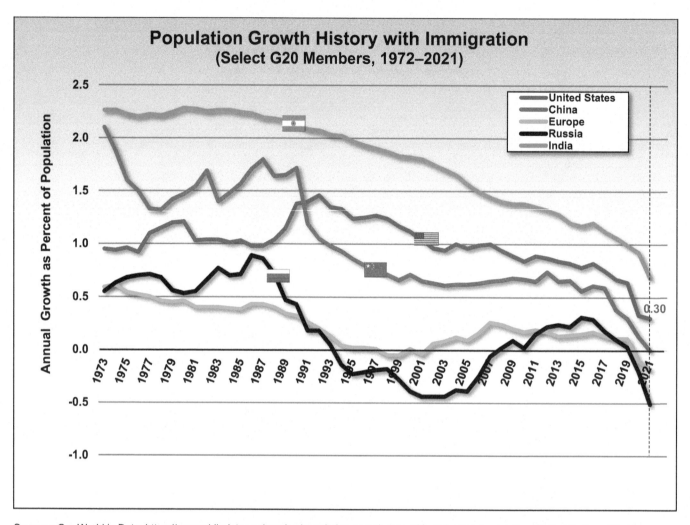

Population Growth History with Immigration
(Select G20 Members, 1972–2021)

Sources: Our World in Data, https://ourworldindata.org/grapher/population-growth-rate-with-and-without-migration, United Nations World Prospect 2022

In 2021, the total population growth rate in the U.S. with net immigration included was 0.30 percent. This was 2.3 times greater than the U.S. natural growth rate, the result of a net positive influx of legal immigrants. The population growth for Russia and Europe including net immigration was not sufficient to reverse the losses of population. Net immigration for both China and India was not sufficient to have any significant impact on their population growth, however, India's natural growth rate was approximately double the total growth rate of the U.S.

Net immigration is the number of people immigrating to a country reduced by the number moving away from that country (immigrants – emigrants).

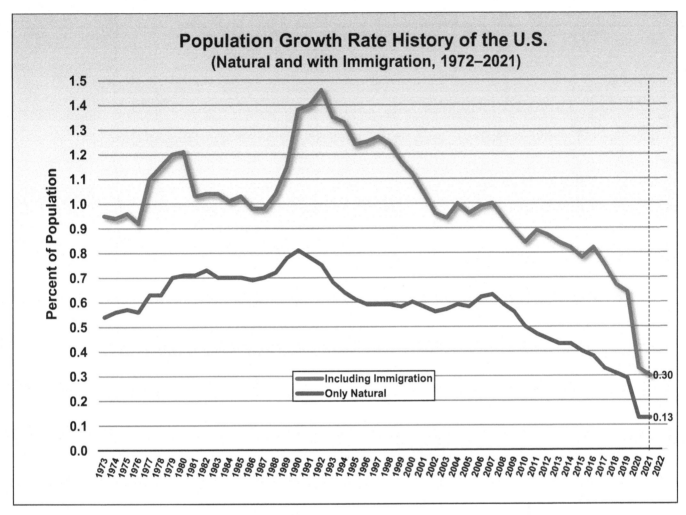

Sources: Our World in Data, https://ourworldindata.org/grapher/population-growth-rate-with-and-without-migration, United Nations World Prospect 2022

In 2021, 60 percent of the population growth in the U.S. was due to immigration. The population growth rate, with and without immigration, was at all-time lows. The COVID-19 pandemic (March 11, 2020, to May 11, 2023) impacted population growth in the U.S. due to 1.35 million "excess deaths" and significant disruptions to immigration. Health care during this period was also significantly disrupted affecting all levels of care, including maternity.

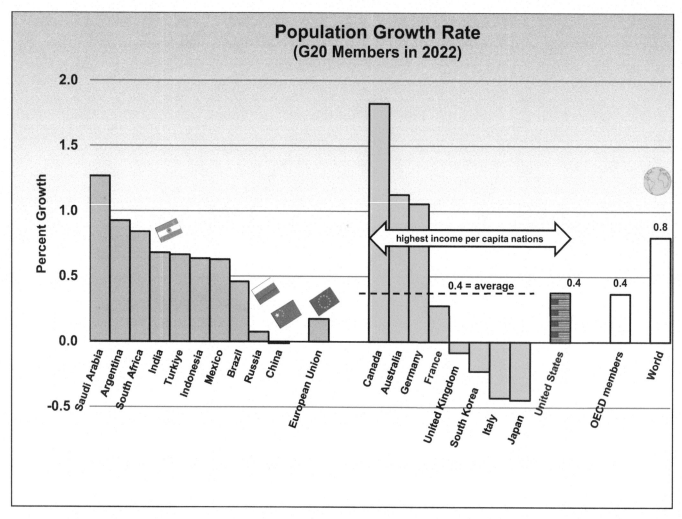

Population Growth Rate
(G20 Members in 2022)

Sources: The World Bank, https://databank.worldbank.org/source/world-development-indicators, SP.POP.GROW, accessed 8/23/23
https://data.worldbank.org/summary-terms-of-use, accessed 7-9-23

In 2022, only half of the G20 members with the highest income per capita (principal U.S. partners) experienced an increase in population that year. The U.S. population growth that year of 0.4 percent was about the average rate for those wealthy members but was half the rate of the world's population growth. About 60 percent of the U.S. population growth is due to legal immigration.

Population is based on the de facto definition of population, which counts all residents regardless of legal status or citizenship.

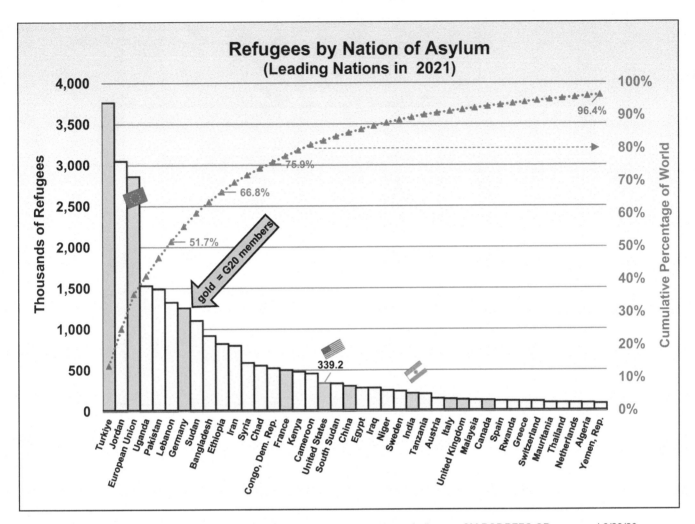

Refugees by Nation of Asylum
(Leading Nations in 2021)

Sources: The World Bank, https://databank.worldbank.org/source/world-development-indicators, SM.POP.REFG.OR, accessed 8/23/23 https://data.worldbank.org/summary-terms-of-use, https://data2.unhcr.org/en/situations/ukraine, https://www.state.gov/russias-strategic-failure-and-ukraines-secure-future/ June 2, 2023, https://www.cia.gov/the-world-factbook/countries/china/#people-and-society

In 2021, more than one quarter of the world's refugee population was being hosted in just two countries, Turkiye and Jordan. The U.S. portion of 339,200 amounted to approximately 1 percent of the estimated 27,119,816 refugees worldwide in 2021. In addition, after Russia's invasion of Ukraine in February 2022, approximately six million Ukrainians became asylum seekers according to the United Nations High Commissioner for Refugees (UNHCR). The number of refugees worldwide increased to 35.3 million by the end of 2022, the largest yearly increase ever recorded, according to UNHCR's statistics on forced displacement. The increase was largely due to refugees from Ukraine.

In fiscal year 2022, according to the CIA, the U.S. admitted 25,465 refugees including: 7,810 (Democratic Republic of the Congo), 4,556 (Syria), 2,156 (Burma), 1,669 (Sudan), 1,618 (Afghanistan), and 1,610 (Ukraine).

A refugee is a person who has fled their own country because they are at risk of serious human rights violations and persecution there. If they apply for protection from abroad and are granted protection, they are considered refugees.

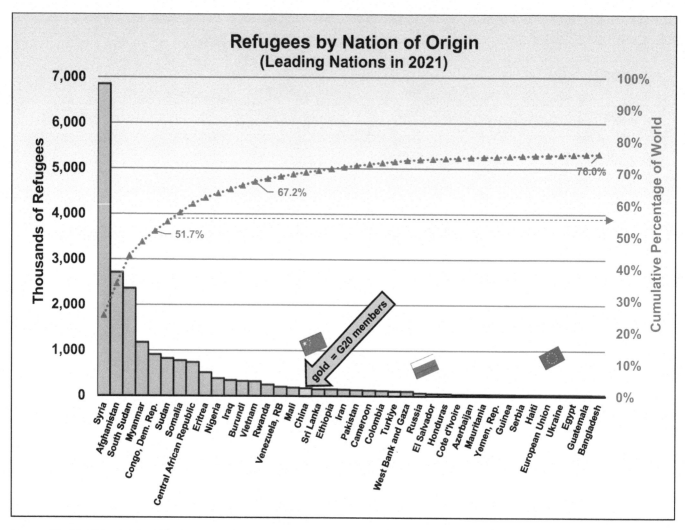

Source: The World Bank, https://databank.worldbank.org/source/world-development-indicators, SM.POP.REFG.OR, accessed 8/23/23
https://data.worldbank.org/summary-terms-of-use, https://www.unhcr.org

According to the United Nations High Commission for Refugees: *"the number of refugees worldwide increased from 27.1 million in 2021 to 35.3 million at the end of 2022, the largest yearly increase ever recorded. The increase was largely due to refugees from Ukraine fleeing the international armed conflict in their country. Overall, 52 percent of all refugees and other people in need of international protection came from just three countries: the Syrian Arab Republic (6.5 million), Ukraine (5.7 million) and Afghanistan (5.7 million)."*

A <u>refugee</u> is a person who has fled their own country because they are at risk of serious human rights violations and persecution there. If they apply for protection from abroad and are granted protection, they are considered refugees.

The countries from where most refugees originated in 2021, are those that are classified as "Not Free" by the Freedom House Organization (www.freedomhouse.org). People who begin their application with a well-founded fear of being persecuted because of their race, religion, nationality, membership of a particular social group or political opinion are considered <u>asylum seekers</u>. If they apply for protection from within the destination country and are granted protection, they are considered <u>asylees</u>.

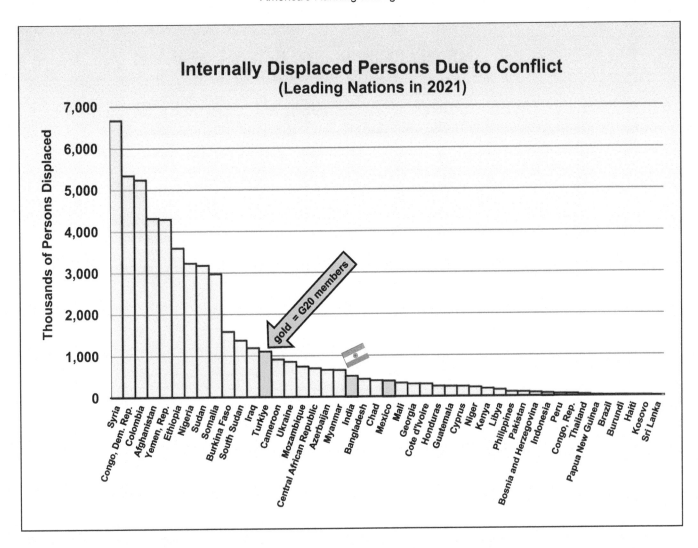

Source: The World Bank, https://databank.worldbank.org/source/world-development-indicators, VC.IDP.TOCV, accessed 8/23/23
https://data.worldbank.org/summary-terms-of-use

The U.S. does not appear on this ranking of countries that have internally displaced persons due to conflict in 2021. The G20 nations that do have portions of their population that fit the definition of internal displacement are Turkiye, India, and Mexico.

Internally displaced persons are people or groups of people who have been forced or obliged to flee or to leave their homes or places of habitual residence, in particular as a result of armed conflict, or to avoid the effects of armed conflict, situations of generalized violence, violations of human rights, or natural or human-made disasters and *who have not crossed an international border.* "People displaced" refers to the number of people living in displacement as of the end of each year, and reflects the stock of people displaced at the end of the previous year, plus inflows of new cases arriving over the year as well as births over the year to those displaced, minus outflows which may include returnees, those who settled elsewhere, those who integrated locally, those who travelled over borders, and deaths.

Most people who are forced to flee never cross an international border, remaining displaced within their own countries. Known as internally displaced people, or IDPs, they account for 58 percent of all forcibly displaced people. The largest number of people displaced within their own country was 6.8 million in Syria, consistent with the end of the previous year.

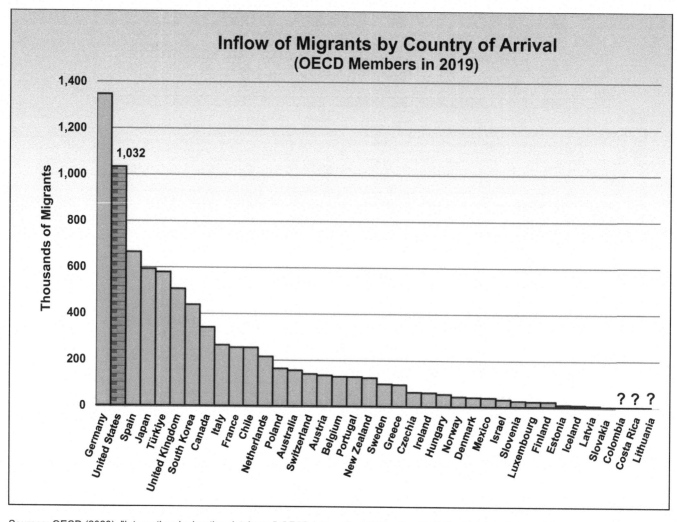

Inflow of Migrants by Country of Arrival
(OECD Members in 2019)

Sources: OECD (2023), "International migration database," *OECD International Migration Statistics* (database), https://doi.org/10.1787/data-00342-en (accessed on 20 May 2023), https://www.oecd-ilibrary.org/social-issues-migration-health/data/oecd-international-migration-statistics/international-migration-database_data-00342-enOf the 38 OECD member nations only

In 2019, prior to the COVID-19 pandemic, the U.S. was the primary destination for over one million migrants. Of the 35 OECD reporting nations only Germany received more.

Migrants are people who choose to leave their own country to live in another, temporarily or permanently, for work, study, joining family, fleeing poverty, fleeing violence or other many other circumstances, whereas a refugee is someone who has been forced from their home.

OECD countries seldom have tools specifically designed to measure the inflows and outflows of the foreign population, and national estimates are generally based either on population registers or residence permit data. This note is aimed at describing more systematically what is measured by each of the sources used.

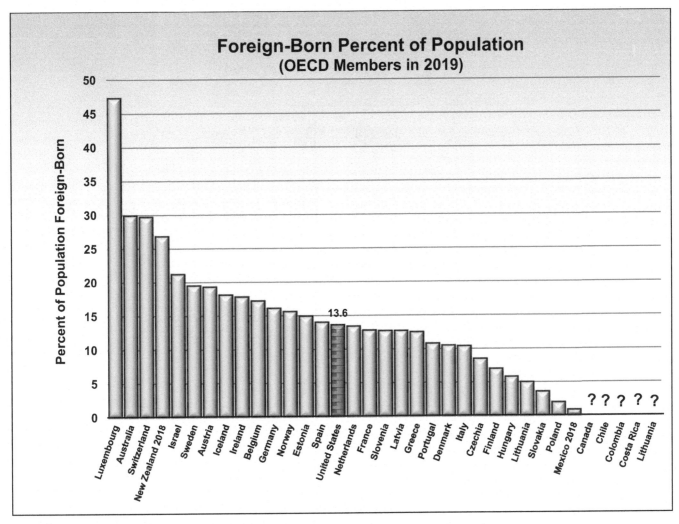

Foreign-Born Percent of Population
(OECD Members in 2019)

Sources: OECD (2023), Foreign-born population (indicator). doi: 10.1787/5a368e1b-en (Accessed on 20 May 2023), https://data.oecd.org/migration/foreign-born-population.htm

Foreign-born residents of the U.S. made up 13.6 percent of the population in 2019. This was approximately average for the 34 reporting OECD nations but approximately half the percentage of the populations of Australia and Switzerland. Luxembourg had the most foreign-born at 47.2 percent.

The foreign-born population covers all people who have ever immigrated from their country of birth to their current country of residence. The foreign-born population data shown here include people born abroad as nationals of their current country of residence. The difference across countries between the size of the foreign-born population and that of the foreign population depends on the rules governing the acquisition of citizenship in each country. This indicator is measured as a percentage of population.

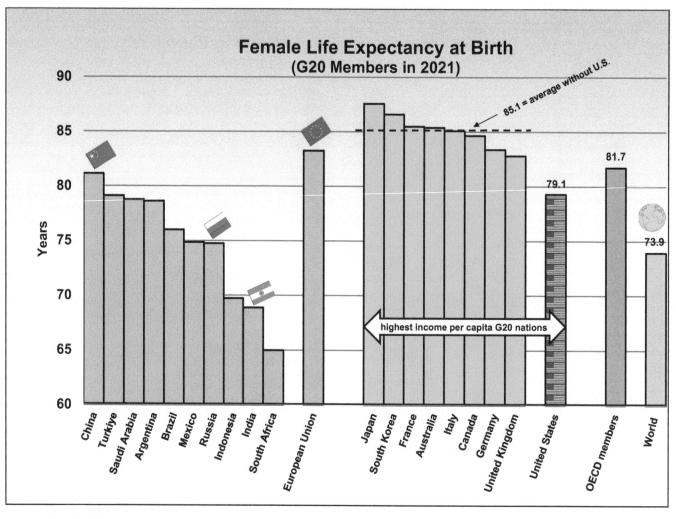

Female Life Expectancy at Birth
(G20 Members in 2021)

Sources: The World Bank, https://databank.worldbank.org/source/world-development-indicators, SP.DYN.LE00.FE.IN, accessed 8/23/23
https://data.worldbank.org/summary-terms-of-use, accessed 7-9-23

In 2021, newborn females in the U.S. had a life expectancy that was 6.0 years lower than the average newborn female in other high income G20 nations (principal U.S. partners).

In August 2022, the CDC reported that excess deaths due to COVID-19 and other causes in 2020, and 2021, led to an overall decline in life expectancy between 2019 and 2021 of 2.7 years for the total U.S. population, and 2.3 years for females.

Life expectancy at birth indicates the number of years a newborn infant would live if prevailing patterns of mortality at the time of its birth were to stay the same throughout its life. High mortality in young age groups significantly lowers the life expectancy at birth. But if a person survives one's childhood of high mortality, one may live much longer. For example, in a population with a life expectancy at birth of 50, there may be few people dying at age 50. The life expectancy at birth may be low due to the high childhood mortality so that once a person survives one's childhood, one may live much longer than 50 years.

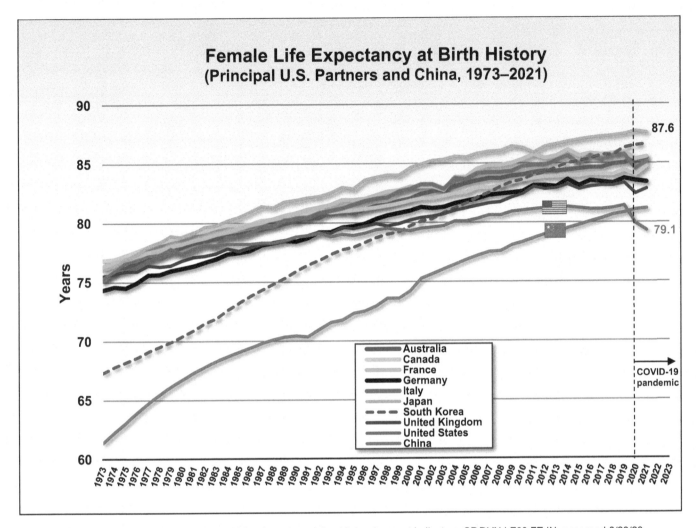

Female Life Expectancy at Birth History
(Principal U.S. Partners and China, 1973–2021)

Sources: The World Bank, https://databank.worldbank.org/source/world-development-indicators, SP.DYN.LE00.FE.IN, accessed 8/23/23
https://data.worldbank.org/summary-terms-of-use; CDC, Vital Statistics Rapid Release, https://www.cdc.gov/nchs/data/vsrr/vsrr023.pdf

In August 2022, the CDC reported that excess deaths due to COVID-19 and other causes in 2020 and 2021 led to a decline in life expectancy between 2019 and 2021, of 2.3 years for females and 2.7 years for all births. The revised female life expectancy of 79.1 years was 8.5 years less than females born in Japan and 2.0 years less than those born in China. That was the largest decline for any of the principal U.S. partners and resulted in the U.S. life expectancy at birth falling below China's for the first time.

Life expectancy at birth does not reflect the mortality pattern that a person actually experiences during his/her life, which can be calculated in a cohort life table. High mortality in young age groups significantly lowers the life expectancy at birth. But if a person survives his/her childhood of high mortality, he/she may live much longer.

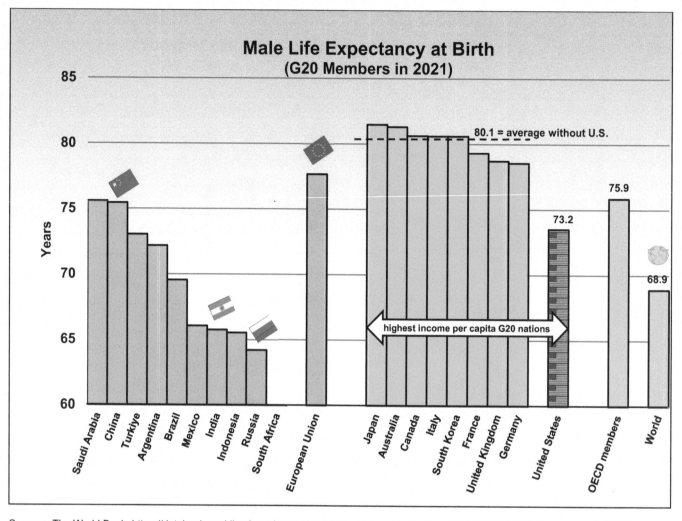

Male Life Expectancy at Birth
(G20 Members in 2021)

Sources: The World Bank, https://databank.worldbank.org/source/world-development-indicators, SP.DYN.LE00.MA.IN, accessed 8/23/23
https://data.worldbank.org/summary-terms-of-use, accessed 7-9-23

In 2021, newborn males in the U.S. had a life expectancy that was 6.9 years lower than the average newborn in the other eight high income per capita G20 nations (principal U.S. partners). In 2022, the CDC's revised life expectancy for newborn males in the U.S. was reduced to 73.2 years, a 3.1 year decline which was attributed primarily to COVID-19 and increases in unintentional injuries including drug overdoses.

Life expectancy at birth indicates the number of years a newborn infant would live if prevailing patterns of mortality at the time of its birth were to stay the same throughout its life. High mortality in young age groups significantly lowers the life expectancy at birth. But if a person survives one's childhood of high mortality, he/she may live much longer. For example, in a population with a life expectancy at birth of 50, there may be few people dying at age 50. The life expectancy at birth may be low due to the high childhood mortality so that once a person survives one's childhood, one may live much longer than 50 years.

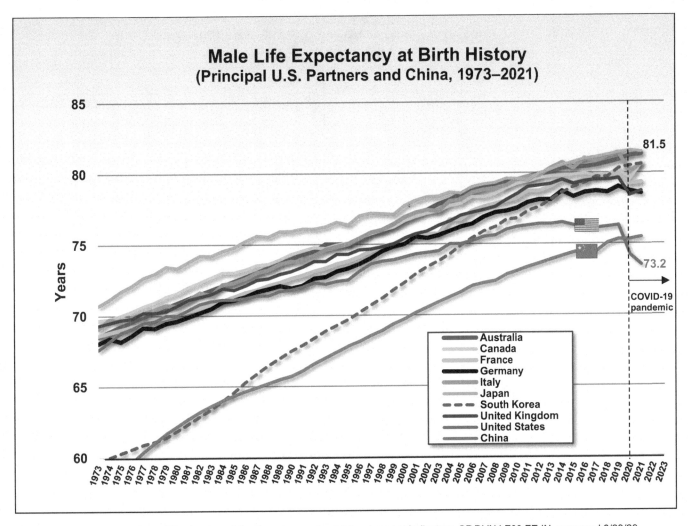

Male Life Expectancy at Birth History
(Principal U.S. Partners and China, 1973–2021)

Sources: The World Bank, https://databank.worldbank.org/source/world-development-indicators, SP.DYN.LE00.FE.IN, accessed 8/23/23
https://data.worldbank.org/summary-terms-of-use; CDC, Vital Statistics Rapid Release, https://www.cdc.gov/nchs/data/vsrr/vsrr023.pdf

In August 2022, the CDC reported that excess deaths due to COVID-19 and other causes in 2020 and 2021 led to a decline in life expectancy between 2019 and 2021 of 3.1 years for males and 2.7 years for all births. The revised male life expectancy of 73.2 years was 8.3 years less than males born in Japan and 2.3 years less than those born in China. That was the largest decline for any of the principal U.S. partners and resulted in the U.S. life expectancy at birth falling below China's for the first time.

Life expectancy at birth used here is the average number of years a newborn is expected to live if mortality patterns at the time of its birth remain constant in the future. It reflects the overall mortality level of a population, and summarizes the mortality pattern that prevails across all age groups in a given year. It is calculated in a period life table which provides a snapshot of a population's mortality pattern at a given time. It therefore does not reflect the mortality pattern that a person actually experiences during his/her life, which can be calculated in a cohort life table. High mortality in young age groups significantly lowers the life expectancy at birth. But if a person survives his/her childhood of high mortality, he/she may live much longer.

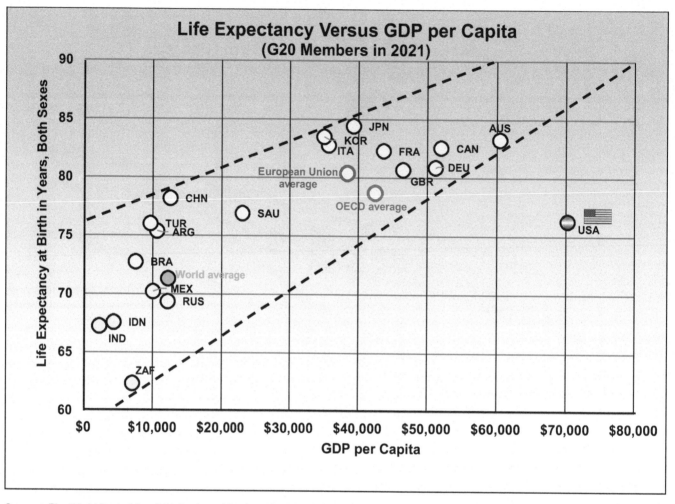

Sources: The World Bank, https://databank.worldbank.org/source/world-development-indicators, NY.GDP.PCAP.CD and SP.DYN.LE00.IN, https://data.worldbank.org/summary-terms-of-use, accessed 8/23/23

In 2021, life expectancy in the U.S. was an outlier and up to ten years lower than would be expected when based only on GDP per capita in comparison with other G20 members including the E.U., OECD nations, and the world's average.

Country Codes

Argentina	ARG
Australia	AUS
Brazil	BRA
Canada	CAN
China	CHN
France	FRA
Germany	DEU
India	IND
Indonesia	IDN
Italy	ITA
Japan	JPN
South Korea	KOR
Mexico	MEX
Russia	RUS
Saudi Arabia	SAU
South Africa	ZAF
Turkiye	TUR
United Kingdom	GBR
United States	USA

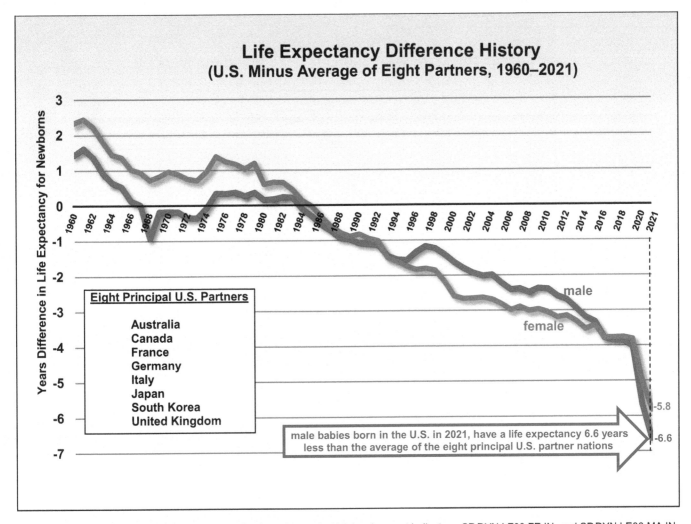

Life Expectancy Difference History
(U.S. Minus Average of Eight Partners, 1960–2021)

Eight Principal U.S. Partners

- Australia
- Canada
- France
- Germany
- Italy
- Japan
- South Korea
- United Kingdom

male

female

-5.8

-6.6

male babies born in the U.S. in 2021, have a life expectancy 6.6 years less than the average of the eight principal U.S. partner nations

Sources: The World Bank, https://databank.worldbank.org/source/world-development-indicators, SP.DYN.LE00.FE.IN, and SP.DYN.LE00.MA.IN, https://data.worldbank.org/summary-terms-of-use, accessed 8/23/23

Between 1960 and 1985, life expectancy for newborns in the U.S. was generally greater compared with the average of the eight principal U.S. partners: Australia, Canada, France, Germany, Italy, Japan, South Korea, and the U. K. (These eight nations and the U.S. had the highest income per capita of the G20 members in 2021.) Then, in approximately 1985, being born in the U.S. started to become a relative disadvantage. Between 1985 and 2019, life expectancy for American newborns continually declined compared to the average of the eight partner nations and by 2019, that disparity had increased to approximately four years for both male and female American newborns. Then in 2020, when the COVID-19 pandemic arrived, the disadvantage accelerated. By 2021, compared with these eight principal U.S. partners the life expectancy deficit for U.S. males had increased to 6.6 years and for females 5.8 years.

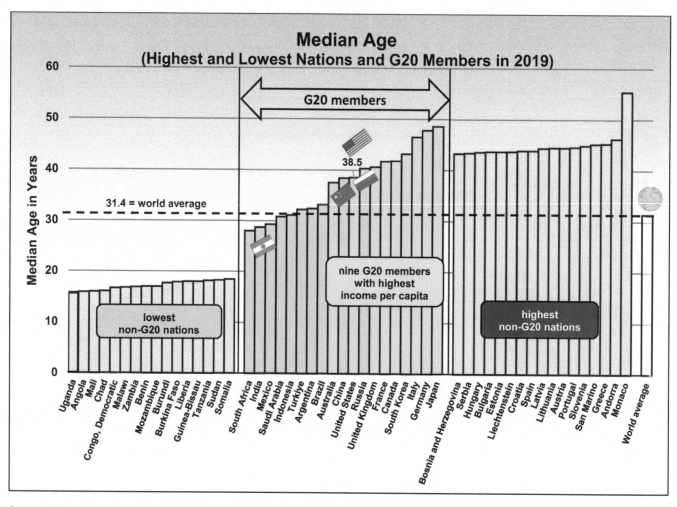

Sources: The World Factbook 2021. Washington, DC: Central Intelligence Agency, 2021, https://www.cia.gov/the-world-factbook/, The Factbook is in the public domain, : U.S. Census Bureau, https://www2.census.gov/programs-surveys/decennial/2000/phc/phc-t-09/tab07.pdf

In 2019, the median age for the U.S. population was 38.5 years which was approximately the average age for G20 members, 7.1 years older than the world's average, and second lowest among the nine highest income per capita G20 members.

By 2022, the median age in the U.S. had increased to 38.9 years according to the U.S. Census Bureau.

Median age is the age that divides a population into two numerically equal groups; that is, half the people are younger than this age and half are older. It is a single index that summarizes the age distribution of a population.

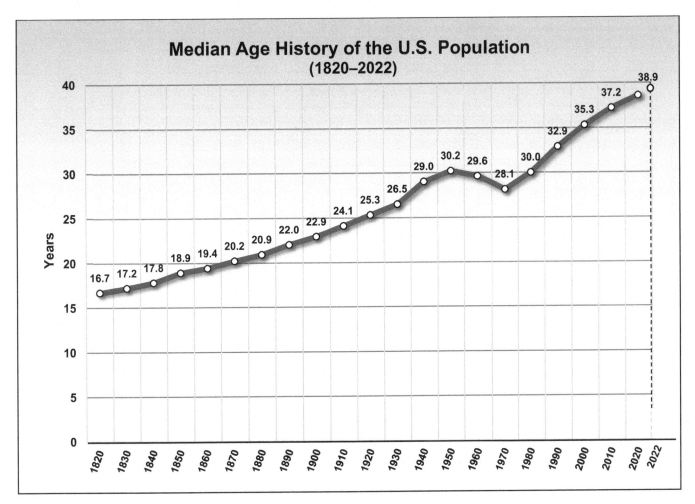

Source: U.S. Census Bureau, https://www2.census.gov/programs-surveys/decennial/2000/phc/phc-t-09/tab07.pdf, accessed on 5-22-23

The median age for the U.S. population has steadily increased over the past 200 years, except for a 30-year period between the mid-fifties to mid-eighties. Since 1860, the median age in the U.S. has doubled.

Median age is the age that divides a population into two numerically equal groups; that is, half the people are younger than this age and half are older. It is a single index that summarizes the age distribution of a population.

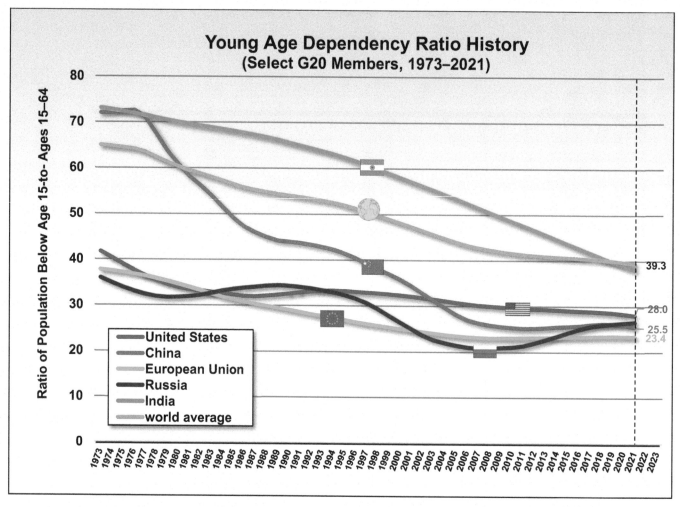

Source: The World Bank, https://databank.worldbank.org/source/world-development-indicators, SP.POP.DPND.YG, accessed 8/23/23
https://data.worldbank.org/summary-terms-of-use

Over the period approximately 2010–2021, the young age dependency ratio for the U.S. and European Union nations have remained relatively flat, whereas India's has steadily declined by 53 percent over the past 48 years. China's ratio dramatically dropped after implementing their one-child policy in 1972.

Data are shown as the proportion of dependents per 100 working-age population. Dependency ratios capture variations in the proportions of children, elderly people, and working-age people in the population that imply the dependency burden that the working-age population bears in relation to children and the elderly. But dependency ratios show only the age composition of a population, not economic dependency. Some children and elderly people are part of the labor force, and many working-age people are not. Patterns of development in a country are partly determined by the age composition of its population. Different age groups have different impacts on both the environment and on infrastructure needs. Therefore, the age structure of a population is useful for analyzing resource use and formulating future policy and planning goals with regards to infrastructure and development.

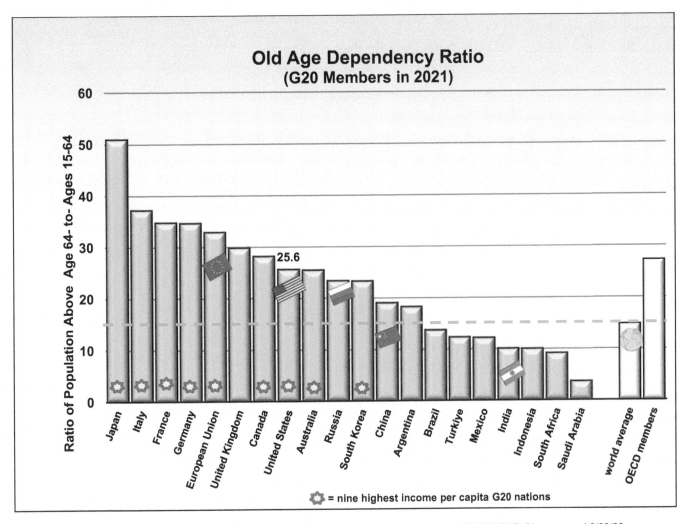

Old Age Dependency Ratio
(G20 Members in 2021)

Ratio of Population Above Age 64- to- Ages 15-64

25.6

☼ = nine highest income per capita G20 nations

Source: The World Bank, https://databank.worldbank.org/source/world-development-indicators, SP.POP.DPND.OL, accessed 8/23/23
https://data.worldbank.org/summary-terms-of-use

Societies with older populations will have high old age dependency ratios since there are high proportions of people above age 64 compared with the rest of the population. In 2021, Japan had a ratio of approximately 50 which is equivalent to every two workers supporting a third person! The ratio in the United States was approximately half of Japan's.

Age dependency ratio, old, is the ratio of older dependents—people older than 64—to the working-age population—those ages 15–64. Data are shown as the proportion of dependents per 100 working-age population. It is important to note that these definitions do not take into account labor force participation rates by age-group. Some portion of the "dependent" population may be employed and not necessarily economically dependent.

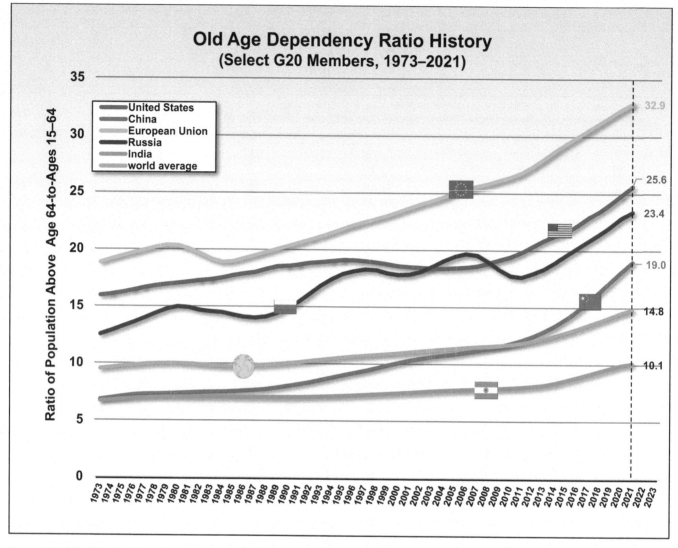

Old Age Dependency Ratio History
(Select G20 Members, 1973–2021)

Source: The World Bank, https://databank.worldbank.org/source/world-development-indicators, SP.POP.DPND.OL, accessed 8/23/23
https://data.worldbank.org/summary-terms-of-use

As populations across the world tend to live longer and have lowering birth rates the old age dependency ratio will climb. This places an economic burden on society especially considering the higher health care required by advanced ages. The ratio in the United States had been relatively flat for several decades until approximately 2007, after which it has continued to rise, and by 2021, it had increased by 38 percent.

Data are shown as the proportion of dependents per 100 working-age population. Dependency ratios capture variations in the proportions of children, elderly people, and working-age people in the population that imply the dependency burden that the working-age population bears in relation to children and the elderly. But dependency ratios show only the age composition of a population, not economic dependency. Some children and elderly people are part of the labor force, and many working-age people are not. Patterns of development in a country are partly determined by the age composition of its population. Different age groups have different impacts on both the environment and on infrastructure needs.

Chapter 3

Healthcare and
Vital Statistics

Overview of Healthcare and Vital Statistics

In 2020, U.S. healthcare expenditures per capita was the highest of any nation and consumed approximately one-sixth of the entire U.S. economy measured at 16.2 percent of GDP. Healthcare expenditures per capita in the United States was $11,702 which was approximately three times higher per capita as the average of the European Union member nations at $3,734. It was also 2.5 times as much as is expended by the average high income per capita G20 nations (principal U.S. partners). However, despite this excessive investment life expectancy for newborns in the U.S. was 6.4 years lower than for these nations. This very low life expectancy was up to ten years lower than would be projected based on the general correlation that exists between life expectancy and healthcare expenditures per capita of other nations.

In 2019, the U.S. age-standardized death rate for all causes was 44 percent above the average rate for the other high income per capita G20 members (principal U.S. partners) and 70 percent above the rate for Japan. Compared with these nations the U.S. had the highest rate for preventable deaths and for noncommunicable disease deaths, but had approximately the same rate for communicable diseases. Then, in 2020, the COVID-19 pandemic hit and the U.S. COVID-19 death rate became the highest of any G20 nation and 17th highest in the world.

Between March 2021 and March 2022, at the end of the second full year of the COVID-19 pandemic, COVID-19 became the third-largest cause of death in the U.S. and was responsible for 11.0 percent of all U.S. deaths during that one-year period for the total population of all ages. Approximately three-fourths of those deaths were people aged 65 years and older.

Preventable deaths is the third category of deaths and the U.S. is the leader of the wealthiest nations in this category also. For the age-group 1–44 years in 2022, unintentional injuries combined with suicide and homicide accounted for 66 percent of all deaths in the U.S. Unintentional injuries were the leading subcategory in this age-group and included opioid overdoses (unintentional poisoning), motor vehicle crashes, drowning, and unintentional falls. Unintentional injuries represented 44 percent of all deaths for this 1–44 years age-group. Suicide was the second leading cause of death followed by homicides.

During the 12 months ending in March 2022, drug overdose was the leading cause of death for Americans aged 35–44 years, the age-group with the highest rate, accounting for 21.7 percent of all deaths in that age-group.

The overall crude death rate in the U.S. between 2000 and 2019, increased by 42.9 deaths per 100,000 people (5.1 percent). This period ended prior to the March 2020, pandemic declaration so these data were not impacted by COVID-19. This net increase occurred despite significant reductions in deaths per 100,000 population in several categories of noncommunicable diseases, especially ischemic heart disease (–61.2) and stroke (–12.9) since they were offset by increased Alzheimer's disease deaths, dementia deaths (+57.2), and drug use disorders (+17.3).

Crude death rate is defined as the actual number of deaths divided by the population size. When comparing death rates between countries that generally have different age distributions the observed differences in rates may be due to age distribution differences and therefore it is common to "adjust" all data to conform to a "standard" age distribution. Age-standardized death rate comparisons remove the age bias so observed differences in the age-standardized rates are due to other factors other than age differences.

In 2021, although 99.5 percent of births in the U.S. were attended by skilled health staff approximately 18,000 births in the U.S. did not have medical oversight. In 2021, U.S. infant mortality rate was higher than Russia's and China's, and the highest among the wealthiest nine G20 nations, based on income per capita. U.S. infant mortality was approximately three times higher than Japan's. If the U.S. rate had been the same as Japan's, then 14,000 infant lives would not have been lost that year.

In 2021, the U.S. neonatal death rate of 3.3 deaths per 1,000 live births was substantially lower than that of many under-developed nations with limited healthcare resources, however, that rate was 48 percent higher than the average rate for E.U. nations. The U.S. under-age-five mortality rate was one-tenth the world's average rate, however, that rate of 6.2 deaths per 1,000 live births was 63 percent above the rate for the E.U. nations.

In 2017, the U.S. ranked fourth among the 38 OECD nations in maternal mortality rate. That rate of 19.0 deaths per 100,000 live births was 88 percent higher than the OECD average of 38 members and 155 percent higher than the average of the other 36 members when Colombia and Mexico are excluded.

The number of maternal mortalities in the U.S. increased by 83 percent between 2018 and 2021. In 2021, the rate of Black women's maternal deaths was 2.6 times greater than the rate of non-Hispanic White maternal deaths.

~

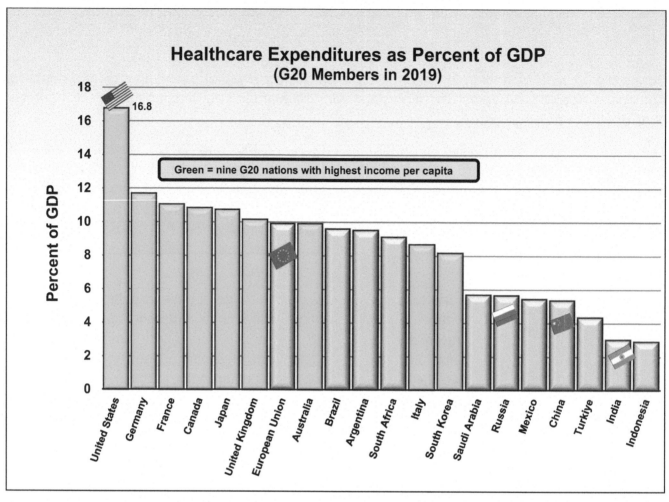

Healthcare Expenditures as Percent of GDP
(G20 Members in 2019)

Green = nine G20 nations with highest income per capita

Source: The World Bank, https://databank.worldbank.org/source/world-development-indicators, SH.XPD.CHEX.GD.ZS, accessed 8/23/23
https://data.worldbank.org/summary-terms-of-use, accessed 8-23-23

The U.S. spent more on health care in 2019, measured as percent of gross domestic product (GDP), than any other G20 nation. Compared with the other high income per capita nations (principal U.S. partners) the U.S. spent 66 percent more.

The level of current healthcare expenditure for the G20 members are expressed as a percentage of GDP. Estimates of current health expenditures include healthcare goods and services consumed during each year. This indicator does not include capital health expenditures such as buildings, machinery, IT and stocks of vaccines for emergencies or outbreaks.

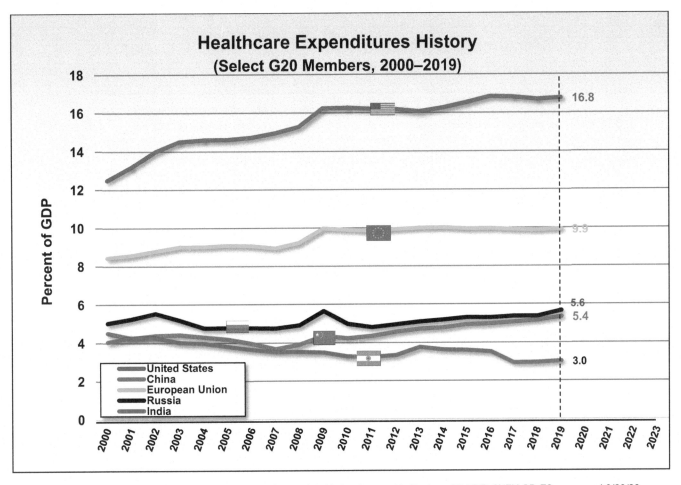

Source: The World Bank, https://databank.worldbank.org/source/world-development-indicators, SH.XPD.CHEX.GD.ZS, accessed 8/23/23
https://data.worldbank.org/summary-terms-of-use, accessed 6-1-23

Whereas the E.U.'s health care expenditures, measured as percent of GDP, have increased 17 percent between 2000 and 2019, the U.S. expenditures increased by 31 percent between 2000 and 2009, and slowed to 3 percent between 2009 and 2019.

The health expenditure estimates have been prepared by the World Health Organization under the framework of the System of Health Accounts 2011 (SHA 2011). The Health SHA 2011 tracks all health spending in a given country over a defined period of time regardless of the entity or institution that financed and managed that spending.

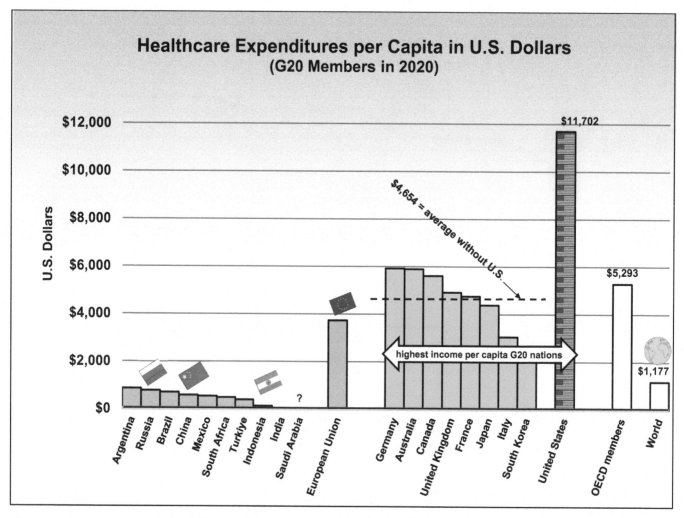

Healthcare Expenditures per Capita in U.S. Dollars
(G20 Members in 2020)

Source: The World Bank, https://databank.worldbank.org/source/world-development-indicators, SH.XPD.CHEX.PC.CD, accessed 8/23/23
https://data.worldbank.org/summary-terms-of-use, accessed 7-9-23

In 2020, the U.S. spent 2.5 times as much per capita for healthcare as the other eight highest income per capita G20 members (principal U.S. partners), 2.2 as much as the average OECD member, and ten times as much as the world's average expenditure.

Current expenditures on health per capita are in 2020 US dollars. Estimates of current health expenditures include healthcare goods and services consumed during each year. The health expenditure estimates have been prepared by the World Health Organization under the framework of the System of Health Accounts 2011 (SHA 2011). The Health SHA 2011, tracks all health spending in a given country over a defined period of time regardless of the entity or institution that financed and managed that spending. It generates consistent and comprehensive data on health spending in a country, which in turn can contribute to evidence-based policymaking.

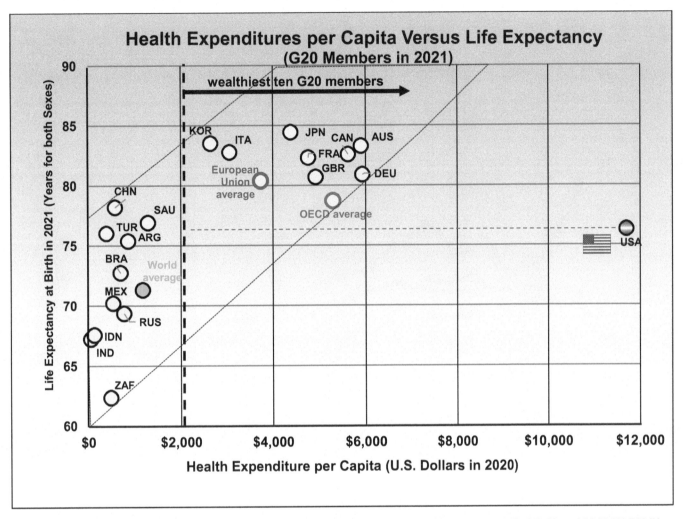

Sources: The World Bank, https://databank.worldbank.org/source/world-development-indicators, SH.XPD.CHEX.PC.CD and SP.DYN.LE00.IN, https://data.worldbank.org/summary-terms-of-use, accessed 8/23/23

In 2021, life expectancy in the U.S. was up to ten years lower than would be expected based on health care expenditure per capita of other nations. U.S. life expectancy was the lowest of the wealthiest ten G20 members, and lower than all OECD members

Country Codes

Country	Code
Argentina	ARG
Australia	AUS
Brazil	BRA
Canada	CAN
China	CHN
France	FRA
Germany	DEU
India	IND
Indonesia	IDN
Italy	ITA
Japan	JPN
South Korea	KOR
Mexico	MEX
Russia	RUS
Saudi Arabia	SAU
South Africa	ZAF
Turkiye	TUR
United Kingdom	GBR
United States	USA

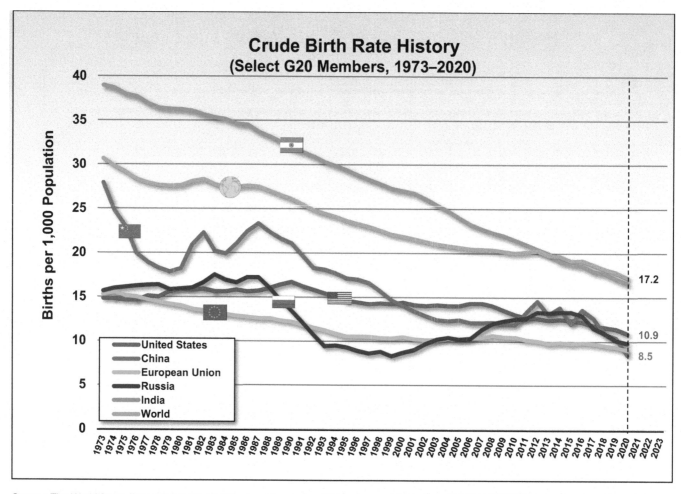

Source: The World Bank, https://databank.worldbank.org/source/world-development-indicators, SP.DYN.CBRT.IN, accessed 8/23/23
https://data.worldbank.org/summary-terms-of-use

Since 1990, the birth rate in the U.S. has been on the decline. By 2020, the U.S. birth rate had declined by one-third but was 10–25 percent above China, Russia, and the E.U. with birth rates that were approximately one-half of the world's average rate of 17.2 percent.

Crude birth rate indicates the number of live births occurring during the year, per 1,000 population estimated at midyear. Subtracting the crude death rate from the crude birth rate provides the rate of natural increase, which is equal to the rate of population change in the absence of migration.

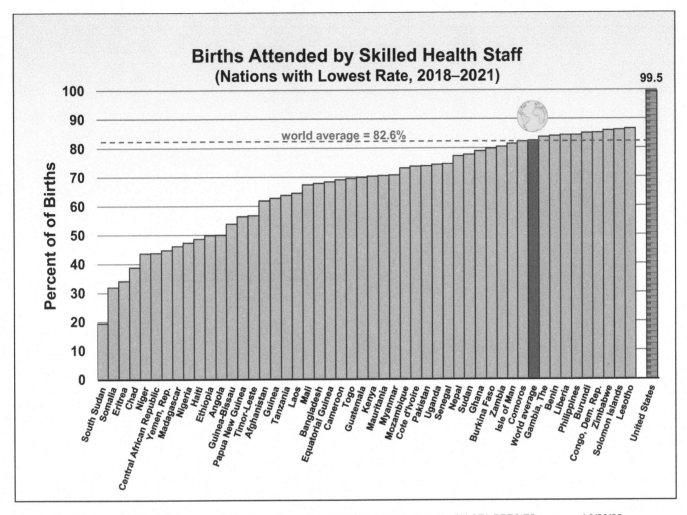

Births Attended by Skilled Health Staff
(Nations with Lowest Rate, 2018–2021)

Source: The World Bank, https://databank.worldbank.org/source/world-development-indicators, SH.STA.BRTC.ZS, accessed 8/23/23
https://data.worldbank.org/summary-terms-of-use

Although the U.S. ranked very high in the world in 2021, for percent of births attended by skilled health staff at 99.5 percent that left approximately 18,000 births in the U.S. that did not have medical oversight. Generally, nations with low oversight percentage tended to experience disproportionate infant, neonatal, and maternal death rates. For example, South Sudan, the country with the lowest oversight rate (19.4 percent ranked highest in the world for maternal death rate and third highest for neonatal death rate.

Births attended by skilled health staff are the percentage of deliveries attended by personnel trained to give the necessary supervision, care, and advice to women during pregnancy, labor, and the postpartum period; to conduct deliveries on their own; and to care for newborns. Reproductive health is a state of physical and mental well-being in relation to the reproductive system and its functions and processes. Means of achieving reproductive health include education and services during pregnancy and childbirth, safe and effective contraception, and prevention and treatment of sexually transmitted diseases. Complications of pregnancy and childbirth are the leading cause of death and disability among women of reproductive age in developing countries. The share of births attended by skilled health staff is an indicator of a health system's ability to provide adequate care for pregnant women. Assistance by trained professionals during birth reduces the incidence of maternal deaths during childbirth.

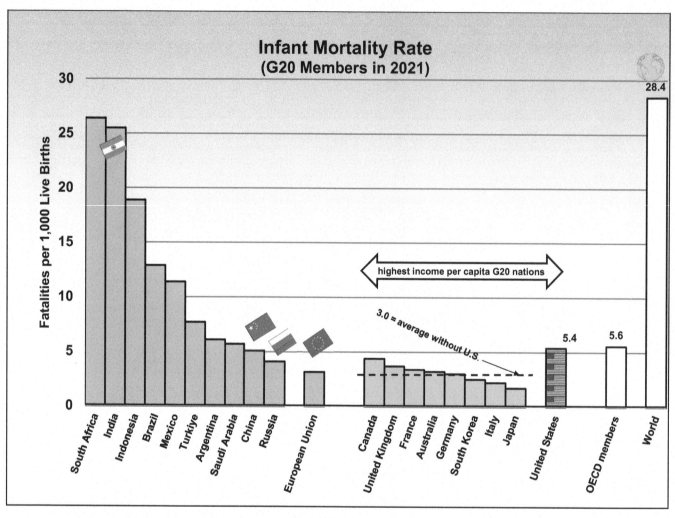

Infant Mortality Rate
(G20 Members in 2021)

Source: The World Bank, https://databank.worldbank.org/source/world-development-indicators, SP.DYN.IMRT.IN, accessed 8/23/23
https://data.worldbank.org/summary-terms-of-use, accessed 7-9-23, https://www.cdc.gov/nchs/fastats/infant-health.htm

In 2021, the infant mortality rate in the U.S. was five time lower than the average rate of all the world's nations, however, it was 80 percent higher than the average rate for the other high income per capita G20 nations (principal U.S. partners). If the U.S. rate had been the same as the other wealthy nations, then instead of 19,921 infants dying there would have been 8,900 fewer.

Infant mortality rate is the number of infants dying before reaching one year of age, per 1,000 live births in a given year. The main sources of mortality data are vital registration systems and direct or indirect estimates based on sample surveys or censuses.

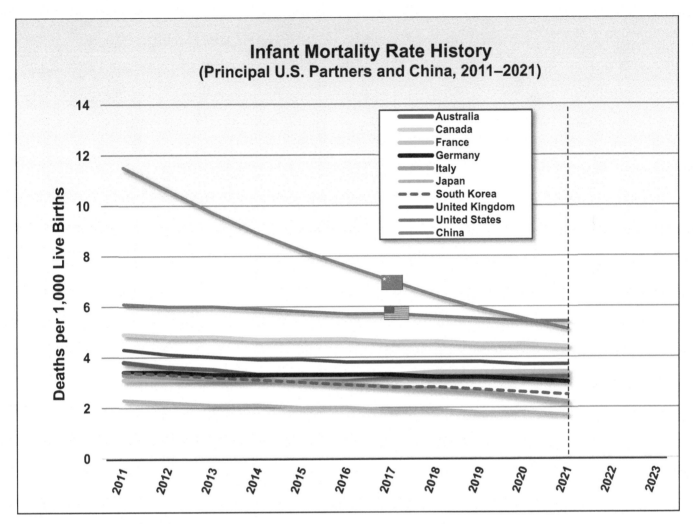

Infant Mortality Rate History
(Principal U.S. Partners and China, 2011–2021)

Source: The World Bank, https://databank.worldbank.org/source/world-development-indicators, SP.DYN.IMRT.IN, accessed 8/23/23
https://data.worldbank.org/summary-terms-of-use

In 2021, the U.S. infant mortality rate was higher than for any of the eight high income per capita principal U.S. partners. Between 2011 and 2021, U.S. infant mortality rate declined from 6.1 deaths per 1,000 live births to 5.4, a 12 percent reduction. However, in that same time period China's infant mortality rate declined by a factor of two, down to 5.1 deaths per 1,000 live births.

Infant mortality rate is the number of infants dying before reaching one year of age, per 1,000 live births in a given year. The main sources of mortality data are vital registration systems and direct or indirect estimates based on sample surveys or censuses. A "complete" vital registration system —covering at least 90 percent of vital events in the population—is the best source of age-specific mortality data. Estimates of neonatal, infant, and child mortality tend to vary by source and method for a given time and place. Years for available estimates also vary by nation, making comparisons across countries and over time difficult.

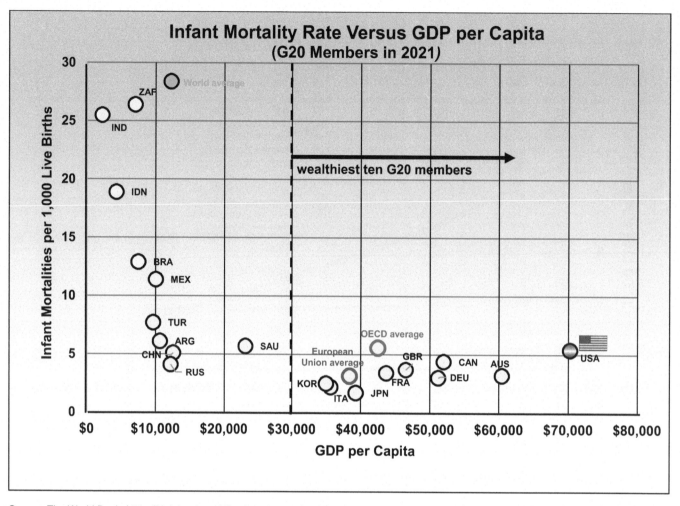

Source: The World Bank, https://databank.worldbank.org/source/world-development-indicators, NY.GDP.PCAP.CD and SP.DYN.IMRT.IN, accessed 8/23/23, https://data.worldbank.org/summary-terms-of-use

In 2021, U.S. infant mortality rate was 70 percent higher than the E.U.'s average rate, based on GDP per capita, and approximately three times higher than Japan's. It was higher than the rate for any principal U.S. partner.

Country Codes

Argentina	ARG
Australia	AUS
Brazil	BRA
Canada	CAN
China	CHN
France	FRA
Germany	DEU
India	IND
Indonesia	IDN
Italy	ITA
Japan	JPN
South Korea	KOR
Mexico	MEX
Russia	RUS
Saudi Arabia	SAU
South Africa	ZAF
Turkiye	TUR
United Kingdom	GBR
United States	USA

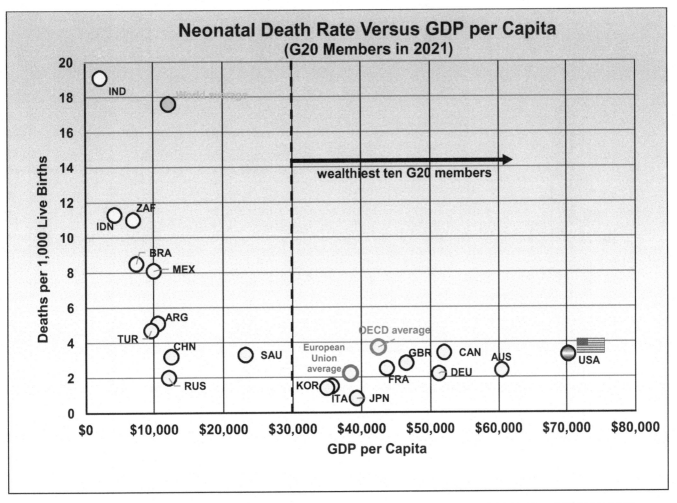

Neonatal Death Rate Versus GDP per Capita
(G20 Members in 2021)

Source: The World Bank, https://databank.worldbank.org/source/world-development-indicators, NY.GDP.PCAP.CD and SH.DYN.NMRT, accessed 8/23/23, https://data.worldbank.org/summary-terms-of-use

In 2021, the U.S. neonatal mortality rate was approximately one-sixth the world's average rate and approximately equal to the average of the E.U. and OECD nations.

Neonatal mortality rate is the number of neonates dying before reaching 28 days of age.

Country Codes

Argentina	ARG
Australia	AUS
Brazil	BRA
Canada	CAN
China	CHN
France	FRA
Germany	DEU
India	IND
Indonesia	IDN
Italy	ITA
Japan	JPN
South Korea	KOR
Mexico	MEX
Russia	RUS
Saudi Arabia	SAU
South Africa	ZAF
Turkiye	TUR
United Kingdom	GBR
United States	USA

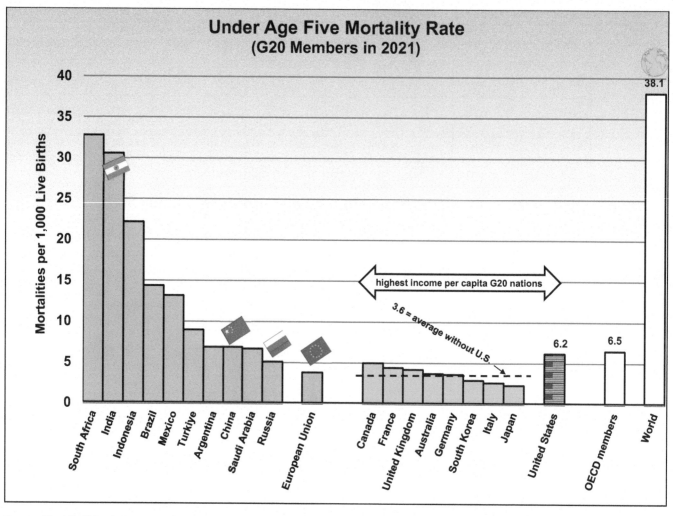

Under Age Five Mortality Rate
(G20 Members in 2021)

Source: The World Bank, https://databank.worldbank.org/source/world-development-indicators, SH.DYN.MORT, https://data.worldbank.org/summary-terms-of-use, accessed 7-9-23

In 2021, newborns in the U.S. that were under age five died at a rate that was 1.7 times higher than the rate for the other eight high income per capita G20 nations (principal U.S. partners).

Under-five mortality rate is the probability per 1,000 that a newborn baby will die before reaching age five, if subject to age-specific mortality rates of the specified year. The main sources of mortality data are vital registration systems and direct or indirect estimates based on sample surveys or censuses. A "complete" vital registration system (covering at least 90 percent of vital events in the population) is the best source of age-specific mortality data.

Estimates of neonatal, infant, and child mortality tend to vary by source and method for a given time and place. Years for available estimates also vary by nation, making comparisons across countries and over time difficult.

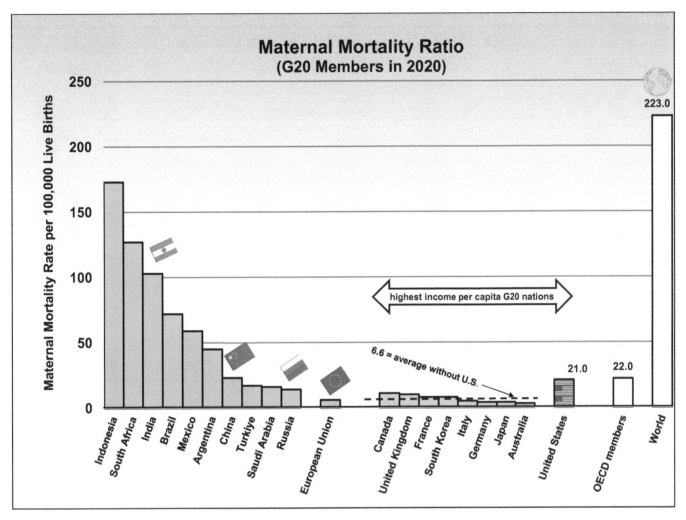

Source: The World Bank, https://databank.worldbank.org/source/world-development-indicators, SH.STA.MMRT, https://data.worldbank.org/summary-terms-of-use, accessed 7-9-23

In 2020, U.S. maternal mortality rates were eleven times lower than the world's average rate. However, the U.S. experienced 21 deaths per 100,000 live births, three times the maternal death rate of the other high income per capita G20 members (principal U.S. partners). In 2021, there were 1,205 maternal deaths in the U.S.

Maternal mortality ratio is the number of women who die from pregnancy-related causes while pregnant or within 42 days of pregnancy termination per 100,000 live births. The data are estimated with a regression model using information on the proportion of maternal deaths among non-AIDS deaths in women ages 15–49, fertility, birth attendants, and GDP measured using purchasing power parities (PPPs).

Maternal mortality is generally of unknown reliability, as are many other cause-specific mortality indicators. Household surveys such as Demographic and Health Surveys attempt to measure maternal mortality by asking respondents about survivorship of sisters. The main disadvantage of this method is that the estimates of maternal mortality that it produces pertain to any time within the past few years before the survey, making them unsuitable for monitoring recent changes or observing the impact of interventions. In addition, measurement of maternal mortality is subject to many types of errors. Even in high-income countries with reliable vital registration systems, misclassification of maternal deaths has been found to lead to serious underestimation.

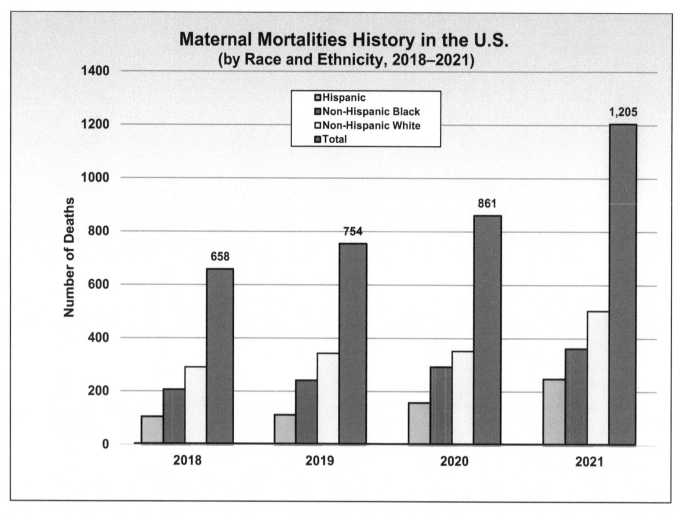

Maternal Mortalities History in the U.S.
(by Race and Ethnicity, 2018–2021)

Source: CDC, National Center for Health Statistics, National Vital Statistics System, Natality and Mortality, https://www.cdc.gov/nchs/data/hestat/maternal-mortality/2021/maternal-mortality-rates-2021.htm, accessed 6-2-23

The number of maternal mortalities in the U.S. has increased by 83 percent between 2018 and 2021. In 2021, the rate of Black maternal deaths was 2.6 times greater than the rate of non-Hispanic White maternal deaths.

Data are from the National Vital Statistics System mortality file. The number of maternal deaths does not include all deaths occurring to pregnant or recently pregnant women, but only deaths with the underlying cause of death assigned to International Statistical Classification of Diseases.

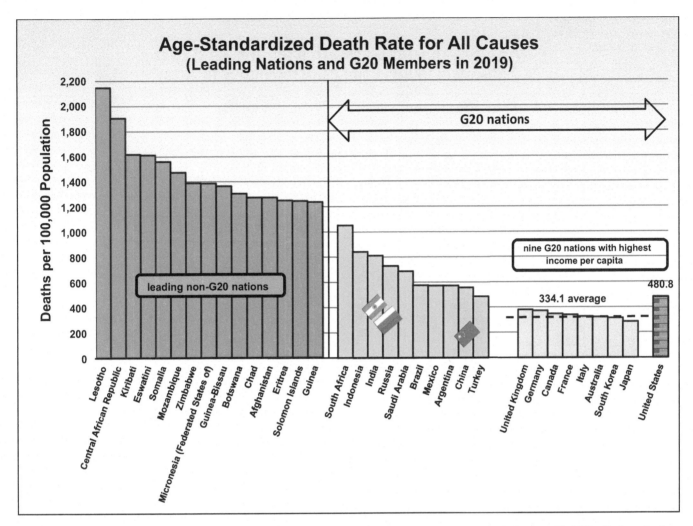

Age-Standardized Death Rate for All Causes
(Leading Nations and G20 Members in 2019)

Source: Global Health Estimates 2019: Deaths by Cause, Age, Sex, by Country and by Region, 2000-2019. Geneva, World Health Organization; 2020. https://www.who.int/data/gho/data/themes/mortality-and-global-health-estimates, Non-exclusive license dated 3/15/23 to use selected WHO published materials.

In 2019, prior to the COVID-19 pandemic, the age-standardized death rate for all causes in the United States was 44 percent above the average of the other eight high income per capita G20 members (principal U.S. partners). The use of age-standardized data removes the age bias inherent in comparing data among nations with different age distributions.

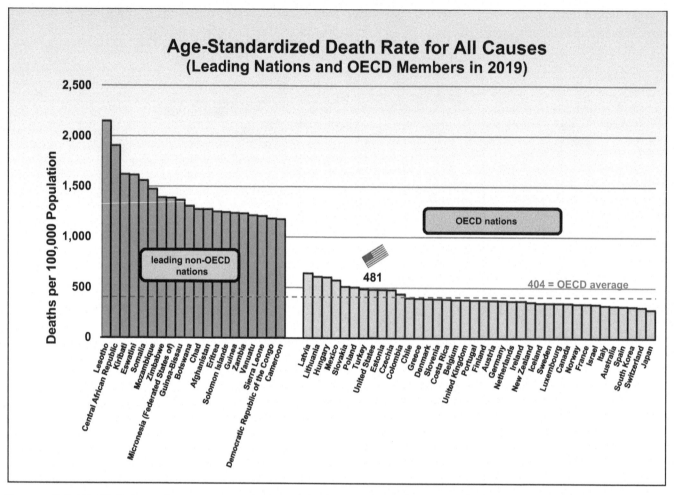

Age-Standardized Death Rate for All Causes
(Leading Nations and OECD Members in 2019)

Sources: Global Health Estimates 2019: Deaths by Cause, Age, Sex, by Country and by Region, 2000-2019. Geneva, World Health Organization; 2020. https://www.who.int/data/gho/data/themes/mortality-and-global-health-estimates, Non-exclusive license dated 3/15/23 to use selected WHO published materials, National Vital Statistics Reports; Vol. 47 No. 3. Hyattsville, Maryland: National Center for Health Statistics

In 2019, the U.S. age-standardized death rate for all causes ranked eighth out of the 38 OECD nations. The table below illustrates how the standard age distributions of the U.S. have changed with time. Age-standardized fatality rates can be used to compare the mortality rates of countries without being affected by the difference in age distributions from country to country.

	U.S. Standard Population Distributions:		
	Proportion of U.S. Population in Age-Group		
Age	1940	1970	2000
Under 1 year	1.5%	1.7%	1.4%
1 - 4 years	6.5%	6.7%	5.5%
5 - 14 years	17.0%	20.1%	14.6%
15 - 24 years	18.2%	17.4%	13.9%
25 - 34 years	16.2%	12.3%	13.6%
35 - 44 years	13.9%	11.4%	16.3%
45 - 54 years	11.8%	11.4%	13.5%
55 - 64 years	8.0%	9.1%	8.7%
65 - 74 years	4.8%	6.1%	6.6%
75 - 84 years	1.7%	3.0%	4.5%
85 and over	0.3%	0.7%	1.6%
All ages	100.0%	100.0%	100.0%

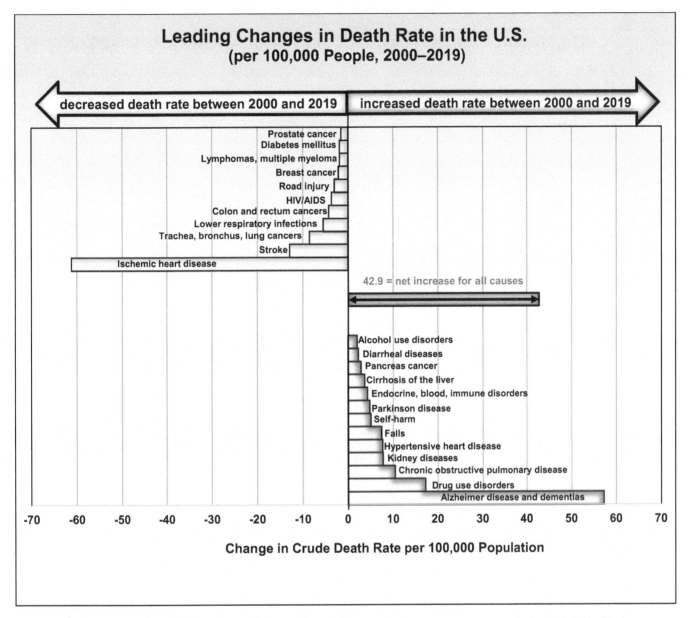

Source: Global Health Estimates 2019: Deaths by Cause, Age, Sex, by Country and by Region, 2000–2019. Geneva, World Health Organization; 2020. https://www.who.int/data/gho/data/themes/mortality-and-global-health-estimates, Non-exclusive license dated 3/15/23 to use selected WHO published materials.

The overall crude death rate in the U.S. between 2000 and 2019, increased by 42.9 deaths per 100,000 people (5.1 percent). This period ended prior to the 2020 pandemic declaration so the data were not impacted by COVID-19. This net increase occurred despite significant reductions in deaths per 100,000 population in several categories of noncommunicable diseases, especially ischemic heart disease (–61.2) and stroke (–12.9) which were offset by increases in Alzheimer's disease, dementias (+57.2), and drug use disorders (+17.3).

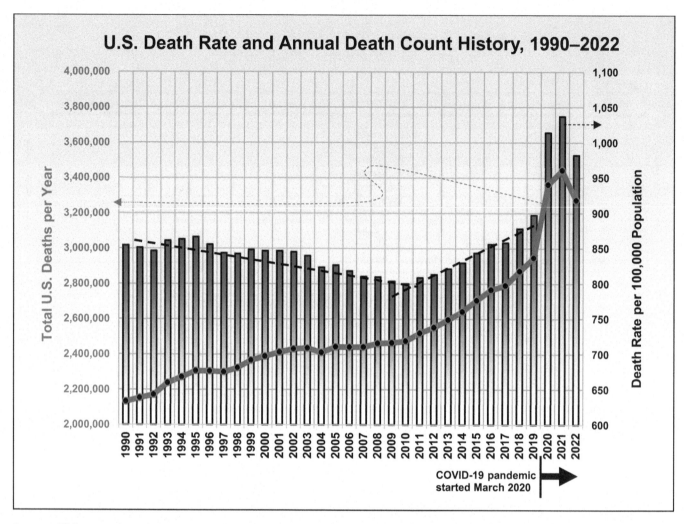

U.S. Death Rate and Annual Death Count History, 1990–2022

COVID-19 pandemic
started March 2020

Sources: CDC, www.cdc.gov/nchs/data/databriefs/db456-tables.pdf#3, and Our World In Data, https://ourworldindata.org/.

In 2010, the death rate in the U.S. had declined to 800 deaths per 100,000 population, the lowest rate since 1990. However, beginning in approximately 2010, there was an abrupt reversal in annual death rate and instead of the rate declining each year it began to increase at a rate that averaged at an additional 40,000 deaths per year over the next ten years. Then, in March 2020, the COVID-19 pandemic dramatically increased the death rate and by 2021, peaked at 1,037 deaths per 100,000 population. Compared to the 2010 low rate of 800 that represented a 29.6 percent increase in rate. In the year 2021, there were 3,443,000 deaths in the U.S. and by 2022, the rate declined to 982 deaths per 100,000 population.

Had the rate of 800 deaths per 100,000 as was experienced in 2010, remained constant through 2022, there would have been 3,419,550 fewer deaths between 2010 and 2022.

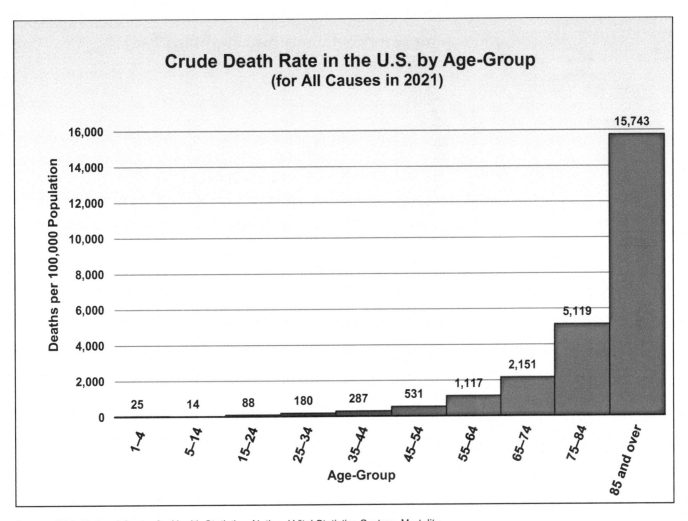

Crude Death Rate in the U.S. by Age-Group
(for All Causes in 2021)

Source: CDC, National Center for Health Statistics, National Vital Statistics System, Mortality,
https://www.cdc.gov/nchs/products/databriefs/db456.htm, accessed 6-2-23

The large death rate level differences between age groups in the U.S. dramatically demonstrates how death rate comparisons between countries can be difficult to compare when age distributions are not the same.

The crude mortality rate is a good indicator of the general health status of a geographic area or population. The crude death rate is not appropriate for comparison of different populations or areas with large differences in age distributions. Higher crude death rates can be found in some developed countries, despite high life expectancy, because typically these countries have a much higher proportion of older people, due to lower recent birth rates and lower age-specific mortality rates. Crude death rate indicates the number of deaths occurring during the year, per 1,000 population estimated at midyear. Subtracting the crude death rate from the crude birth rate provides the rate of natural increase, which is equal to the rate of population change in the absence of migration.

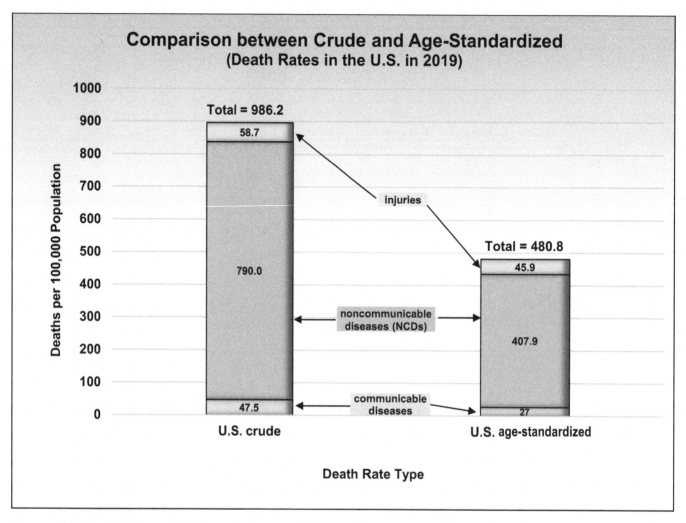

Comparison between Crude and Age-Standardized
(Death Rates in the U.S. in 2019)

Sources: Global Health Estimates 2019: Deaths by Cause, Age, Sex, by Country and by Region, 2000-2019. Geneva, World Health Organization; 2020. https://www.who.int/data/gho/data/themes/mortality-and-global-health-estimates, Non-exclusive license dated 3/15/23 to use selected WHO published materials, National Vital Statistics Reports; Vol. 47 No. 3. Hyattsville, Maryland: National Center for Health Statistics

The table below illustrates how the age distributions in the U.S. have changed with time. Age-standardized fatality rates can be used to compare the mortality rates of countries without being affected by the difference in age distributions between countries.

	U.S. Standard Population Distributions:		
	Proportion of U.S. Population in Age-Group		
Age	**1940**	**1970**	**2000**
Under 1 year	1.5%	1.7%	1.4%
1 - 4 years	6.5%	6.7%	5.5%
5 - 14 years	17.0%	20.1%	14.6%
15 - 24 years	18.2%	17.4%	13.9%
25 - 34 years	16.2%	12.3%	13.6%
35 - 44 years	13.9%	11.4%	16.3%
45 - 54 years	11.8%	11.4%	13.5%
55 - 64 years	8.0%	9.1%	8.7%
65 - 74 years	4.8%	6.1%	6.6%
75 - 84 years	1.7%	3.0%	4.5%
85 and over	0.3%	0.7%	1.6%
All ages	100.0%	100.0%	100.0%

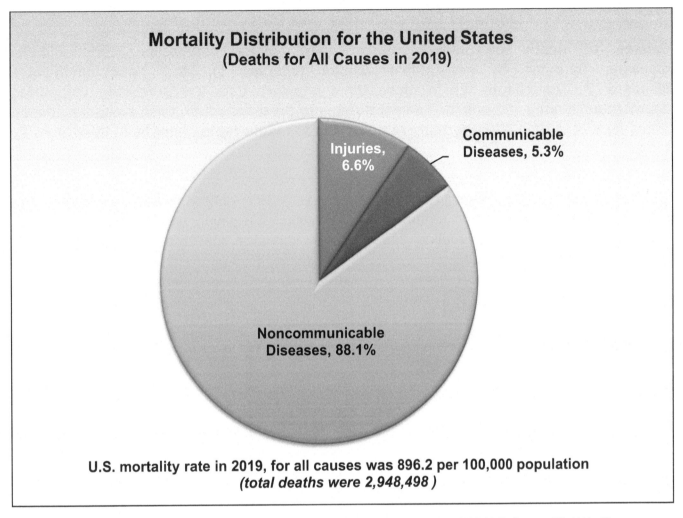

Mortality Distribution for the United States
(Deaths for All Causes in 2019)

Injuries, 6.6%

Communicable Diseases, 5.3%

Noncommunicable Diseases, 88.1%

U.S. mortality rate in 2019, for all causes was 896.2 per 100,000 population
(total deaths were 2,948,498)

Sources: Global Health Estimates 2019: Deaths by Cause, Age, Sex, by Country and by Region, 2000-2019. Geneva, World Health Organization; 2020. https://www.who.int/data/gho/data/themes/mortality-and-global-health-estimates, Non-exclusive license dated 3/15/23 to use selected WHO published materials.

In 2019, prior to the COVID-19 pandemic, noncommunicable diseases (NCDs) were the cause of death for 2,597,626 lives (88.1 percent) in the U.S. The largest subcategories of NCDs were cardiovascular diseases (872,755 lives) followed by malignant neoplasms (616,236 lives).

Mortality Comparisons and Classifications

Causes of death fall under one of three major categories: communicable diseases (chapter 4), preventable deaths (chapter 5), and noncommunicable diseases (NCDs, chapter 6). In these three chapters data are presented comparing death rates among nations for a select number of diseases within each category, chosen primarily due to their high mortality rates or due to recent rapid changes in their morality rates.

The hierarchy of causes of death, including their major categories and subcategories, consists of 203 named causes. The World Health Organization (WHO) publishes rules adopted by the World Health Assembly (WHA) regarding the selection of a single cause or condition, from death certificates, for the routine tabulation of mortality statistics to standardize the production of mortality data.

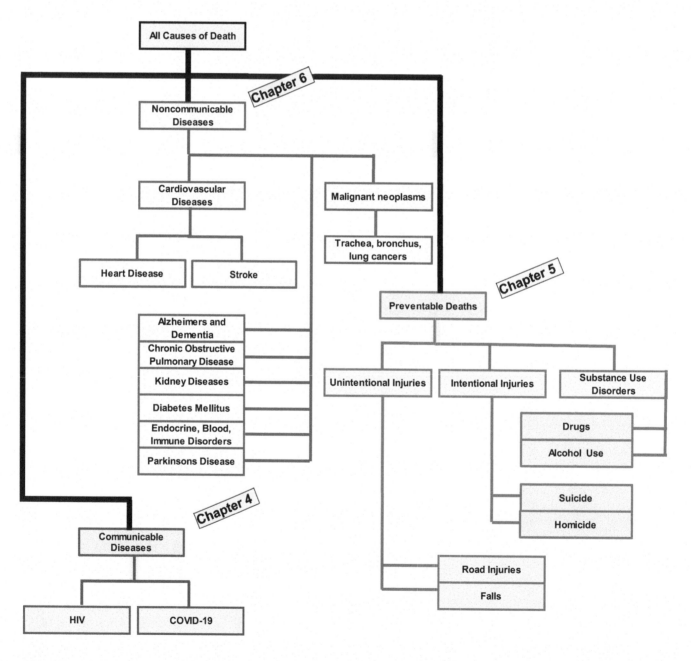

Chapter 4

Communicable Diseases

Overview of Communicable Diseases

Communicable disease death rates are typically disproportionately high in the poorest countries that lack disease prevention methods and readily available quality health care. In 2019—prior to the COVID-19 pandemic—the wealthiest nine G20 nations (the U.S. plus principal U.S. partners) had an average communicable disease death rate of 22.7 deaths per 100,000 population. In contrast some of the "poorest" nations averaged communicable disease death rates that were 20 times higher.

Communicable diseases accounted for 5.2 percent of all deaths in the U.S. in 2019, however, after the first year of the COVID-19 pandemic that began in March 2020, the percentage jumped from 5.2 percent to 16.7 percent. The U.S. reached the highest death count of any nation for COVID-19, estimated to be one-sixth of all COVID-19 deaths in the world. Total age-standardized death rate in the U.S. increased by 22.4 percent in the one-year period between March 2020 and March 2021.

The following pages in this chapter contextualize the COVID-19 fatalities in the U.S. and illustrate the failure by the U.S. to fully benefit from the available scientific guidelines, protections and vaccinations, thereby making the U.S. the world's leader in COVID-19 deaths and placing the U.S. in the top 8 percent of nations for the highest COVID-19 death rates in the world of 193 nations.

On May 5, 2023, the World Health Organization (WHO) declared that the global COVID-19 pandemic had ended, after 37 months that killed an estimated 6.94 million people globally. The U.S. experienced 1.13 million COVID-19 deaths which was the highest level in the world, estimated to be 16.2 percent of the world's total COVID-19 death count. Of the 1.13 million deaths 75.5 percent were for people aged 65 years and more.

On June 30, 2023, the CDC published the U.S. statistics showing that 1,135,793 had died of COVID-19 since February 1, 2020, and during that period the number of "excess deaths" was 1,349,355. Excess mortality is defined as the difference between the total number of deaths estimated for a specific place and given time period and the number that would have been expected in the absence of a crisis (*e.g., COVID-19 pandemic*). This difference is assumed to include deaths attributable directly to COVID-19 as well as deaths indirectly associated with COVID-19 through impacts on health systems and society, minus any deaths that would have occurred under normal circumstances but were averted due to pandemic-related changes in social conditions and personal behaviors.

In early 2020, the efficacy of the initial COVID-19 mRNA vaccines to prevent death was estimated to be 95 percent, however, as new variants of the virus emerged that efficacy was reduced and reformulated vaccine boosters were required to maintain protection. In the U.S. public trust in scientific data and in the nation's health institutions—including the CDC and National Institute of Health—was diminished due to disinformation spread by conspiracy theorists about the dangers posed by these vaccines. The result was that many people choose not to be vaccinated resulting in possibly hundreds of thousands of deaths that may have been prevented.

There is a significant statistical correlation between U.S. states with lower vaccination rates having higher COVID-19 death rates. There is also a significant correlation between states with lower vaccination rates and states with higher percentage vote counts for the Republican 2020 presidential candidate Donald Trump. Cross-correlating the data shows that states with the highest percentage votes for Trump over Biden had the highest COVID-19 death rates.

In 2019, prior to the COVID-19 pandemic, HIV/AIDS accounted for 0.19 percent of all deaths in the U.S. However, the reliability of HIV infection level statistics is considered low since many with HIV have not been tested and many people do not know they are infected. In poor countries, HIV testing and medications that can lower levels of HIV in the blood and help prevent transmission risk have limited availability. Poor countries, especially in Africa, have infection rates among adults of more than 20 percent. In South Africa, a G20 member, the rate is 18.3 percent which is 45 times higher than the U.S. rate. Between 2003 and 2023, the U.S. funded over $100 billion for global HIV/AIDS treatment and prevention saving an estimated 20 million lives, predominately in Africa.

In 2023, according to the CDC, prior to polio vaccines becoming available in the 1950s, polio paralyzed more than 15,000 people each year in the U.S. Thanks to widespread polio vaccinations in the U.S., wild polio has been eliminated—with no cases occurring in the country between 1979 and 2022. The CDC also reported that in 2018, 92.5 percent of all children in the U.S. had received polio vaccinations. If the polio vaccine had been politicized as was the COVID-19 vaccine there most likely would have been a completely different outcome.

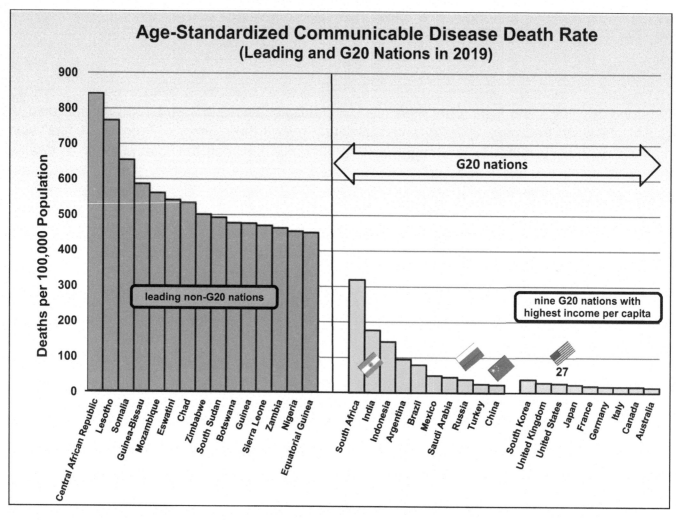

Age-Standardized Communicable Disease Death Rate
(Leading and G20 Nations in 2019)

Source: Global Health Estimates 2019: Deaths by Cause, Age, Sex, by Country and by Region, 2000-2019. Geneva, World Health Organization; 2020. https://www.who.int/data/gho/data/themes/mortality-and-global-health-estimates, Non-exclusive license dated 3/15/23 to use selected WHO published materials

Communicable disease death rates are disproportionately high in poor countries. In 2019— prior to the COVID-19 pandemic—the "wealthiest" nine G20 nations had an average age-standardized communicable disease death rate of 22.7 deaths per 100,000 population. In contrast the "poorest" nations averaged death rates that were 20 time higher. All communicable diseases accounted for 5.2 percent of all deaths in the U.S. in 2019, however, during the COVID-19 pandemic (March 2020–May 2023) that percentage jumped from 5.2 percent to 16.7 percent. The U.S. had the highest death count of any nation for COVID-19.

Pages 81-87 present the COVID-19 fatalities in the U.S. and show the failure by the U.S. to fully benefit from the scientific guidelines and protections of vaccinations, thereby making the U.S. the world's leader in COVID-19 deaths and placing the U.S. in the top 8 percent of nations for the highest COVID-19 death rate.

A communicable disease is one that is spread from one person to another through a variety of ways that include: contact with blood and bodily fluids; breathing in an airborne virus; or by being bitten by an insect. Age-standardized mortality rates can be used to compare the mortality rates of countries without being affected by the difference in age distributions from country to country.

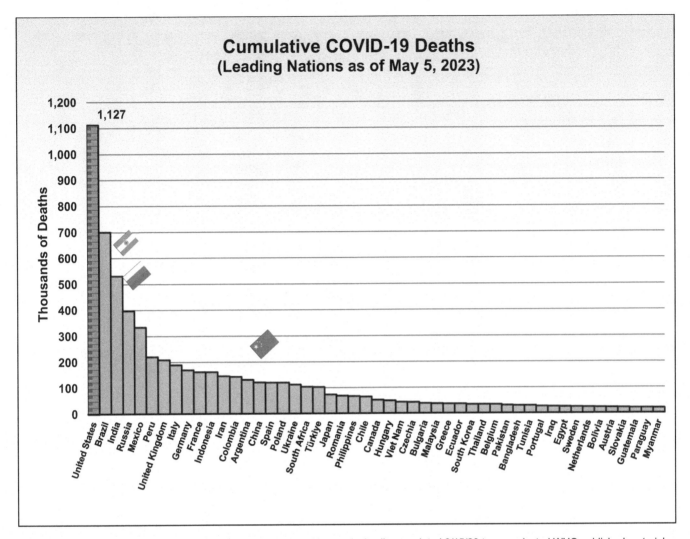

Cumulative COVID-19 Deaths
(Leading Nations as of May 5, 2023)

Source: World health Organization, https://covid19.who.int/data. Non-exclusive license dated 3/15/23 to use selected WHO published materials, https://data.cdc.gov/widgets/9bhg-hcku?mobile_redirect=true

On May 5 2023, the World Health Organization declared that the global COVID-19 pandemic had ended, after 37 months during which COVID-19 killed an estimated 6.94 million people globally. The U.S. experienced 1.13 million deaths which was the highest level in the world, estimated to be 16.2 percent of the world's total deaths. According to the CDC, between January 1, 2020 and June 24, 2023, 75.5 percent of the 1,136,057 deaths due to COVID-19 in the U.S. were people aged over 65 years.

COVID-19 is a disease caused by a virus named SARS-CoV-2. It can be very contagious and spreads quickly. COVID-19 most often causes respiratory symptoms that can feel much like a cold, the flu, or pneumonia. COVID-19 may attack more than your lungs and respiratory system. Other parts of your body may also be affected by the disease. COVID-19 spreads when an infected person breathes out droplets and very small particles that contain the virus. Other people can breathe in these droplets and particles, or these droplets and particles can land on their eyes, nose, or mouth. In some circumstances, these droplets may contaminate surfaces they touch. Anyone infected with COVID-19 can spread it, even if they do NOT have symptoms. In January 2021, vaccines became available that reduced the risk of severe COVID symptoms by up to 95 percent. By the end of the pandemic an estimated 13.3 billion doses, including boosters, had been administered throughout the world.

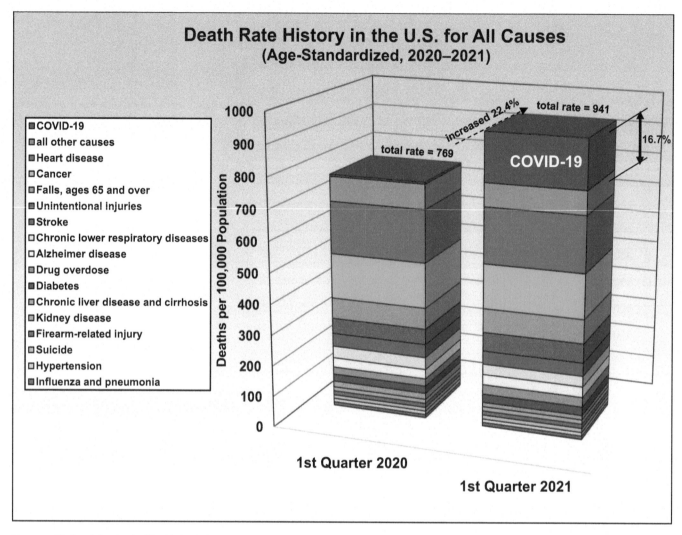

Death Rate History in the U.S. for All Causes
(Age-Standardized, 2020–2021)

Legend:
- COVID-19
- all other causes
- Heart disease
- Cancer
- Falls, ages 65 and over
- Unintentional injuries
- Stroke
- Chronic lower respiratory diseases
- Alzheimer disease
- Drug overdose
- Diabetes
- Chronic liver disease and cirrhosis
- Kidney disease
- Firearm-related injury
- Suicide
- Hypertension
- Influenza and pneumonia

Y-axis: Deaths per 100,000 Population

total rate = 769 (1st Quarter 2020)
increased 22.4%
total rate = 941 (1st Quarter 2021)
16.7%
COVID-19

Sources: National Center for Health Statistics, https://www.cdc.gov/nchs/nvss/vsrr/mortality-dashboard.htm, Ahmad FB, Cisewski JA. Quarterly provisional estimates for selected indicators of mortality, 2020-Quarter 3, 2022. National Center for Health Statistics. National Vital Statistics System, Vital Statistics Rapid Release Program. 2023.

On February 29, 2020, the first person in the U.S. died of COVID-19 and on March 11, 2020, the World Health Organization (WHO) declared a pandemic. By the end of the first year of the pandemic COVID-19 accounted for 16.7 percent of all deaths in the U.S. and COVID-19 had become the second leading cause of death in the U.S. That year the death rate for COVID-19 was 158 per 100,000, after the number one cause of death, heart disease and before third place, cancer. The total death rate in the U.S. increased by 22.3 percent during that one-year period.

COVID-19 spreads when an infected person breathes out droplets and very small particles that contain the virus. Other people can breathe in these droplets and particles, or these droplets and particles can land on their eyes, nose, or mouth. In some circumstances, these droplets may contaminate surfaces they touch. Anyone infected with COVID-19 can spread it, even if they do not have symptoms.

In January 2021, vaccines became available that reduced the risk of severe COVID symptoms by up to 95 percent. By the end of the pandemic an estimated 13.3 billion doses, including boosters, had been administered throughout the world.

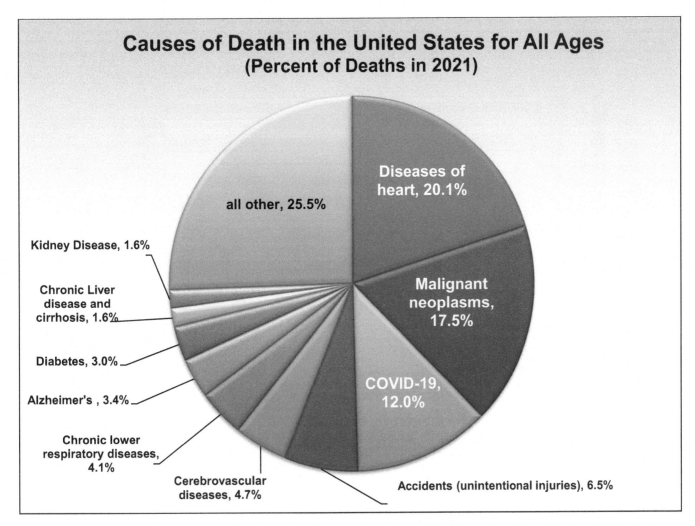

Causes of Death in the United States for All Ages
(Percent of Deaths in 2021)

Diseases of heart, 20.1%

Malignant neoplasms, 17.5%

COVID-19, 12.0%

Accidents (unintentional injuries), 6.5%

Cerebrovascular diseases, 4.7%

Chronic lower respiratory diseases, 4.1%

Alzheimer's , 3.4%

Diabetes, 3.0%

Chronic Liver disease and cirrhosis, 1.6%

Kidney Disease, 1.6%

all other, 25.5%

Sources: National Center for Health Statistics, https://www.cdc.gov/nchs/nvss/vsrr/mortality-dashboard.htm, Ahmad FB, Cisewski JA. Quarterly provisional estimates for selected indicators of mortality, 2020-Quarter 3, 2022. National Center for Health Statistics. National Vital Statistics System, Vital Statistics Rapid Release Program. 2023.

At the end of 2021, the first full calendar year of the pandemic, COVID-19 became the third-largest cause of death in the U.S., responsible for 12.0 percent of all deaths in the U.S.

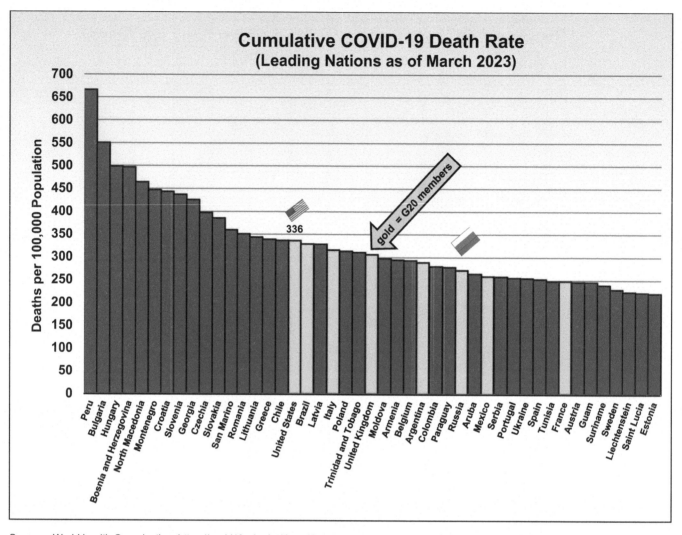

Cumulative COVID-19 Death Rate
(Leading Nations as of March 2023)

Sources: World health Organization, https://covid19.who.int/data. Non-exclusive license dated 3/15/23 to use selected WHO published materials, https://www.cdc.gov/nchs/covid19/mortality-overview.htm, https://www.ncbi.nlm.nih.gov/pmc/articles/PMC7488823/

In 2023, the cumulative death rate from COVID-19 in the U.S. was 336 per 100,000 population. That rate was the highest of any G20 member and ranked 17th in the world.

On June 30, 2023, the CDC published the U.S. statistics showing that 1,135,793 had died of COVID-19 since February 1, 2020, and during that period the number of "excess deaths" was 1,349,355.

Excess deaths provides an estimate of the additional number of deaths within a given time period, compared to the number of deaths expected in a specified time period. In encompassing deaths from all causes, excess mortality overcomes the variation between countries in reporting and testing of COVID-19 and in the misclassification of the cause of death on death certificates. Under the assumption that the incidence of other diseases remains steady over time, then excess deaths can be viewed as those caused both directly and indirectly by COVID-19 and gives a summary measure of the "whole system" impact.

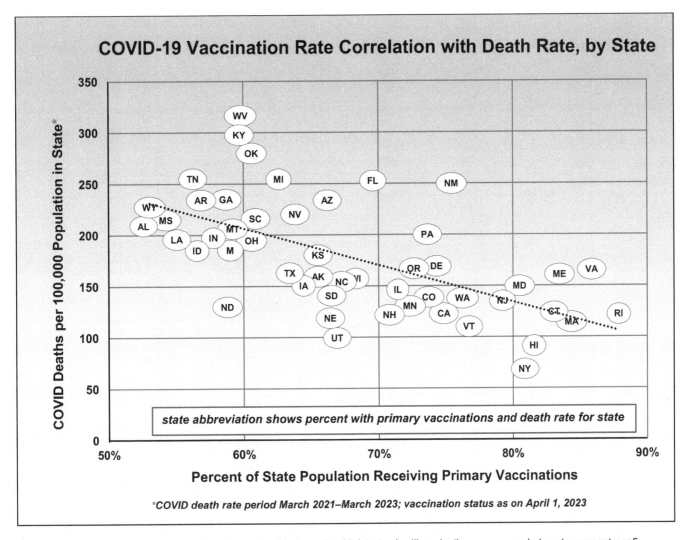

COVID-19 Vaccination Rate Correlation with Death Rate, by State

state abbreviation shows percent with primary vaccinations and death rate for state

COVID death rate period March 2021–March 2023; vaccination status as on April 1, 2023

Sources: National Center for Health Statistics, https://covid.cdc.gov/covid-data-tracker/#vaccinations_vacc-people-booster-percent-pop5

In early 2020, the efficacy of the initial COVID-19 mRNA vaccines to prevent death was estimated to be 95 percent, however, as new variants emerged that efficacy was reduced and reformulated vaccine boosters were required to maintain protection. In the U.S. trust in scientific data and in the nation's health institutions, including the CDC and National Institute of Health, were diminished due to misinformation spread by conspiracy theorists about the dangers posed by these vaccines. The result was that many people did not become vaccinated resulting in possibly hundreds of thousands of deaths that were preventable. The strong inverse correlation between COVID-19 death rates with vaccination rates for the 50 states is apparent from the data plot.

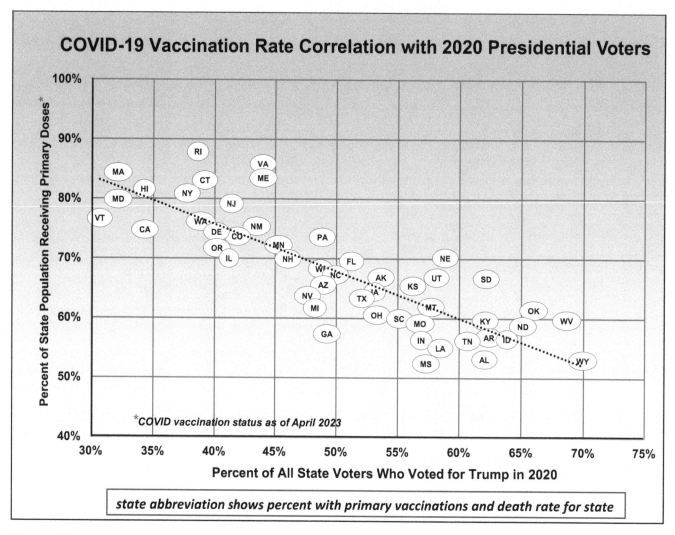

COVID-19 Vaccination Rate Correlation with 2020 Presidential Voters

Percent of State Population Receiving Primary Doses*

Percent of All State Voters Who Voted for Trump in 2020

*COVID vaccination status as of April 2023

state abbreviation shows percent with primary vaccinations and death rate for state

Sources: (1) Federal Election Commission, https://www.FEC.gov/resources/cms-content/documents/2020presgeresults.pdf, (2) National Center for Health Statistics, https://covid.cdc.gov/covid-data-tracker/#vaccinations_vacc-people-booster-percent-pop5

During the pandemic disinformation about the dangers of the mRNA vaccines became primary political talking points for factions of the Republican party. The result was that a significant portion of the U.S. public chose not to become vaccinated. There is a strong inverse correlation between vaccination rates in those states where a high percent of voters chose the Republican 2020 presidential candidate, Donald Trump over Joseph Biden, as evidenced by the data plot.

Trust in scientific data and in U.S. health institutions, including the CDC and National Institute of Health, were diminished due to misinformation spread by conspiracy theorists about the dangers posed by these vaccines. The result was that many people did not become vaccinated resulting in possibly hundreds of thousands of deaths that were preventable.

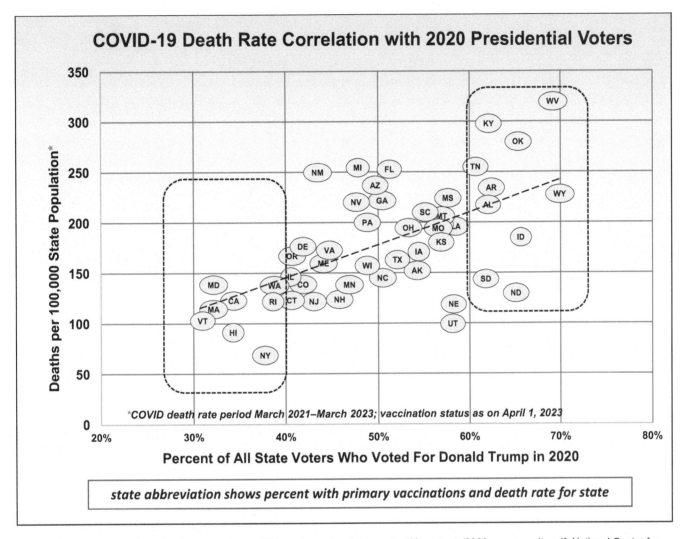

COVID-19 Death Rate Correlation with 2020 Presidential Voters

state abbreviation shows percent with primary vaccinations and death rate for state

Sources: Federal Elections Commission, https://www.FEC.gov/resources/cms-content/documents/2020presgeresults.pdf, National Center for Health Statistics, https://covid.cdc.gov/covid-data-tracker/#vaccinations_vacc-people-booster-percent-pop5, U.S. Census Bureau, https://www.census.gov/data/tables/time-series/demo/popest/2020s-state-total.html

Combining the data from the prior two charts showing the inverse correlation between vaccination rate and death rate (page 85), and the direct correlation between vaccination rate and voter choice of 2020 presidential candidate (page 86), leads to the observation that states with the highest percent of votes for Donald Trump were the states with the highest COVID-19 death rate.

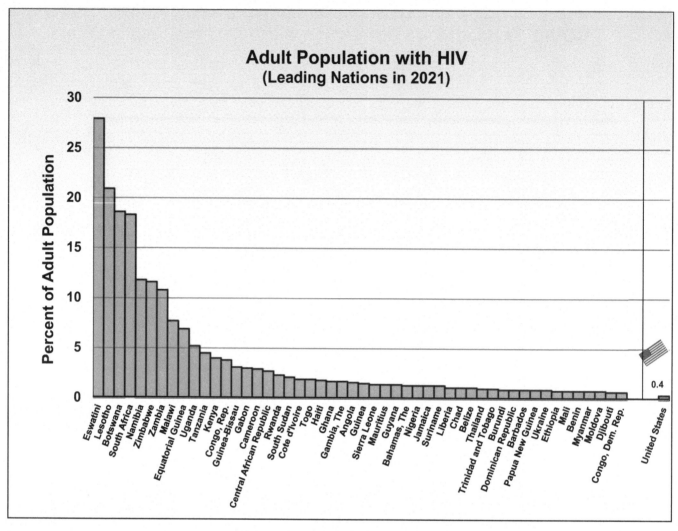

Adult Population with HIV
(Leading Nations in 2021)

Sources: The World Bank, https://databank.worldbank.org/source/world-development-indicators, SH.DYN.AIDS.ZS, accessed 8/23/23, U.S. Department of Health and Human Services, https://data.worldbank.org/summary-terms-of-use, https://www.hiv.gov/hiv-basics/overview/data-and-trends/statistics/, https://www.gao.gov/products/gao-23-105347

In 2019, prior to the COVID-19 pandemic, HIV/AIDS accounted for 0.19 percent of all deaths in the U.S. The reliability of HIV infection level statistics is low since many with HIV have not been tested and many people do not know they are infected. In poor countries, HIV testing and medications that can lower levels of HIV in the blood and help prevent transmission risk have limited availability. Poor countries, especially in Africa, have infection rates among adults of more than 20 percent. In South Africa, a G20 member, the rate is 18.3 percent which is 45 times higher than in the United States.

Since the beginning of the HIV/AIDS epidemic in 1981, an estimated 84.2 million people have been infected with the HIV virus and about 40.1 million people have died of HIV. Globally, 38.4 million people were living with HIV at the end of 2021. Since the beginning of the HIV epidemic, more than 700,000 people in the U.S. have died from HIV-related illness. In 2021, approximately 1.2 million people in the U.S. have HIV. About 13 percent of them don't know it and need testing.

Since 2003, the U.S. program "President's Emergency Plan for AIDS Relief" (PEPFAR) has provided over $100 billion for combating HIV/AIDS globally and saved an estimated 20 million lives, predominately in Africa.

Chapter 5

Preventable Deaths

Overview of Preventable Deaths

The five leading causes of preventable deaths in the U.S in 2021 accounted for over one-quarter million deaths:

Preventable Deaths in U.S., 2021

Drug overdose	106,688
Suicide	48,183
Road Injury	42,914
Falls	38,700
Homicides	22,900
Total	**259,385**

This chapter on preventable deaths has two major subcategories: unintentional and intentional injuries. Unintentional injuries include: road injury, falls, fire, heat and hot substances, drowning, exposure to mechanical forces, and natural disasters. This subcategory is the same as classified by the World Health Organization (WHO) except in this chapter on preventable deaths we added substance abuse (drug overdose and alcohol abuse) as a type of unintentional injury whereas WHO classifies it under "mental and substance use disorders"—a subdivision of "noncommunicable diseases" (NCDs).

Intentional injuries in this chapter are the same as classified by WHO and include: self-harm (suicide), interpersonal violence, collective violence, and legal intervention.

Unintentional Injuries:

Substance Abuse:

Between 2000 and 2019, the death rate in the U.S. due to opioid use increased by 470 percent, compared with an average 44 percent increase for the remaining G20 nations. In 2019, the death rate due to opioids was 16.6 per 100,000 population and accounted for 73 percent of all drug overdose deaths in the U.S. By 2019, prior to the COVID-19 pandemic, the U.S. experienced the highest drug overdose death rate in the world, 6.5 times higher than that of the age-standardized death rate for the average G20 nation.

By 2021, the drug overdose deaths in the U.S. reached an all-time high level of 106,699 and according to the CDC: "*Of the drug overdose deaths in 2021, 92.1 percent were unintentional, 4.1 percent were suicides, 3.6 percent were of undetermined intent, and less than 1.0 percent were homicides.*" The drug overdose age-standardized death rate reached 32.4 deaths per 100,000 population. Adults aged 65 years and over had the largest percentage increase in rates from 2020, through 2021. Between 2020 and 2021, drug overdose death rates increased for each race and Hispanic-origin group in the U.S. except non-Hispanic Asian people. The rate of drug overdose deaths involving synthetic opioids other than methadone increased 22 percent.

In 2021, 27 percent of drug overdose deaths in the U.S. were for people aged 35-44 years, the age-group with the largest death level. The Non-Hispanic White population accounted for 67 percent of all drug overdose deaths, whereas according to the U.S. Census Bureau only 58.9 percent of the U.S. population identified as Non-Hispanic White that year.

Heroin deaths peaked in 2017 at 15,482 deaths, and declined by 40 percent by 2021.

In 2019, deaths in the U.S. due to alcohol use increased 88 percent since 2000, placing the U.S. in fourth place among the G20 nations. This rate was approximately one-fourth the alcohol death rate in Russia.

Other Unintentional Injuries:

The second leading cause of death under *unintentional injury* category in 2019 was road injuries. The road injury death rate in the U.S. was the highest among the nine highest income per capita G20 nations, 2.3 times higher than the average rate in the E.U. nations, and 3.5 times higher than Japan's. However, many underdeveloped nations experienced significantly higher traffic fatality rates than the high income nations, led by the Dominican Republic which experienced six times the rate of the average G20 nation.

Between 2000 and 2019, the average crude death rate due to road injuries for G20 nations decreased by 17 percent while the U.S. experienced a 20 percent reduction in that same period. However, the U.S. rate was approximately double the rate of the eight high income per capita G20 nations. Despite achieving the lowest traffic fatality death rate in U.S. history in 2014, that rate had climbed 24 percent by 2021, during the COVID-19 pandemic.

NHTSA estimated that 42,915 people died in motor vehicle traffic crashes in the U.S. in 2021, a 10.5 percent increase from the 38,824 fatalities in 2020. That is the highest number of fatalities since 2005, and the largest annual percentage increase in the Fatality Analysis Reporting System's history.

Falls is another preventable risk and killed 38,700 people in the U.S. in 2021. Between 2012 and 2021, the age-standardized death rate in the U.S. due to falls increased by 41 percent, from 55.3 per 100,000 adults aged 65 years or more to 78.0 per 100,000 in 2021.

Intentional Injuries: In 2019, suicide in the U.S., a subcategory of intentional injuries, was approximately at the same age-standardized rate as the average for all G20 nations and approximately one-third the rate of the G20 nation with the highest rate, Saudi Arabia. The suicide rate for many underdeveloped nations was three to seven times higher than the G20 average, however, the U.S. suicide rate was 32 percent above the average rate for the other eight high income per capita G20 nations (principal U.S. partners). In the 19 years between 2000 and 2019, G20 members experienced a reduction of crude death rate due to suicide, averaging 11 percent. In contrast, the U.S. crude death rate due to suicide increased by 46 percent during that period.

In 2021, the U.S. experienced 48,183 deaths by suicide with an age-standardized rate of 14.0 per 100,000 individuals. Within the U.S. the rate of suicide is highest for middle-aged white males.

The U.S. also experienced the highest suicide by firearm rate in the world according to the latest data available in 2016.

In 2020, the U.S. ranked as the fifth highest among G20 nations for the rate of intentional homicide. That rate was six times the average rate for the E.U. nations. The highest rates in the world were in some Central America nations, led by El Salvador with a rate approximately 15 times higher than that of the U.S.

In 2019, the U.S experienced the fourth-highest homicide rate out of the 38 OECD member nations, which was approximately one-fifth the rate of Mexico's, the leading rate among OECD nations.

During the period 1991–2020, the intentional homicide rate in the U.S. reached its lowest level in 2014, at 4.4 deaths per 100,000 population. By 2020, the rate had climbed by 48 percent to 6.5 deaths per 100,000 population, a rate not seen since 1997, equal to 21,570 deaths. By 2021, that level had increased to 22,900 deaths.

In 2016, the U.S. experienced the second-highest number of firearm-related deaths in the world. Firearm-related deaths are the aggregate of homicides, suicides, and accidental injuries. The CDC has reported that in 2021, the number of firearm related fatalities in the U.S. increased to 48,830, a rate of 14.7 per 100,000 population. This was 14 percent higher than the 42,915 that died in traffic accidents that year. In 2016, the latest data available, the U.S. experienced the seventh-highest rate of firearm-related deaths in the world. The CDC has reported that in 2021, the crude firearm-related fatality rate in the U.S. increased to 14.7 per 100,000 population.

~

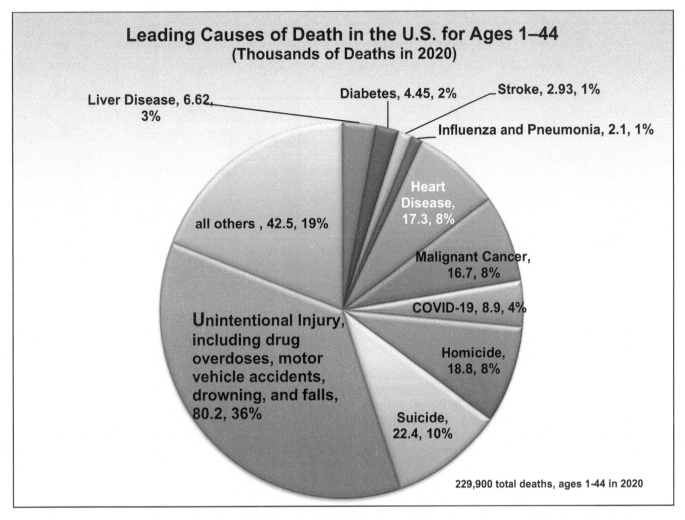

Leading Causes of Death in the U.S. for Ages 1–44
(Thousands of Deaths in 2020)

Liver Disease, 6.62, 3%

Diabetes, 4.45, 2%

Stroke, 2.93, 1%

Influenza and Pneumonia, 2.1, 1%

Heart Disease, 17.3, 8%

all others , 42.5, 19%

Malignant Cancer, 16.7, 8%

COVID-19, 8.9, 4%

Unintentional Injury, including drug overdoses, motor vehicle accidents, drowning, and falls, 80.2, 36%

Homicide, 18.8, 8%

Suicide, 22.4, 10%

229,900 total deaths, ages 1-44 in 2020

Sources: National Center for Health Statistics, https://www.cdc.gov/nchs/nvss/vsrr/mortality-dashboard.htm, Ahmad FB, Cisewski JA. Quarterly provisional estimates for selected indicators of mortality, 2020-Quarter 3, 2022. National Center for Health Statistics. National Vital Statistics System, Vital Statistics Rapid Release Program. 2023, https://wisqars.cdc.gov/cgi-bin/broker.exe?_service=v8prod&_server=ASPV-wisq-10.cdc.gov&_port=5099&_sessionid=tE9cfl4sR52&_program=wisqars.dd_percents10.sas&age1=1&age2=44&agetext=1-44&category=ALL&_debug=0

In 2020, unintentional injuries, suicide and homicide altogether accounted for 55 percent of all deaths in the U.S. for the age-group 1–44 years. Unintentional injuries were the leading single cause in this age-group and included opioid overdoses (unintentional poisoning), motor vehicle crashes, drowning, and unintentional falls. Unintentional injuries are "preventable" and represented 36 percent of all deaths for this 1–44 years age-group. Suicide was the second leading cause of death for this age-group, followed by homicides in third place. Together, these three categories accounted for 54.5 percent of deaths ages 1–44, (121,480 deaths out of 229,000 total deaths for the 1–44 age-group in 2020).

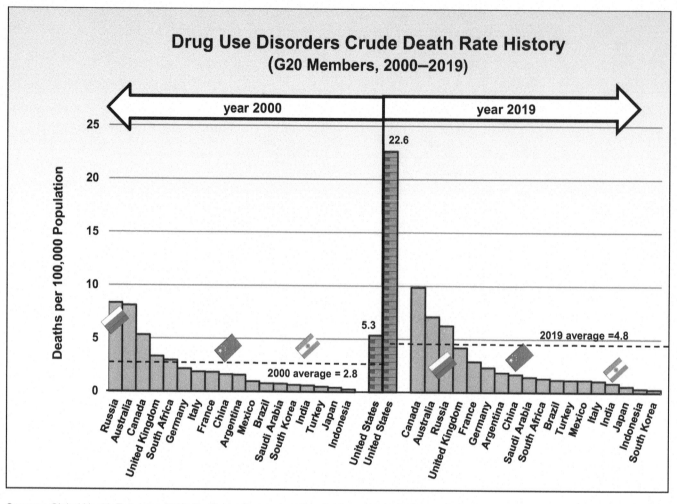

Drug Use Disorders Crude Death Rate History
(G20 Members, 2000–2019)

Sources: Global Health Estimates 2019: Deaths by Cause, Age, Sex, by Country and by Region, 2000-2019. Geneva, World Health Organization; 2020. https://www.who.int/data/gho/data/themes/mortality-and-global-health-estimates, Non-exclusive license dated 3/15/23 to use selected WHO published materials; CDC, https://www.cdc.gov/nchs/products/databriefs/db457.htm

In 2019, the drug epidemic in the U.S. reached 470 percent above the G20 average, approximately a fourfold increase since 2000. According to the CDC "By 2021, 106,699 drug overdose deaths occurred, resulting in an age-standardized rate of 32.4 per 100,000 population in the U.S. Adults aged 65 and over had the largest percentage increase in rates from 2020 through 2021. Drug overdose death rates increased for each race and Hispanic-origin group except non-Hispanic Asian people between 2020 and 2021. The rate of drug overdose deaths involving synthetic opioids other than methadone increased 22 percent, while the rate of deaths involving heroin declined 32 percent between 2020 and 2021. Of the drug overdose deaths in 2021, 92.1 percent were unintentional, 4.1 percent were suicides, 3.6 percent were of undetermined intent, and less than 1.0 percent were homicides."

Drug use disorders are classified by the World Health Organization under mental and substance use disorders and include: opioid use disorders, cocaine use disorders, amphetamine use disorders, and cannabis use disorders.

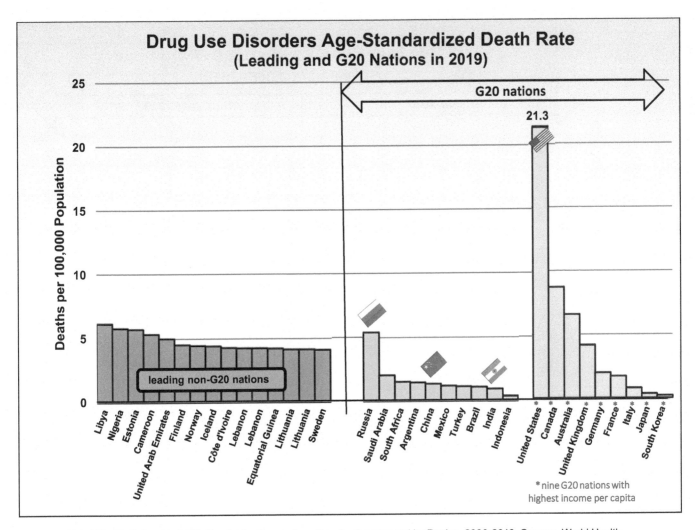

Drug Use Disorders Age-Standardized Death Rate
(Leading and G20 Nations in 2019)

Sources: Global Health Estimates 2019: Deaths by Cause, Age, Sex, by Country and by Region, 2000-2019. Geneva, World Health Organization; 2020. https://www.who.int/data/gho/data/themes/mortality-and-global-health-estimates, Non-exclusive license dated 3/15/23 to use selected WHO published materials, https://nida.nih.gov/research-topics/trends-statistics/overdose-death-rates

In 2019, the U.S. experienced the highest drug overdose age-standardized death rate in the world, 6.5 times higher than the average G20 member and 2.6 times higher than the second highest nation, Canada.

Drug use disorders are classified under mental and substance use disorders by the World Health Organization (WHO and include: opioid use disorders, cocaine use disorders, amphetamine use disorders, and cannabis use disorders.

According to the NIH, "There were 106,699 drug-involved overdose deaths reported in the U.S. in 2021; 69 percent of cases occurred among males. Synthetic opioids other than methadone (primarily fentanyl) were the main driver of drug overdose deaths with a nearly 7.5-fold increase from 2015 to 2021."

Age-standardized mortality rates can be used to compare the mortality rates of countries without being affected by the difference in age distributions from country to country. Without using this standardization, it would be unclear if differing mortality rates were due to age or as a result of other factors.

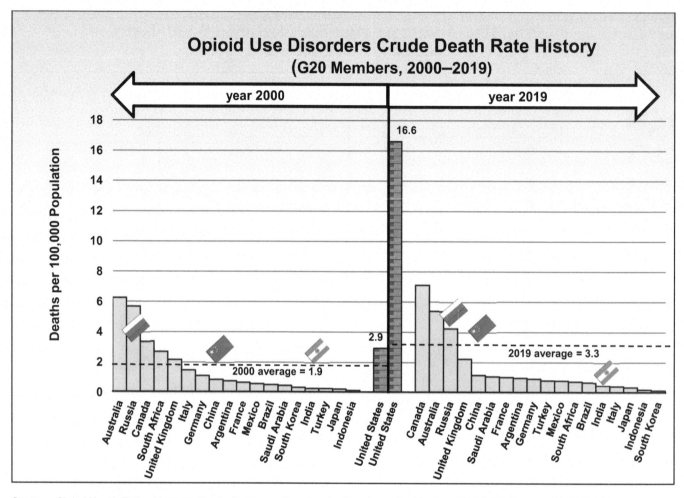

Sources: Global Health Estimates 2019: Deaths by Cause, Age, Sex, by Country and by Region, 2000-2019. Geneva, World Health Organization; 2020. https://www.who.int/data/gho/data/themes/mortality-and-global-health-estimates, Non-exclusive license dated 3/15/23 to use selected WHO published materials.

Between 2000 and 2019, opioid use death rate in the U.S. increased by 470 percent, compared with an average 44 percent increase for the remaining G20 nations. In 2019, the opioid death rate of 16.6 per 100,000 population represented 73 percent of all drug overdose deaths in the U.S.

Opioid use disorder is classified by the World Health Organization (WHO) as a subdivision of mental and substance use disorders, which is a subdivision of noncommunicable diseases (NCD).

The crude mortality rate is a good indicator of the general health status of a geographic area or population. The crude death rate is not appropriate for comparison of different populations or areas with large differences in age distributions. Higher crude death rates can be found in some developed countries, despite high life expectancy, because typically these countries have a much higher proportion of older people, due to lower recent birth rates and lower age-specific mortality rates.

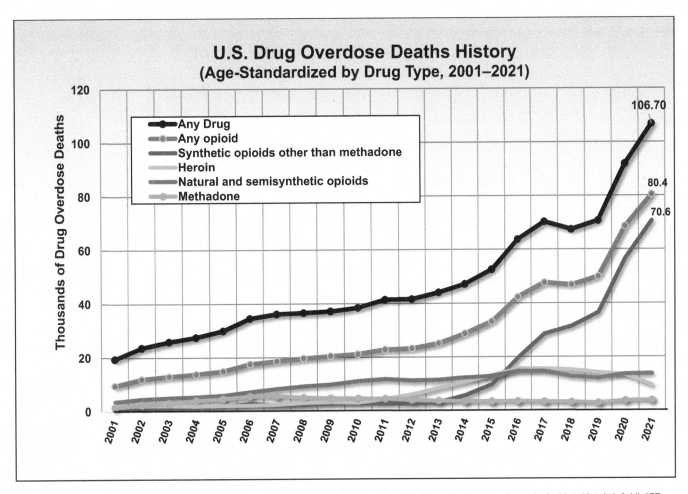

U.S. Drug Overdose Deaths History
(Age-Standardized by Drug Type, 2001–2021)

Sources: National Center for Health Statistics, National Vital Statistics System, Mortality File, https://www.cdc.gov/nchs/data/databriefs/db457-tables.pdf#2, accessed 5-22-23; CDC, https://www.cdc.gov/nchs/products/databriefs/db457.htm

Between 2001 and 2021, the drug overdose death level in the U.S. increased by 460 percent, reaching an all-time high of 106,699 deaths in 2021. By contrast, deaths due to heroin had peaked in 2017, at 15,482 deaths, and declined by 40 percent by 2021.

According to the CDC "By 2021, 106,699 drug overdose deaths occurred, resulting in an age-adjusted rate of 32.4 per 100,000 standard population in the United States. Adults aged 65 and over had the largest percentage increase in rates from 2020 through 2021. Drug overdose death rates increased for each race and Hispanic-origin group except non-Hispanic Asian people between 2020 and 2021. The rate of drug overdose deaths involving synthetic opioids other than methadone increased 22 percent, while the rate of deaths involving heroin declined 32 percent between 2020 and 2021. Of the drug overdose deaths in 2021, 92.1 percent were unintentional, 4.1 percent were suicides, 3.6 percent were of undetermined intent, and less than 1.0 percent were homicides."

Age-adjusted death rates were calculated using the direct method and the 2000 U.S. standard population.

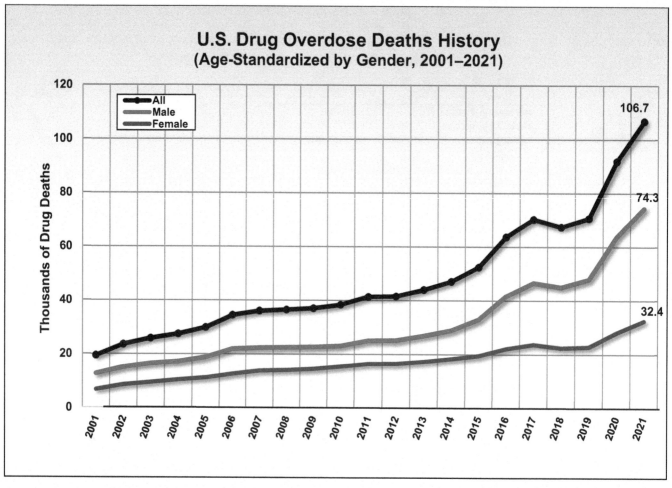

U.S. Drug Overdose Deaths History
(Age-Standardized by Gender, 2001–2021)

Source: National Center for Health Statistics, National Vital Statistics System, Mortality File, https://www.cdc.gov/nchs/data/databriefs/db457-tables.pdf#2, accessed 5-22-23

Between 2001 and 2021, the male-to-female proportion of total drug overdose deaths in the U.S remained relatively unchanged at approximately 2:1 throughout the period.

Drug overdose deaths were identified using International Classification of Diseases, 10th Revision underlying cause-of-death codes X40–X44, X60–X64, X85, and Y10–Y14. Age-standardized death rates were calculated using the direct method and the 2000 U.S. standard population.

On May 31, 2023, the Department of Homeland Security (DHS) published a news report (https://www.dhs.gov/news/2023/05/31/dhs-operations-blue-lotus-and-four-horsemen-stopped-nearly-10000-pounds-fentanyl) stating that:

> Operation Blue Lotus consisted of a focused deployment of HSI personnel alongside CBP Officers at ports of entry, where over 90 percent of fentanyl is trafficked in cars and trucks, so that HSI could immediately pursue investigations as contraband was discovered. Working with federal, state, tribal and local partners, the investigations in turn helped expose the networks. The complementary U.S. Border Patrol operation, Operation Four Horsemen, focused between ports of entry and at check points near the border.

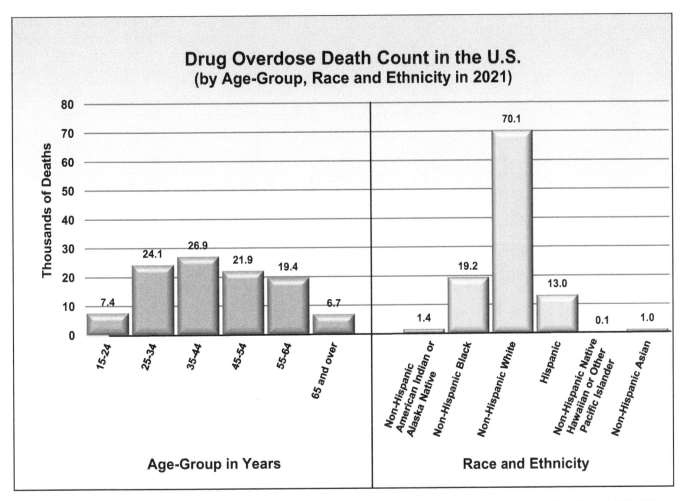

Source: National Center for Health Statistics, National Vital Statistics System, Mortality File, https://www.cdc.gov/nchs/data/databriefs/db457-tables.pdf#2, accessed 5-22-23, https://www.census.gov/quickfacts/fact/table/US/PST045222

In 2021, 27 percent of drug overdose deaths in the U.S. were between the ages of 35–44, the largest age-group. The Non-Hispanic White population accounted for 67 percent of all drug overdose deaths, whereas according to the U.S. Census Bureau only 58.9 percent of the U.S. population identify as Non-Hispanic White that year.

Drug overdose deaths were identified using International Classification of Diseases, tenth Revision underlying cause-of-death codes X40–X44, X60–X64, X85, and Y10–Y14. Age-standardized death rates were calculated using the direct method and the 2000 U.S. standard population (*see page 70*).

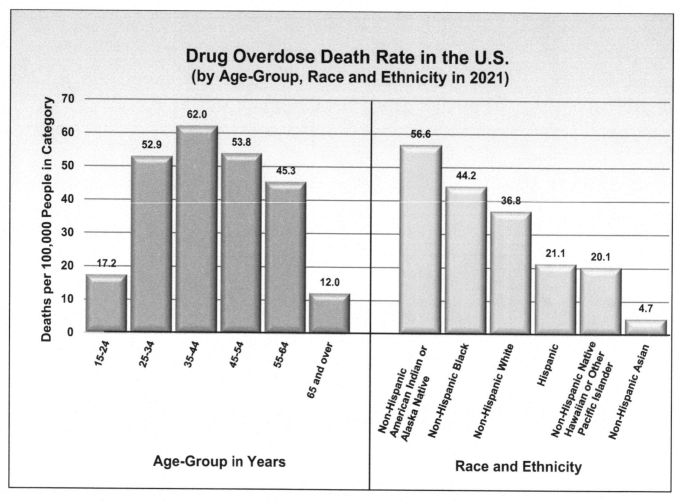

Source: National Center for Health Statistics, National Vital Statistics System, Mortality File, https://www.cdc.gov/nchs/data/databriefs/db457-tables.pdf#2, accessed 5-22-23

In 2021, 27 percent of drug overdose deaths in the U.S. were persons between the ages of 35–44, the largest age-group. The Non-Hispanic White population accounted for 67 percent of all drug overdose deaths while the American Indian or Alaska native population group rate was 1.5 times higher.

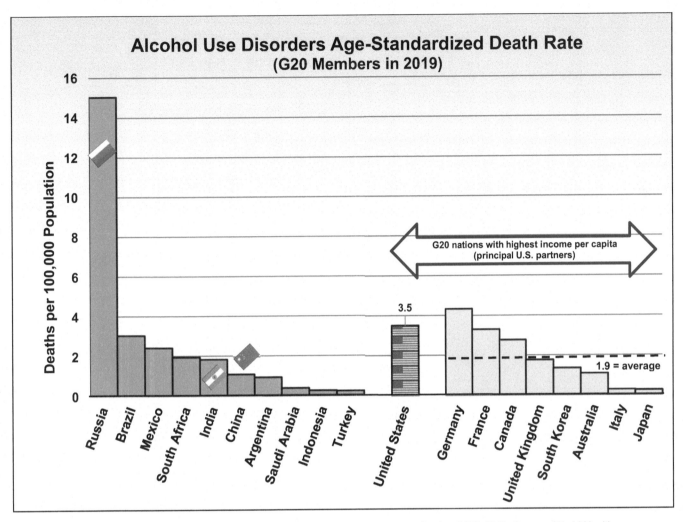

Sources: Global Health Estimates 2019: Deaths by Cause, Age, Sex, by Country and by Region, 2000-2019. Geneva, World Health Organization; 2020. https://www.who.int/data/gho/data/themes/mortality-and-global-health-estimates, Non-exclusive license dated 3/15/23 to use selected WHO published materials.

In 2019, the U.S. experienced an age-standardized death rate due to alcohol abuse that was almost twice as high as the average high income per capita G20 nations, second only to Germany among those nations.

Alcohol use disorders are classified by the WHO under mental and substance use disorders.

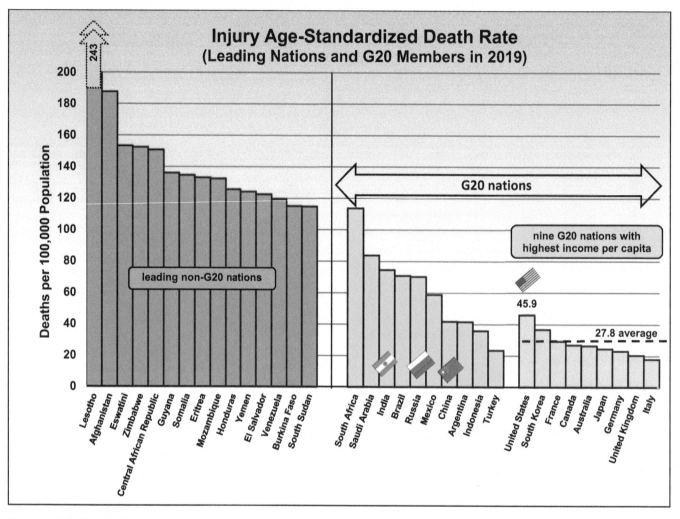

Sources: Global Health Estimates 2019: Deaths by Cause, Age, Sex, by Country and by Region, 2000-2019. Geneva, World Health Organization; 2020. https://www.who.int/data/gho/data/themes/mortality-and-global-health-estimates, Non-exclusive license dated 3/15/23 to use selected WHO published materials.

In 2019, the death rate due to injuries in the U.S. was at the average level for G20 nations, but that rate was 65 percent higher than the nine highest income per capita G20 nations (principal U.S. partners).

Injuries are divided into the following subcategories:

<u>Unintentional injuries</u> include: road injury, poisonings, falls, fire, heat and hot substances, drowning, exposure to mechanical forces natural disasters.

(Note that the World Health Organization (WHO) includes substance abuse as a subclassification of noncommunicable diseases (NCD), whereas the U.S. Centers for Disease Control and Prevention (CDC) classifies drug abuse as an unintentional injury which is why it is included in this chapter. Substance abuse includes drug abuse and alcohol abuse.)

<u>Intentional injuries</u> include: self-harm, interpersonal violence, collective violence and legal intervention

Age-standardized mortality rates can be used to compare the mortality rates of countries without being affected by the difference in age distributions from country to country. Without using this standardization, it would be unclear if differing mortality rates were due to age or as a result of other factors.

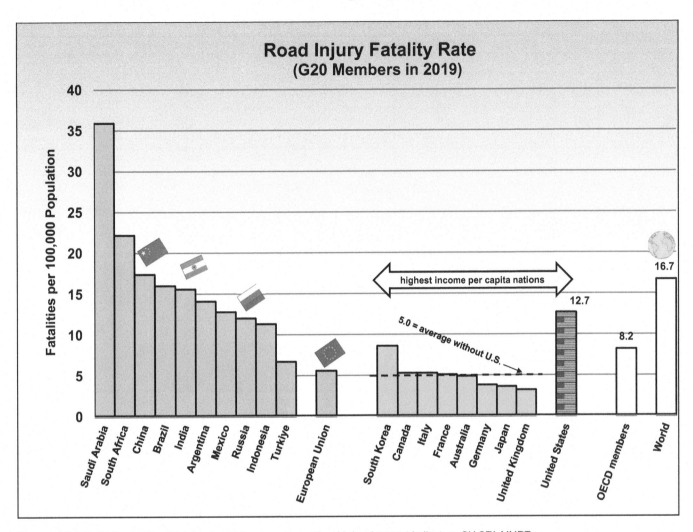

Road Injury Fatality Rate
(G20 Members in 2019)

Fatalities per 100,000 Population

highest income per capita nations

5.0 = average without U.S.

16.7

12.7

8.2

Saudi Arabia · South Africa · China · Brazil · India · Argentina · Mexico · Russia · Indonesia · Turkiye · European Union · South Korea · Canada · Italy · France · Australia · Germany · Japan · United Kingdom · United States · OECD members · World

Sources: The World Bank, https://databank.worldbank.org/source/world-development-indicators, SH.STA.MMRT, https://data.worldbank.org/summary-terms-of-use, accessed 7-9-23, https://www.nhtsa.gov/risky-driving/seat-belts#:~:text=In percent202021 percent2C percent2026 percent2C325 percent20passenger percent20vehicle,seat percent20belts percent2C percent20in percent202017 percent20alone.

In 2019, before the COVID-19 pandemic, the U.S. experienced 2.5 times higher road fatality death rates than the other eight high income per capita G20 members (principal U.S. partners). Then, in 2021, that high rate increased again by 10 percent during the pandemic. The 2019 rate was already at three-fourths the average world's rate which included all the developing nations on the planet. Most of these deaths were preventable if the efficacy of the available lifesaving automobile technology was understood and utilized by the driving public. For example, according to the National Highway Traffic Administration (NHTSA) it was estimated that in 50 percent of fatalities the victim was not wearing a seatbelt*.

In 2023, the CDC published research that found that the U.S. had higher rates of motor vehicle crash deaths than most other high-income countries in 2019, and lagged behind these other countries in saving lives on the road. The U.S. rate was 2.3 times higher than the average rate for 28 other high-income countries (4.8 per 100,000 population). In addition, the number of crash deaths in the U.S. further increased in 2020 and 2021. The CDC concluded that the U.S. could save more than 20,500 lives if we could reduce the population-based crash death rate to match the average rate of 28 other high-income countries in 2019.

*https://injuryfacts.nsc.org/motor-vehicle/occupant-protection/seat-belts/

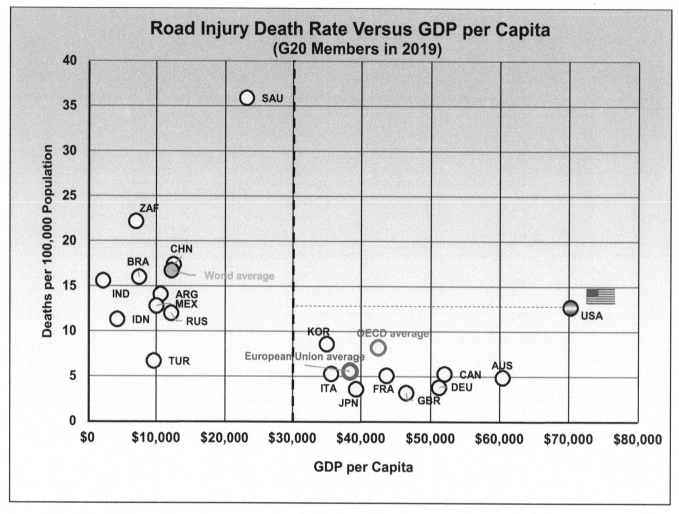

Sources: The World Bank, https://databank.worldbank.org/source/world-development-indicators, NY.GDP.PCAP.CD and SH.STA.TRAF.P5, accessed 8/23/23, https://data.worldbank.org/summary-terms-of-use

In 2019, the road injury death rate in the U.S. was the highest among the wealthiest ten G20 members, based on GDP per capita, 2.3 times higher than the average rate in the E.U., and 3.5 times higher than Japan's.

Country Codes	
Argentina	ARG
Australia	AUS
Brazil	BRA
Canada	CAN
China	CHN
France	FRA
Germany	DEU
India	IND
Indonesia	IDN
Italy	ITA
Japan	JPN
South Korea	KOR
Mexico	MEX
Russia	RUS
Saudi Arabia	SAU
South Africa	ZAF
Turkiye	TUR
United Kingdom	GBR
United States	USA

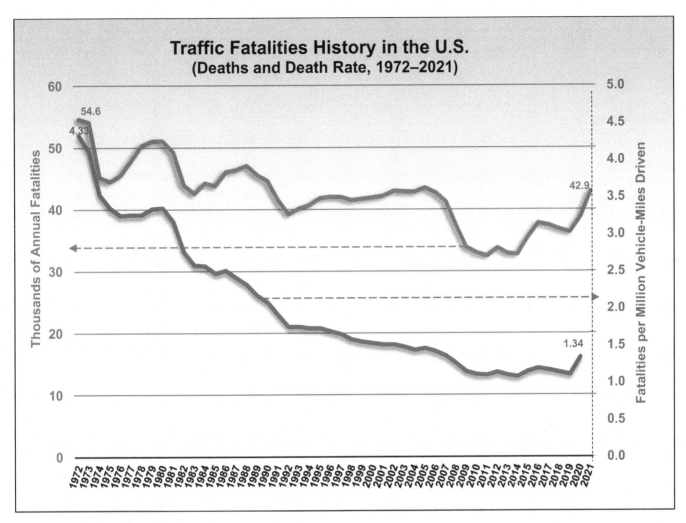

Traffic Fatalities History in the U.S.
(Deaths and Death Rate, 1972–2021)

Source: National Highway Traffic Safety Administration, https://cdan.nhtsa.gov/tsftables/Fatalities percent20and percent20Fatality percent20Rates.pdf, accessed 5/22/23

Despite achieving the lowest traffic fatality death rate in U.S. history in 2014, that rate had climbed 24 percent by 2021, during the COVID-19 pandemic.

NHTSA has estimated that 42,915 people died in motor vehicle traffic crashes in 2021, a 10.5 percent increase from the 38,824 fatalities in 2020. The projection is the highest number of fatalities since 2005, and the largest annual percentage increase in the Fatality Analysis Reporting System's history.

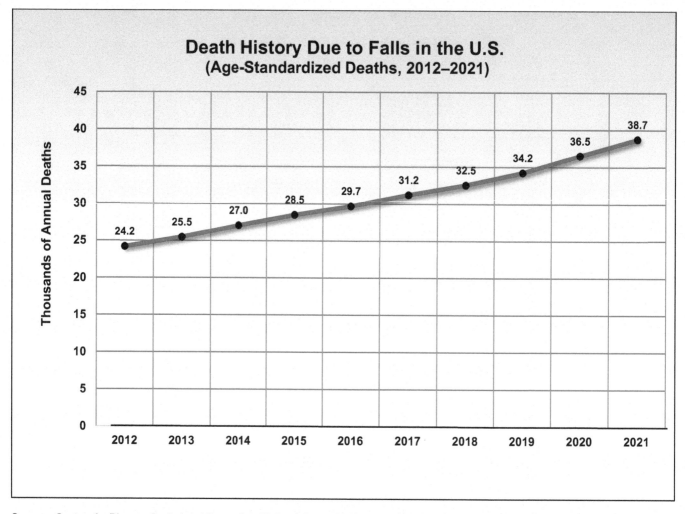

Death History Due to Falls in the U.S.
(Age-Standardized Deaths, 2012–2021)

Sources: Centers for Disease Control and Prevention, National Center for Health Statistics. National Vital Statistics System, Mortality 1999-2021 on CDC WONDER Online Database. Accessed January 24, 2023. http://wonder.cdc.gov/ucd-icd10.html, https://www.cdc.gov/falls/data/fall-deaths.html

Between 2012 and 2021, the age-standardized death rate due to "falls" in the U.S. increased by 41 percent, from 55.3 per 100,000 adults aged 65 years or more to 78.0 per 100,000 in 2021, killing 38,700 people that year.

Falls are the leading cause of injury-related death among adults age 65 and older, and the age-standardized fall death rate is increasing. Each year at least 300,000 older people are hospitalized for hip fractures. More than 95 percent of hip fractures are caused by falling, usually by falling sideways. Falls are the most common cause of traumatic brain injuries.

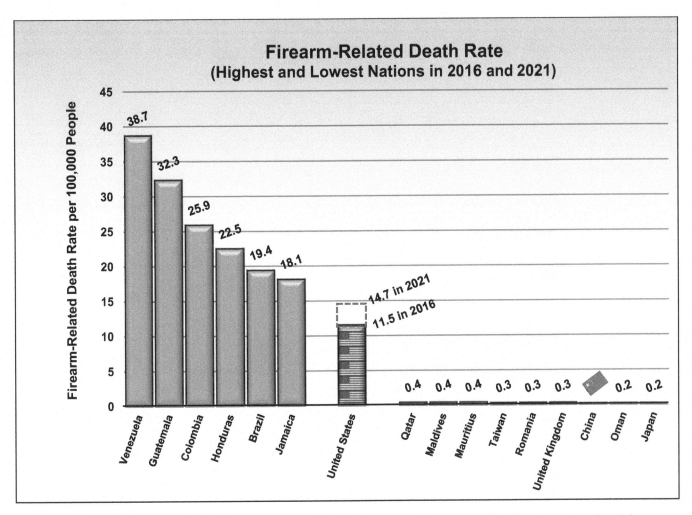

Firearm-Related Death Rate
(Highest and Lowest Nations in 2016 and 2021)

Sources: Institute for Health Metrics Evaluation. Used with permission. All rights preserved. https://www.healthdata.org/news-release/six-countries-americas-account-half-all-firearm-deaths, data accessed 4/5/23. Centers for Disease Control and Prevention, National Center for Health Statistics. National Vital Statistics System, Mortality 2018-2021 on CDC WONDER Online Database, released in 2021. Data are from the Multiple Cause of Death Files, 2018-2021, as compiled from data provided by the 57 vital statistics jurisdictions through the Vital Statistics Cooperative Program. Accessed at http://wonder.cdc.gov/ucd-icd10-expanded.html on June 19, 2023

In 2016, the latest data available, the U.S. experienced the seventh-highest rate of firearm-related deaths in the world. Firearm-related deaths are the aggregate of homicides, suicides, and accidental injuries. The CDC has reported that in 2021, the crude firearm-related fatality rate in the U.S. had increased to 14.7 per 100,000.

According to the Institute for Health Metrics Evaluation, "A new study reveals more than a quarter-million people died from firearm-related injuries in 2016, with half of those deaths occurring in only six countries in the Americas: Brazil, the United States, Mexico, Colombia, Venezuela, and Guatemala. A part of the Global Burden of Disease, the study assesses firearm-related mortality between 1990 and 2016, for 195 countries and territories by age and by sex. It is the most extensive study ever conducted on global firearm-related deaths. Deaths from conflict and terrorism, executions, and law enforcement shootings were not included in the total estimates."

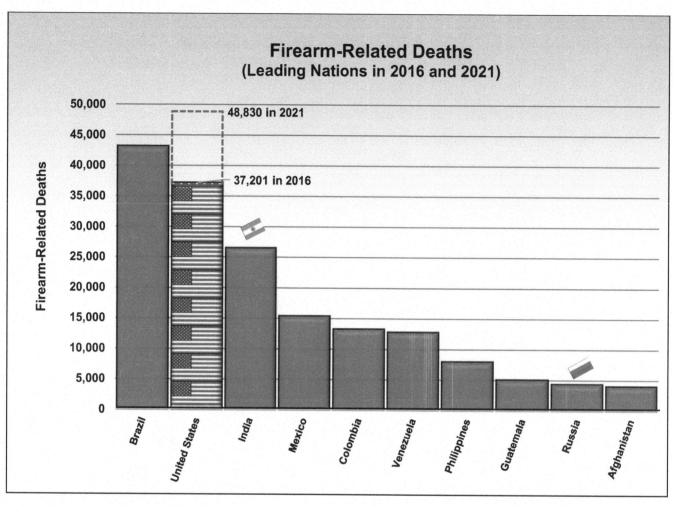

Firearm-Related Deaths
(Leading Nations in 2016 and 2021)

Sources: Institute for Health Metrics Evaluation. Used with permission. All rights preserved. https://www.healthdata.org/news-release/six-countries-americas-account-half-all-firearm-deaths, data accessed 6/15/23, Centers for Disease Control and Prevention, National Center for Health Statistics. National Vital Statistics System, Mortality 2018-2021 on CDC WONDER Online Database, released in 2021. Data are from the Multiple Cause of Death Files, 2018-2021, as compiled from data provided by the 57 vital statistics jurisdictions through the Vital Statistics Cooperative Program. Accessed at http://wonder.cdc.gov/ucd-icd10-expanded.html on June 19, 2023

In 2016, the U.S. experienced the second highest number of firearm-related deaths in the world, behind Brazil. Firearm-related deaths are the aggregate of homicides, suicides, and accidental injuries. The CDC has reported that in 2021, the number of firearm-related fatalities in the U.S. had increased to 48,830.

According to the Institute for Health Metrics Evaluation: ". . . more than a quarter-million people died from firearm-related injuries in 2016, with half of those deaths occurring in only six countries in the Americas: Brazil, the United States, Mexico, Colombia, Venezuela, and Guatemala."

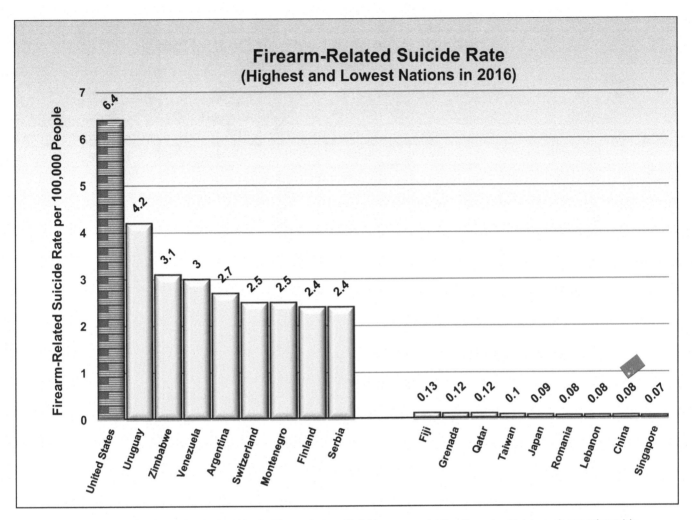

Firearm-Related Suicide Rate
(Highest and Lowest Nations in 2016)

In 2016, the latest data available, the U.S. experienced the highest suicide by firearm rate in the world.

In June 2023, according to the National Institute of Health (NIH): "Firearm suicide receives relatively little public attention in the U.S., however, the U.S. is in the midst of a firearm suicide crisis. Most suicides are completed using a firearm. The age-standardized firearm suicide rate increased 22.6 percent from 2005 to 2017, and globally the U.S. firearm suicide rate is eight times higher than the average firearm suicide rate of 22 other developed countries."

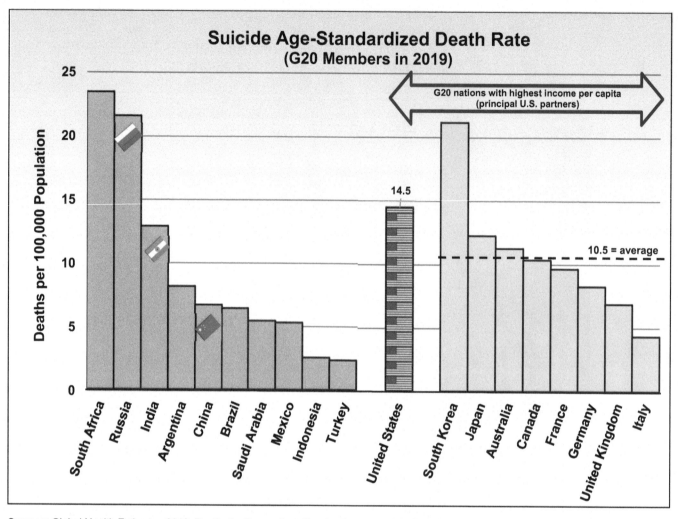

Suicide Age-Standardized Death Rate
(G20 Members in 2019)

Sources: Global Health Estimates 2019: Deaths by Cause, Age, Sex, by Country and by Region, 2000-2019. Geneva, World Health Organization; 2020. https://www.who.int/data/gho/data/themes/mortality-and-global-health-estimates, Non-exclusive license dated 3/15/23 to use selected WHO published materials, https://www.cdc.gov/suicide/facts/index.html

In 2019, the U.S. experienced an age-standardized suicide rate that was 38 percent above the average rate for the other high income per capita G20 nations, and in second place behind South Korea among those nations.

Suicide (self-harm is a subcategory of Intentional injuries).

In June 2023, according to the CDC: "Suicide rates increased in the U.S. approximately 36 percent between 2000 and 2021. Suicide was responsible for 48,183 deaths in 2021, which is about one death every 11 minutes. The number of people who think about or attempt suicide is even higher. In 2021, an estimated 12.3 million American adults seriously thought about suicide, 3.5 million planned a suicide attempt, and 1.7 million attempted suicide."

Suicide is death caused by injuring oneself with the intent to die. (A suicide attempt is when someone harms themselves with any intent to end their life, but they do not die as a result of their actions.)

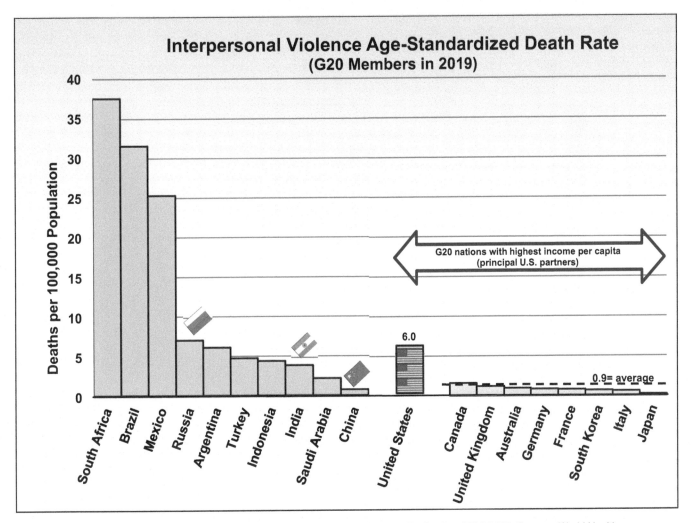

Interpersonal Violence Age-Standardized Death Rate
(G20 Members in 2019)

Sources: Global Health Estimates 2019: Deaths by Cause, Age, Sex, by Country and by Region, 2000-2019. Geneva, World Health Organization; 2020. https://www.who.int/data/gho/data/themes/mortality-and-global-health-estimates, Non-exclusive license dated 3/15/23 to use selected WHO published materials, https://www.cdc.gov/suicide/facts/index.html

In 2019, the U.S. experienced deaths due to interpersonal violence at a rate that was more than six time greater than the average for the other high income per capita G20 nations.

Interpersonal violence involves the intentional use of physical force or power against other persons by an individual or small group of individuals. Acts of interpersonal violence can be further divided into family or partner violence and community violence.

- Family or partner violence refers to violence within the family or between intimate partners. It includes child maltreatment, dating and intimate partner violence, and elder maltreatment.

- Community violence occurs among individuals who are not related by family ties but who may know each other. It includes youth violence, bullying, assault, rape or sexual assault by acquaintances or strangers, and violence that occurs in institutional settings such as schools, workplaces, and prisons.

WHO's Global Health Estimates (GHE) indicate that approximately 504,587 died due to interpersonal violence in 2011. In 2011, the estimated rate of deaths due to interpersonal violence or homicide in low-to-middle income countries was 8.0 per 100,000 people, compared with 3.3 per 100,000 in high-income countries.

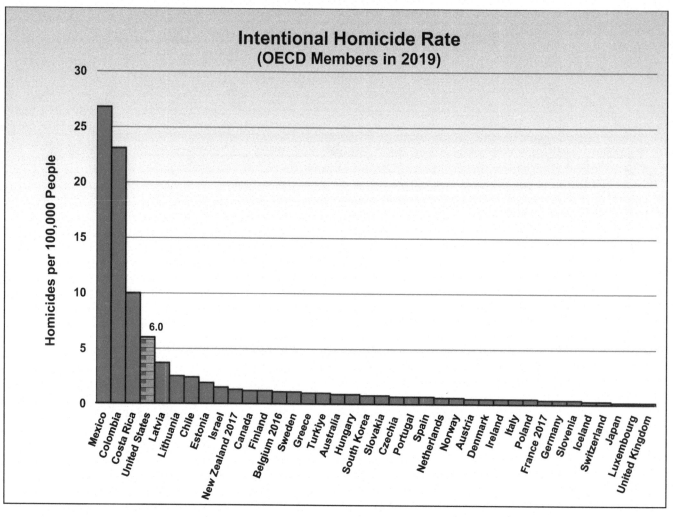

Intentional Homicide Rate
(OECD Members in 2019)

Source: OECD Health Data: Causes of Mortality, http://stats.oecd.org/Index.aspx?DataSetCode=HEALTH_STAT, accessed 5-20-23

In 2019, the U.S experienced the fourth-highest intentional homicide rate out of the 38 OECD member nations, which was approximately one-fifth the rate of Mexico, the leading OECD nation.

Age-standardized rate per 100,000 population is shown. Data refer to 2019, for Austria, Brazil, Costa Rica, the Czech Republic, Estonia, Germany, Korea, the Russia, Slovenia, and Turkiye; 2017-19 for Hungary and Lithuania; 2016 for Canada, Colombia, Italy, Mexico, Spain, Switzerland and the U.S.; 2015 for Belgium, France, New Zealand, Norway and the U.K.; 2015, for Ireland and South Africa; 2014, for the Slovak Republic; and 2018, for all the other countries.

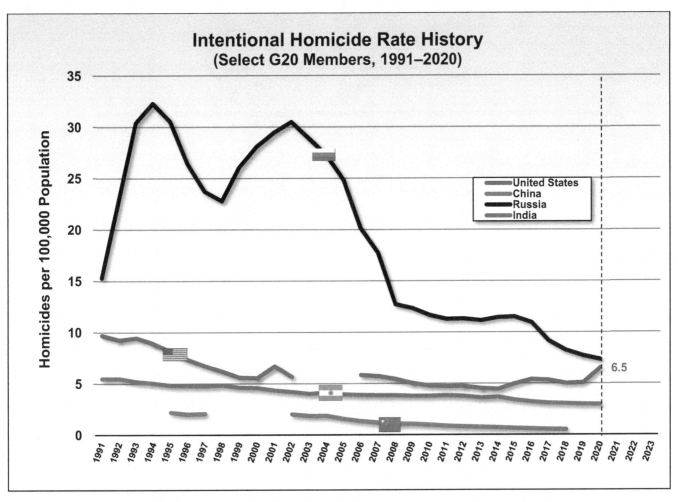

Source: The World Bank, https://databank.worldbank.org/source/world-development-indicators, VC.IHR.PSRC.P5, https://data.worldbank.org/summary-terms-of-use

Over the period 1991–2020, the intentional homicide rate in the U.S. reached its lowest level in 2014, at 4.4 deaths per 100,000 population. By 2020, the rate had climbed by 48 percent to 6.5, a rate not seen since 1997. Between 2014 and 2020, India, Russia, and China all experienced reductions in homicide rates.

All existing data sources on intentional homicides, both at national and international level, stem from either criminal justice or public health systems. In the former case, data are generated by law enforcement or criminal justice authorities in the process of recording and investigating a crime event. In the latter, data are produced by health authorities certifying the cause of death of an individual. Statistics reported to the United Nations in the context of its various surveys on crime levels and criminal justice trends are incidents of victimization that have been reported to the authorities in any given country.

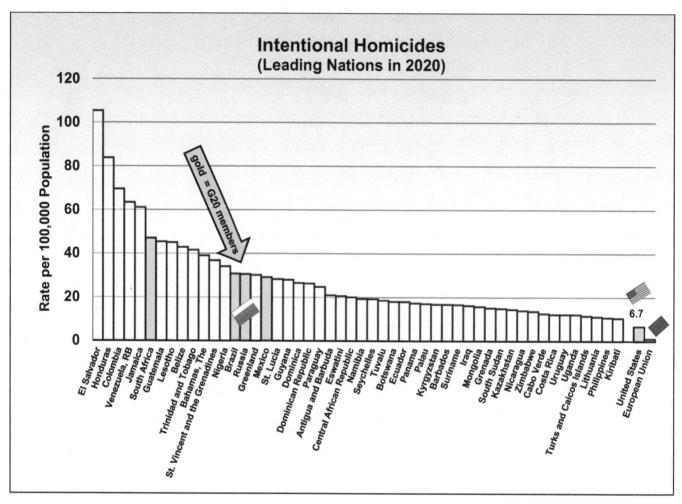

Intentional Homicides
(Leading Nations in 2020)

gold = G20 members

6.7

Sources: The World Bank, https://databank.worldbank.org/source/world-development-indicators, VC.IHR.PSRC.P5, https://data.worldbank.org/summary-terms-of-use

In 2020, the U.S. ranked as the fifth highest among G20 members for intentional homicide rate with 21,570 deaths. That rate was six times the average rate for the E.U. nations. The highest rates in the world were in some Central America nations, led by El Salvador with a rate approximately 15 times higher than in the United States.

Intentional homicides are estimates of unlawful homicides purposely inflicted as a result of domestic disputes, interpersonal violence, violent conflicts over land resources, inter-gang violence over turf or control, and predatory violence and killing by armed groups. Intentional homicide does not include all intentional killing; the difference is usually in the organization of the killing. Individuals or small groups usually commit homicide, whereas killing in armed conflict is usually committed by fairly cohesive groups of up to several hundred members and is thus usually excluded.

The degree to which different societies apportion the level of culpability to acts resulting in death is also subject to variation. Consequently, the comparison between countries and regions of "intentional homicide," or unlawful death purposefully inflicted on a person by another person, is also a comparison of the extent to which different countries deem that a killing be classified as such, as well as the capacity of their legal systems to record it. Caution should therefore be applied when evaluating and comparing homicide data.

Chapter 6

Noncommunicable Diseases

Overview of Noncommunicable Diseases (NCDs)

Note that the World Health Organization classifies substance abuse—drug abuse and alcohol abuse—as a subclassification of noncommunicable diseases (NCDs), whereas the U.S. Centers for Disease Control and Prevention (CDC) classifies drug abuse as an unintentional injury and is covered in the previous chapter 5 "Preventable Deaths."

In 2019, prior to the COVID-19 pandemic, noncommunicable diseases (NCDs) accounted for 88.1 percent of the 2,948,498 deaths in the U.S., compared with 5.3 percent for communicable diseases. In contrast, during the first year of the pandemic, COVID-19 alone accounted for 16.7 percent of all U.S. deaths. Due to the major distortions of mortalities caused by the COVID-19 pandemic the data presented in this chapter for purposes of comparing (NCDs) among nations are generally from the pre-pandemic year 2019.

Most NCD mortality rates—including cardiac diseases, cancers and Alzheimer's disease—increase with aging populations which is why age-standardized rates are used to compare countries thereby removing the inherent age bias in mortality statistics between countries with different age distributions. When differences are observed in age-standardized death rates among nations it is indicative of factors other than age causing those differences.

In 2019, the U.S. experienced an overall age-standardized death rate due to NCDs that was 36 percent above the average rate experienced by the other eight high income per capita G20 nations (principal U.S. partners). Compared with these other nations the U.S. death rates were above average in most subcategories of NCDs including: heart disease—where the U.S. rate was approximately twice as high, and above average for Alzheimer's disease, COPD, kidney disease, diabetes, blood disorders, and Parkinson's disease. The age-standardized death rate for the U.S. and these nations was approximately the same for most cancers, whereas the U.S. rate was approximately 20 percent lower for colon and rectum cancers.

The leading subcategory for U.S. NCD death rate was cardiovascular diseases (CVDs), responsible for 29.6 percent of all U.S. deaths at a rate 60 percent above the rate experienced by the nine highest income per-capita G20 nations (principal U.S. partners). The major categories of fatal cardiovascular diseases were heart disease (accounting for 24.2 percent of all U.S. deaths) and stroke (accounting for 5.4 percent of all U.S. deaths).

Between 2000 and 2019, the U.S. experienced a 20 percent reduction in the crude rate of fatal heart disease and stroke. Despite this reduction, in 2019, the age-standardized death rate for NCDs in the U.S. was 73 percent higher than Japan's and was 36 percent above the average of the nine highest income per capita G20 nations.

In 2019, malignant neoplasms (cancer) was the second-highest age-standardized death rate category of noncommunicable diseases (NCDs in the U.S.—after cardiovascular diseases (CVDs)—accounting for 20.9 percent of all deaths in the U.S. at 103 deaths per 100,000 population. This level was 3 percent below the average of all G20 nations.

In 2019, lung, trachea and bronchus cancer deaths were the largest subcategory of malignant neoplasms, accounting for 5.3 percent of all deaths in the U.S.

In 2019, Alzheimer's disease and other dementias were the third-highest death rate subcategory of NCDs and accounted for 9.7 percent of all deaths in the U.S. Unlike heart disease, stroke, and malignant neoplasms—all of which declined between 2000 and 2019 in the U.S.—the death rate for Alzheimer's disease and other dementias increased 191 percent during this period.

In 2019, COPD (chronic obstructive pulmonary disease was the fourth-highest death rate subcategory of NCDs, and accounted for 9.6 percent of all deaths in the U.S.

In 2019, kidney disease was the fifth-highest death rate subcategory of NCDs for the U.S., accounting for 2.9 percent of all deaths; diabetes mellitus was in sixth place; endocrine, blood and immune disorders were in seventh place; Parkinson's disease was in eighth place for death rate due to NCDs.

~

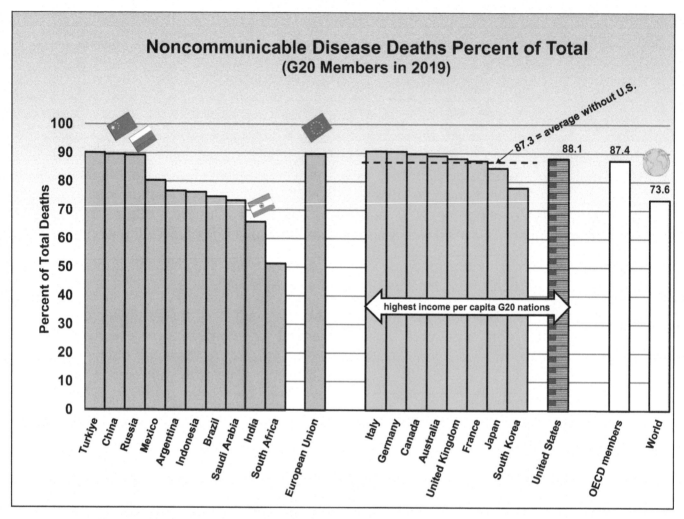

Noncommunicable Disease Deaths Percent of Total
(G20 Members in 2019)

Sources: The World Bank, https://databank.worldbank.org/source/world-development-indicators, SH.DTH.NCOM.ZS, accessed 8/23/23
https://data.worldbank.org/summary-terms-of-use, accessed 7-9-23

In 2019, prior to the COVID-19 pandemic, the proportion of noncommunicable diseases (NCDs) deaths to total deaths for all causes in the U.S. was approximately the same as the average of the wealthiest G20 nations but about 14 percentage points above the world's average. Wealthy nations have historically controlled infectious diseases better than poorer nations and therefore experience higher percentage of NCDs attributed to aging, including cardiovascular diseases, cancers and Alzheimer's. Wealthy nations have a lower proportion of communicable diseases than do poor nations.

Cause of death refers to the share of all deaths for all ages by underlying causes. Non-communicable diseases include cancer, diabetes mellitus, cardiovascular diseases, digestive diseases, skin diseases, musculoskeletal diseases, and congenital anomalies. Derived based on the data from Global Health Estimates 2020: Deaths by Cause, Age, Sex, by Country and by Region, 2000–2019. Geneva, World Health Organization; 2020.

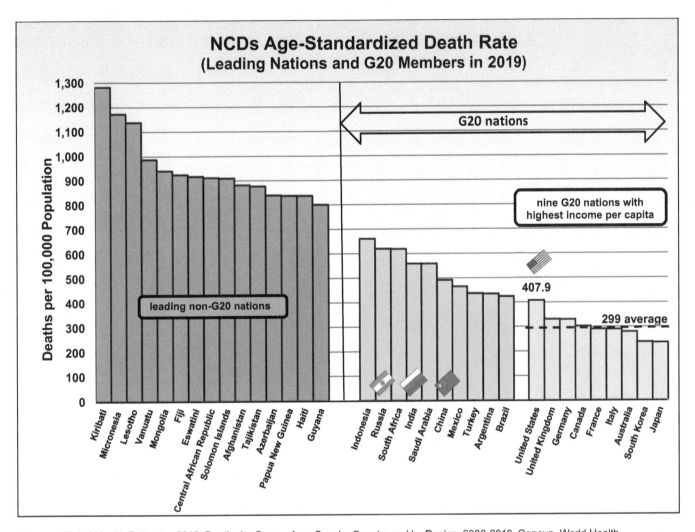

NCDs Age-Standardized Death Rate
(Leading Nations and G20 Members in 2019)

Sources: Global Health Estimates 2019: Deaths by Cause, Age, Sex, by Country and by Region, 2000-2019. Geneva, World Health Organization; 2020. https://www.who.int/data/gho/data/themes/mortality-and-global-health-estimates, Non-exclusive license dated 3/15/23 to use selected WHO published materials.

In 2019, prior to the COVID-19 pandemic, noncommunicable diseases (NCDs) accounted for 88.1 percent of all deaths in the U.S. The age-standardized death rate for NCDs in the U.S. in 2019 was 73 percent higher than Japan's and 36 percent above the average of the nine high income per capita G20 members and less than half the rate for poor and developing countries, including Mongolia, Central African Republic, and Afghanistan.

The noncommunicable subgroups with the highest mortalities in the U.S. were: cardiovascular diseases (29.6 percent), malignant neoplasms (20.9 percent), Alzheimer's disease and other dementia (9.7 percent), chronic obstructive pulmonary disease (6.6 percent), kidney disease (2.9 percent), and diabetes (2.1 percent).

Noncommunicable diseases (NCDs), including heart disease, stroke, cancer, diabetes and chronic lung disease, are collectively responsible for 74 percent of all deaths worldwide. More than three-quarters of all NCD deaths, and 86 percent of the 17 million people who died prematurely, or before reaching 70 years of age, occur in low- and middle-income countries. NCDs share four major risk factors: tobacco use, physical inactivity, the harmful use of alcohol and unhealthy diets. Noncommunicable diseases (NCDs) kill 41 million people each year, equivalent to 74 percent of all deaths globally.

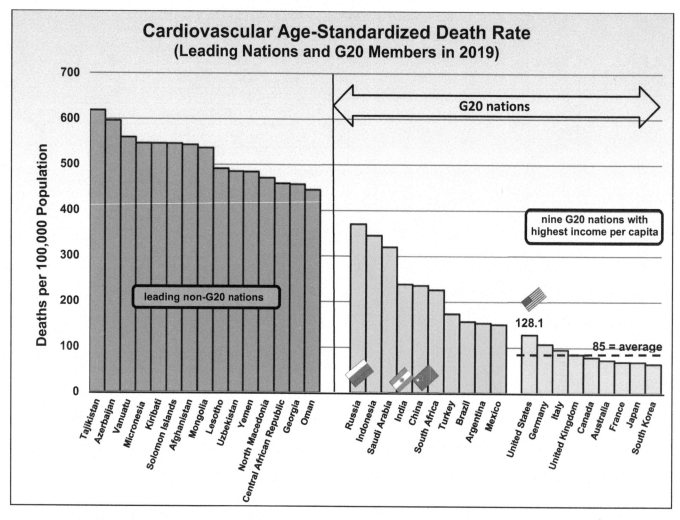

Source: Global Health Estimates 2019: Deaths by Cause, Age, Sex, by Country and by Region, 2000-2019. Geneva, World Health Organization; 2020. https://www.who.int/data/gho/data/themes/mortality-and-global-health-estimates, Non-exclusive license dated 3/15/23 to use selected WHO published materials.

In 2019, prior to the COVID-19 pandemic, cardiovascular diseases (CVDs) accounted for 29.6 percent of all deaths in the U.S. and were the leading causes of death within all noncommunicable diseases. Based on age-standardized death rates the ten G20 nations with the lowest GDP per capita were also the ten G20 nations with the highest cardiovascular death rates. The U.S. ranked 11th, which was 60 percent above the average death rate for the nine highest income per capita G20 member nations while ten percent below the average of all G20 nations.

Cardiovascular diseases account for most noncommunicable diseases (NCD deaths, or 17.9 million people annually. Age-standardized mortality rates can be used to compare the mortality rates of countries without being affected by the difference in age distributions from country to country. Without using this standardization, it would be unclear if differing mortality rates were due to age or as a result of other factors. Cardiovascular diseases (CVDs are the leading cause of death globally, taking an estimated 17.9 million lives each year. CVDs are a group of disorders of the heart and blood vessels and include coronary heart disease, cerebrovascular disease, rheumatic heart disease and other conditions.

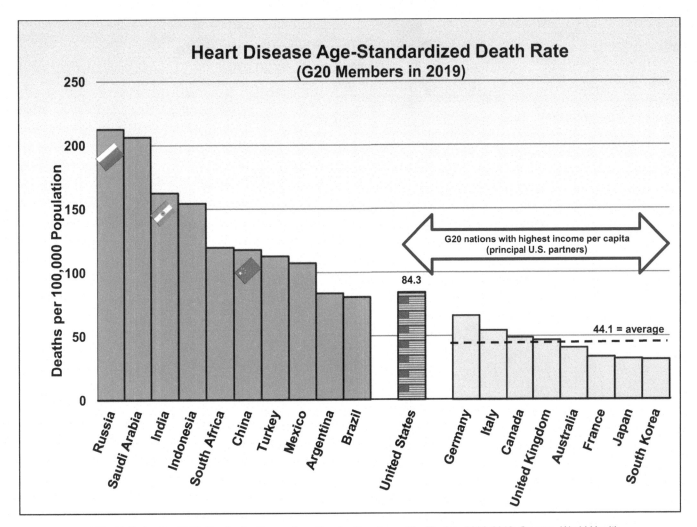

Heart Disease Age-Standardized Death Rate
(G20 Members in 2019)

Sources: Global Health Estimates 2019: Deaths by Cause, Age, Sex, by Country and by Region, 2000-2019. Geneva, World Health Organization; 2020. https://www.who.int/data/gho/data/themes/mortality-and-global-health-estimates, Non-exclusive license dated 3/15/23 to use selected WHO published materials.

In 2019, heart diseases—including circulatory diseases other than stroke—was the leading subgroup of cardiovascular disease (CVD) deaths in the U.S. and accounted for 24.2 percent of all U.S. deaths. Stroke made up the remaining subgroup of cardiovascular diseases and accounted for 5.4 percent of all deaths in the U.S.

The U.S. age-standardized death rate due to heart disease was approximately twice as high as the other eight high income per capita G20 members but only half the rate experienced by India.

The term "heart disease" refers to several types of heart conditions. The most common type of heart disease in the U.S. is coronary artery disease (CAD), which affects the blood flow to the heart. Decreased blood flow can cause a heart attack. Heart disease includes: ischemic heart disease, rheumatic heart disease, hypertensive heart disease, cardiomyopathy, myocarditis, endocarditis, and other circulatory diseases, however, a separate category of CAD is stroke and is not included in the data for this chart. More than four out of five CVD deaths in the U.S. are due to heart attacks and strokes, and one third of these deaths occur prematurely in people under 70 years of age.

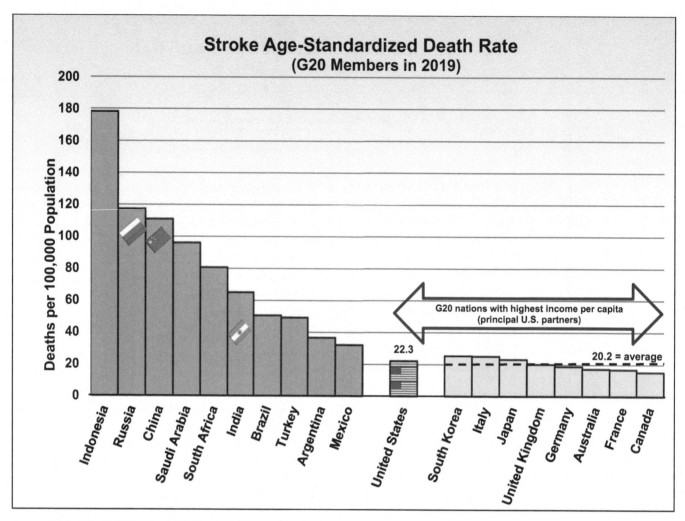

Source: Global Health Estimates 2019: Deaths by Cause, Age, Sex, by Country and by Region, 2000-2019. Geneva, World Health Organization; 2020. https://www.who.int/data/gho/data/themes/mortality-and-global-health-estimates, Non-exclusive license dated 3/15/23 to use selected WHO published materials.

In 2019, stroke, the second-largest subgroup of cardiovascular diseases (CVDs), accounted for 5.4 percent of all deaths in the U.S. The U.S. age-standardized death rate due to stroke was approximately the same as for the other high income per capita G20 members while only one-third the rate of India.

A stroke, sometimes called a brain attack, occurs when something blocks blood supply to part of the brain or when a blood vessel in the brain bursts. In either case, parts of the brain become damaged or die. A stroke can cause lasting brain damage, long-term disability, or even death. Stroke does not include heart disease which is also categorized as a cardiovascular disease (CAD. Stroke includes ischemic stroke and hemorrhagic stroke.

More than four out of five CVD deaths in the U.S. are due to heart attacks and strokes, and one-third of these deaths occur prematurely in people under 70 years of age.

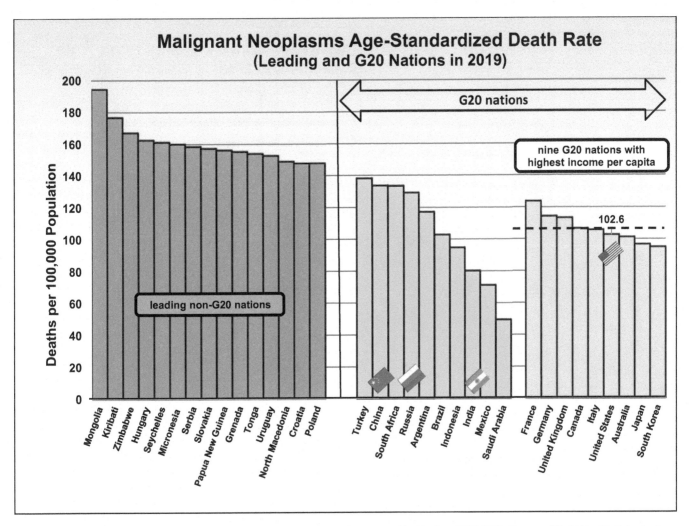

Malignant Neoplasms Age-Standardized Death Rate
(Leading and G20 Nations in 2019)

Source: Global Health Estimates 2019: Deaths by Cause, Age, Sex, by Country and by Region, 2000-2019. Geneva, World Health Organization; 2020. https://www.who.int/data/gho/data/themes/mortality-and-global-health-estimates, Non-exclusive license dated 3/15/23 to use selected WHO published materials.

In 2019, malignant neoplasms (cancer) was the second-highest category of noncommunicable diseases (NCDs)—after cardiovascular diseases (CVDs)—and accounted for 20.9 percent of all deaths in the U.S. at 103 deaths per 100,000 population. This level was three percent below the average of all G20 nations.

Neoplasms may be benign (not cancer or malignant (cancer. Benign neoplasms may grow large but do not spread into, or invade, nearby tissues or other parts of the body. Malignant neoplasms can spread into, or invade, nearby tissues. They can also spread to other parts of the body through the blood and lymph systems.

Age-standardized mortality rates can be used to compare the mortality rates of countries without being affected by the difference in age distributions from country to country. Without using this standardization, it would be unclear if differing mortality rates were due to age or as a result of other factors. A neoplasm is composed of atypical neoplastic, often pleomorphic cells that invade other tissues. Malignant neoplasms often metastasize to distant anatomic sites and may recur after excision. The most common malignant neoplasms are carcinomas, Hodgkin's and non-Hodgkin's lymphomas, leukemia, melanomas, and sarcomas.

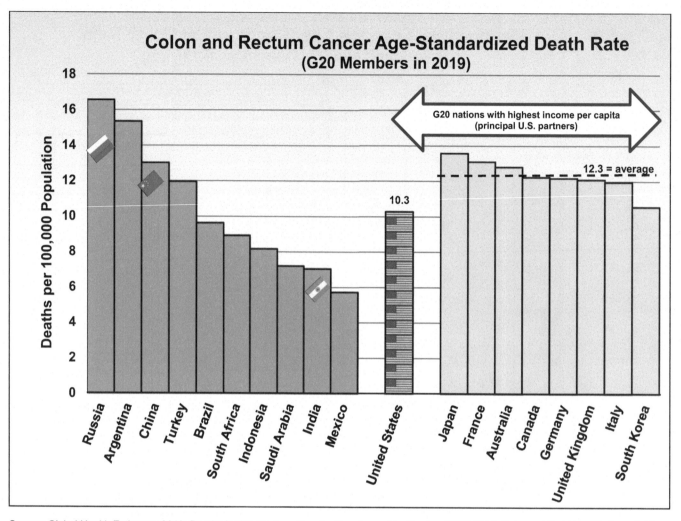

Colon and Rectum Cancer Age-Standardized Death Rate
(G20 Members in 2019)

Source: Global Health Estimates 2019: Deaths by Cause, Age, Sex, by Country and by Region, 2000-2019. Geneva, World Health Organization; 2020. https://www.who.int/data/gho/data/themes/mortality-and-global-health-estimates, Non-exclusive license dated 3/15/23 to use selected WHO published materials.

In 2019, the U.S. experienced an age-standardized death rate due to colon and rectum cancer that was approximately 20 percent below the rate experienced by the other high income per capita G20 nations.

A neoplasm is composed of atypical neoplastic, often pleomorphic cells that invade other tissues. Malignant neoplasms often metastasize to distant anatomic sites and may recur after excision. The most common malignant neoplasms are carcinomas, Hodgkin's and non-Hodgkin's lymphomas, leukemias, melanomas, and sarcomas.

The crude mortality rate is a good indicator of the general health status of a geographic area or population. The crude death rate is not appropriate for comparison of different populations or areas with large differences in age distributions. Higher crude death rates can be found in some developed countries, despite high life expectancy, because typically these countries have a much higher proportion of older people, due to lower recent birth rates and lower age-specific mortality rates.

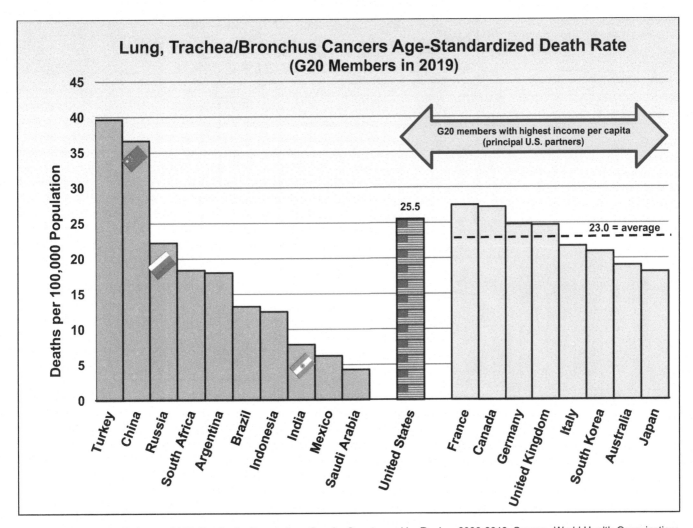

Lung, Trachea/Bronchus Cancers Age-Standardized Death Rate
(G20 Members in 2019)

Source: Global Health Estimates 2019: Deaths by Cause, Age, Sex, by Country and by Region, 2000-2019. Geneva, World Health Organization; 2020. https://www.who.int/data/gho/data/themes/mortality-and-global-health-estimates, Non-exclusive license dated 3/15/23 to use selected WHO published materials.

In 2019, Lung, trachea and bronchus cancer deaths were the largest subcategory of malignant neoplasms, accounting for 5.3 percent of all deaths in the U.S. The U.S. age-standardized death rate due to these cancers was approximately 10 percent above the rate for the other high income per capita G20 nations.

Cancer is a disease in which cells in the body grow out of control. When cancer starts in the lungs, it is called lung cancer. Lung cancer begins in the lungs and may spread to lymph nodes or other organs in the body, such as the brain. Cancer from other organs also may spread to the lungs. When cancer cells spread from one organ to another, they are called metastases. Lung cancers usually are grouped into two main types called small-cell and non-small-cell (including adenocarcinoma and squamous cell carcinoma). These types of lung cancer grow differently and are treated differently. Non-small-cell lung cancer is more common than small-cell lung cancer. The crude mortality rate is a good indicator of the general health status of a geographic area or population. The crude death rate is not appropriate for comparison of different populations or areas with large differences in age distributions.

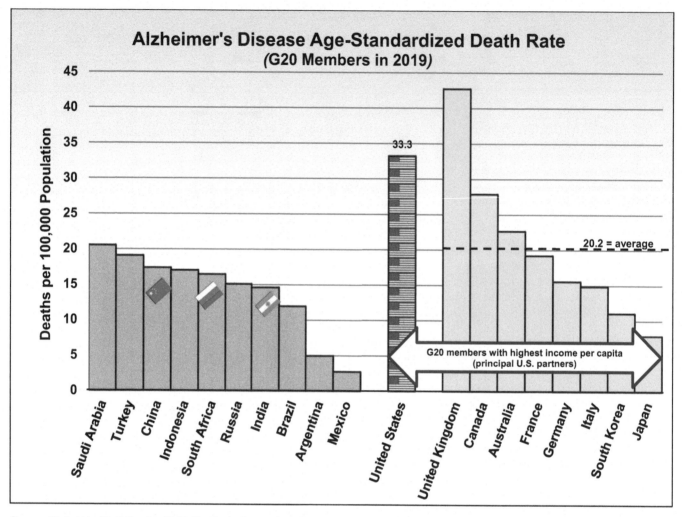

Alzheimer's Disease Age-Standardized Death Rate
(G20 Members in 2019)

Source: Global Health Estimates 2019: Deaths by Cause, Age, Sex, by Country and by Region, 2000-2019. Geneva, World Health Organization; 2020. https://www.who.int/data/gho/data/themes/mortality-and-global-health-estimates, Non-exclusive license dated 3/15/23 to use selected WHO published materials.

In 2019, Alzheimer's disease and other dementias were the third-highest death rate subcategory under noncommunicable diseases, accounting for 9.7 percent of all deaths in the U.S. That rate was 65 percent higher than the average age-standardized rate for the other high income per capita G20 nations and approximately twice as high as for India.

Dementia is a general term for conditions that cause loss of memory severe enough that they may impact a person's ability to carry out daily activities. There are many kinds of dementia, but Alzheimer's is the most common type. Alzheimer's disease is a type of dementia that causes problems with memory, thinking, language, and behavior. It may begin with mild memory loss, and symptoms can slowly worsen over time. The crude mortality rate is a good indicator of the general health status of a geographic area or population.

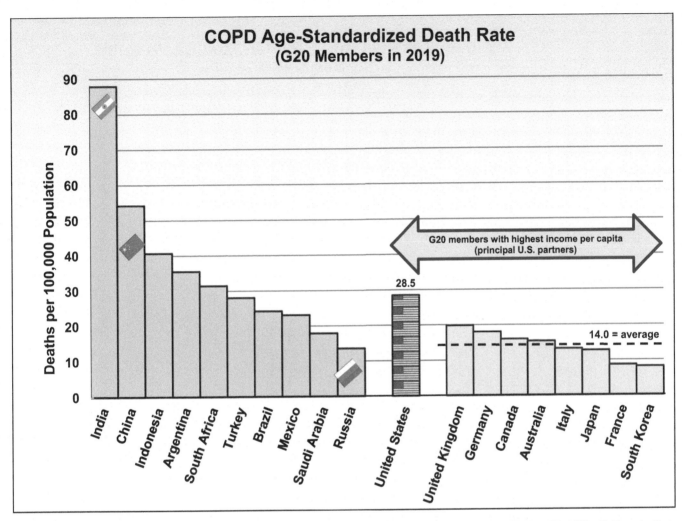

COPD Age-Standardized Death Rate
(G20 Members in 2019)

Source: Global Health Estimates 2019: Deaths by Cause, Age, Sex, by Country and by Region, 2000-2019. Geneva, World Health Organization; 2020. https://www.who.int/data/gho/data/themes/mortality-and-global-health-estimates, Non-exclusive license dated 3/15/23 to use selected WHO published materials.

In 2019, COPD (chronic obstructive pulmonary disease) was the fourth-highest death rate subcategory in the U.S. under noncommunicable diseases, accounting for 9.6 percent of all deaths in the U.S. That age-standardized death rate was twice as high as that experienced by the other high income per capita nations.

Chronic obstructive pulmonary disease, or COPD, refers to a group of diseases that cause airflow blockage and breathing-related problems. It includes emphysema and chronic bronchitis. COPD makes breathing difficult for the 16 million Americans who have this disease.

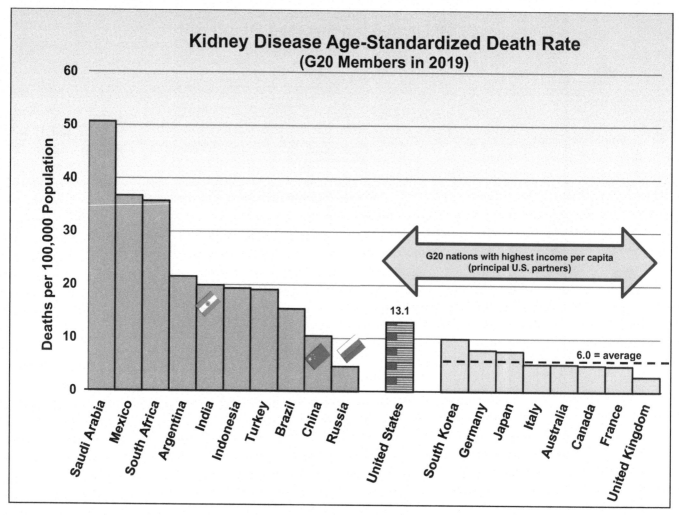

Source: Global Health Estimates 2019: Deaths by Cause, Age, Sex, by Country and by Region, 2000-2019. Geneva, World Health Organization; 2020. https://www.who.int/data/gho/data/themes/mortality-and-global-health-estimates, Non-exclusive license dated 3/15/23 to use selected WHO published materials.

In 2019, kidney disease was the fifth-highest death rate subcategory under noncommunicable diseases (NCDs) for the U.S., accounting for 2.9 percent of all deaths in the U.S. The U.S. experienced an age-standardized death rate for kidney diseases approximately double the rate experienced by the other high income per capita G20 nations.

Chronic kidney disease (CKD) means your kidneys are damaged and can't filter blood the way they should. The disease is called "chronic" because the damage to your kidneys happens slowly over a long period of time. This damage can cause wastes to build up in your body. CKD can also cause other health problems.

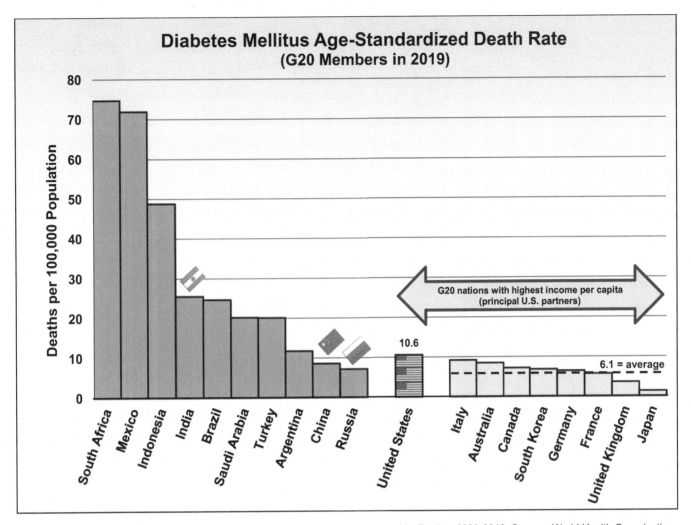

Diabetes Mellitus Age-Standardized Death Rate
(G20 Members in 2019)

Source: Global Health Estimates 2019: Deaths by Cause, Age, Sex, by Country and by Region, 2000-2019. Geneva, World Health Organization; 2020. https://www.who.int/data/gho/data/themes/mortality-and-global-health-estimates, Non-exclusive license dated 3/15/23 to use selected WHO published materials.

In 2019, diabetes mellitus was the sixth-highest death rate subcategory under noncommunicable diseases (NCDs) in the U.S., accounting for 2.1 percent of all deaths in the U.S. The U.S. age-standardized death rate was 74 percent higher than the rate experienced by the other high income per capita G20 nations while half the rate experienced by India.

The technical name for diabetes is diabetes mellitus. Diabetes is a chronic, metabolic disease characterized by elevated levels of blood glucose (or blood sugar), which leads over time to serious damage to the heart, blood vessels, eyes, kidneys and nerves. The most common is type 2 diabetes, usually in adults, which occurs when the body becomes resistant to insulin or doesn't make enough insulin. In the past three decades the prevalence of type 2 diabetes has risen dramatically in countries of all income levels. Type 1 diabetes, once known as juvenile diabetes or insulin-dependent diabetes, is a chronic condition in which the pancreas produces little or no insulin by itself.

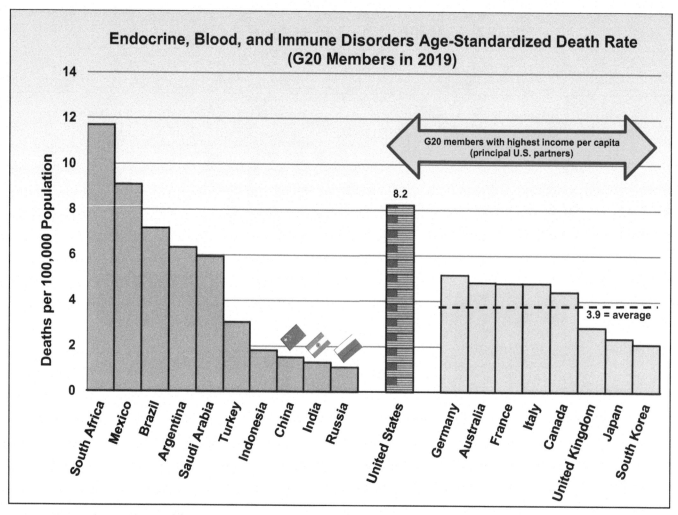

Endocrine, Blood, and Immune Disorders Age-Standardized Death Rate
(G20 Members in 2019)

Sources: Global Health Estimates 2019: Deaths by Cause, Age, Sex, by Country and by Region, 2000-2019. Geneva, World Health Organization; 2020. https://www.who.int/data/gho/data/themes/mortality-and-global-health-estimates, Non-exclusive license dated 3/15/23 to use selected WHO published materials.

In 2019, endocrine, blood, immune disorders were the seventh-highest death rate subcategory under noncommunicable diseases (NCDs) in the U.S., accounting for 1.6 percent of all deaths in the U.S. The age-standardized death rate experienced by the U.S. was approximately double the level experienced by the other high income per capita G20 nations and six times higher than experienced by India.

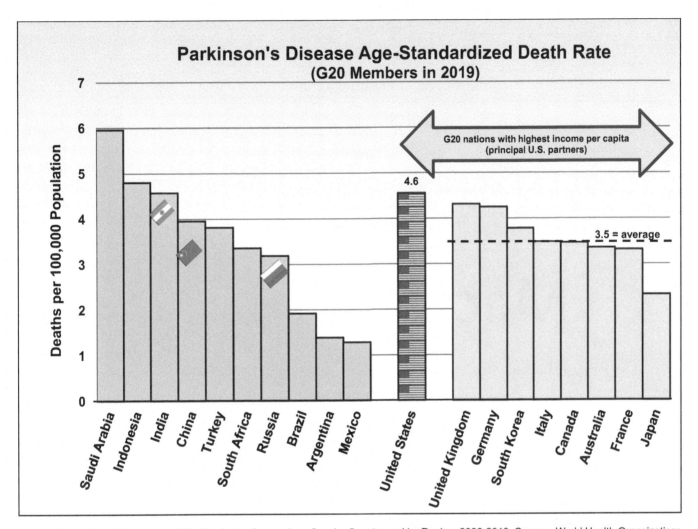

Parkinson's Disease Age-Standardized Death Rate
(G20 Members in 2019)

Source: Global Health Estimates 2019: Deaths by Cause, Age, Sex, by Country and by Region, 2000-2019. Geneva, World Health Organization; 2020. https://www.who.int/data/gho/data/themes/mortality-and-global-health-estimates, Non-exclusive license dated 3/15/23 to use selected WHO published materials.

In 2019, Parkinson's disease was the eighth-highest death rate subcategory under noncommunicable diseases (NCDs) in the U.S., and accounted for 1.2 percent of all deaths in the U.S. The age-standardized death rate in the U.S. was 31 percent above the rate experienced by the other high income per capita G20 nations and approximately the same as experienced by India.

Parkinson's disease is a brain disorder that causes unintended or uncontrollable movements, such as shaking, stiffness, and difficulty with balance and coordination. Symptoms usually begin gradually and worsen over time. As the disease progresses, people may have difficulty walking and talking. They may also have mental and behavioral changes, sleep problems, depression, memory difficulties, and fatigue.

Chapter 7

Macroeconomics

Overview of Macroeconomics

In 2022, the U.S. GDP ranked as the leading economy in the world, at $25.5 trillion U.S. dollars, 44 percent larger than China's, which ranked in second place. Together, the U.S. and China accounted for 43 percent of the world's GDP. Collectively, the G20 member nations comprised 85.2 percent of the world's GDP. The U.S. also had the highest gross national income per capita of the G20 nations. Australia was almost as high at 97 percent of the U.S. level.

During the period 2010–2019, prior to the COVID-19 pandemic, the U.S. economy, measured in constant 2015 U.S. dollars, experienced very consistent annual GDP growth of approximately 2.2 percent. During that same period China's growth experienced a nearly steady decline from approximately 14 percent to six percent. In 2022, after the initial economic disruption due to COVID-19 the U.S. GDP grew at 2.2 percent while China's had declined to 3.0 percent. That was the smallest difference in GDP growth between these nations since 1989.

When comparing GDP, or GDP per capita, an alternative measurement to the U.S. dollar is the international dollar. The international dollar is calculated based on Purchasing Power Parity (PPP) and on that basis China's GDP is the largest in the world. In 2017, China's GDP based on PPP was equal to the U.S. and by 2021, had grown to be 18 percent larger than the U.S. The CIA has judged that using PPP for evaluation of China's economy may be the better indicator of China's economic size than the U.S. dollar since China tends to depreciate the yuan to improve their export business.

In 2021, GDP growth for most of the world was disrupted due to the COVID-19 pandemic, however, by 2021 most economies had begun to recover. Most notably, the E.U.'s GDP had stagnated beginning in 2009, and didn't begin to grow again until 2021, which was also after the departure of the U.K. from the Union in January, 2020 (called "Brexit").

Over the arc of time, 1960–2022, the U.S. portion of world's GDP declined by approximately one-third, from 39 percent to 25 percent, while China gained approximately as much of the world's share as the U.S. lost over that period.

Another overarching trend has been the accumulation of U.S. federal debt that reached unprecedented levels. By January 1, 2024, U.S. federal debt had climbed to $34.0 trillion, which was 120.2 percent of GDP—the highest percentage since World War II—and 30 percent of that debt was held by foreigners. In 2022, the foreign portion of U.S. debt was $7.3 trillion which was a reduction from the all-time peak in 2020, of $7.7 trillion. In January 2023, 36 percent of foreign debt was held by just three countries: Japan, ($1.1 trillion), China, ($.86 trillion), and the United Kingdom, ($.67 trillion).

In 2022, the Organization for Economic Cooperation and Development (OECD), comprised of 38 nations, had a total GDP of $58.3 trillion in U.S. dollars, accounting for 61 percent of the world's GDP. Two-thirds of the world's top 30 nations with the highest GDP are OECD members.

Between 1982 and 2022, on average the U.S. added 2.2 GDP percentage points per year to its debt and there is no off-ramp in sight. Deficit spending has become a standard federal funding method in the U.S. For fiscal year 2023, the U.S. government interest payments on federal debt held by the public reached a new high level of $720.6 billion. That level was a 22 percent increase since the previous high in 2018, and was equivalent to 88 percent of the U.S. Defense Department budget for that year.

In 2022, the U.S. GDP was $25.46 trillion in U.S. dollars, of which 68.2 percent was consumer spending. Consumer spending for services was almost two-thirds of that total. The federal government consumption and investment portion of GDP exceeded state and local amounts by 70 percent. External trade with other countries resulted in a reduction of GDP by $975 billion (3.8 percent). GDP is equal to: Consumption + Investment + Government Purchases + (Exports – Imports). For the year 2020, after the COVID-19 pandemic was declared on March 11th that year, U.S. real GDP growth for the year declined from 2.58 percent in 2019, to 1.18 percent. In 2021, GDP growth spiked to 5.75 percent but then declined to .90 percent in 2022.

In 2022, the top 50 nations with the highest GDP per capita in U.S. dollars, all voted "In Favor" of the February 23, 2023, U.N. resolution for Russia to withdraw from Ukraine. The U.S. GDP per capita ranked 8th in the world at $76,400 per capita. Monaco was the world's leader at $234,000 per capita.

In 2021, the U.S. ranked 15th out of the 19 G20 member nations for production growth rate. Economic growth and supply chains across the globe were stunted during the COVID-19 pandemic between March 2020 and May 2023.

China's value of foreign reserves, measured in U.S. dollars, fluctuates as the exchange rate between the U.S. dollar and other currencies fluctuate. The increased value of the U.S. dollar in 2015, may have contributed to the 21 percent reduction in value of China's reserves which occurred in 2015.

On February 23, 2023—the eve of the one-year anniversary of Russia's invasion of Ukraine—the U.N. General Assembly voted on a resolution for Russia to withdraw. Of the 180 votes cast, those 141 nations that voted "In Favor" of withdrawal were nations that accounted for 71 percent of the world's GDP.

~

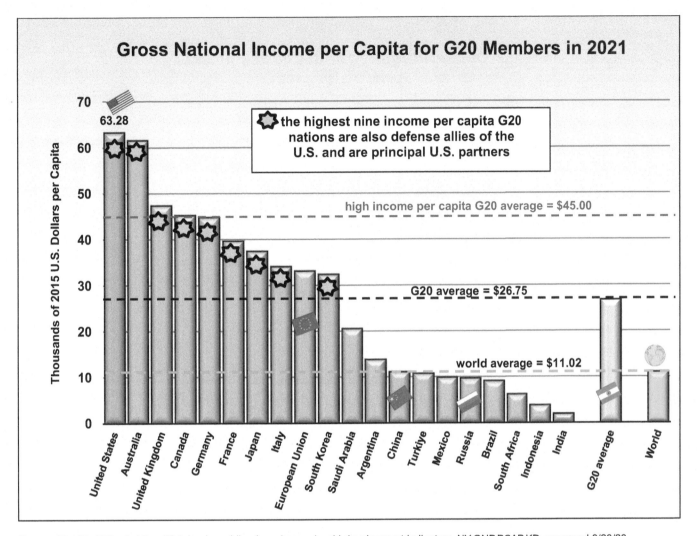

Source: The World Bank, https://databank.worldbank.org/source/world-development-indicators, NY.GNP.PCAP.KD, accessed 8/23/23
https://data.worldbank.org/summary-terms-of-use gross national income of $432.

In 2021, the U.S. was the G20 nation with the highest gross national income per capita. Australia was almost as high at 97 percent of the U.S. level. China was approximately 18 percent as large as the U.S. level. The nine highest income G20 member nations had an average per capita gross national income of $45,045, which was 3.7 times higher than the world's average and 4.7 times higher than the average of the other ten G20 nations. Those members with the highest gross national income per capita are also principal U.S. partners.

GNI is the total dollar value of everything produced by a country and the income its residents receive—whether it is earned at home or abroad. In contrast, GDP is the sum of all goods and services with the borders of the country.

GNI is the sum of value added by all resident producers plus any product taxes (less subsidies) not included in the valuation of output plus net receipts of primary income (compensation of employees and property income) from abroad. Data are in constant 2015 U.S. dollars. Gross National Income (GNI) per capita is gross national income divided by midyear population.

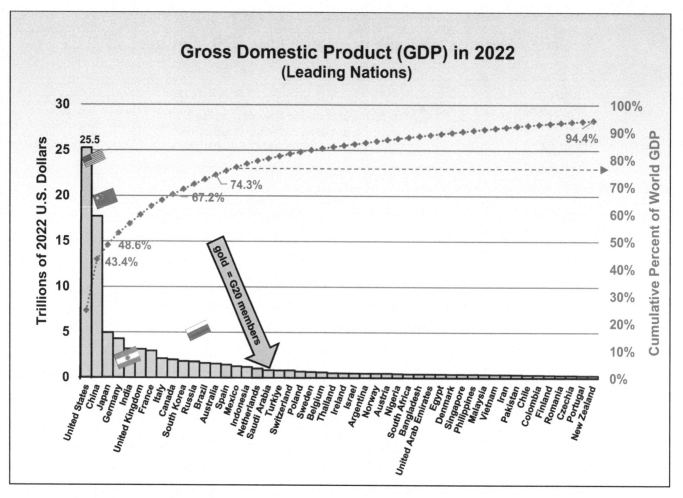

Source: The World Bank, https://databank.worldbank.org/source/world-development-indicators, NY.GDP.MKTP.CD, accessed 8/23/23
https://data.worldbank.org/summary-terms-of-use

In 2022, U.S. GDP ranked as the highest in the world, at $25.5 trillion U.S. dollars, 44 percent larger than China's GDP, which ranked in second place. Of the 19 G20 nations 13 held the top 13 rankings for highest GDP in the world, and included the eight principal U.S. partners. The 13 top ranked nations accounted for three-fourths of the world's entire GDP. Collectively, the G20 member nations comprised 85.2 percent of the world's GDP.

Dollar figures for GDP are converted from domestic currencies using single-year official exchange rates. For a few countries where the official exchange rate does not reflect the rate effectively applied to actual foreign exchange transactions, an alternative conversion factor is used. Gross domestic product (GDP) represents the sum of value added by all its producers. Value added is the value of the gross output of producers less the value of intermediate goods and services consumed in production, before accounting for consumption of fixed capital in production. The United Nations System of National Accounts calls for value added to be valued at either basic prices (excluding net taxes on products) or producer prices (including net taxes on products paid by producers but excluding sales or value added taxes).

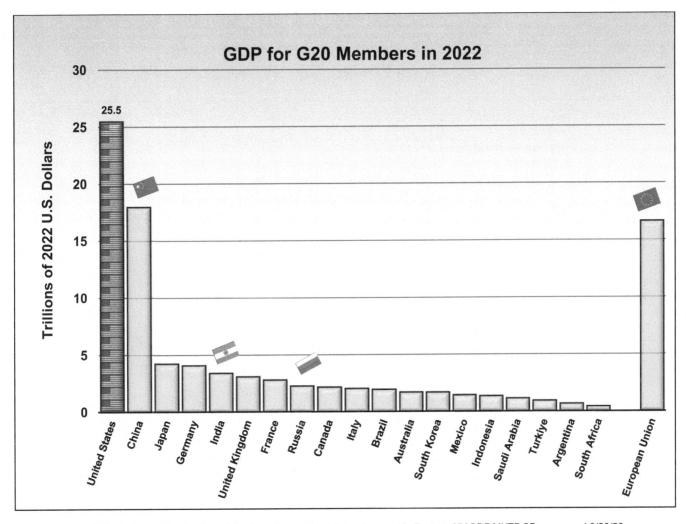

GDP for G20 Members in 2022

Trillions of 2022 U.S. Dollars

United States: 25.5

Source: The World Bank, https://databank.worldbank.org/source/world-development-indicators, NY.GDP.MKTP.CD, accessed 8/23/23
https://data.worldbank.org/summary-terms-of-use

In 2022, the G20 members—comprised of 19 nations plus the European Union (E.U.)—accounted for 85.2 percent of the world's GDP, based on 2022 U.S. dollars. However, when comparing GDP, or GDP per capita, an alternative measurement to the U.S. dollar is the international dollar. The international dollar is calculated based on Purchasing Power Parity (PPP) and on that basis China's GDP is greater than the U.S. In 2017, China's GDP based on PPP was equal to the U.S. and has grown to be 18 percent larger than the U.S. GDP as of 2021 (see page 139). The six G20 nations with the lowest GDP are South Africa, Argentina, Turkiye, Saudi Arabia, Indonesia, and Mexico, with a combined GDP of approximately $5 trillion dollars—which is less than one-fifth the GDP of the U.S.

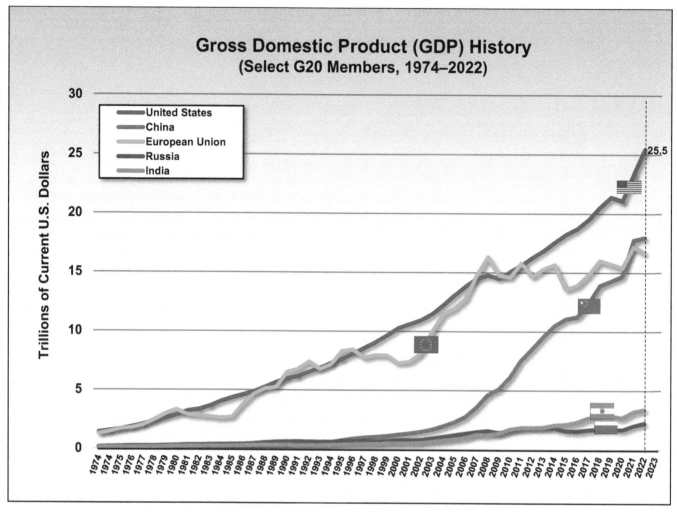

Gross Domestic Product (GDP) History
(Select G20 Members, 1974–2022)

Legend:
- United States
- China
- European Union
- Russia
- India

Y-axis: Trillions of Current U.S. Dollars (0, 5, 10, 15, 20, 25, 30)

25.5

X-axis years: 1974 through 2023

Source: The World Bank, https://databank.worldbank.org/source/world-development-indicators, NY.GDP.MKTP.CD, accessed 8/23/23
https://data.worldbank.org/summary-terms-of-use

GDP growth for most G20 members was disrupted in 2020, due to the COVID-19 pandemic, however, by 2021, most economies had begun to recover. Most notably, the E.U.'s GDP had stagnated beginning in 2009, and didn't begin to grow again until 2021, after the departure of the U.K. from the Union in January 2020 (Brexit).

When GDP is measured in U.S. dollars, U.S. GDP was 42 percent higher than China's in 2022, however, an alternate method for calculating GDP is using Purchasing Power Parity (PPP) by which China's GDP surpassed the U.S. in 2017, (as shown on page 139).

GDP at purchaser's prices is the sum of gross value added by all resident producers in the economy plus any product taxes and minus any subsidies not included in the value of the products. It is calculated without making deductions for depreciation of fabricated assets or for depletion and degradation of natural resources. Data are in current U.S. dollars. Dollar figures for GDP are converted from domestic currencies using single-year official exchange rates.

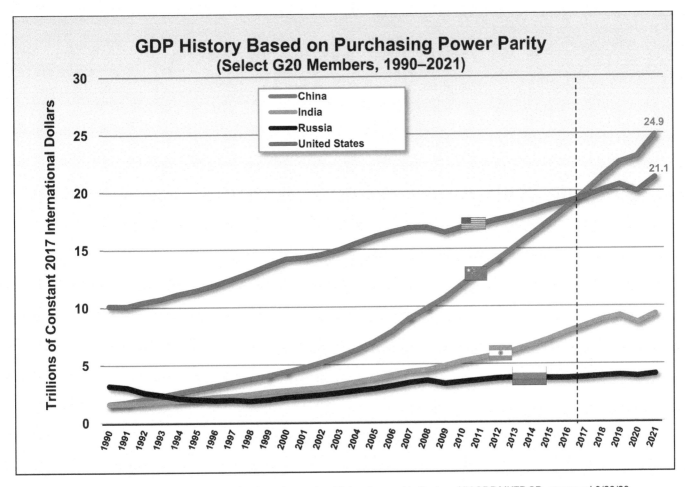

GDP History Based on Purchasing Power Parity
(Select G20 Members, 1990–2021)

Sources: The World Bank, https://databank.worldbank.org/source/world-development-indicators, NY.GDP.MKTP.CD, accessed 8/23/23
https://data.worldbank.org/summary-terms-of-use, CIA, World Factbook, https://www.cia.gov/the-world-factbook/countries/china/#economy

In 2017, GDP for China surpassed the U.S. when measured based on purchasing power parity (PPP). In 2021, China's GDP, based on 2017 international dollars, was 18 percent larger than of the U.S.

According to the CIA, "Because China's exchange rate is determined by fiat rather than by market forces, the official exchange rate measure of GDP is not an accurate measure of China's output; GDP at the official exchange rate substantially understates the actual level of China's output vis-a-vis the rest of the world; in China's situation, GDP at purchasing power parity provides the best measure for comparing output across countries."

Purchasing power parity (PPP) GDP is gross domestic product converted to international dollars using purchasing power parity rates. An international dollar has the same purchasing power over GDP as the U.S. dollar has in the U.S. GDP is the sum of gross value added by all resident producers in the country plus any product taxes and minus any subsidies not included in the value of the products. It is calculated without making deductions for depreciation of fabricated assets or for depletion and degradation of natural resources. Data are in constant 2017 international dollars. The major use of purchasing power parity (PPP) is as a first step in making inter-country comparisons in real terms of gross domestic product (GDP) and its component expenditures.

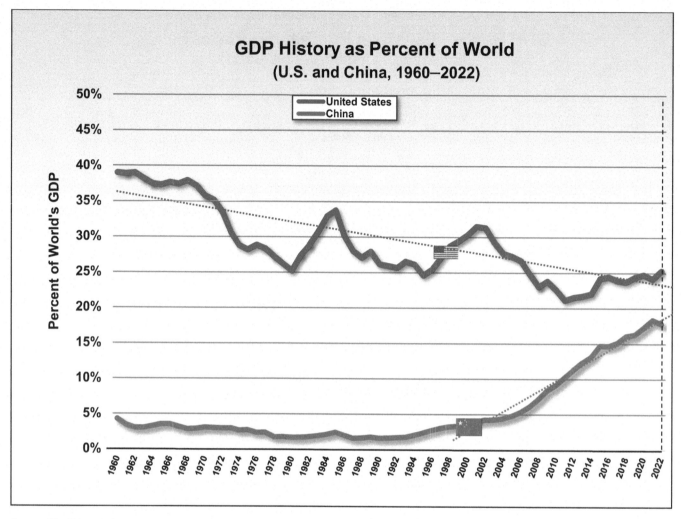

Source: The World Bank, https://databank.worldbank.org/source/world-development-indicators, NY.GDP.MKTP.CD, accessed 8/23/23
https://data.worldbank.org/summary-terms-of-use

From the post-Korean War era to 2022, the combined GDP for the U.S. plus China has been approximately one-half of the worlds' total GDP when measured as percentage of GDP in U.S. dollars. Over the arc of time, 1960–2022, the U.S. portion of world GDP has declined by approximately one-third, from 39 percent to 25 percent, while China has gained approximately as much of the world's share as the U.S. lost during that period.

GDP at purchaser's prices is the sum of gross value added by all resident producers in the economy plus any product taxes and minus any subsidies not included in the value of the products. It is calculated without making deductions for depreciation of fabricated assets or for depletion and degradation of natural resources. Data are in current U.S. dollars. Dollar figures for GDP are converted from domestic currencies using single year official exchange rates.

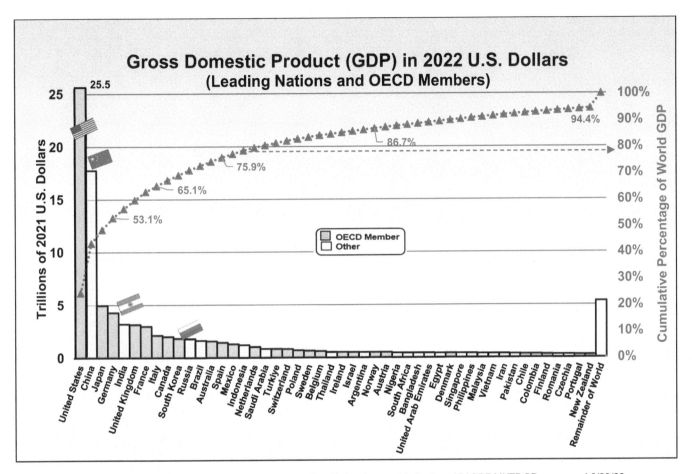

Source: The World Bank, https://databank.worldbank.org/source/world-development-indicators, NY.GDP.MKTP.CD, accessed 8/23/23
https://data.worldbank.org/summary-terms-of-use

In 2022, the Organization for Economic Cooperation and Development (OECD) was comprised of 38 nations, with a total GDP of $58.3 trillion U.S. dollars. Two-thirds of the world's top 30 nations with the highest GDP are OECD members.

Data are in current U.S. dollars. Dollar figures for GDP are converted from domestic currencies using single-year official exchange rates. For a few countries where the official exchange rate does not reflect the rate effectively applied to actual foreign exchange transactions, an alternative conversion factor is used. Gross domestic product (GDP) represents the sum of value added by all its producers. Value added is the value of the gross output of producers less the value of intermediate goods and services consumed in production, before accounting for consumption of fixed capital in production.

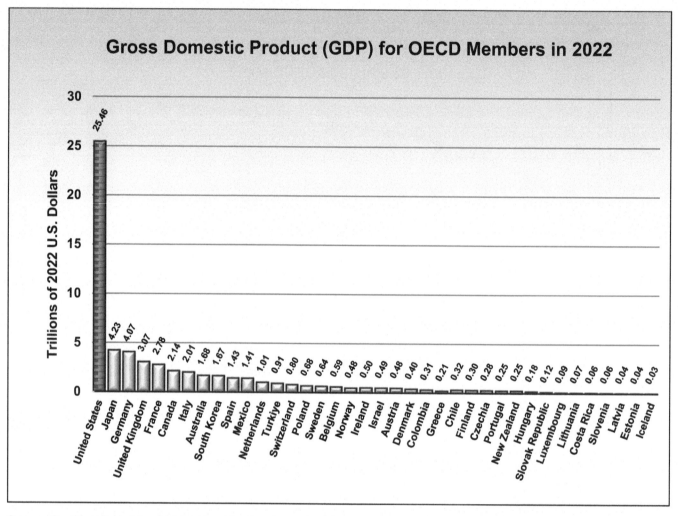

Gross Domestic Product (GDP) for OECD Members in 2022

Sources: The World Bank, https://databank.worldbank.org/source/world-development-indicators, NY.GDP.MKTP.CD, accessed 8/23/23
https://data.worldbank.org/summary-terms-of-use

In 2022, the Organization for Economic Cooperation and Development (OECD) members accounted for 61 percent of the world's GDP. OECD was comprised of 38 nations, with a total GDP of $58.3 trillion in U.S. dollars, of which the U.S. accounted for $25.5 trillion.

GDP at purchaser's prices is the sum of gross value added by all resident producers in the economy plus any product taxes and minus any subsidies not included in the value of the products. It is calculated without making deductions for depreciation of fabricated assets or for depletion and degradation of natural resources. Data are in current U.S. dollars. Dollar figures for GDP are converted from domestic currencies using single-year official exchange rates. For a few countries where the official exchange rate does not reflect the rate effectively applied to actual foreign exchange transactions, an alternative conversion factor is used. Gross domestic product (GDP) represents the sum of value added by all its producers. Value added is the value of the gross output of producers less the value of intermediate goods and services consumed in production, before accounting for consumption of fixed capital in production.

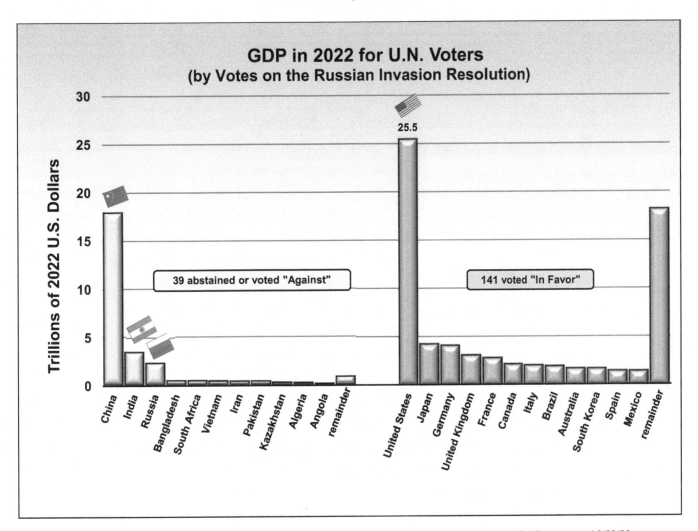

Source: The World Bank, https://databank.worldbank.org/source/world-development-indicators, NY.GDP.MKTP.CD, accessed 8/23/23
https://data.worldbank.org/summary-terms-of-use

On February 23, 2023—the eve of the one-year anniversary of Russia's invasion of Ukraine—the U.N. General Assembly voted on a resolution for Russia to withdraw. Of the 180 votes cast, those that voted "In Favor" of withdrawal were nations that accounted for 71 percent of the world's GDP.

Gross domestic product (GDP) represents the sum of value added by all its producers. Value added is the value of the gross output of producers less the value of intermediate goods and services consumed in production, before accounting for consumption of fixed capital in production. The United Nations System of National Accounts calls for value added to be valued at either basic prices (excluding net taxes on products) or producer prices (including net taxes on products paid by producers but excluding sales or value added taxes). Both valuations exclude transport charges that are invoiced separately by producers. Total GDP is measured at purchaser prices. Value added by industry is normally measured at basic prices.

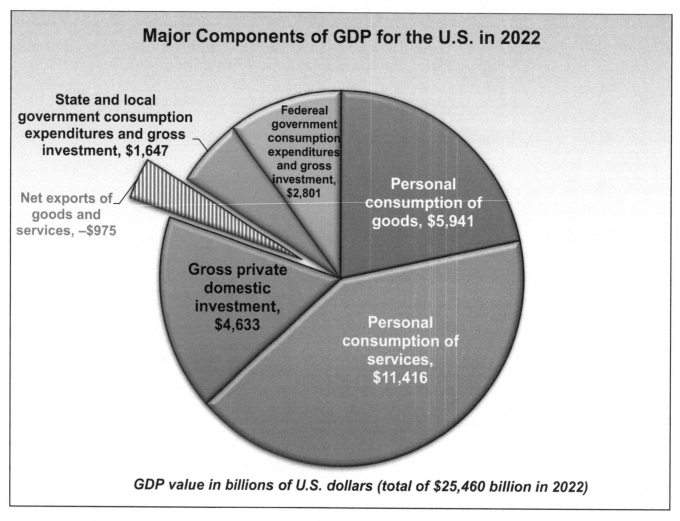

Major Components of GDP for the U.S. in 2022

State and local government consumption expenditures and gross investment, $1,647

Federeal government consumption expenditures and gross investment, $2,801

Personal consumption of goods, $5,941

Net exports of goods and services, –$975

Gross private domestic investment, $4,633

Personal consumption of services, $11,416

GDP value in billions of U.S. dollars (total of $25,460 billion in 2022)

Source: U.S. Bureau of Economic Analysis. https://www.bea.gov/data/gdp/gdp-industry

In 2022, the U.S. GDP was $25.46 trillion in U.S. dollars, of which 68.2 percent was consumer spending. Consumer spending for services was almost double (92 percent more) the amount for consumer spending for goods. Federal government consumption and investment exceeded state and local amounts by 70 percent. External trade with other countries resulted in a deficit which reduced GDP by $975 billion (3.8 percent).

GDP equals: Consumption + Investment + Government Purchases + (Exports – Imports)

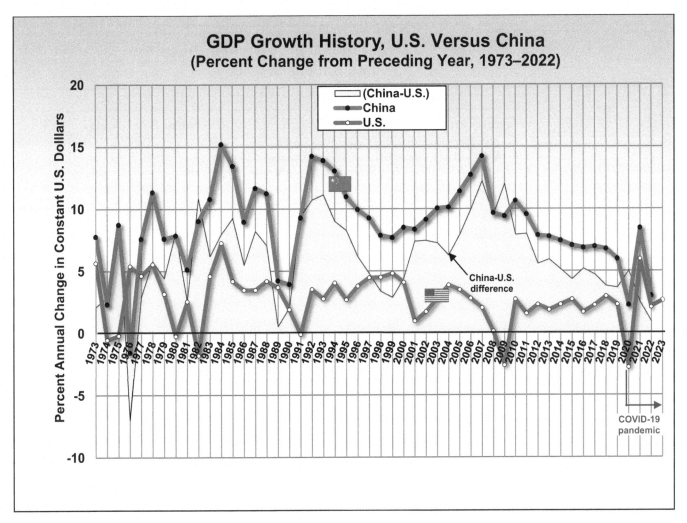

GDP Growth History, U.S. Versus China
(Percent Change from Preceding Year, 1973–2022)

Sources: The World Bank, https://databank.worldbank.org/source/world-development-indicators, NY.GDP.MKTP.KD.ZG, accessed 9/10/23 https://data.worldbank.org/summary-terms-of-use, U.S. Bureau of Economic Analysis, https://www.bea.gov/sites/default/files/2024-01/gdp4q23-adv.pdf, FRED, Federal Reserve Bank of St. Louis; https://fred.stlouisfed.org/series/A191RL1Q225SBEA

From the period 2010–2019, prior to the COVID-19 pandemic, the U.S. economy, measured in constant 2015 U.S. dollars, experienced stable annual GDP growth of approximately 2.2 percent. Then in 2020—after the COVID-19 pandemic was declared on March 11th—U.S. GDP growth dropped precipitously to –2.7 percent for that year. In 2021, growth spiked to 5.8 percent, followed by 1.9 percent in 2022, and 2.5 percent in 2023.

During the period 2010–2019, China's annual GDP growth experienced a nearly steady decline from approximately 14 percent to 6 percent, then dropping in the first year of the pandemic to 2.2 percent, recovering to 3.0 percent by 2022, after a spike in 2021.

The five-to-ten percent GDP growth advantage over the U.S. that China had enjoyed for nearly three decades during 1978–2008, diminished to 1 percent by 2022.

Gross domestic product (GDP) is the value of the goods and services produced by the nation's economy less the value of the goods and services used up in production. GDP is also equal to the sum of personal consumption expenditures, gross private domestic investment, net exports of goods and services, and government consumption expenditures and gross investment. Real values are inflation-adjusted estimates—that is, estimates that exclude the effects of price changes.

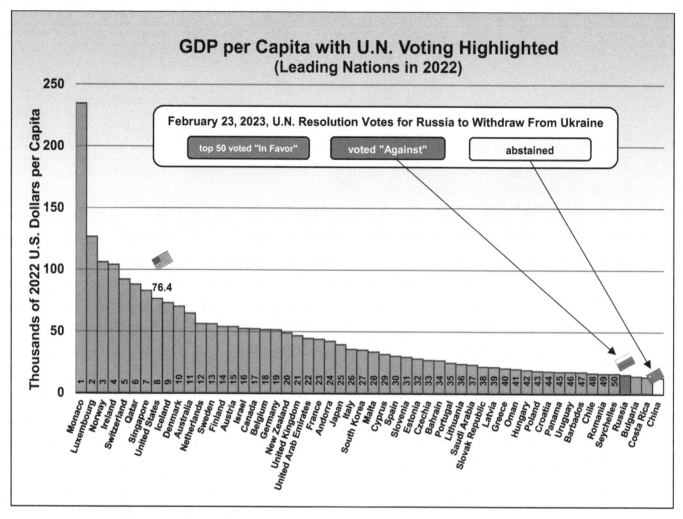

Sources: The World Bank, https://databank.worldbank.org/source/world-development-indicators, NY.GDP.PCAP.CD, accessed 8/23/23
https://data.worldbank.org/summary-terms-of-use

In 2022, the world's top 50 nations, based on GDP per capita measured in U.S. dollars, voted "In Favor" of the February 23, 2023, U.N. resolution for Russia to withdraw from Ukraine.

GDP per capita is gross domestic product divided by midyear population. GDP is the sum of gross value added by all resident producers in the economy plus any product taxes and minus any subsidies not included in the value of the products. It is calculated without making deductions for depreciation of fabricated assets or for depletion and degradation of natural resources. Data are in current U.S. dollars.

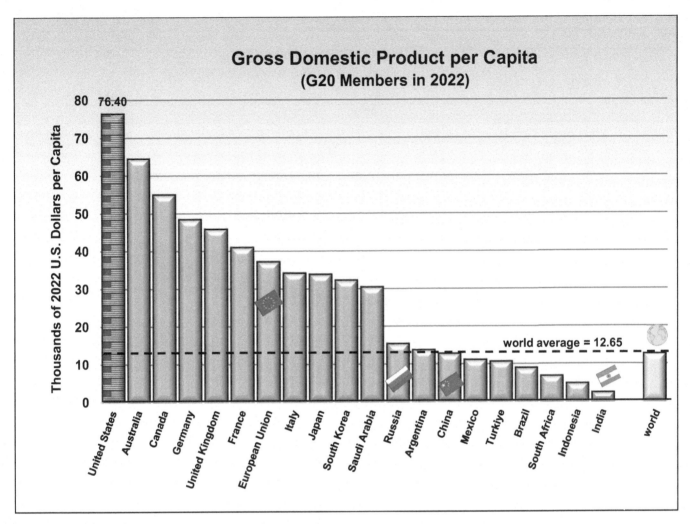

Sources: The World Bank, https://databank.worldbank.org/source/world-development-indicators, NY.GDP.PCAP.CD, accessed 8/23/23
https://data.worldbank.org/summary-terms-of-use

In 2022, the U.S. was the G20 nation with the highest GDP per capita of $76,400, measured in U.S. dollars, which was 6.4 times higher than the world's average. China's GDP per capita was approximately 17 percent as large as the U.S. The nine G20 nations with the highest GDP per capita (the U.S. and its eight primary partners) were the same nine that had the highest gross national income (GNI) per capita (see page 135).

GDP per capita is gross domestic product divided by midyear population. GDP is the sum of gross value added by all resident producers in the economy plus any product taxes and minus any subsidies not included in the value of the products. It is calculated without making deductions for depreciation of fabricated assets or for depletion and degradation of natural resources. Data are in current U.S. dollars.

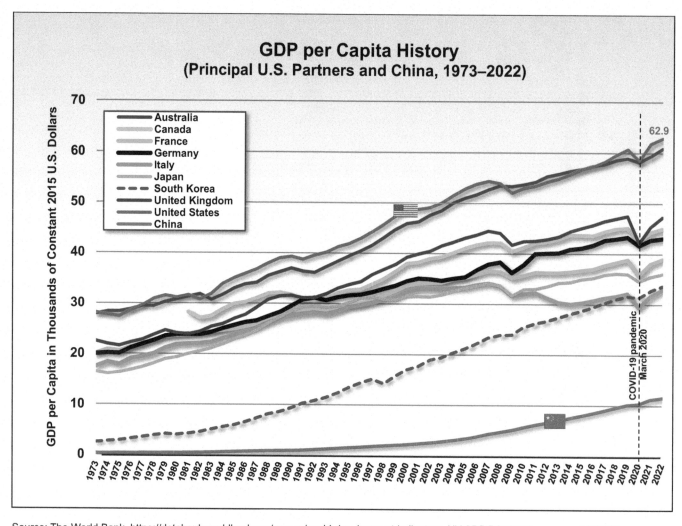

Source: The World Bank, https://databank.worldbank.org/source/world-development-indicators, NY.GDP.PCAP.CD, accessed 8/23/23
https://data.worldbank.org/summary-terms-of-use

Between 1973 and 2022, U.S. GDP per capita grew by 123 percent in constant U.S. dollars and in 2022, was the highest among the wealthiest nine G20 members (principal U.S. partners). Throughout that entire period Australia and the U.S. GDP per capita tracked at almost identical levels.

GDP per capita is gross domestic product divided by midyear population. GDP is the sum of gross value added by all resident producers in the economy plus any product taxes and minus any subsidies not included in the value of the products. It is calculated without making deductions for depreciation of fabricated assets or for depletion and degradation of natural resources. Data are in current U.S. dollars.

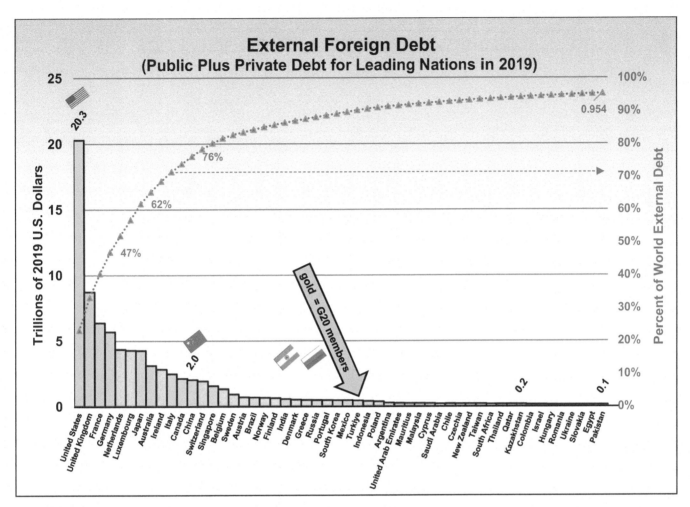

Source: CIA, The World Factbook 2021. Washington, DC: Central Intelligence Agency, 2021, https://www.cia.gov/the-world-factbook/, The Factbook is in the public domain.

In 2021, the U.S. was the world's leader for total foreign debt, both public and private, of $20.3 trillion U.S. dollars which was 22.3 percent of the total world external debt.

External debt compares the total public and private debt owed to nonresidents repayable in foreign currency, goods, or services. These figures are calculated on an exchange rate basis.

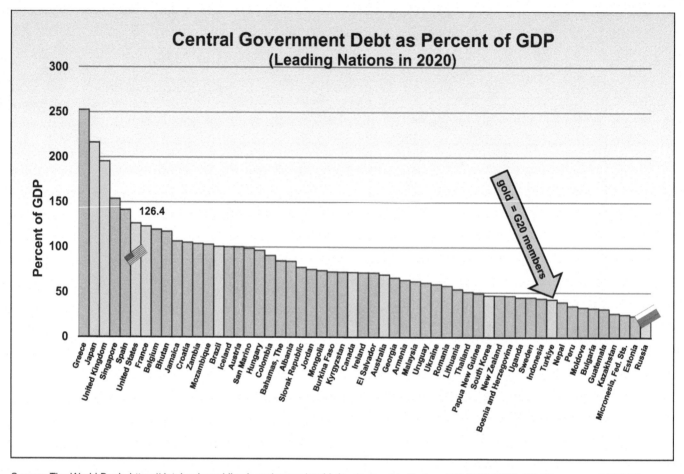

Source: The World Bank, https://databank.worldbank.org/source/world-development-indicators, GC.DOD.TOTL.GD.ZS, accessed 8/23/23
https://data.worldbank.org/summary-terms-of-use

In 2020, the U.S. ranked sixth in the world and third among G20 members, for federal debt expressed as a percentage of GDP. U.S. federal debt was 126.4 percent of GDP, the highest level since world war II.

Debt is the entire stock of direct government fixed-term contractual obligations to others outstanding on a particular date. It includes domestic and foreign liabilities such as currency and money deposits, securities other than shares, and loans. It is the gross amount of government liabilities reduced by the amount of equity and financial derivatives held by the government. Because debt is a stock rather than a flow, it is measured as of a given date, usually the last day of the fiscal year. For most countries central government finance data have been consolidated into one account, but for others only budgetary central government accounts are available. Countries reporting budgetary data are noted in the country metadata. Because budgetary accounts may not include all central government units (such as social security funds), they usually provide an incomplete picture. In federal states the central government accounts provide an incomplete view of total public finance.

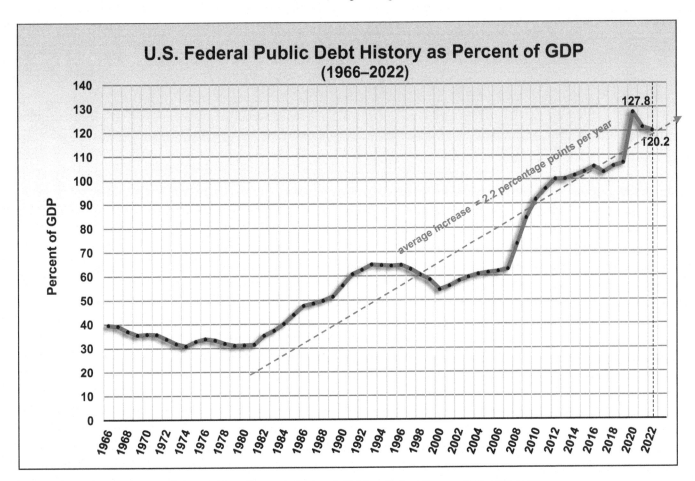

Source: FRED, Federal Reserve Economic Data, Economic Research Division, Federal Reserve Bank of St. Louis, https://fred.stlouisfed.org/series/GFDEGDQ188S, data accessed 4/23/23. The Bank grants a non-exclusive, limited right and license to display and reproduce the charts and graphs.

In 2022, U.S. federal public debt in proportion to GDP was 120.2 percent, a reduction from the peak of 127.8 percent which occurred in 2020. Since 1981, the debt has increased an average of 2.2 percentage points per year.

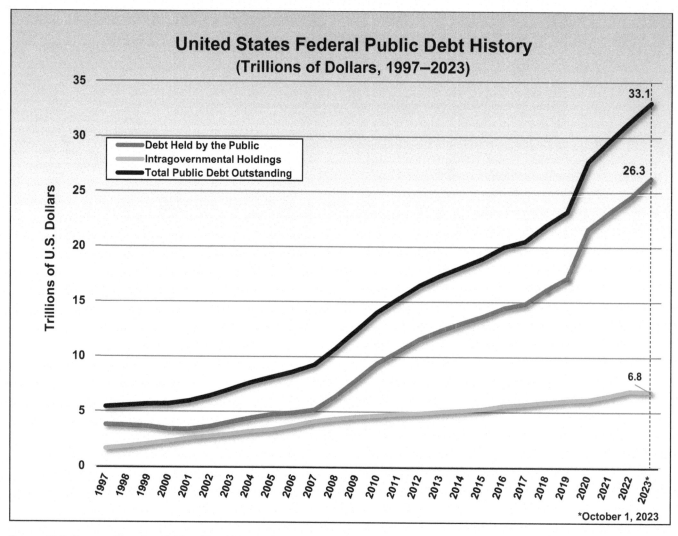

United States Federal Public Debt History
(Trillions of Dollars, 1997–2023)

*October 1, 2023

Source: U.S. Treasury Department, https://fiscaldata.treasury.gov/datasets/debt-to-the-penny/debt-to-the-penny

All data shown are as of December 31st, except for the year 2023, which was on October 1st, the latest data available. On that date the U.S. federal debt level reached $33.1 trillion, which had doubled since 2012. The public portion of that debt was $26.3 trillion.

The Debt to the Penny dataset provides information about the total outstanding public debt and is reported each day. Debt to the Penny is made up of intragovernmental holdings and debt held by the public, including securities issued by the U.S. Treasury. Total public debt outstanding is composed of Treasury Bills, Notes, Bonds, Treasury Inflation-Protected Securities (TIPS), Floating Rate Notes (FRNs), and Federal Financing Bank (FFB) securities, as well as Domestic Series, Foreign Series, State and Local Government Series (SLGS), U.S. Savings Securities, and Government Account Series (GAS) securities. Debt to the Penny is updated at the end of each business day with data from the previous business day.

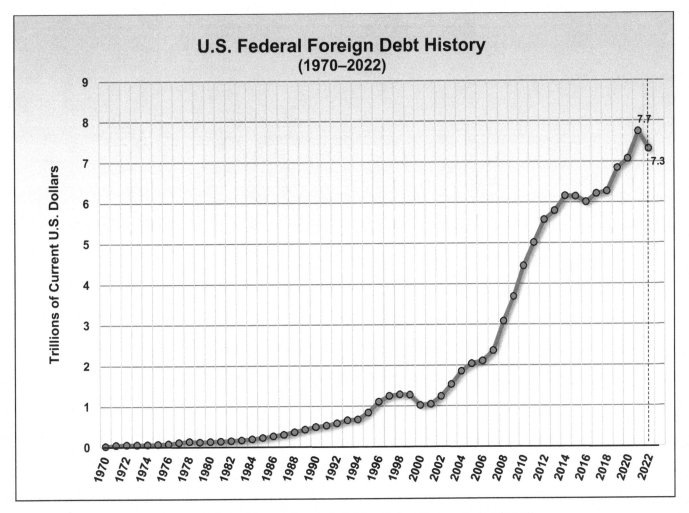

Source: FRED, Federal Reserve Economic Data, Economic Research Division, Federal Reserve Bank of St. Louis, https://fred.stlouisfed.org/series/FDHBFIN, data accessed 4/23/23. The Bank grants a non-exclusive, limited right and license to display and reproduce the charts and graphs.

In 2022, U.S. foreign debt of $7.3 trillion had declined since the all-time peak in 2020, of $7.7 trillion.

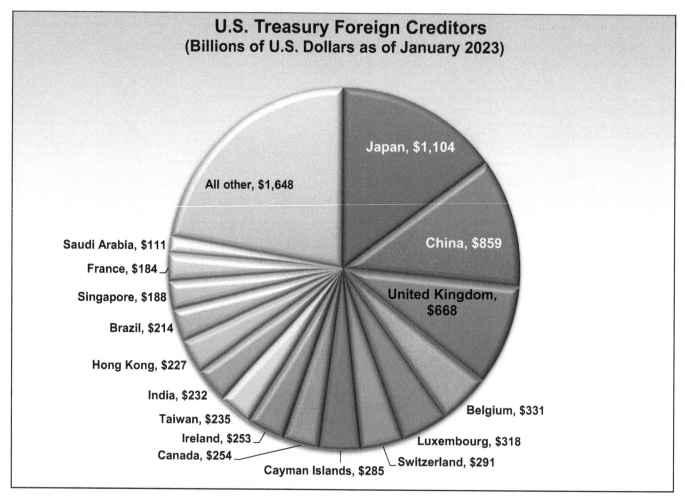

U.S. Treasury Foreign Creditors
(Billions of U.S. Dollars as of January 2023)

Japan, $1,104

All other, $1,648

China, $859

United Kingdom, $668

Saudi Arabia, $111

France, $184

Singapore, $188

Brazil, $214

Hong Kong, $227

India, $232

Taiwan, $235

Ireland, $253

Canada, $254

Cayman Islands, $285

Switzerland, $291

Luxembourg, $318

Belgium, $331

Source: U.S. Department of the Treasury/Federal Reserve Board,
https://ticdata.treasury.gov/resource-center/data-chart-center/tic/Documents/mfh.txt, accessed on 5-22-23

in January 2023, over one-third (36.0 percent) of U.S. total foreign debt was held by just three countries: Japan ($1.1 trillion), China ($.86 trillion), and the United Kingdom ($.67 trillion).

The data in this chart are collected primarily from U.S.-based custodians and broker-dealers. Since U.S. securities held in overseas custody accounts may not be attributed to the actual owners, the data may not provide a precise accounting of individual country ownership of Treasury securities

Estimated foreign holdings of U.S. Treasury marketable and non-marketable bills, bonds, and notes reported under the Treasury International Capital (TIC) reporting system are based on monthly data on holdings of Treasury bonds and notes as reported on TIC Form SLT, Aggregate Holdings of Long-Term Securities by U.S. and Foreign Residents and on TIC Form BL2, Report of Customers' U.S. Dollar Liabilities to Foreign Residents.

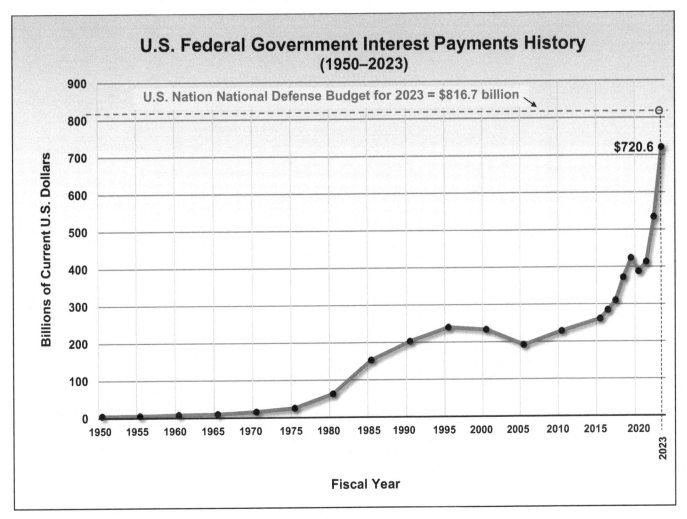

Sources: U.S. White House, https://www.whitehouse.gov/wp-content/uploads/2023/03/ap_20_borrowing_fy2024.pdf, accessed 10/1/23, https://www.defense.gov/News/News-Stories/Article/Article/3252968/biden-signs-national-defense-authorization-act-into-law/

For the fiscal year 2023, the U.S. government interest payments on federal debt held by the public reached a new high level of $720.6 billion. This amount was equivalent to 88 percent of the U.S. national defense budget for that year. According to the U.S. Department of Defense the fiscal 2023 National Defense Authorization Act allotted $816.7 billion to the Defense Department.

Fiscal year 2023, was the period between October 1, 2022 and September 30, 2023.

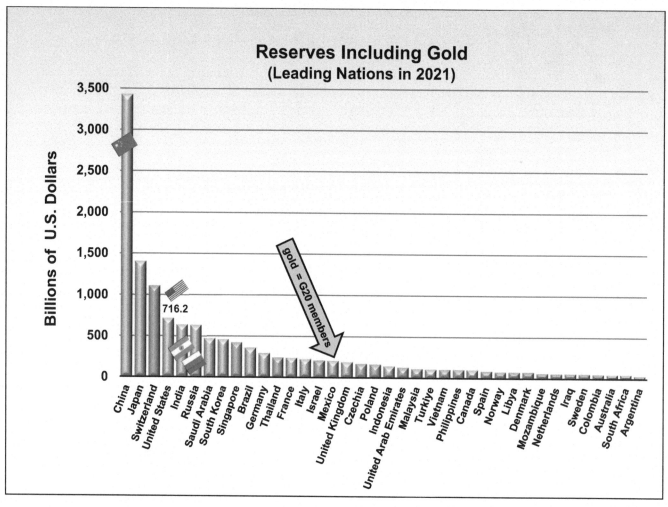

Reserves Including Gold
(Leading Nations in 2021)

Sources: The World Bank, https://databank.worldbank.org/source/world-development-indicators, FI.RES.TOTL.CD, accessed 8/23/23
https://data.worldbank.org/summary-terms-of-use

In 2021, the U.S. reserves holding was the fourth largest in the world at $716 billion. That level was 21 percent as large as China's reserves. Most of the world uses the U.S. dollar as the reserve currency.

Total reserves comprise holdings of monetary gold, special drawing rights, reserves of IMF members held by the IMF, and holdings of foreign exchange under the control of monetary authorities. The gold component of these reserves is valued at year-end (December 31) London prices. Data are in current U.S. dollars.

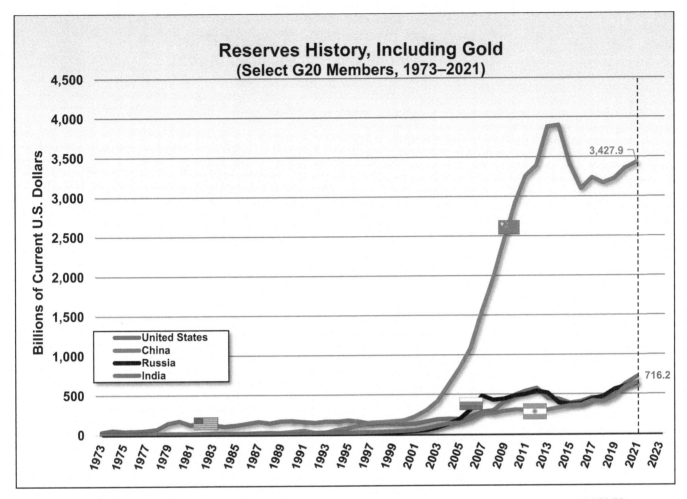

Sources: The World Bank, https://databank.worldbank.org/source/world-development-indicators, FI.RES.TOTL.CD, accessed 8/23/23
https://data.worldbank.org/summary-terms-of-use

China's value of foreign reserves, measured in U.S. dollars, fluctuates as the exchange rate between U.S. dollar and other currencies fluctuate. The increased value of the U.S. dollar in 2015 may have contributed to the 21 percent reduction in value of China's reserves which occurred in 2015.

Total reserves comprise holdings of monetary gold, special drawing rights, reserves of the International Monetary Fund (IMF) members held by the IMF, and holdings of foreign exchange under the control of monetary authorities. The gold component of these reserves is valued at year-end (December 31) London prices. Data are in current U.S. dollars.

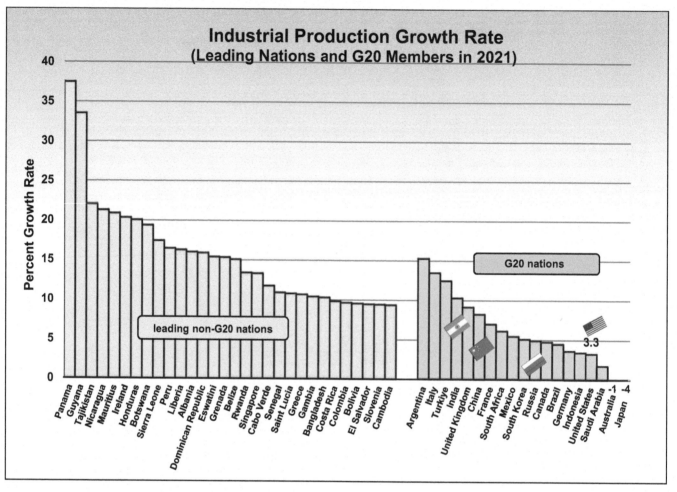

Source: The World Factbook 2021. Washington, DC: Central Intelligence Agency, 2021, https://www.cia.gov/the-world-factbook/, The Factbook is in the public domain.

In 2021, the U.S. ranked 15th out of the 19 G20 member nations in production growth rate. Economic growth and supply chains across the globe were stunted during the COVID-19 pandemic between March 2020 and May 2023.

Industrial production growth rate compares the annual percentage increase in industrial production (includes manufacturing, mining, and construction).

Chapter 8

Trade

Overview of Trade

The value of U.S. international trade in 2021—equal to the sum of goods and services, both imported and exported—comprised 10.9 percent of the world's total trade, in second place to China's 12.2 percent. However, these portions of world trade were dwarfed by the European Union (E.U.) that accounted for 29.2 percent. The E.U. is comprised of 27 nations. (*See Appendix VI, page 318.*)

U.S. trade was fueled by imports of consumer and capital goods and exports of industrial supplies. Approximately one-third of U.S. exports in 2022 were shipped to Canada and Mexico. The U.S. imported the most goods from China, valued at $537 billion, followed by Canada and Mexico. Based on the U.S. dollar exchange rate index, a basket of currencies from 25 nations plus the Euro, the value of the U.S. dollar in 2022 was near the record high looking back two decades, making U.S. imports for Americans more affordable while making exports of goods and services to foreign customers more expensive.

In 2021, the balance of payments for the United States due to international trade resulted in a deficit of $861.7 billion—the largest in the world—which directly reduced U.S. GDP by 3.8 percent. In contrast, China enjoyed a net trade surplus of $462 billion—the largest surplus in the world.

In 2022, the trade deficit for the United States due to trade with China alone was $366 billion which had the direct effect of adding 2.0 percentage points to China's GDP while reducing U.S. GDP by 1.4 percentage points. For China that 2.0 percent contribution to GDP was equivalent to over one-fourth (28 percent) of their 7.0 percent average GDP annual growth rate experienced over the entire decade prior to the COVID-19 pandemic (2010–2019). By comparison the U.S experienced an average real GDP annual growth over that decade of only 2.3 percent which hypothetically could have been 1.4 points higher without the China trade deficit. In other words, in the hypothetical absence of trade between the U.S. and China, China's average real GDP growth would have been only 5.0 percent and the U.S. real GDP growth would have been raised to 3.7 percent.

In 2021, the level of exports of goods and services for the United States was equivalent to 10.9 percent of GDP, the lowest of any G20 member, indicating that the U.S. economy was the least dependent on external trade for its economic strength. The U.S. external trade balance deficit was the largest in the world at $862 billion, an all-time high, and 11 times higher than India's. That year the U.S. imported the least amount of goods and services of any G20 nation, when measured as percent of GDP (14.6 percent).

In 2022, the leading trade partner for goods and services with the United States was China, resulting in a $366 billion U.S. trade deficit. The second-largest trade deficit for the U.S. was with Mexico, at $138 billion. Trade with the Netherlands resulted in the largest trade surplus for the U.S at $51 billion.

In 2022, the U.S. exported $2.6 trillion in goods and services. Almost one-third (31 percent) of exports were for services, of which financial services was the largest subcategory. Canada was the number one customer for U.S. exports of goods, accounting for 17.1 percent of all U.S. goods exported that year. The leading exports were machinery and mechanical appliances (23.8 percent), and transportation equipment (17.8 percent). Mexico was the second-largest export customer at 15.6 percent. Together, Canada and Mexico accounted for approximately one-third of all U.S. exports of goods.

Ireland was the leading customer for U.S. services, valued at $83.4 billion. U.S. services exports to Ireland included intellectual property licenses, research and development, and management consulting services.

In 2022, the U.S. imported $3,402 billion in goods and services, led by consumer goods (23 percent), capital goods (22 percent), and industrial supplies (19 percent). Services accounted for 16 percent of total U.S. imports. Five nations, led by China, accounted for 53.3 percent of all goods imported. The U.S. imported the most services from U.K., valued at $70.8 billion. Leading services were financial, insurance, telecommunications, information services and travel.

In 2022, the U.S. Geological Survey published their annual listing of the top 50 most critical minerals to the U.S., of which ten were 100 percent outsourced to other nations, including eight where China is the leading producer. This raises serious national security concerns. The U.S. is also reliant on imports for some critical materials and electronic components, including Taiwan's supply for the most advanced semiconductors. Taiwan is the world's leading exporter for advanced integrated circuits and had become the world's leading location for semiconductor foundry manufacturing.

The U.S is one of the world's most visited tourist destinations. In 2019, the last data available and prior to the COVID-10 pandemic, the U.S. was the second-most-visited nation in the world, after France, and hosted approximately the same number of visitors as China. This popularity is despite the strong value of the U.S. dollar which disincentivizes travel to the U.S. The U.S. is also the most popular destination for foreign students to attend college. In 2018, prior to the COVID-19 pandemic, approximately 1.1 million foreign students attended college in the U.S.

~

U.S. Dollar Exchange Rate Index History
(Nominal, Broad Index, 2006–2023)

Source: Board of Governors of the Federal Reserve System (US), Nominal Broad U.S. Dollar Index [DTWEXBGS], retrieved from FRED, Federal Reserve Bank of St. Louis; https://fred.stlouisfed.org/series/DTWEXBGS, June 17, 2023

The exchange rate index is based upon a basket of currencies from 25 nations plus the Euro. Based on data between 2006 and 2022, the value of the U.S. dollar in 2022, was near the record high making U.S. imports more affordable and exports more expensive.

The exchange rates are certified by the Federal Reserve Bank of New York for customs purposes as required by section 522 of the amended Tariff Act of 1930. These rates are also those required by the SEC for the integrated disclosure system for foreign private issuers. The information is based on data collected by the Federal Reserve Bank of New York from a sample of market participants.

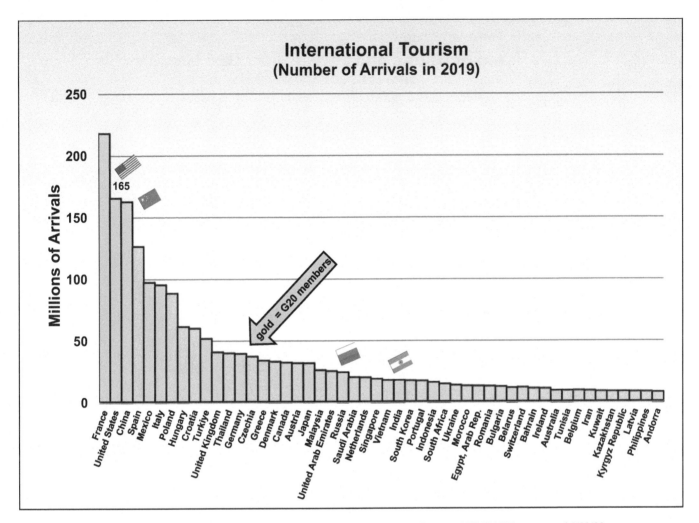

International Tourism
(Number of Arrivals in 2019)

Source: The World Bank, https://databank.worldbank.org/source/world-development-indicators, ST.INT.ARVL, accessed 8/23/23
https://data.worldbank.org/summary-terms-of-use

In 2019, prior to the COVID-10 pandemic, the U.S. was the second-most-visited nation in the world, after France, with approximately the same number of visitors as China.

International inbound tourists (overnight visitors) are the number of tourists who travel to a nation other than that in which they have their usual residence, but outside their usual environment, for a period not exceeding 12 months and whose main purpose in visiting is other than an activity remunerated from within the nation visited. When data on number of tourists are not available, the number of visitors, which includes tourists, same-day visitors, cruise passengers, and crew members, is shown instead. Sources and collection methods for arrivals differ across countries. In some cases, data are from border statistics (police, immigration, and the like) and supplemented by border surveys. In other cases, data are from tourism accommodation establishments. For some countries number of arrivals is limited to arrivals by air and for others to arrivals staying in hotels. Some countries include arrivals of nationals residing abroad while others do not. Caution should thus be used in comparing arrivals across countries. The data on inbound tourists refer to the number of arrivals, not to the number of people traveling. Thus, a person who makes several trips to a nation during a given period is counted each time as a new arrival.

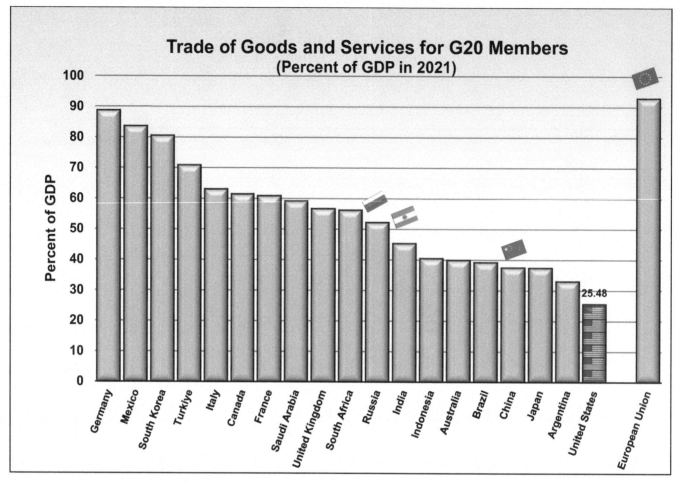

Source: The World Bank, https://databank.worldbank.org/source/world-development-indicators, NE.TRD.GNFS.ZS, accessed 8/23/23
https://data.worldbank.org/summary-terms-of-use

In 2021, U.S. trade, as measured in proportion to GDP, was the least amount compared with any of the G20 members, indicating that the U.S. economy was the least dependent on external trade for its economic strength. U.S. trade accounted for 10.9 percent of global trade, second to China at 12.2 percent. Both nations were dwarfed by the E.U. which accounted for 29.2 percent. The E.U. is comprised of 27 nations. (See Appendix VI, page 318.)

Trade is the sum of exports and imports of goods and services measured as a share of gross domestic product.

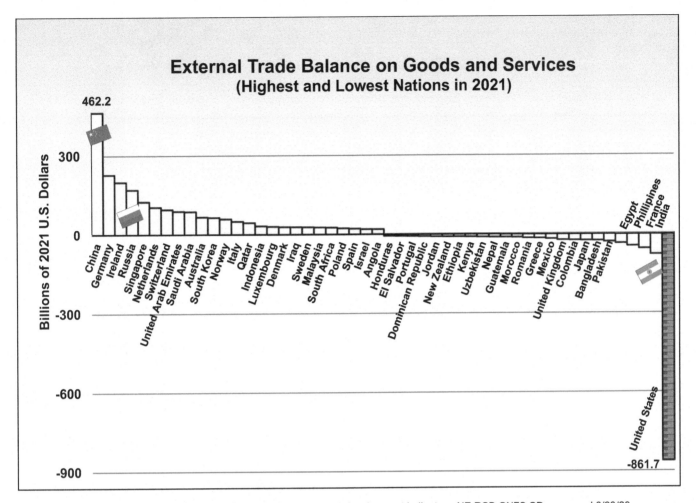

External Trade Balance on Goods and Services
(Highest and Lowest Nations in 2021)

Source: The World Bank, https://databank.worldbank.org/source/world-development-indicators, NE.RSB.GNFS.CD, accessed 8/23/23
https://data.worldbank.org/summary-terms-of-use

In 2021, the U.S. external trade balance deficit was the largest in the world at $861.7 billion and 11 times higher than India's, the second highest. Russia's surplus of $169 billion contributed 9.4 percent of GDP to their economy.

External balance on goods and services (formerly resource balance) equals exports of goods and services minus imports of goods and services. Data are in current U.S. dollars.

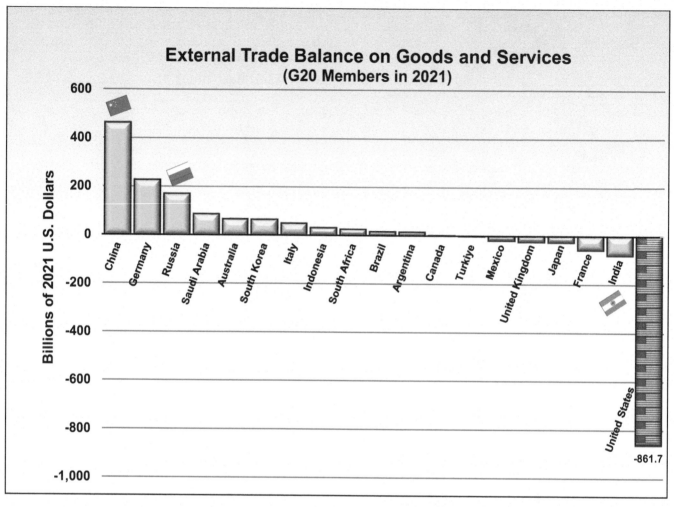

External Trade Balance on Goods and Services
(G20 Members in 2021)

Source: The World Bank, https://databank.worldbank.org/source/world-development-indicators, NE.RSB.GNFS.CD, accessed 8/23/23
https://data.worldbank.org/summary-terms-of-use

In 2021, the U.S. was one of five G20 members with a deficit external trade balance, the largest in the world at $861.7 billion. Both Canada and Turkiye had balances that were near nil while the remaining members had surpluses, led by China at $462 billion.

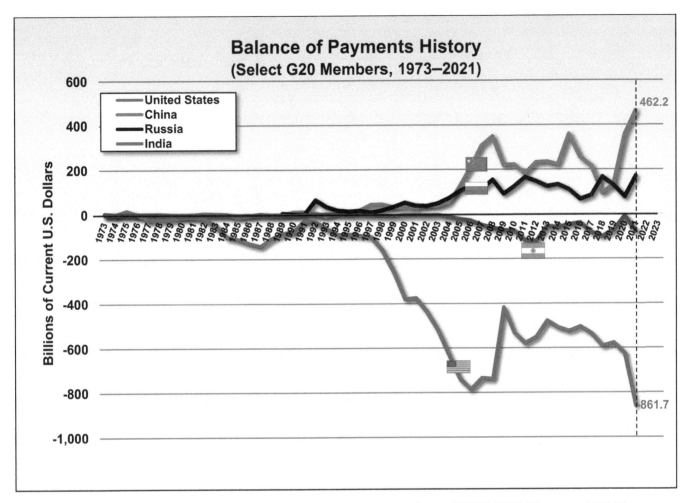

Source: The World Bank, https://databank.worldbank.org/source/world-development-indicators, NE.RSB.GNFS.CD, accessed 8/23/23
https://data.worldbank.org/summary-terms-of-use

In 2021, the U.S. balance of payments deficit reached an all-time high of $862 billion, while China reached an all-time high surplus of $462 billion.

External balance on goods and services (formerly resource balance) equals exports of goods and services minus imports of goods and services (previously nonfactor services). Data are in current U.S. dollars.

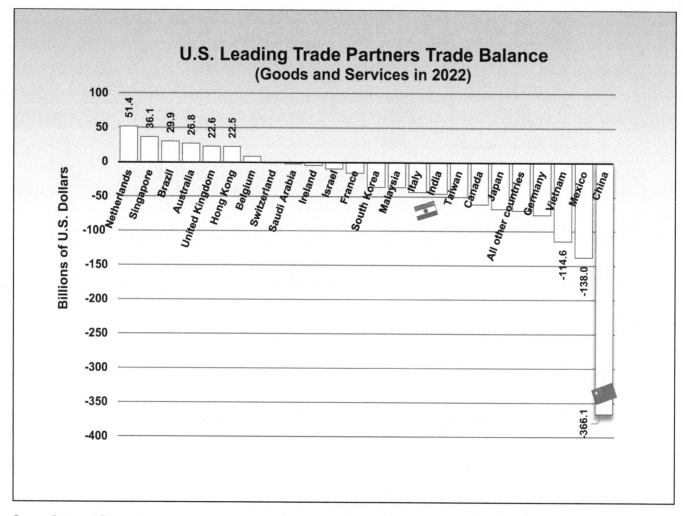

U.S. Leading Trade Partners Trade Balance
(Goods and Services in 2022)

Source: Bureau of Economic Analysis, https://apps.bea.gov/international/factsheet/factsheet.html#650, accessed on 4/1/23

In 2022, U.S. leading trade partner for goods and services was China, resulting a $366 billion trade deficit. This deficit with China alone reduced U.S. GDP by 1.45 percent in 2022. The second-largest trade deficit with the U.S. was with Mexico, at $138 billion. Trade with the Netherlands resulted in the largest trade surplus for the U.S at $51 billion.

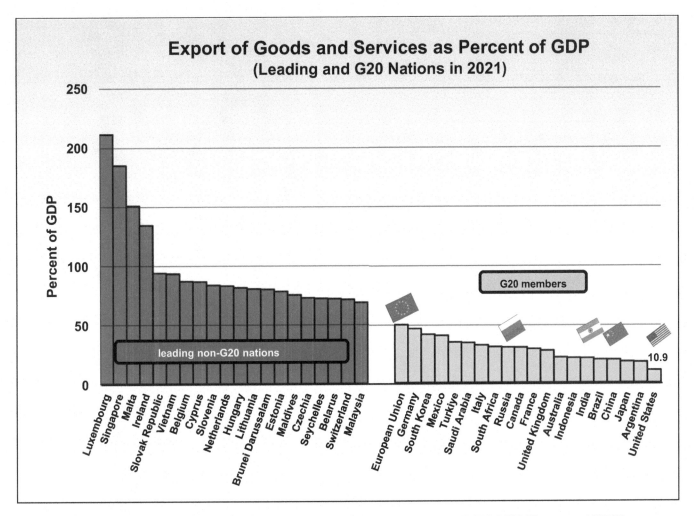

Source: The World Bank, https://databank.worldbank.org/source/world-development-indicators, NE.EXP.GNFS.ZS, accessed 8/23/23
https://data.worldbank.org/summary-terms-of-use

In 2021, the U.S. value for exports for goods and services was equivalent to 10.9 percent of GDP, the lowest percentage of any G20 member. That was valued at $2.6 trillion in U.S. dollars, second to China at $3.6 trillion.

Exports of goods and services represent the value of all goods and other market services provided to the rest of the world. They include the value of merchandise, freight, insurance, transport, travel, royalties, license fees, and other services, such as communication, construction, financial, information, business, personal, and government services. They exclude compensation of employees and investment income (formerly called factor services) and transfer payments.

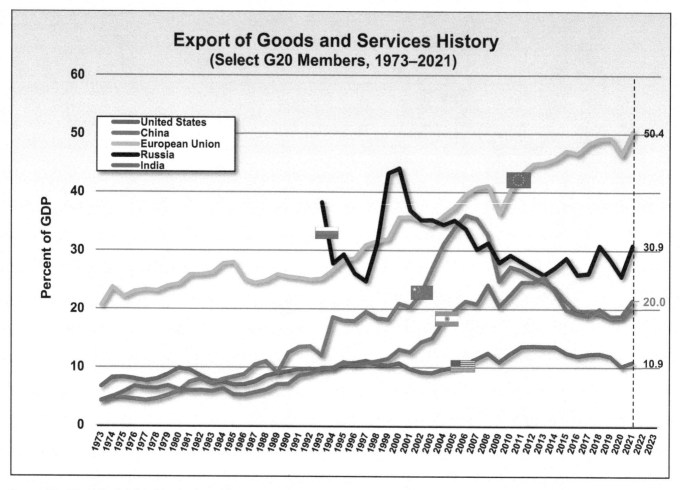

Export of Goods and Services History
(Select G20 Members, 1973–2021)

Source: The World Bank, https://databank.worldbank.org/source/world-development-indicators, E.EXP.GNFS.ZS, accessed 8/23/23
https://data.worldbank.org/summary-terms-of-use

During the period 1973–2021, U.S. exports of goods and services measured as percent of GDP doubled between 1973 and 2014, then declined 20 percent between 2014 and 2021. In contrast, the E.U's exports reached a new high of 50.4 percent in 2021.

Exports of goods and services represent the value of all goods and other market services provided to the rest of the world. They include the value of merchandise, freight, insurance, transport, travel, royalties, license fees, and other services, such as communication, construction, financial, information, business, personal, and government services. They exclude compensation of employees and investment income (formerly called factor services) and transfer payments.

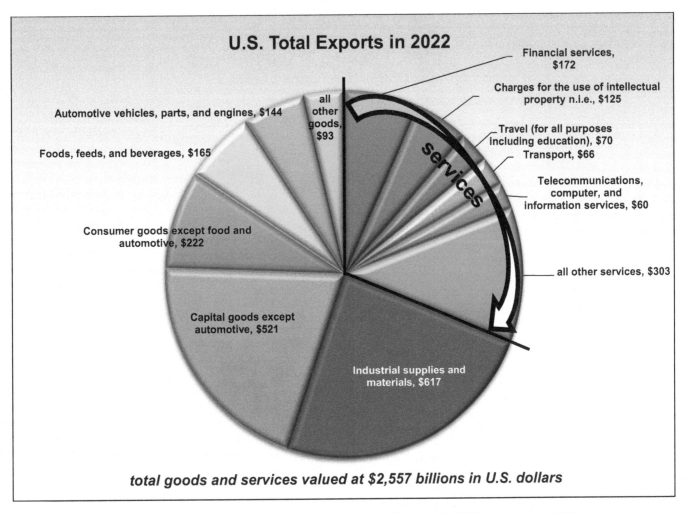

U.S. Total Exports in 2022

Financial services, $172

Charges for the use of intellectual property n.i.e., $125

Travel (for all purposes including education), $70

Transport, $66

Telecommunications, computer, and information services, $60

all other services, $303

all other goods, $93

Automotive vehicles, parts, and engines, $144

Foods, feeds, and beverages, $165

Consumer goods except food and automotive, $222

Capital goods except automotive, $521

Industrial supplies and materials, $617

services

total goods and services valued at $2,557 billions in U.S. dollars

Source: Bureau of Economic Analysis, https://apps.bea.gov/international/factsheet/factsheet.html#650, accessed on 4/1/23

In 2022, U.S. exported $2.6 trillion in goods and services. Almost one-third (31 percent) of exports were for services, of which financial services was the largest category.

The largest U.S. export segment for "goods" was industrial supplies and materials followed by capital goods except automotive.

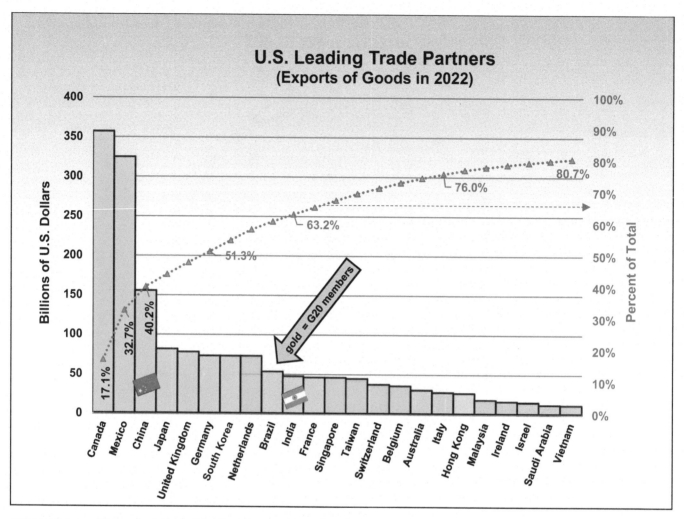

U.S. Leading Trade Partners
(Exports of Goods in 2022)

Sources: Bureau of Economic Analysis, https://apps.bea.gov/international/factsheet/factsheet.html#650, accessed on 4/1/23, https://www.bis.doc.gov/index.php/component/docman/?task=doc_download&gid=2785#:~:text=In percent202020 percent2C percent20of percent20the percent20 percent24255.1,and percent20Leather percent20products percent20(15.3 percent25).

In 2022, Canada was the number one customer for U.S. exports of goods, accounting for 17.1 percent of all goods exported that year. The leading exports were: machinery and mechanical appliances (23.8 percent), transportation equipment (17.8 percent), and chemicals, plastics and leather products (15.3 percent).

Mexico was the second-largest export customer at 15.6 percent. Together, these two countries accounted for approximately one-third of all U.S. exports of goods.

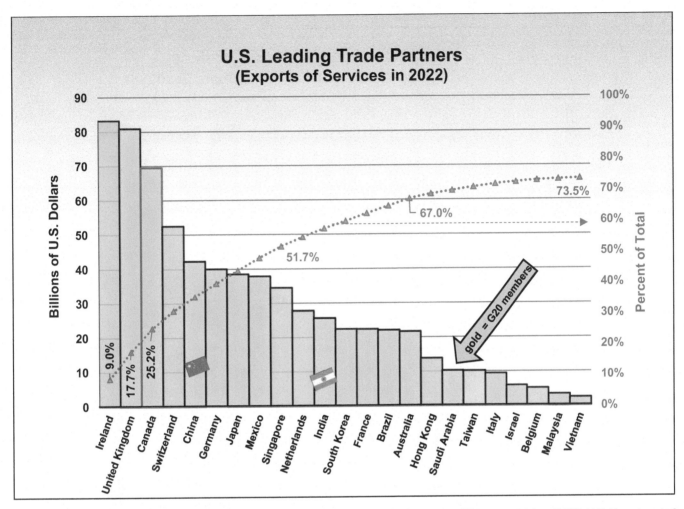

U.S. Leading Trade Partners
(Exports of Services in 2022)

Sources: Bureau of Economic Analysis, https://apps.bea.gov/international/factsheet/factsheet.html#650, accessed on 4/1/23, U.S. Department of State, https://www.state.gov/u-s-relations-with-ireland/

In 2022, Ireland was the leading customer of U.S. services, valued at $83.4 billion. U.S. services exports to Ireland included intellectual property licenses, research and development, and management consulting services.

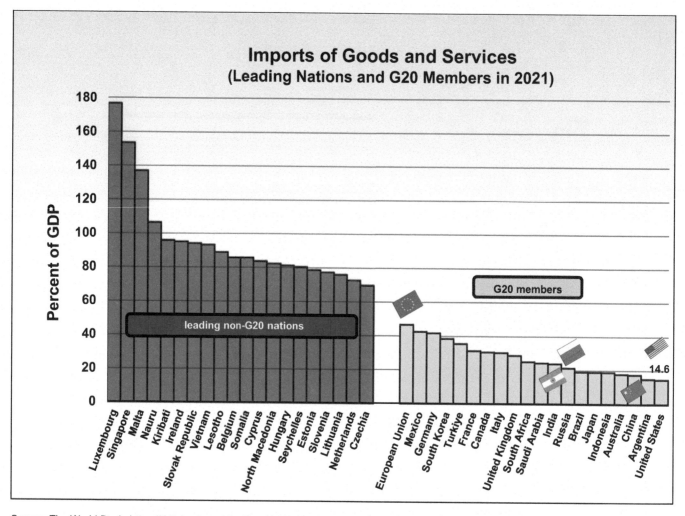

Imports of Goods and Services
(Leading Nations and G20 Members in 2021)

Source: The World Bank, https://databank.worldbank.org/source/world-development-indicators, NE.IMP.GNFS.ZS, accessed 8/23/23
https://data.worldbank.org/summary-terms-of-use

In 2021, the U.S. imported the least amount of goods and services of any G20 nation, measured as 14.6 percent of GDP. Despite this low percentage of GDP the total value of U.S. imports at $3.4 trillion was the largest of any nation.

Imports of goods and services represent the value of all goods and other market services received from the rest of the world. They include the value of merchandise, freight, insurance, transport, travel, royalties, license fees, and other services, such as communication, construction, financial, information, business, personal, and government services. They exclude compensation of employees and investment income (formerly called factor services) and transfer payments.

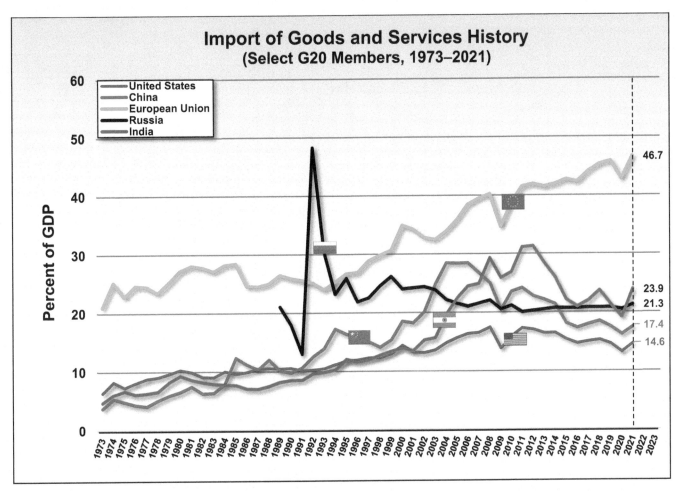

Import of Goods and Services History
(Select G20 Members, 1973–2021)

Sources: The World Bank, https://databank.worldbank.org/source/world-development-indicators, NE.IMP.GNFS.ZS, https://data.worldbank.org/summary-terms-of-use

In 2020, imports of goods and services by the leading G20 nations declined during the early phases of the COVID-19 pandemic partly due to supply chain disruptions. By 2020, most had recovered to near pre-pandemic levels. Throughout that period Russia's imports remained relatively flat at approximately 21 percent of GDP.

Imports of goods and services represent the value of all goods and other market services received from the rest of the world. They include the value of merchandise, freight, insurance, transport, travel, royalties, license fees, and other services, such as communication, construction, financial, information, business, personal, and government services. They exclude compensation of employees and investment income (formerly called factor services) and transfer payments.

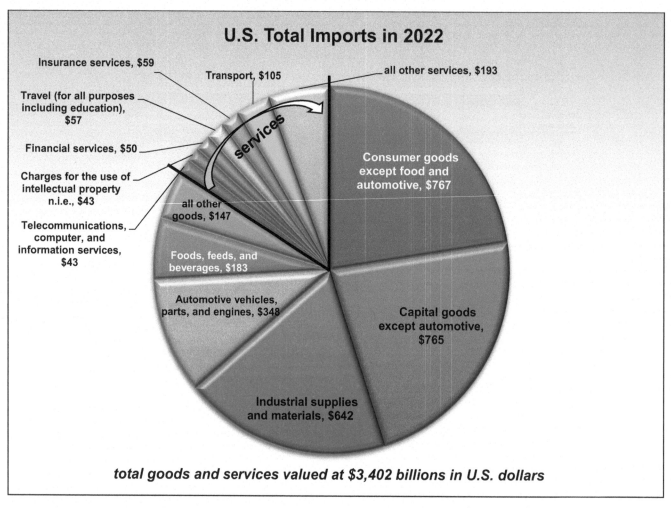

U.S. Total Imports in 2022

Insurance services, $59

Transport, $105

all other services, $193

Travel (for all purposes including education), $57

Financial services, $50

Charges for the use of intellectual property n.i.e., $43

Telecommunications, computer, and information services, $43

services

all other goods, $147

Consumer goods except food and automotive, $767

Foods, feeds, and beverages, $183

Automotive vehicles, parts, and engines, $348

Capital goods except automotive, $765

Industrial supplies and materials, $642

total goods and services valued at $3,402 billions in U.S. dollars

Source: Bureau of Economic Analysis, https://apps.bea.gov/international/factsheet/factsheet.html#650, accessed on 4/1/23

In 2022, the U.S. imported $3,402 billion in goods and services, led by consumer goods (23 percent), capital goods (22 percent), and industrial supplies (19 percent). Services accounted for 16 percent of total U.S. imports. The U.S. was the world's largest customer.

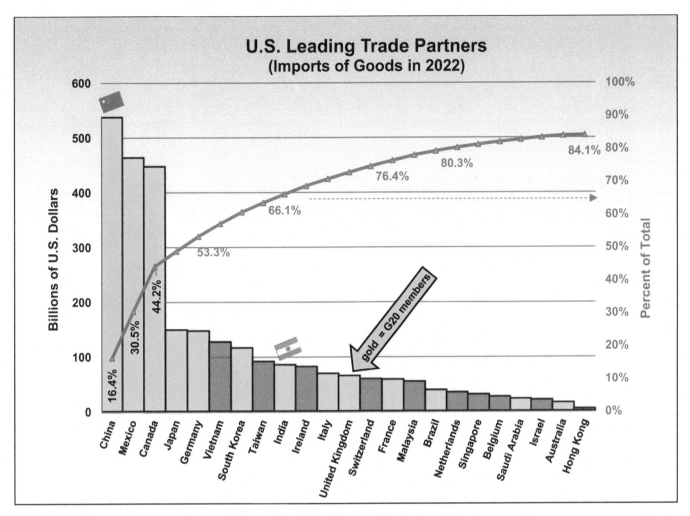

Source: Bureau of Economic Analysis, https://apps.bea.gov/international/factsheet/factsheet.html#650, accessed on 4/1/23

In 2022, the U.S. imported $3.27 trillion in goods of which 16.7 percent were from China. Five nations—China, Mexico, Canada, Japan, and Germany—accounted for 53.3 percent of all goods imported.

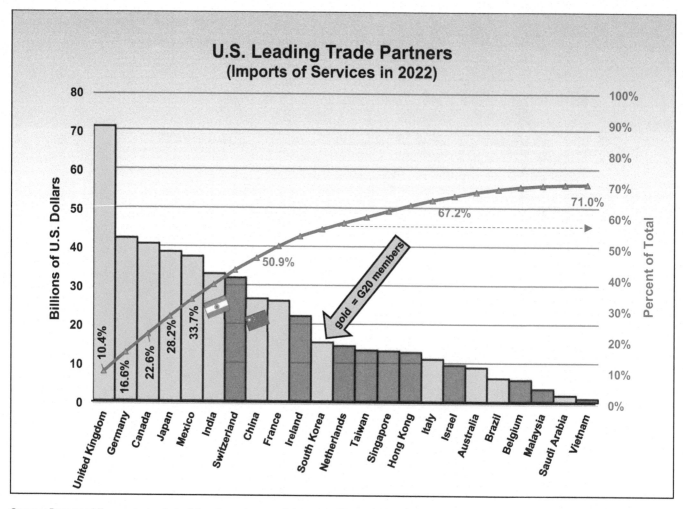

U.S. Leading Trade Partners
(Imports of Services in 2022)

Source: Bureau of Economic Analysis, https://apps.bea.gov/international/factsheet/factsheet.html#650, accessed on 4/1/23

In 2022, the U.S. imported the most services from the U.K., valued at $70.8 billion. The leading services were financial, Insurance, telecommunications, information services and travel.

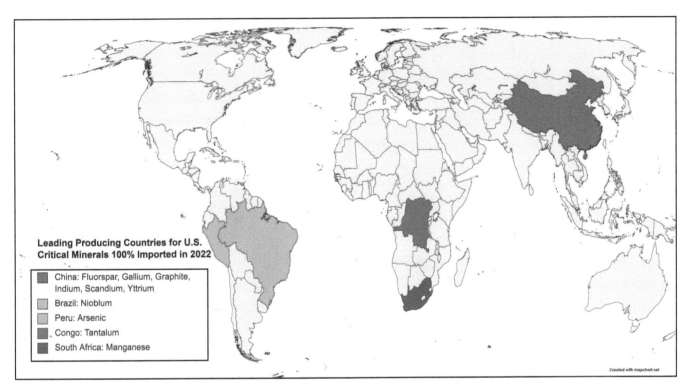

Sources: U.S. Geological Survey, 2023, Mineral Commodities Summaries 2023, https://www.usgs.gov/centers/national-minerals-information-center/international-minerals-statistics-and-information, accessed on 5-1-23

Leading Producing Countries for U.S. Critical Minerals 100 Percent Imported in 2022

In 2022, the U.S. Geological Survey published their annual listing of the most critical minerals to the U.S., of which the following ten are 100 percent outsourced to other nations, including eight where China is the leading producer.

For ten of 50 critical minerals the U.S. is 100 percent dependent on imports, published on February 24, 2022, by U.S. Geological Survey (87 FR 10381), and listed below.

Leading Producer	Mineral	Applications
China	Fluorspar	Cement, industrial chemical, and metallurgy.
China	Gallium	Integrated circuits and optical devices.
China	Graphite	Batteries, fuel cells, and lubricants.
China	Indium	Liquid crystal displays.
China	Scandium	Ceramics, fuel cells, and metallurgy.
China	Yttrium	Catalysts, ceramics, lasers, metallurgy, and phosphors
Brazil	Niobium	Metallurgy.
Peru	Arsenic	Semiconductors.
Congo	Tantalum	Capacitors and metallurgy
South Africa	Manganese	Batteries and metallurgy.

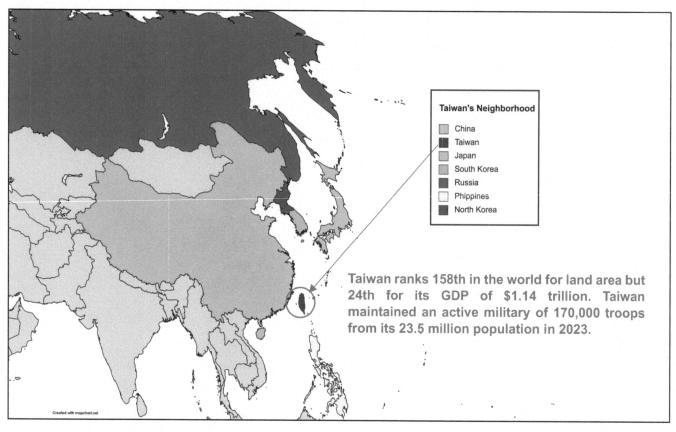

Taiwan ranks 158th in the world for land area but 24th for its GDP of $1.14 trillion. Taiwan maintained an active military of 170,000 troops from its 23.5 million population in 2023.

Sources: U.S. Department of State, https://www.state.gov/u-s-relations-with-taiwan/, CIA World Factbook, https://www.cia.gov/the-world-factbook/countries/taiwan/, Congressional Research Service, Semiconductors: U.S. Industry, Global Competition, and Federal Policy, October 26, 2020, https://crsreports.congress.gov/product/pdf/R/R46581, Report to the President, Revitalizing the U.S. Semiconductor Ecosystem, September, 2022, https://www.whitehouse.gov/wp-content/uploads/2022/09/PCAST_Semiconductors-Report_Sep2022.pdf,

Map Showing Taiwan's Neighborhood

Taiwan has outsized importance due to its advanced semiconductor industry considering its relatively small population and land area. Taiwan's leading export is integrated circuits and Taiwan has become the world's leading location for semiconductor foundry manufacturing.

Due to Taiwan's strategic importance to the U.S., it has been informally granted the status of Major Non-NATO Ally (MNNA). This status provides military and economic privileges but does not entail any security commitments to Taiwan. (See page 180 for description of MNNA privileges).

Taiwan is the major supplier for the most advanced semiconductors and is a strategic partner to the U.S. The U.S.–Taiwan Relations Act of April 1979 states that the U.S. shall provide Taiwan with arms of a defensive character and shall maintain the capacity of the U.S. to resist any resort to force or other forms of coercion that would jeopardize the security, or social or economic system, of the people of Taiwan. However, due to China's claim that Taiwan is part of China the U.S. does not have an embassy in Taiwan; commercial and cultural relations with the people of Taiwan are maintained through an unofficial instrumentality, the American Institute in Taiwan (AIT), a private nonprofit corporation that performs citizen and consular services similar to those at diplomatic posts.

Chapter 9

Investments and Infrastructure

Overview of Investments and Infrastructure

Direct foreign investment is based on ownership of 10 percent or more of the ordinary shares of voting stock of a corporation. The direct foreign investment by Americans in 2021 was below the level of the eight high income per capita G20 nations (principal U.S. partners) and approximately one-half the level by E.U. investors, measured as percent of GDP. The investment in the U.S. by foreigners was almost completely offset by the 1.71 percent investments made by Americans in other countries, measured as percent of GDP.

The direct foreign investment in the U.S. by residents of other nations was approximately average for G20 nations, including the E.U., but accounted for only one-third the investment level—measured as percent of GDP—foreigners made in Brazil.

Foreign investment levels in some G20 nations have been very volatile over the past 30 years. In 2021, foreign investments in the E.U. ranged from zero-to-ten percent of GDP while foreign investments in the U.S. ranged between 0.5–3.4 percent. Foreign investments in the leading G20 nations were all at approximately 2 percent of GDP.

In 2020, the U.S. was the world's leader for receiving the most patent applications by nonresidents, with approximately double the number of nonresidents filing patent applications in China, the second-largest nation. Between 2015 and 2020, China's rate of annual patent applications filings by residents tripled. During that same period the U.S. annual rate increased by 28 percent.

Patent applications refer to worldwide patent applications filed through the Patent Cooperation Treaty procedure or with a national patent office.

In 2020, China's residents filed over nine million trademark applications. That level was 62 percent of the total number of applications filed by residents throughout the world and approximately 17 times the number filed by U.S. residents. The U.S. was the world's leader in trademark applications being filed by nonresidents. That level was 40 percent above the level filed by nonresidents in China, the nation with the second largest.

In 2020, the U.S. was the world's leader in amount of freight carried by air transport. That amount was 60 percent greater than the amount carried by E.U. carriers, the second largest, and approximately double the amount carried by China's carriers.

In 2019, before the COVID-19 pandemic disrupted air travel, the U.S. was the world's leader in numbers of passengers carried by air transport. That number was 15 percent greater than the number carried by the E.U. and 40 percent greater than the number of passengers carried by China's aircraft.

In 2021, the U.S. was the world's leader in length of rail lines. The U.S. total route length was 35 percent greater than the route length in China, the second-longest rail length. That year approximately three-fourths of all nations had more cellular subscriptions than people in their nation, led by United Arab Emirates (UAE) at 221 subscriptions per 100 people. The U.S. subscription rate was approximately the same as the world's average of 110 per 100 population. It was also estimated that 91 percent of the U.S. population had internet access, compared with the world's average of 60 percent.

In 2020, the U.S. ranked seventh highest among G20 members with 91 percent of its population having internet access. India ranked last among G20 members with only 43 percent. The U.S. ranked 21st among the 38 OECD members for internet access. Colombia ranked last among OECD members with only 70 percent.

In 2021, the U.S. provided $50 billion in foreign aid to over 150 countries and territories. Six of the nations that received aid were G20 members: South Africa, India, Indonesia, Mexico, Brazil and Turkiye.

~

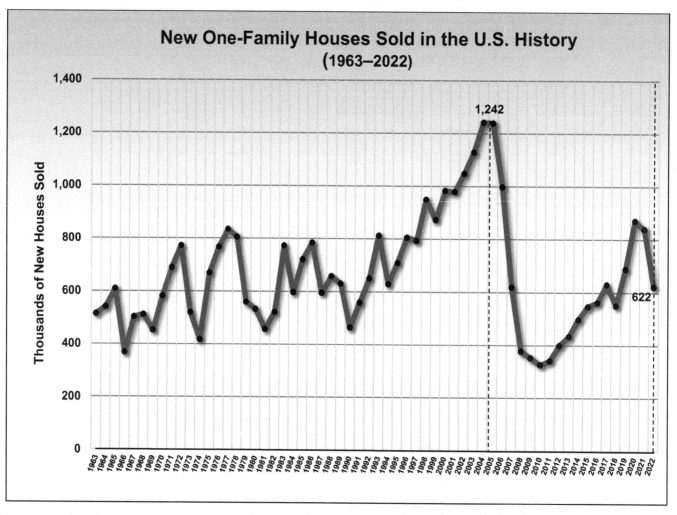

New One-Family Houses Sold in the U.S. History
(1963–2022)

Source: FRED, Federal Reserve Economic Data, Economic Research Division, Federal Reserve Bank of St. Louis, https://fred.stlouisfed.org/series/FDHBFIN, data accessed 4/23/23. The Bank grants a non-exclusive, limited right and license to display and reproduce the charts and graphs.

Over the period 1963–2005, the annual number of new single-family homes sold in the U.S. increased by approximately threefold, reaching a peak of 1,242,000 units in 2005. By 2010, that level had plummeted by 74 percent to 326,000 units, the lowest level since 1963. Subsequently sales recovered to 871,000 units in 2020, but declined to 622,000 units in 2022, during the COVID-19 pandemic.

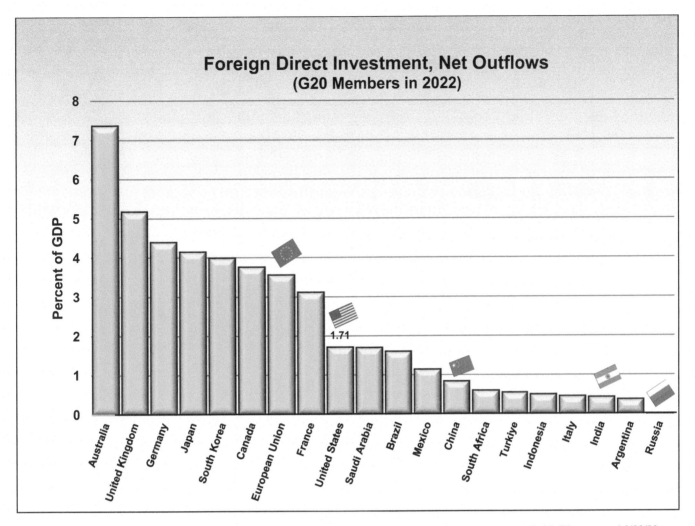

Foreign Direct Investment, Net Outflows
(G20 Members in 2022)

Percent of GDP

1.71

Australia, United Kingdom, Germany, Japan, South Korea, Canada, European Union, France, United States, Saudi Arabia, Brazil, Mexico, China, South Africa, Turkiye, Indonesia, Italy, India, Argentina, Russia

Source: The World Bank, https://databank.worldbank.org/source/world-development-indicators, BM.KLT.DINV.WD.GD.ZS, accessed 8/23/23
https://data.worldbank.org/summary-terms-of-use

The direct foreign investment by Americans in 2022 was approximately one-half the level of direct foreign investments by E.U. investors, measured as percent of GDP.

Foreign direct investment refers to direct investment equity flows in an economy. It is the sum of equity capital, reinvestment of earnings, and other capital. Direct investment is a category of cross-border investment associated with a resident in one economy having control or a significant degree of influence on the management of an enterprise that is resident in another economy. Ownership of 10 percent or more of the ordinary shares of voting stock is the criterion for determining the existence of a direct investment relationship. This series shows net outflows of investment from the reporting economy to the rest of the world, and is divided by GDP.

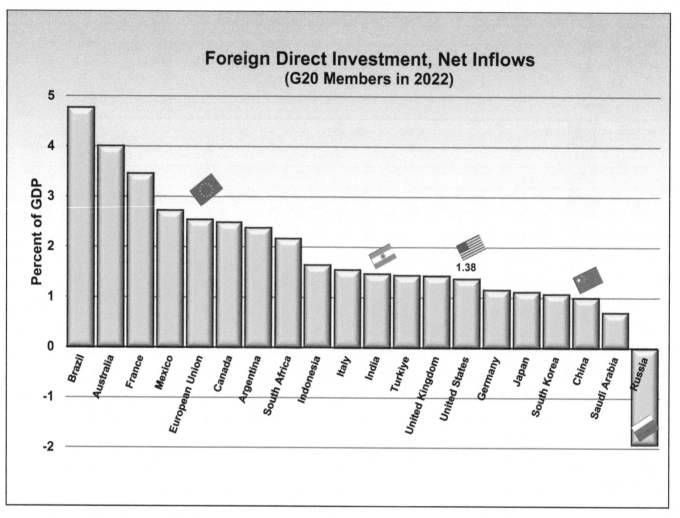

Foreign Direct Investment, Net Inflows
(G20 Members in 2022)

Source: The World Bank, https://databank.worldbank.org/source/world-development-indicators, BX.KLT.DINV.WD.GD.ZS, accessed 8/23/23
https://data.worldbank.org/summary-terms-of-use

The direct foreign investment in the U.S. by residents of other nations in 2022, measured as 1.38 percent of GDP, was in the bottom one-third of the other G20 members, including the E.U.

The investment in the U.S. was more than offset by the 1.71 percent investments made by Americans in other countries.

Foreign direct investment are the net inflows of investment to acquire a lasting management interest (10 percent or more of voting stock) in an enterprise operating in an economy other than that of the investor. It is the sum of equity capital, reinvestment of earnings, other long-term capital, and short-term capital as shown in the balance of payments. This series shows net inflows (new investment inflows less disinvestment) in the reporting economy from foreign investors, and is divided by GDP.

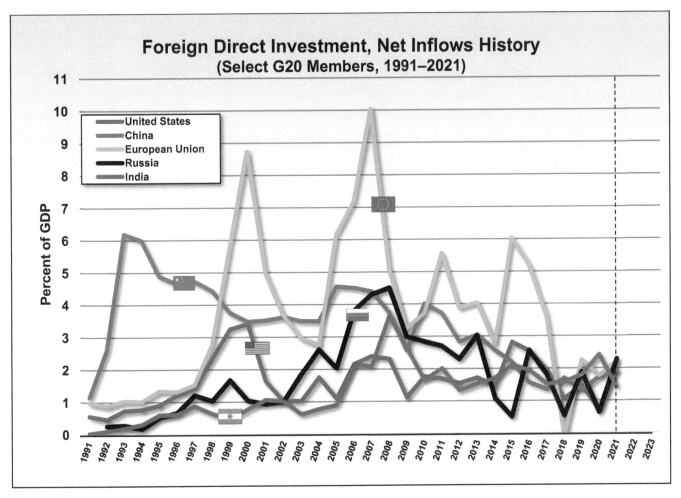

Foreign Direct Investment, Net Inflows History
(Select G20 Members, 1991–2021)

Source: The World Bank, https://databank.worldbank.org/source/world-development-indicators, BX.KLT.DINV.WD.GD.ZS, accessed 8/23/23
https://data.worldbank.org/summary-terms-of-use

Foreign investments in select G20 nations have been very volatile over the past 30 years. Measured as a percent of GDP, foreign investments in the E.U. ranged from zero-to-ten percent, while foreign investments in the U.S. ranged between .5-to-3.4 percent. As of 2021, investments in the leading G20 nations were all approximately at two percent of GDP.

Foreign direct investment are the net inflows of investment to acquire a lasting management interest (10 percent or more of voting stock) in an enterprise operating in an economy other than that of the investor. It is the sum of equity capital, reinvestment of earnings, other long-term capital, and short-term capital as shown in the balance of payments. This series shows net inflows (new investment inflows less disinvestment) in the reporting economy from foreign investors, and is divided by GDP.

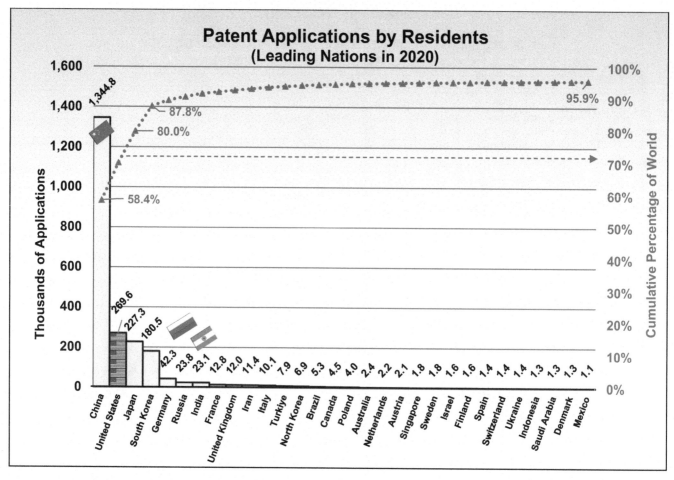

Source: The World Bank, https://databank.worldbank.org/source/world-development-indicators, IP.PAT.RESD, accessed 8/23/23
https://data.worldbank.org/summary-terms-of-use

In 2020, China led the world in numbers of patents filed by residents. That level was five times the level filed by U.S. residents, the second-highest nation. China's filings by residents accounted for 58 percent of all patents filed by residents worldwide in 2020.

Patent applications are worldwide patent applications filed through the Patent Cooperation Treaty procedure or with a national patent office.

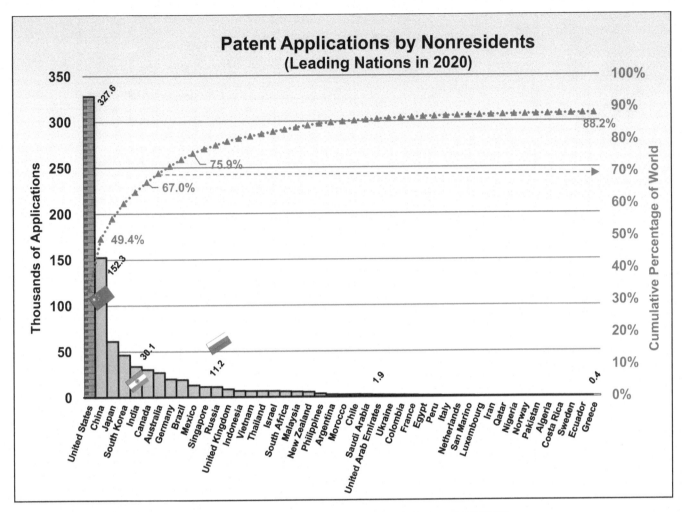

Patent Applications by Nonresidents
(Leading Nations in 2020)

Source: The World Bank, https://databank.worldbank.org/source/world-development-indicators, IP.PAT.NRES, https://data.worldbank.org/summary-terms-of-use

In 2020, the U.S. was the world's leader for receiving the most patent applications by nonresidents, approximately double the number of nonresidents filing patent applications in China, the second-largest nation. The number of nonresidents filing in the U.S. was 20 percent higher than the number of residents filing in the U.S.

Patent applications are worldwide patent applications filed through the Patent Cooperation Treaty procedure or with a national patent office.

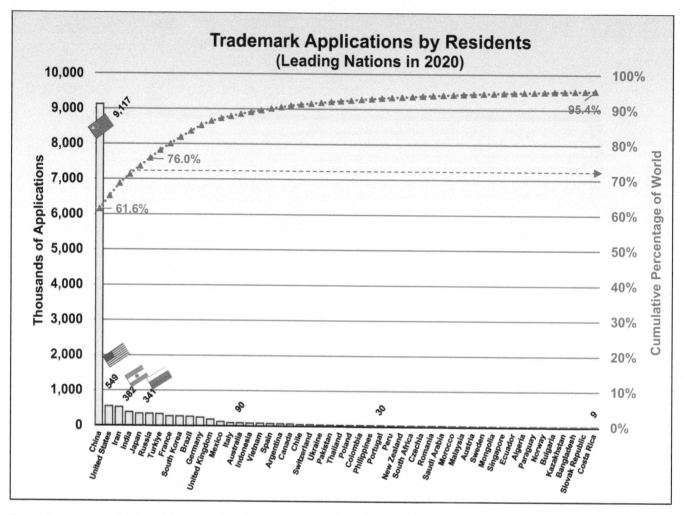

Trademark Applications by Residents
(Leading Nations in 2020)

Source: The World Bank, https://databank.worldbank.org/source/world-development-indicators, IP.TMK.RSCT, accessed 8/23/23
https://data.worldbank.org/summary-terms-of-use

In 2020, China's residents filed over nine million trademark applications. That level was 62 percent of all the applications filed by residents in the world and approximately 17 time the number filed by U.S. residents.

A trademark provides protection to the owner of the mark by ensuring the exclusive right to use it to identify goods or services, or to authorize another to use it in return for payment. The period of protection varies, but a trademark can be renewed indefinitely beyond the time limit on payment of additional fees. Resident application refers to an application filed with the IP office of or acting on behalf of the state or jurisdiction in which the first-named applicant in the application has residence. Class count is used to render application data for trademark applications across offices comparable, as some offices follow a single-class/single-design filing system while other have a multiple class/design filing system.

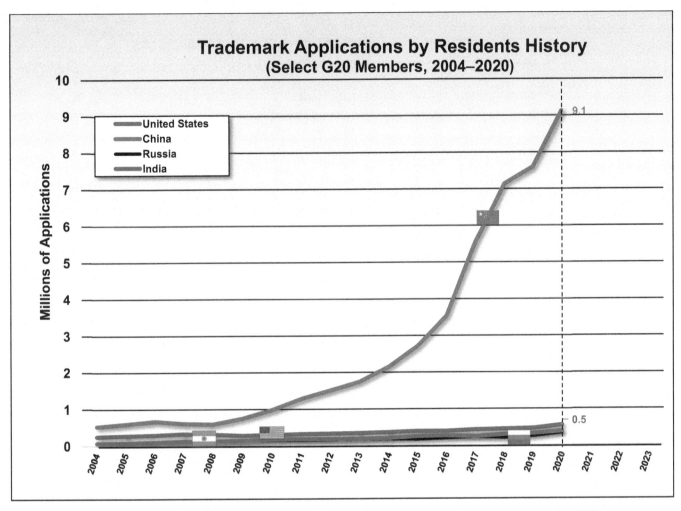

Trademark Applications by Residents History
(Select G20 Members, 2004–2020)

Source: The World Bank, https://databank.worldbank.org/source/world-development-indicators, IP.TMK.RSCT, accessed 8/23/23
https://data.worldbank.org/summary-terms-of-use

Between 2015 and 2020, China's rate of annual trademark applications filings by residents tripled. During that same period the U.S. annual rate increased by 28 percent.

Trademark applications filed are applications to register a trademark with a national or regional Intellectual Property (IP) office and designations received by relevant offices through the Madrid System. A trademark is a distinctive sign which identifies certain goods or services as those produced or provided by a specific person or enterprise. A trademark provides protection to the owner of the mark by ensuring the exclusive right to use it to identify goods or services, or to authorize another to use it in return for payment. The period of protection varies, but a trademark can be renewed indefinitely beyond the time limit on payment of additional fees. Resident application refers to an application filed with the IP office of or acting on behalf of the state or jurisdiction in which the first-named applicant in the application has residence. Class count is used to render application data for trademark applications across offices comparable, as some offices follow a single-class/single-design filing system while other have a multiple class/design filing system.

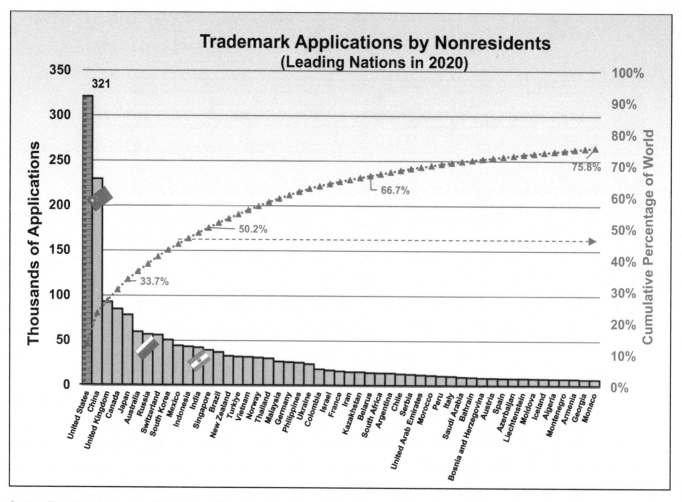

Trademark Applications by Nonresidents
(Leading Nations in 2020)

Source: The World Bank, https://databank.worldbank.org/source/world-development-indicators, IP.TMK.NRCT, accessed 8/23/23
https://data.worldbank.org/summary-terms-of-use

In 2020, the U.S. was the world's leader in applications being filed by nonresidents for trademarks. That level was 58 percent as many as filed in the U.S. by U.S. residents and 40 percent above the level filed by nonresidents in China, the nation with the second largest.

A trademark is a distinctive sign which identifies certain goods or services as those produced or provided by a specific person or enterprise. A trademark provides protection to the owner of the mark by ensuring the exclusive right to use it to identify goods or services, or to authorize another to use it in return for payment. The period of protection varies, but a trademark can be renewed indefinitely beyond the time limit on payment of additional fees. Nonresident application refers to an application filed with the IP office of or acting on behalf of a state or jurisdiction in which the first-named applicant in the application is not domiciled. Class count is used to render application data for trademark applications across offices comparable, as some offices follow a single-class/single-design filing system while other have a multiple class/design filing system.

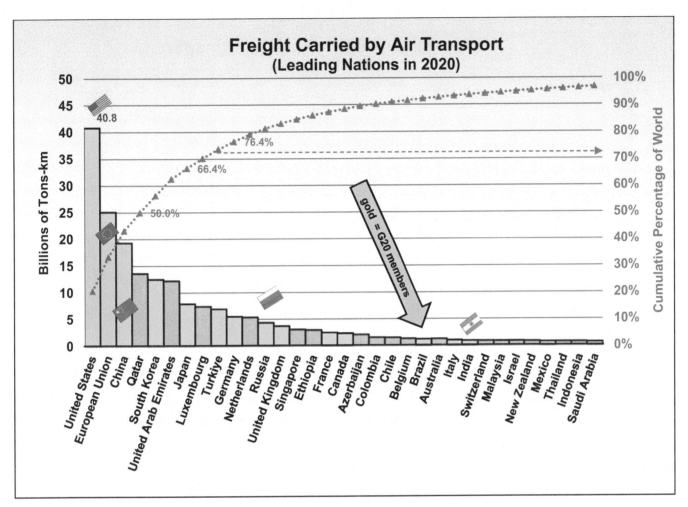

Freight Carried by Air Transport
(Leading Nations in 2020)

Sources The World Bank, https://databank.worldbank.org/source/world-development-indicators, IS.AIR.GOOD.MT.K1, accessed 8/23/23
https://data.worldbank.org/summary-terms-of-use

In 2020, the U.S. was the world's leader in amount of freight carried by air transport. That amount was 60 percent greater than the amount carried by European Union carriers, the second largest, and approximately double the amount carried by China's carriers.

Air freight is the volume of freight, express, and diplomatic bags carried on each flight stage (operation of an aircraft from takeoff to its next landing), measured in metric tons times kilometers traveled.

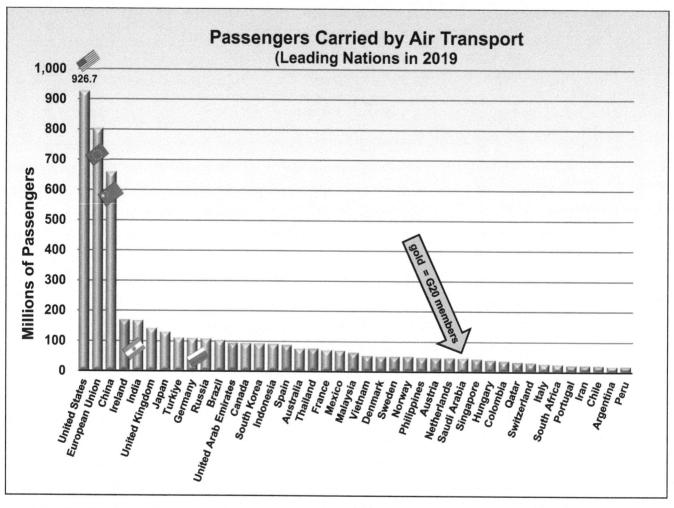

Source: The World Bank, https://databank.worldbank.org/source/world-development-indicators, IS.AIR.PSGR, accessed 8/23/23
https://data.worldbank.org/summary-terms-of-use

In 2019, before the COVID-19 pandemic that disrupted air travel, the U.S. was the world's leader in numbers of passengers carried by air transport. That number was 15 percent greater than the number carried by the E.U. and 40 percent greater than the number of passengers carried by China's aircraft.

Air passengers carried include both domestic and international aircraft passengers of air carriers registered in the nation.

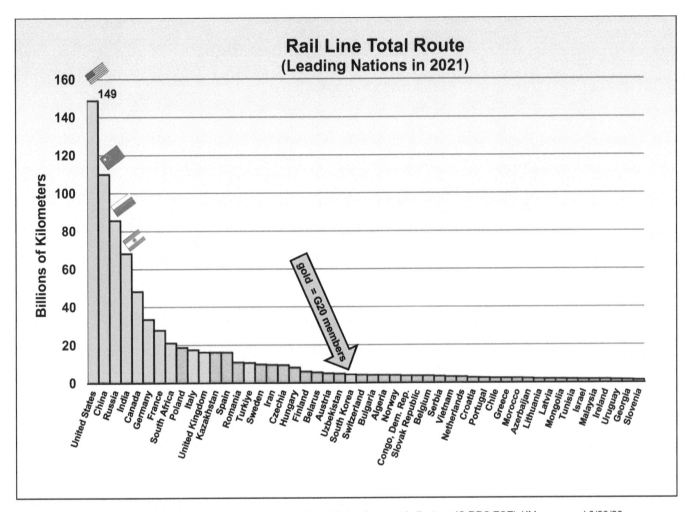

Rail Line Total Route
(Leading Nations in 2021)

Source: The World Bank, https://databank.worldbank.org/source/world-development-indicators, IS.RRS.TOTL.KM, accessed 8/23/23
https://data.worldbank.org/summary-terms-of-use

In 2021, the U.S. was the world's leader in length of rail lines. The total route length in the U.S. was 35 percent greater than the route length in China, the second-longest rail length.

Rail lines are the length of railway route available for train service, irrespective of the number of parallel tracks. It includes railway routes that are open for public passenger and freight services and excludes dedicated private resource railways.

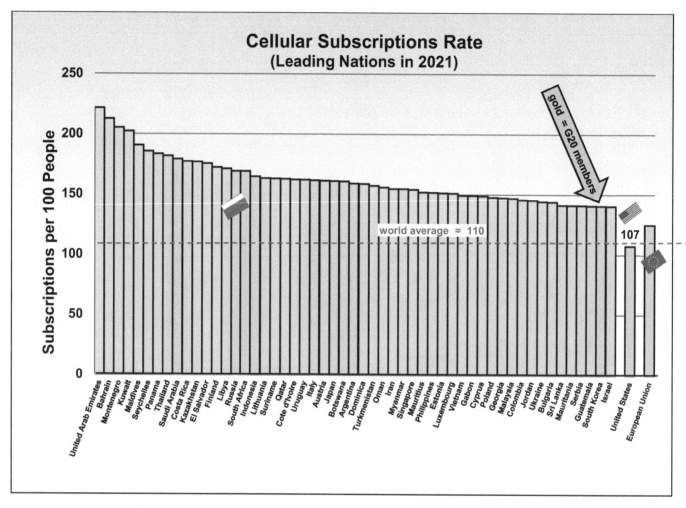

Source: The World Bank, https://databank.worldbank.org/source/world-development-indicators, IT.CEL.SETS.P2, accessed 8/23/23
https://data.worldbank.org/summary-terms-of-use

In 2021, approximately three-fourths of all nations had more cellular subscriptions than people in their nation, led by United Arab Emirates (UAE) at 221 subscriptions per 100 people. The U.S. subscription rate was approximately the same as the world's average of 110 per 100 population.

Cellular subscriptions rate refers to the subscriptions to a public mobile telephone service and provides access to Public Switched Telephone Network (PSTN) using cellular technology, including prepaid SIM cards active during the most recent three months. The data include all mobile cellular subscriptions that offer voice communications but exclude mobile broadband subscriptions via data cards or USB modems. Subscriptions to public mobile data services, private trunked mobile radio, telepoint or radio paging, and telemetry services are also excluded.

Data on mobile cellular subscribers are derived using administrative data that countries (usually the regulatory telecommunication authority or the ministry in charge of telecommunications) regularly, and at least annually, collect from telecommunications operators.

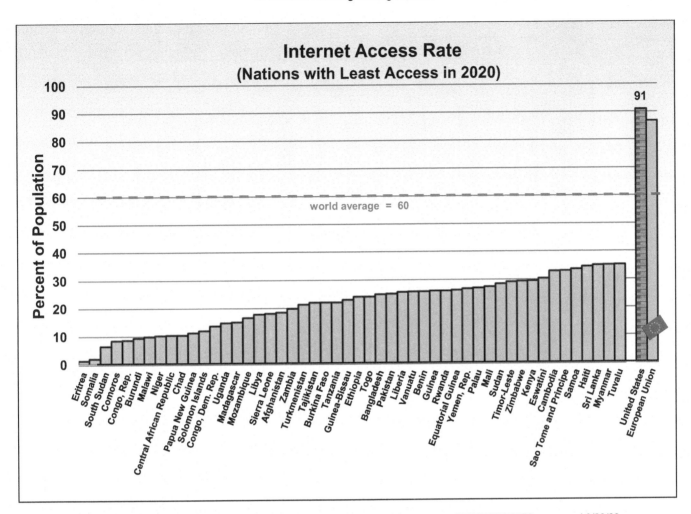

Internet Access Rate
(Nations with Least Access in 2020)

Source: The World Bank, https://databank.worldbank.org/source/world-development-indicators, IT.NET.USER.ZS, accessed 8/23/23
https://data.worldbank.org/summary-terms-of-use

In 2020, it was estimated that 91 percent of the U.S. population had internet access, compared with 60 percent of the world's population.

The internet is a worldwide public computer network. It provides access to a number of communication services including the World Wide Web and carries email, news, entertainment and data files, irrespective of the device used (not assumed to be only via a computer—it may also be by mobile phone, PDA, games machine, digital TV etc.). Access can be via a fixed or mobile network.

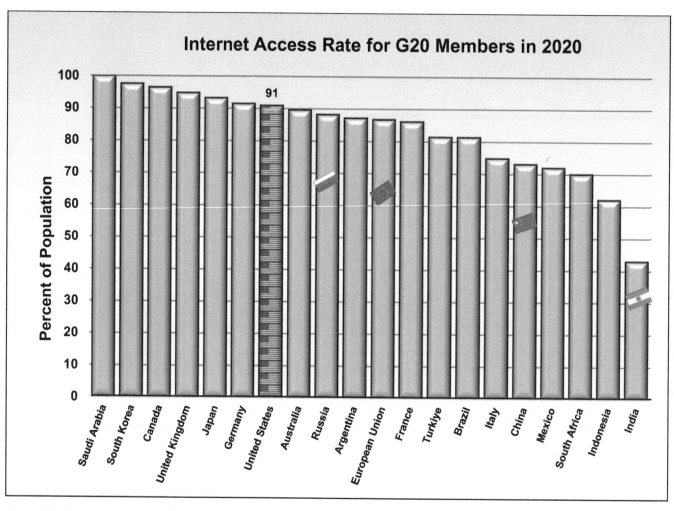

Internet Access Rate for G20 Members in 2020

Percent of Population

91

(Bars, left to right: Saudi Arabia, South Korea, Canada, United Kingdom, Japan, Germany, United States, Australia, Russia, Argentina, European Union, France, Turkiye, Brazil, Italy, China, Mexico, South Africa, Indonesia, India)

Source: The World Bank, https://databank.worldbank.org/source/world-development-indicators, IT.NET.USER.ZS, accessed 8/23/23
https://data.worldbank.org/summary-terms-of-use

In 2020, the U.S. ranked seventh among G20 members for 91 percent of population having internet access. Almost everyone in Saudi Arabia had access while India ranked last among G20 members with only 43 percent.

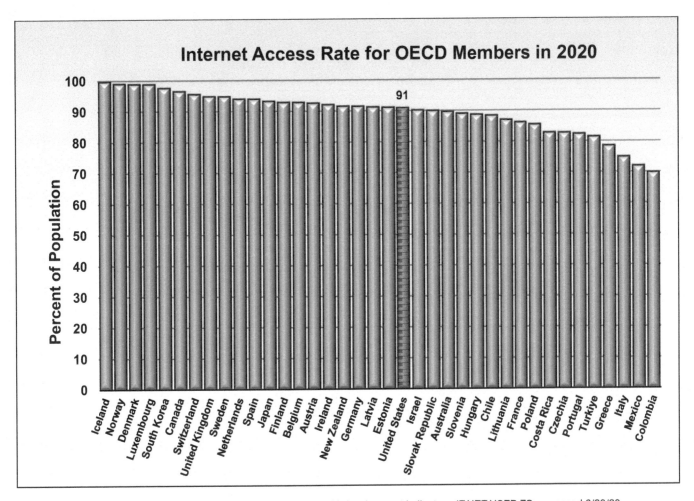

Source: The World Bank, https://databank.worldbank.org/source/world-development-indicators, IT.NET.USER.ZS, accessed 8/23/23
https://data.worldbank.org/summary-terms-of-use

In 2020, the U.S. ranked 21st among the 38 OECD members for internet access, at 91 percent of the population. Almost everyone in Iceland and the Nordic countries had access while Colombia ranked last among OECD members with only 70 percent.

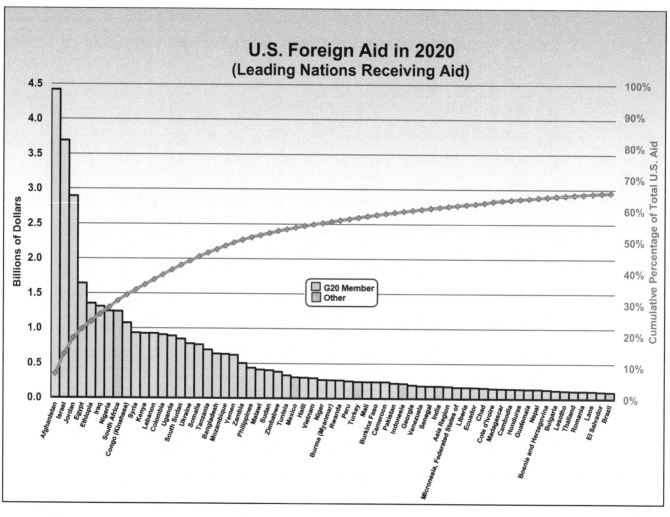

U.S. Foreign Aid in 2020
(Leading Nations Receiving Aid)

Sources: USAID, U.S. Department of State, ForeignAssistance.gov, accessed 7-17-23

In 2020, the U.S. provided $57 billion in foreign aid to over 150 countries and territories. Six of the nations that received aid were G20 members: South Africa, India, Indonesia, Mexico, Brazil, and Turkiye.

Foreign assistance is provided by the U.S. to other countries to support global peace, security, and development efforts, as well as to provide humanitarian relief during times of crisis. The U.S. government provides foreign assistance because it is strategically, economically, and morally imperative for the U.S. and vital to U.S. national security.

The data on the ForeignAssistance.gov website can be found dating back to 1946, when data was collected and reported by predecessor agencies. President Kennedy signed the Foreign Assistance Act of 1961 which created the United States Agency for International Development. This Act, as amended, requires USAID, as the successor to the Development Coordination Committee created under the Act, to report U.S. foreign assistance data to Congress. These data are used for publication of the annual U.S. Overseas Loans and Grants (informally known as the Greenbook) report to Congress.

Chapter 10

Military

Overview of Military

In 2022, there were an estimated 12,706 nuclear warheads in the world, of which an estimated 3,732 were considered to be deployed—meaning they are on operational military bases. These warheads were controlled by nine nations, three of which, the U.S., the U.K., and France, are members of NATO. Of the nine nations that possessed these warheads Russia and the U.S. held approximately 90 percent of them.

In 2022, the U.S. had approximately 1,375,000 active-duty military personnel which was estimated to be 5.0 percent of world's total of 27.7 million. The distribution among U.S. defense departments is estimated to be: 475,000 Army; 345,000 Navy; 335,000 Air Force (includes about 8,000 Space Force); 180,000 Marine Corps; 40,000 Coast Guard. In addition, it is also estimated that there are 335,000 Army National Guard and 105,000 Air National Guard.

In 2023, the 39 nations who abstained or voted "*Against*" the February 23, 2023, U.N. resolution that "*Russia withdraw from Ukraine*" had an estimated 13.4 million armed forces personnel versus 13.3 million for the 141 Nations voting "*In Favor*" of withdrawal. Three G20 members abstained from voting on the resolution (India, China, and South Africa) and Russia voted "*Against*" withdrawal (of course). These four members comprised 47 percent of the military personnel of the G20 members.

As of October 1, 2023, after Russia launched its war against Ukraine, the U.S. had provided Ukraine with $43.9 billion in security assistance and more than $2.1 billion in humanitarian assistance for the people of Ukraine, both inside Ukraine and in the region. Also, the E.U., its member states and its financial institutions, had made available €38.8 billion to support Ukraine's overall economic, social and financial needs and in addition military assistance of approximately €25 billion. That brought the total E.U. support made available to Ukraine since the beginning of Russia's aggression to around €64 billion. (64 billion euros was equivalent to 67 billion U.S. dollars.) The total, combined support by the U.S. and E.U. was $113 billion.

Between 1991 and 2019, four of the five G20 members with the largest number of military personnel (U.S., E.U., China, and Russia) had collectively reduced their armed forces by one-third, while India increased their forces by 140 percent.

In 2019, OECD's 38 members comprised 21.4 percent of the world's 27.7 million armed forces personnel. Although OECD is not a military alliance it is significant that all members voted "*In Favor*" of the February 23, 2023, U.N. resolution for Russia to withdraw from Ukraine. OECD members collectively controlled 60.4 percent of the world's GDP in 2021, and were responsible for 60.1 percent of the world's exports.

The North Atlantic Treaty Organization (NATO has become a stalwart deterrent of aggression against its members due to article five in its founding document that states: any attack on a NATO member in Europe or North America "*shall be considered an attack against them all.*" On February 23, 2023, all 30 NATO member nations voted "In Favor" of the U.N. resolution for Russia to withdraw from Ukraine. Sweden and Finland—not yet members—had also voted "In Favor." Of these 32 nations, 26 were designated "Free" by Freedom House in 2023; North Macedonia, Albania, Montenegro, and Hungary were designated "Partly Free"; Turkiye as "Not Free."

In 2022, the U.S. population comprised over one-third of the combined population of the 30 NATO members. NATO members' combined population comprised 12.0 percent of the world's population, accounted for 47.1 percent of the world's GDP of $101.5 trillion, with an average GDP per capita of $37,000. The U.S. ranked third at $70,250 per capita—behind Luxembourg ($134,000 and Norway ($89,000. In 2019, NATO's 30 members comprised 14.4 percent of the world's estimated 27.7 million armed forces. In April 2023, Finland became a newly admitted member adding 27,000 armed forces and Sweden joined in March 2024, adding an additional 15,000.

In 2023, the U.S. had dual partnerships with 22 nations that belonged to both NATO and OECD. Of those 22, six were also G20 members: Canada, France, Germans, Italy, Turkiye, and the U.K. The U.S. also had in place bilateral/trilateral defense treaties with nations in Asia that were established immediately after either World War II or the Korean War. Three of these nations—Australia, Japan, and South Korea—were also OECD and G20 members. These bilateral agreements incorporate language that states: the parties will ". . . *to meet the common danger in accordance with its constitutional processes.*"

The U.S. is also part of the multilateral "Rio" treaty with 18 Latin American countries, including Venezuela. Article three of The Rio treaty asserts that: "*an armed attack by any State against an American State shall be considered as an attack against all American States.*" Former members that have withdrawn from the Rio treaty are, Cuba, Nicaragua, Mexico, Ecuador, and Bolivia.

In 2021, the U.S. spent 3.5 percent of GDP on military defense programs, which was the third most of the G20 members, after Saudi Arabia and Russia, and in the top 10 percent of nations worldwide.

In 2020, the U.S. was the leading arms exporter in the world, responsible for approximately one-third of all arms exports and more than twice as much as China and Russia combined. Japan purchased more military equipment from the U.S. government than any other nation.

In 2020, India was the world leader in arms imports. Of the $2.8 billion India imported only $.32 billion (11 percent was from the U.S. Twelve nations received approximately two-thirds of the world's arms imports.

~

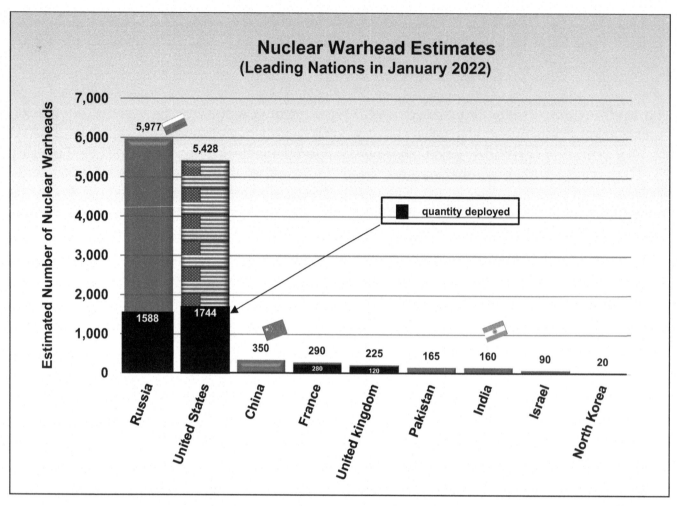

Nuclear Warhead Estimates
(Leading Nations in January 2022)

Source: Information from the Stockholm International Peace Research Institute (SIPRI), https://www.sipri.org/media/press-release/2022/global-nuclear-arsenals-are-expected-grow-states-continue-modernize-new-sipri-yearbook-out-now, accessed on 4/22/23

In 2022, there were an estimated 12,706 nuclear warheads in the world, of which an estimated 3,732 were considered to be deployed. These warheads were controlled by nine nations, three of which—U.S., U.K., and France—are members of NATO. Out of the nine nations that possessed these warheads Russia and the U.S. held approximately 90 percent of them.

"Deployed" warheads refers to warheads placed on missiles or located on bases with operational forces.

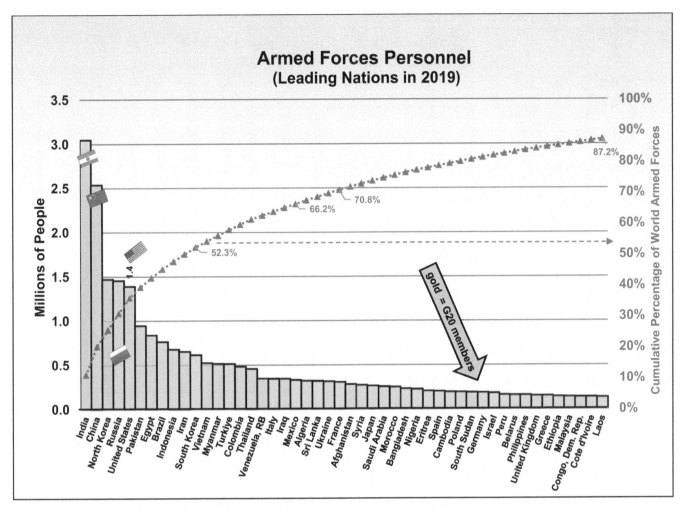

Sources: The World Bank, https://databank.worldbank.org/source/world-development-indicators, MS.MIL.TOTL.P1, accessed 8-15-23, https://data.worldbank.org/summary-terms-of-use, CIA, The World Factbook, https://www.cia.gov/the-world-factbook/countries/united-states/#military-and-security

The G20 member nations comprise 85.2 percent of the world's armed forces. The U.S. active-duty military personnel are estimated to be 1,375,000, with distribution among defense departments of: 475,000 Army; 345,000 Navy; 335,000 Air Force (includes about 8,000 Space Force); 180,000 Marine Corps; 40,000 Coast Guard). In addition, it is estimated there are 335,000 Army National Guard and 105,000 Air National Guard.

Military data on manpower represent quantitative assessment of the personnel strengths of the world's armed forces. The IISS collects the data from a wide variety of sources. The numbers are based on the most accurate data available, or on the best estimate that can be made by the International Institute for Strategic Studies (IISS) at the time of its annual publication.

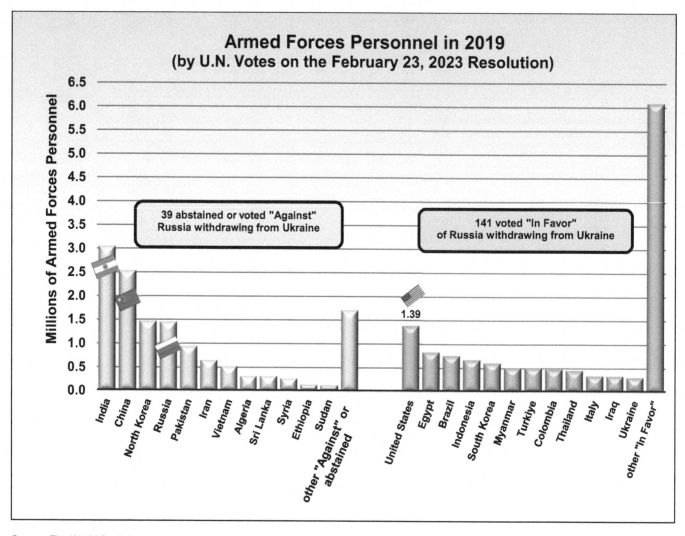

Armed Forces Personnel in 2019
(by U.N. Votes on the February 23, 2023 Resolution)

Millions of Armed Forces Personnel

39 abstained or voted "Against" Russia withdrawing from Ukraine

141 voted "In Favor" of Russia withdrawing from Ukraine

1.39

India, China, North Korea, Russia, Pakistan, Iran, Vietnam, Algeria, Sri Lanka, Syria, Ethiopia, Sudan, other "Against" or abstained

United States, Egypt, Brazil, Indonesia, South Korea, Myanmar, Turkiye, Colombia, Thailand, Italy, Iraq, Ukraine, other "In Favor"

Source: The World Bank, https://databank.worldbank.org/source/world-development-indicators, MS.MIL.TOTL.P1, accessed 8-15-23, https://data.worldbank.org/summary-terms-of-use

In 2023, the 39 nations who abstained or voted "Against" the February 23, 2023 U.N. resolution that "Russia withdraw from Ukraine" have an estimated 13.4 million armed forces personnel versus 13.3 million for the 141 Nations voting "In Favor."

The data include active armed forces and active paramilitary (but not reservists). Armed forces personnel comprise all servicemen and servicewomen on full-time duty, including conscripts and long-term assignments from the Reserves. ("Reserves" describes formations and units not fully manned or operational in peacetime, but which can be mobilized by recalling reservists in an emergency.) The indicator includes paramilitary forces.

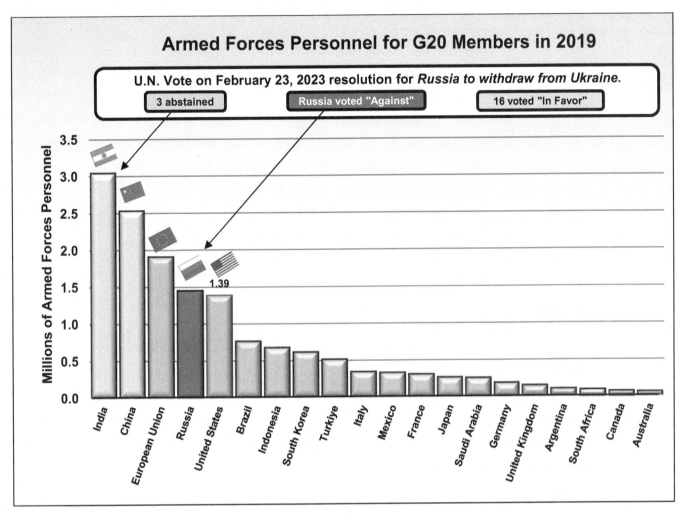

Source: The World Bank, https://databank.worldbank.org/source/world-development-indicators, MS.MIL.TOTL.P1, accessed 8-15-23, https://data.worldbank.org/summary-terms-of-use

In 2019, G20 members comprised 54 percent of the world's estimated 27.7 million armed forces. All members were present for the February 23, 2023, U.N. resolution for *Russia to withdraw from Ukraine*. Three G20 members abstained from voting on the resolution (India, China, and South Africa) and Russia voted "*Against*" withdrawal. These four members comprised 47 percent of the military personnel of the G20 members.

Armed forces personnel comprise all servicemen and servicewomen on full-time duty, including conscripts and long-term assignments from the Reserves. ("Reserves" describes formations and units not fully manned or operational in peacetime, but which can be mobilized by recalling reservists in an emergency.) The indicator includes paramilitary forces.

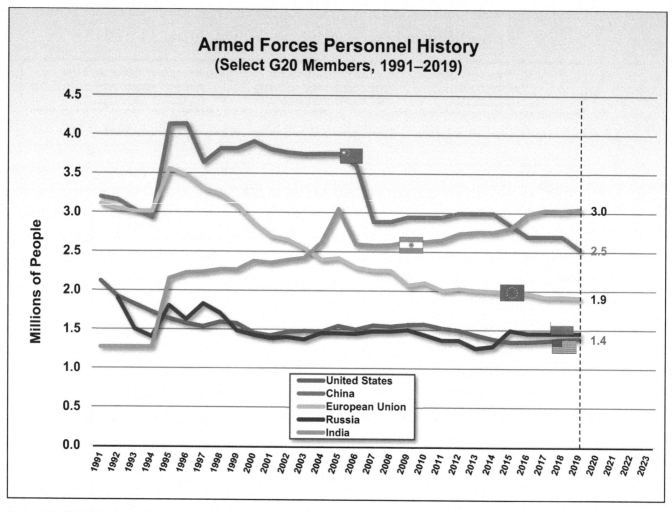

Armed Forces Personnel History
(Select G20 Members, 1991–2019)

Source: The World Bank, https://databank.worldbank.org/source/world-development-indicators, MS.MIL.TOTL.P1, accessed 8-15-23, https://data.worldbank.org/summary-terms-of-use

Between 1991 and 2019, four of the five G20 members with the largest number of military personnel (U.S., E.U., China, and Russia) have collectively reduced their armed forces by one-third, while India increased their forces by 140 percent.

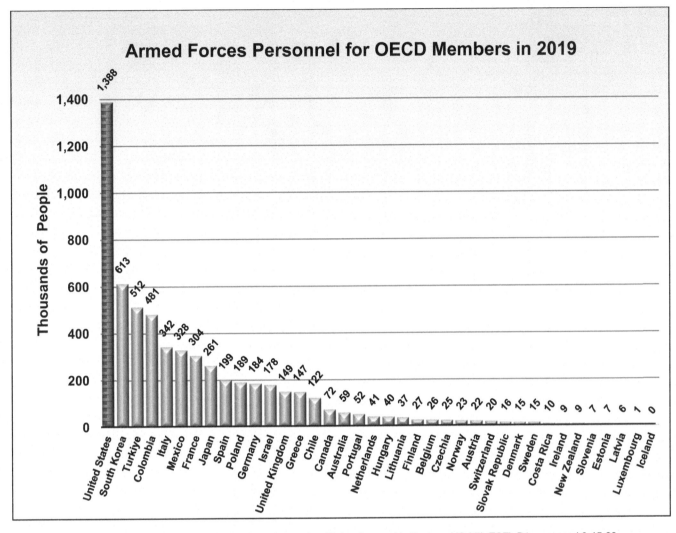

Armed Forces Personnel for OECD Members in 2019

Thousands of People

United States	1,388
South Korea	613
Turkiye	512
Colombia	481
Italy	342
Mexico	328
France	304
Japan	261
Spain	199
Poland	189
Germany	184
Israel	178
United Kingdom	149
Greece	147
Chile	122
Canada	72
Australia	59
Portugal	52
Netherlands	41
Hungary	40
Lithuania	37
Finland	27
Belgium	26
Czechia	25
Norway	23
Austria	22
Switzerland	20
Slovak Republic	16
Denmark	15
Sweden	15
Costa Rica	10
Ireland	9
New Zealand	9
Slovenia	7
Estonia	7
Latvia	6
Luxembourg	1
Iceland	0

Source: The World Bank, https://databank.worldbank.org/source/world-development-indicators, MS.MIL.TOTL.P1, accessed 8-15-23, https://data.worldbank.org/summary-terms-of-use

In 2019, OECD's 38 members comprised 21.4 percent of the world's 27.7 million armed forces personnel. Although OECD is not a military alliance it is significant that all members voted "*In Favor*" of the February 23, 2023, U.N. resolution for Russia to withdraw from Ukraine since the OECD members collectively controlled 60.4 percent of the world's GDP in 2021, and were responsible for 60.1 percent of the world's exports. Iceland was the only OECD member without a military force.

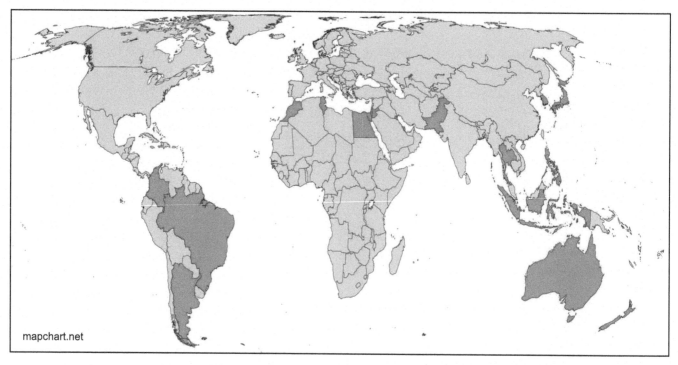

mapchart.net

Source: U.S. Department of State, https://www.state.gov/major-non-nato-ally-status/, accessed 5-28-23

World Map Showing MNNA Nations in March 2024

Major Non-NATO Ally (MNNA) status is a designation under U.S. law that provides foreign partners with certain benefits in the areas of defense trade and security cooperation. The Major Non-NATO Ally designation is a powerful symbol of the close relationship the U.S. shares with those designated countries and demonstrates the U.S. deep respect for the friendship it has for the countries to which it is extended. While MNNA status provides military and economic privileges, it does not entail any security commitments to the designated nation. Those privileges are:

- Entry into cooperative research and development projects with the Department of Defense (DoD) on a shared-cost basis.
- Participation in certain counter-terrorism initiatives.
- Purchase of depleted uranium anti-tank rounds.
- Priority delivery of military surplus (ranging from military rations to ships).
- Possession of War Reserve Stocks of DoD-owned equipment that are kept outside of American military bases.
- Loans of equipment and materials for cooperative research and development projects and evaluations.
- Permission to use American financing for the purchase or lease of certain defense equipment.
- Reciprocal training.
- Expedited export processing of space technology.
- Permission for the nation's corporations to bid on certain DoD contracts for the repair and maintenance of military equipment outside the U.S.

As of 2024, 18 countries are designated as MNNAs: Argentina, Australia, Bahrain, Brazil, Colombia, Egypt, Israel, Japan, Jordan, Kuwait, Morocco, New Zealand, Pakistan, the Philippines, Qatar, South Korea, Thailand, and Tunisia. In addition, it is U.S. policy that Taiwan shall be treated as an MNNA, without formal designation as such. (See page 180 for further explanation.)

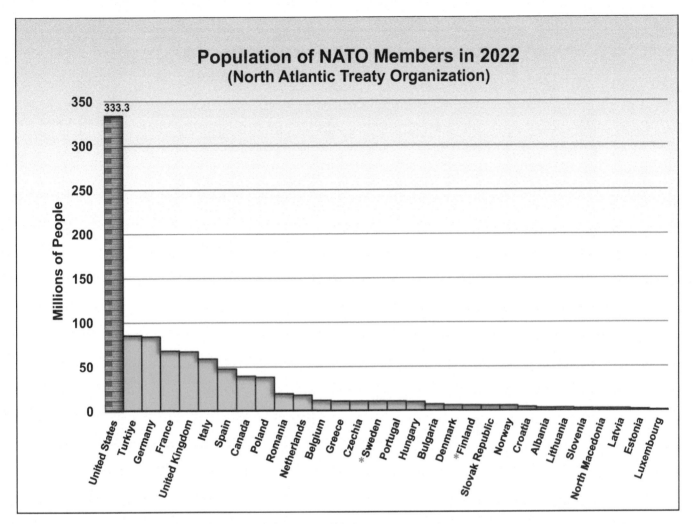

Population of NATO Members in 2022
(North Atlantic Treaty Organization)

Source: The World Bank, https://databank.worldbank.org/source/world-development-indicators, SP.POP.TOTL, accessed 8-15-23, https://data.worldbank.org/summary-terms-of-use

In 2022, the U.S. population comprised over one-third of the combined population of the 30 NATO members. NATO members' population comprised 12.0 percent of the world's population. *With the addition of Finland in 2023, and Sweden in March 2024, the 32 NATO members' portion of the world's population increased to 12.2 percent.

Total population is based on the de facto definition of population, which counts all residents regardless of legal status or citizenship. The values shown are midyear estimates. Population estimates are usually based on national population censuses. Errors and undercounting occur even in high-income countries. In developing countries errors may be substantial because of limits in the transport, communications, and other resources required to conduct and analyze a full census. The quality and reliability of official demographic data are also affected by public trust in the government, government commitment to full and accurate enumeration, confidentiality and protection against misuse of census data, and census agencies' independence from political influence.

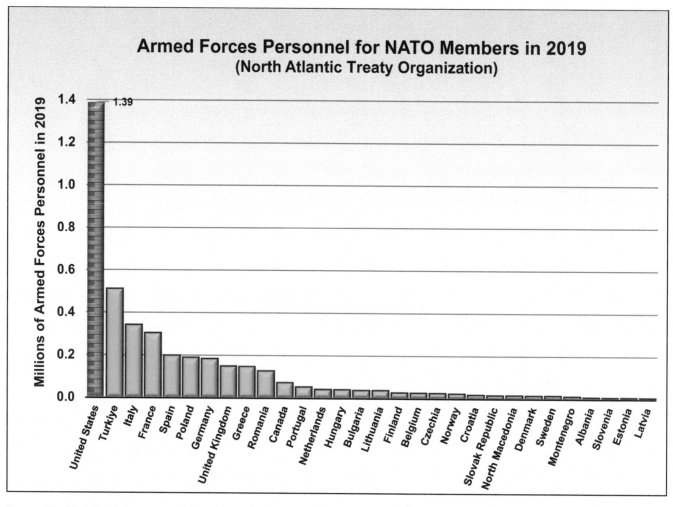

Armed Forces Personnel for NATO Members in 2019
(North Atlantic Treaty Organization)

Source: The World Bank, https://databank.worldbank.org/source/world-development-indicators, MS.MIL.TOTL.P1, accessed 8-15-23, https://data.worldbank.org/summary-terms-of-use

In 2019, NATO's 30 members comprised 14.4 percent of the world's estimated 27.7 million armed forces. In 2023, Finland joined NATO increasing membership to 31 nations which added 27,000 armed forces. Sweden joined in March 2024, becoming the 32nd NATO member, adding an additional 15,000 armed forces.

Military data on manpower represent quantitative assessment of the personnel strengths of the world's armed forces. The IISS collects the data from a wide variety of sources. The numbers are based on the most accurate data available on the best estimate that can be made by the International Institute for Strategic Studies (IISS) at the time of its annual publication. The current WDI indicator includes active armed forces and active paramilitary (but not reservists). Armed forces personnel comprise all servicemen and servicewomen on full-time duty, including conscripts and long-term assignments from the Reserves. ("Reserves" describes formations and units not fully manned or operational in peacetime, but which can be mobilized by recalling reservists in an emergency.) The indicator includes paramilitary forces.

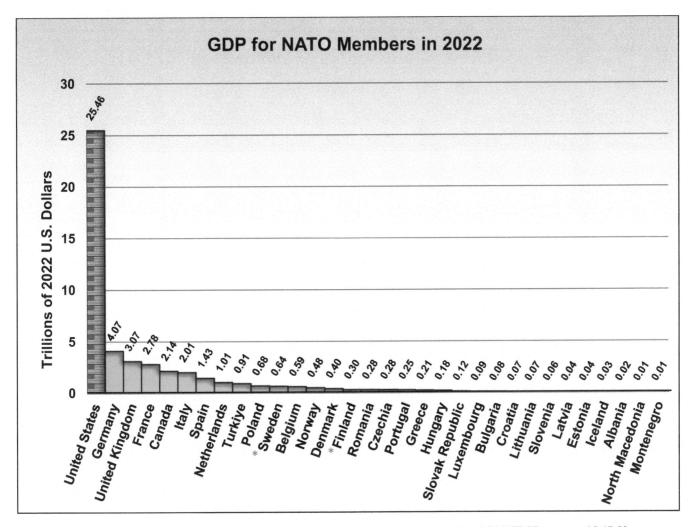

GDP for NATO Members in 2022

Source: The World Bank, https://databank.worldbank.org/source/world-development-indicators, NY.GDP.MKTP.CD, accessed 8-15-23, https://data.worldbank.org/summary-terms-of-use

In 2022, NATO's 30 members accounted for 47.1 percent of the world's GDP of $101.5 trillion. *After Finland joined NATO in 2023, followed by Sweden in March 2024, NATO's percentage of the world's GDP increased to 48.0 percent.

GDP at purchaser's prices is the sum of gross value added by all resident producers in the economy plus any product taxes and minus any subsidies not included in the value of the products. It is calculated without making deductions for depreciation of fabricated assets or for depletion and degradation of natural resources. Data are in current U.S. dollars. Dollar figures for GDP are converted from domestic currencies using single-year official exchange rates.

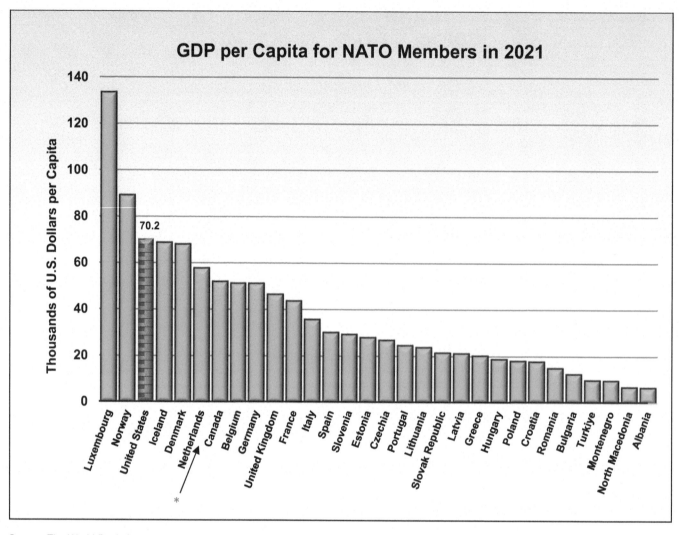

GDP per Capita for NATO Members in 2021

Source: The World Bank, https://databank.worldbank.org/source/world-development-indicators, NY.GDP.PCAP.CD, accessed 8-15-23, https://data.worldbank.org/summary-terms-of-use

In 2021, NATO's members' average GDP per capita was $36,892. The U.S. ranked third at $70,250 per capita, nearly two times the NATO average, and behind Luxembourg and Norway. *(In 2023, Finland joined NATO increasing membership to 31 nations, and in March 2024, Sweden's application for membership was approved. Finland's GDP per capita in 2021, was $55,700—ranking seventh among NATO nations, and Sweden's GDP per capita was approximately the same as Finland's at $55,900.

GDP per capita is gross domestic product divided by midyear population. GDP is the sum of gross value added by all resident producers in the economy plus any product taxes and minus any subsidies not included in the value of the products. It is calculated without making deductions for depreciation of fabricated assets or for depletion and degradation of natural resources. Data are in current U.S. dollars.

U.S. Dual Partnerships with OECD Members and NATO Members

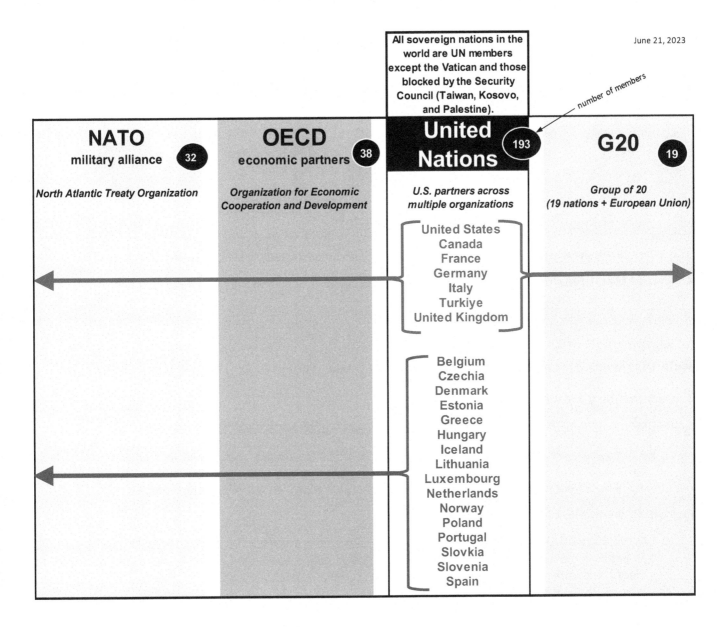

In April 2023, Finland became the 31st member of NATO and in March 2024, Sweden became the 32nd, thereby increasing total membership to 32 of which 26 members were also members of the OECD. Seven of those 32 members were also G20 members: U.S., Canada, France, Germany, Italy, Turkiye, and the U.K.

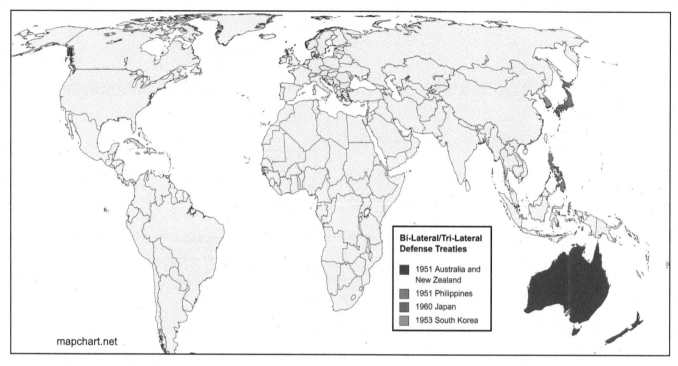

Source: The U.S. Department of State, https://2009-2017.state.gov/s/l/treaty/collectivedefense/index.htm, accessed 5-28-23

World Map of Major Bilateral/Trilateral U.S. Defense Treaty Partners in Asia in 2024

In March 2024, the U.S. had in place bilateral/trilateral defense treaties with nations in Asia that were established immediately after either World War II or the Korean War.

Those primary treaties are:

AGREEMENT BETWEEN THE UNITED STATES AND AUSTRALIA AND NEW ZEALAND

A Treaty signed September 1, 1951, whereby each of the parties recognizes that an armed attack in the Pacific Area on any of the Parties would be dangerous to its own peace and safety and declares that it would ***act to meet the common danger*** in accordance with its constitutional processes.

REPUBLIC OF KOREA TREATY (BILATERAL)

A treaty signed October 1, 1953, whereby each party recognizes that an armed attack in the Pacific area on either of the Parties would be dangerous to its own peace and safety and that each Party would ***act to meet the common danger*** in accordance with its constitutional processes.

JAPANESE TREATY (BILATERAL)

A treaty signed January 19, 1960, whereby each party recognizes that an armed attack against either Party in the territories under the administration of Japan would be dangerous to its own peace and safety and declares that it would ***act to meet the common danger*** in accordance with its constitutional provisions and processes.

PHILIPPINE TREATY (BILATERAL)

A treaty signed August 30, 1951, by which the parties recognize that an armed attack in the Pacific Area on either of the Parties would be dangerous to its own peace and safety and each party agrees that it will ***act to meet the common danger*** in accordance with its constitutional processes.

U.S. Dual Partnerships with OECD Members and Asian Defense Allies

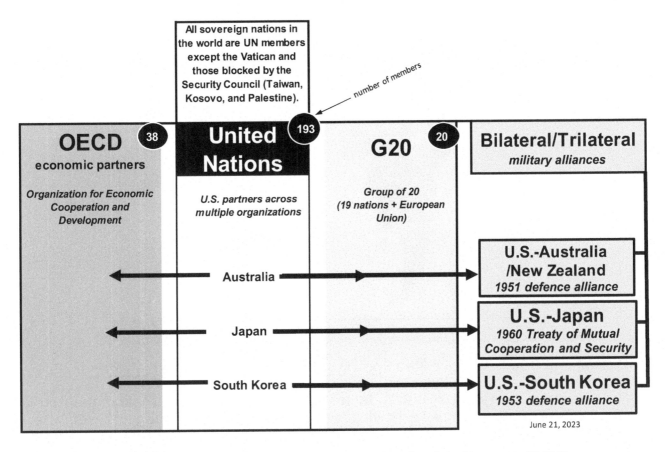

Source: The U.S. Department of State, https://2009-2017.state.gov/s/l/treaty/collectivedefense/index.htm, accessed 5-28-23

In March 2024, three nations, Australia, Japan and South Korea—all three G20 members—had dual partnerships with the U.S. as members of the OECD and also bilateral/trilateral defense treaties.

These defense treaties state that the parties will:

". . . act to meet the common danger in accordance with its constitutional processes"

language that is less explicit about military actions than the NATO charter which states:
 "an armed attack against one or more of them in Europe or North America shall be considered an attack against them all."

mapchart.net

Source: Congressional Research Service, 12/19, https://crsreports.congress.gov/product/pdf/IN/IN11116, accessed 5-28-23

Central and South America Map Showing U.S. Rio Treaty Partners in March 2024

The Rio Treaty was signed in 1947, in the city of Rio de Janeiro and entered into force in 1948. The treaty is a collective security pact among 19 of the 35 countries of the Western Hemisphere. The U.S. ratified the treaty in 1947. Article three of the treaty asserts than "an armed attack by any State against an American State shall be considered as an attack against all American States," and it calls on each party to the treaty to assist in collective self-defense. Article six of the treaty empowers states parties to collectively respond to any other "situation that might endanger the peace" of the region.

The treaty establishes a Meeting of Consultation of Ministers of Foreign Affairs as the principal forum through which states parties are to address collective security threats. Any treaty signatory may request such a meeting but must secure the votes of an absolute majority of parties to the treaty within the Permanent Council of the Organization of American States (OAS, to which the U.S. is also a member.

<table>
<tr><td colspan="3" align="center">**Current Rio Members**</td><td align="center">**Former Rio Members**</td></tr>
<tr><td>Argentina</td><td>Dominican Republic</td><td>Paraguay</td><td>Bolivia (1948–2014)</td></tr>
<tr><td>The Bahamas</td><td>El Salvador</td><td>Peru</td><td>Ecuador (1948–2016)</td></tr>
<tr><td>Brazil</td><td>Guatemala</td><td>Trinidad and Tobago</td><td>Mexico (1948–2004)</td></tr>
<tr><td>Chile</td><td>Haiti</td><td>United States</td><td>Nicaragua (1948–2014)</td></tr>
<tr><td>Colombia</td><td>Honduras</td><td>Uruguay</td><td>Cuba (1948–1962)</td></tr>
<tr><td>Costa Rica</td><td>Panama</td><td>Venezuela</td><td></td></tr>
</table>

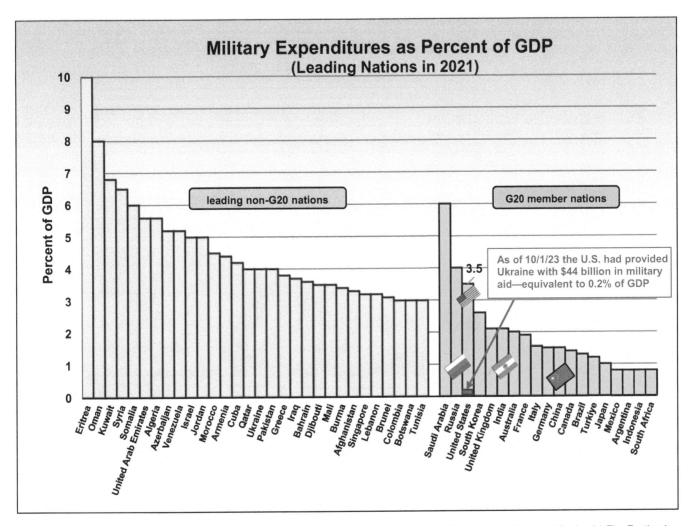

Military Expenditures as Percent of GDP
(Leading Nations in 2021)

leading non-G20 nations

G20 member nations

As of 10/1/23 the U.S. had provided Ukraine with $44 billion in military aid—equivalent to 0.2% of GDP

3.5

Source: The World Factbook 2021. Washington, DC: Central Intelligence Agency, 2021, https://www.cia.gov/the-world-factbook/, The Factbook is in the public domain.

In 2021, the U.S. spent 3.5 percent of GDP on military defense programs, which was the third most of the G20 members, after Saudi Arabia and Russia.

Military expenditures are comparisons of spending on defense programs as a percent of gross domestic product (GDP; calculated on an exchange rate basis).

As of October 1, 2023, according to the U.S. Department of State* since Russia launched its war against Ukraine the U.S. had provided Ukraine with $43.9 billion in security assistance and more than $2.1 billion in humanitarian assistance for the people of Ukraine, both inside Ukraine and in the region. Also, according to the E.U.** the E.U., its Member States and its financial institutions, had made available €38.8 billion to support Ukraine's overall economic, social and financial resilience. This had been in the form of macro-financial assistance, budget support, emergency assistance, crisis response and humanitarian aid. In addition, military assistance measures provided were approximately €25 billion, of which €5.6 billion have been mobilized under the European Peace Facility. That brings the total E.U. support made available to Ukraine since the beginning of Russia's aggression to around €64 billion. (64 billion euros was equivalent to 67 billion U.S. dollars.)

* *https://www.state.gov/u-s-security-cooperation-with-ukraine/* and *https://www.state.gov/united-states-announces-additional-humanitarian-assistance-for-the-people-of-ukraine/* , ** *https://eu-solidarity-ukraine.ec.europa.eu/eu-assistance-ukraine_en*

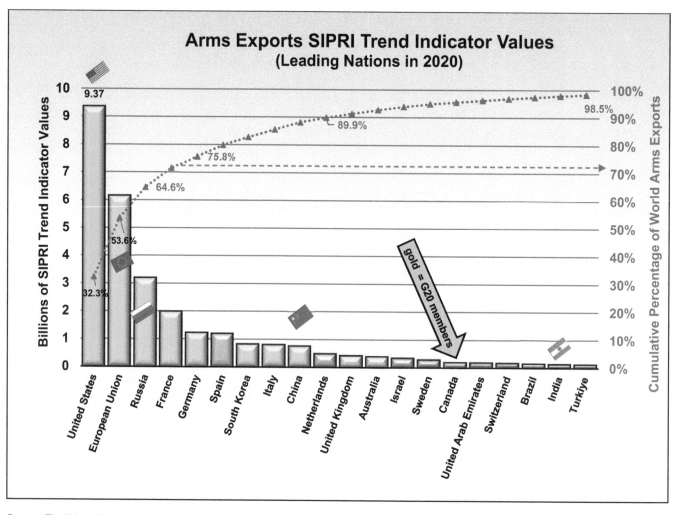

Arms Exports SIPRI Trend Indicator Values
(Leading Nations in 2020)

Source: The World Bank, https://databank.worldbank.org/source/world-development-indicators, MS.MIL.XPRT.KD, accessed 8-15-23,
https://data.worldbank.org/summary-terms-of-use

In 2020, the U.S. was the leading arms exporter in the world, responsible for approximately one-third of all arms exports and more than twice as much as China and Russia combined.

Stockholm International Peace Research Institute (SIPRI)'s Arms Transfers Program collects data on arms transfers from open sources. Since publicly available information is inadequate for tracking all weapons and other military equipment, SIPRI covers only what it terms major conventional weapons. Data cover the supply of weapons through sales, aid, gifts, and manufacturing licenses; therefore, the term arms transfers rather than arms trade is used. SIPRI data also cover weapons supplied to or from rebel forces in an armed conflict as well as arms deliveries for which neither the supplier nor the recipient can be identified with acceptable certainty; these data are available in SIPRI's database.

Data cover major conventional weapons such as aircraft, armored vehicles, artillery, radar systems and other sensors, missiles, and ships designed for military use as well as some major components such as turrets for armored vehicles and engines. Excluded are other military equipment such as most small arms and light weapons, trucks, small artillery, ammunition, support equipment, technology transfers, and other services.

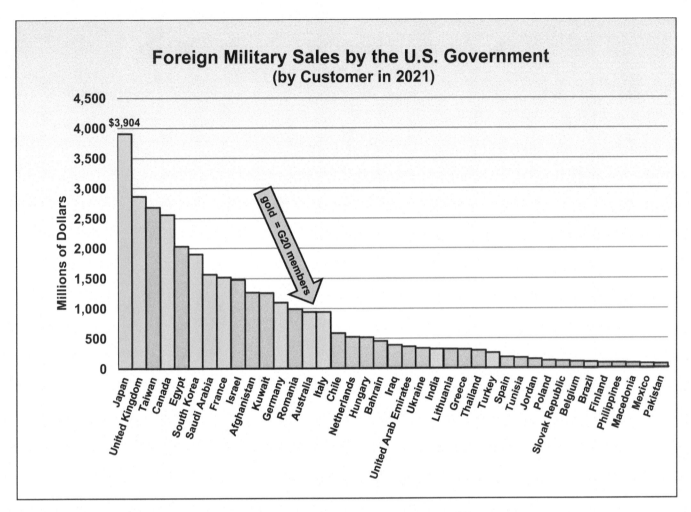

Foreign Military Sales by the U.S. Government
(by Customer in 2021)

gold = G20 members

Sources: The Defense Security Cooperation Agency, https://www.dsca.mil/foreign-military-sales-faq

In 2021, Japan purchased more military equipment from the U.S. government than any other nation—valued at $3.9 billion.

Foreign Military Sales (FMS) is the U.S. Government's program for transferring defense articles, services, and training to our international partners and international organizations. The FMS program is funded by administrative charges to foreign purchasers and is operated at no cost to taxpayers. The Defense Security Cooperation Agency (DSCA) administers the FMS program for the Department of Defense (DoD). Under FMS, the U.S. Government uses DoD's acquisition system to procure defense articles and services on behalf of its partners. Eligible countries may purchase defense articles and services with their own funds or with funds provided through U.S. government-sponsored assistance programs. The President designates countries and international organizations eligible to participate in FMS. The Department of State approves individual programs on a case-by-case basis. In 2021, some 189 countries and international organizations participate in FMS.

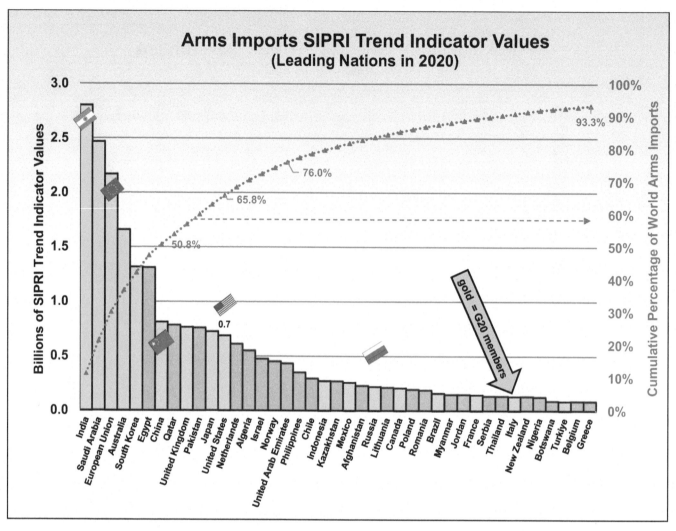

Arms Imports SIPRI Trend Indicator Values
(Leading Nations in 2020)

Source: The World Bank, https://databank.worldbank.org/source/world-development-indicators, MS.MIL.MPRT.KD, accessed 8-15-23, https://data.worldbank.org/summary-terms-of-use

In 2020, India was the world leader in arms imports. Of the $2.8 billion India imported only $.32 billion (11 percent) was from the U.S. Twelve nations received approximately two-thirds of the world's arms imports, nine of which were G20 members.

Stockholm International Peace Research Institute (SIPRI)'s Arms Transfers Program collects data on arms transfers from open sources. Since publicly available information is inadequate for tracking all weapons and other military equipment, SIPRI covers only what it terms major conventional weapons. Data cover the supply of weapons through sales, aid, gifts, and manufacturing licenses; therefore, the term arms transfers rather than arms trade is used. SIPRI data also cover weapons supplied to or from rebel forces in an armed conflict as well as arms deliveries for which neither the supplier nor the recipient can be identified with acceptable certainty; these data are available in SIPRI's database.

Data cover major conventional weapons such as aircraft, armored vehicles, artillery, radar systems and other sensors, missiles, and ships designed for military use as well as some major components such as turrets for armored vehicles and engines. Excluded are other military equipment such as most small arms and light weapons, trucks, small artillery, ammunition, support equipment, technology transfers, and other services.

Chapter 11

Poverty

Overview of Poverty

One of several measurements of poverty used by the World Bank is income below $6.85 per day. At this level, during the period between 2016 and 2021—based on availability of data—52 percent of the world's population was below this poverty income threshold, compared with 2.0 percent of the U.S. population. In 2021, three G20 nations had income below this poverty threshold, India (83 percent), Indonesia (75 percent), and South Africa (62 percent).

The poverty rate as defined by the OECD was the ratio of the number of people (in a given age -group) whose income falls below the poverty line; taken as half the median household income of the total population. In 2019, for the U.S. population aged above 66 years, 23 percent met that criterion, the seventh-highest level of all 35 OECD members for which data existed.

The official poverty measure in the U.S. according to the U.S. Bureau of Labor Statistics, defines poverty by comparing pretax money income to a poverty threshold that is adjusted by family composition. However, the Supplemental Poverty Measure (SPM), first released in 2011, extends the official poverty measure by taking account of many government programs that are designed to assist low-income families but are not included in the official poverty measure. The SPM also includes federal and state taxes and work and medical expenses. In addition, the SPM accounts for geographic variation in poverty thresholds, while the official poverty measure does not.

In 2021, the official poverty rate in the U.S. was 11.6 percent, with 37.9 million people in poverty, whereas the SPM rate in 2021, was 7.8 percent. In 2022, the SPM poverty rate rose to 12.4 percent, the largest one-year jump on record. This coincided with the ending of direct payments to households due to the COVID-19 pandemic, which had included enhanced unemployment and nutrition benefits, increased rental assistance and an expanded child tax credit, which briefly provided a guaranteed income to families with children.

In 2021, the poverty income threshold in the U.S. for a single person was defined as $13,788 per year. (That is the annual amount that a worker would earn at $6.63 per hour for 40 hours per week. This amount was only 8.6 percent below what one would earn at the federal minimum wage of $7.25 per hour.)

Between 1987 and 2021, the percentage of people in the U.S. aged 18–64 years with income below the poverty threshold had remained nearly unchanged at 10.5 percent, the average level for all races and ethnicities.

In 2021, poverty for Black Americans aged 18–64 years was at 17.8 percent, more than double the rate for White Americans (8.0 percent). Americans aged under 18 years experienced the highest poverty level among all age groups at 15.3 percent. Between 1987 and 2021, the percent living in poverty in the under age 18 group had declined by approximately one-third across all races and ethnicities.

The Gini index is an internationally widely used measure of inequality of income among countries. A Gini index value of zero represents perfect equality of income distribution, while an index of 100 implies perfect inequality. In the time period 2019–2021, inequality in the U.S. as measured by the Gini index ranked highest (least equality) of the nine G20 members with the highest income-per-capita (*eight with available data*). The U.S. level of 41.5 points was approximately 22 points below South Africa's, the highest score in the world. Between 1991 and 2020, inequality in the U.S. as measured by the Gini index had increased by 9 percent.

Another measure of income inequality is income share. In 2021, the income share held by the top 10 percent in the U.S. was 31.2 percent, the highest (least equality) among the nine wealthiest G20 nations. The U.S. had continually been near the highest level among the wealthiest G20 nations over the previous 30 years.

In the 2019–2021, period, the share of income for the lowest 10 percent in the U.S. was 1.9 percent, placing the U.S. in the bottom (least equality) among the nine G20 members with the highest income.

In 2019, the U.S. ranked second highest, after Luxembourg, for household wealth among the 29 OECD members for whom data existed. In 2022, Luxembourg also had the second-highest GDP per capita of any nation in the world at $126,000, behind Monaco at $234,000. The U.S. was in eighth place at $76,000 per capita.

~

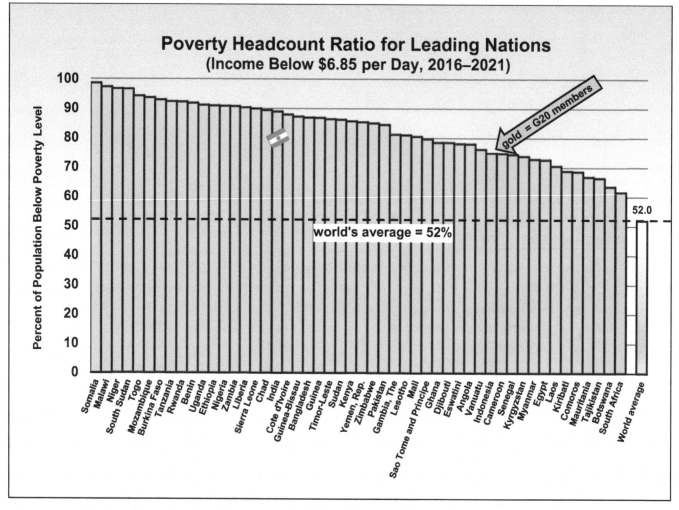

Poverty Headcount Ratio for Leading Nations
(Income Below $6.85 per Day, 2016–2021)

Source: The World Bank, https://databank.worldbank.org/source/world-development-indicators, SI.POV.UMIC, accessed 8-15-23, https://data.worldbank.org/summary-terms-of-use

One of several measurements of poverty used by the World Bank is income below $6.85 per day. At this level, in the period 2016–2021—based on availability of data— 52 percent of the world's population was below this poverty income threshold. In contrast, only 2.0 percent of the U.S. population was below this threshold.

The majority of the populations for three G20 nations had income below this poverty threshold, India (83 percent), Indonesia (75 percent), and South Africa (62 percent).

The welfare of people living in different countries can be measured on a common scale by adjusting for differences in the purchasing power of currencies. As differences in the cost of living across the world evolve, the international poverty line has to be periodically updated using new PPP price data to reflect these changes. The $6.85 poverty line is derived from typical national poverty lines in countries classified as Upper Middle Income.

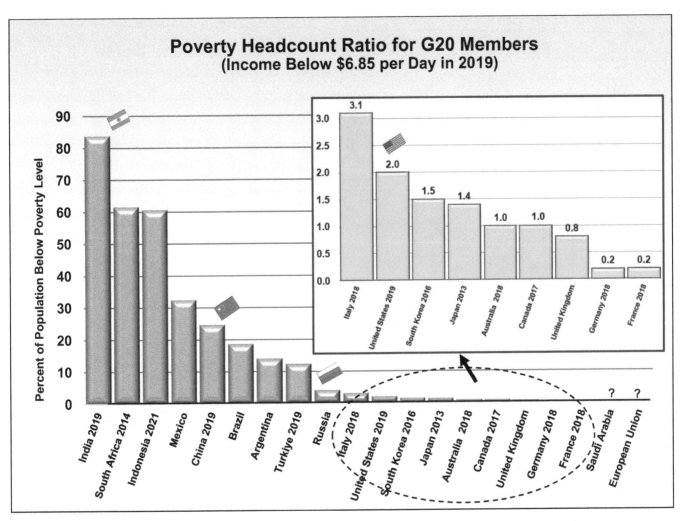

Poverty Headcount Ratio for G20 Members
(Income Below $6.85 per Day in 2019)

Source: The World Bank, https://databank.worldbank.org/source/world-development-indicators, SI.POV.UMIC, accessed 8-15-23, https://data.worldbank.org/summary-terms-of-use

One of several measurements of poverty used by the World Bank is income below $6.85 per day. At that level, in 2019, only 2.0 percent of the U.S. population was below this threshold for poverty. However, of the nine highest income per capita G20 members rated, the U.S. placed as second highest after Italy. By contrast, 83 percent of India's population lived in poverty, the highest of any G20 member. Also, over one half the population of both South Africa and Indonesia are below this poverty threshold.

International comparisons of poverty estimates entail both conceptual and practical problems. Countries have different definitions of poverty, and consistent comparisons across countries can be difficult. Local poverty lines tend to have higher purchasing power in rich countries, where more generous standards are used, than in poor countries.

The welfare of people living in different countries can be measured on a common scale by adjusting for differences in the purchasing power of currencies. As differences in the cost of living across the world evolve, the international poverty line has to be periodically updated using new PPP price data to reflect these changes. The $6.85 poverty line is derived from typical national poverty lines in countries classified as Upper Middle Income.

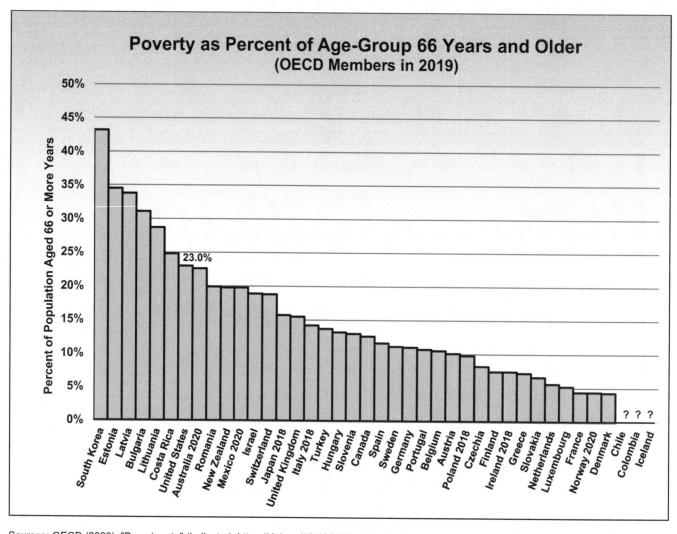

Sources: OECD (2023), "Poverty rate" (indicator), https://doi.org/10.1787/0fe1315d-en (accessed on 20 May 2023).

In 2019, the poverty rate as defined by OECD for the population aged above 66 years, was 23 percent for the U.S., the seventh-highest level of the 35 OECD members for which data existed. (Note that dates shown as suffix to nation names specify any exceptions to the 2019 date of data.)

The poverty rate is the ratio of the number of people (in a given age-group whose income falls below the poverty line; taken as half the median household income of the total population. However, two countries with the same poverty rates may differ in terms of the relative income-level of the poor.

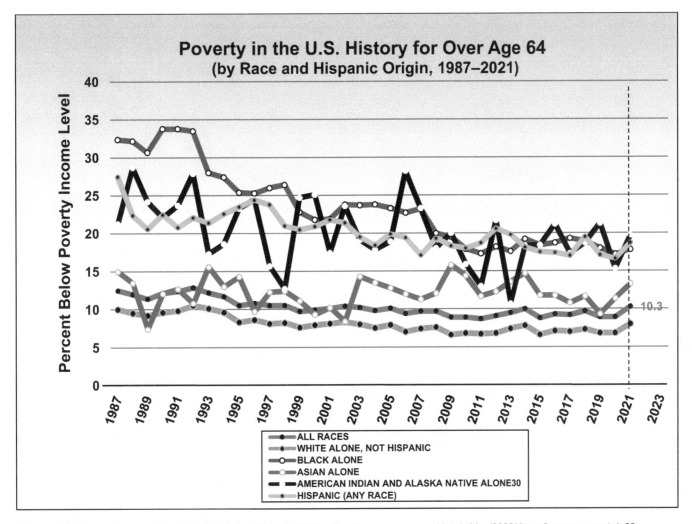

Poverty in the U.S. History for Over Age 64
(by Race and Hispanic Origin, 1987–2021)

Source: U.S. Census Bureau, Poverty in the United States in 2021, https://www.census.gov/data/tables/2022/demo/income-poverty/p60-277.html, accessed on 5-22-23

Between 1990 and 2021, poverty among Black Americans aged over 64 years dropped by 50 percent, however, in 2021, the Black poverty level was 17.8 percent compared with 8.0 percent in that age-group for White. In 2021, the poverty income threshold in the U.S. for a single person was defined as $13,788 per year. That was the annual amount that a worker would earn at $6.63 per hour for 40 hours per week. That amount was below the federal minimum wage of $7.25.

Poverty Thresholds for 2021 by Size of Family and Number of Related Children Under 18 Years
(In dollars)

Size of family unit	Weighted average thresholds	Related children under 18 years								
		None	One	Two	Three	Four	Five	Six	Seven	Eight or more
One person (unrelated individual):	13,788									
Under 65 years............................	14,097	14,097								
65 years and over........................	12,996	12,996								
Two people:	17,529									
Householder under 65 years.......	18,231	18,145	18,677							
Householder 65 years and over...	16,400	16,379	18,606							
Three people..................................	21,559	21,196	21,811	21,831						
Four people....................................	27,740	27,949	28,406	27,479	27,575					
Five people....................................	32,865	33,705	34,195	33,148	32,338	31,843				
Six people......................................	37,161	38,767	38,921	38,119	37,350	36,207	35,529			
Seven people.................................	42,156	44,606	44,885	43,925	43,255	42,009	40,554	38,958		
Eight people..................................	47,093	49,888	50,329	49,423	48,629	47,503	46,073	44,585	44,207	
Nine people or more......................	56,325	60,012	60,303	59,501	58,828	57,722	56,201	54,826	54,485	52,386

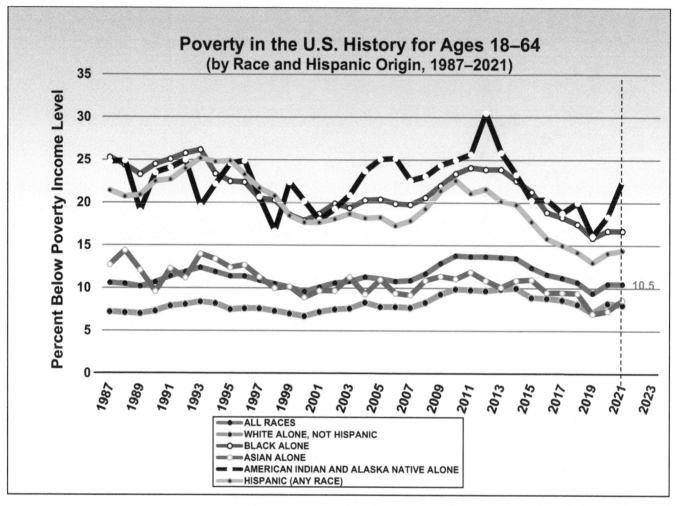

Source: U.S. Census bureau, Poverty in the United States in 2021, https://www.census.gov/data/tables/2022/demo/income-poverty/p60-277.html, accessed on 5-22-23

Between 1987 and 2021, the percentage of people in the U.S. aged 18–64 years with income below the poverty threshold had remained nearly unchanged at 10.5 percent, the average level for all races and ethnicities. In 2021, poverty for American Indians and Alaska Natives was more than double the average of all races and ethnicities in that age-group.

The official poverty measure, in use since the 1960's, defines poverty by comparing pretax money income to a poverty threshold that is adjusted by family composition. The Supplemental Poverty Measure (SPM), first released in 2011, and produced with support from the U.S. Bureau of Labor Statistics (BLS), extends the official poverty measure by taking account of many government programs that are designed to assist low-income families but are not included in the official poverty measure. The SPM also includes federal and state taxes and work and medical expenses. In addition, the SPM accounts for geographic variation in poverty thresholds, while the official poverty measure does not.

The official poverty rate for all ages in 2021, was 11.6 percent, with 37.9 million people in poverty, whereas the SPM rate in 2021, was 7.8 percent. However, the SPM poverty rate rose to 12.4 percent in 2022, the largest one-year jump on record. This coincided with the ending of direct payments to households in 2020, and 2021, plus other COVID-19 pandemic-related benefits.

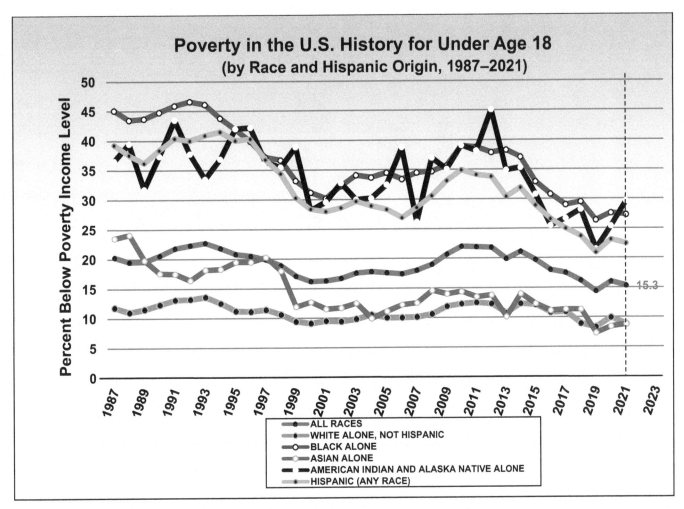

Poverty in the U.S. History for Under Age 18
(by Race and Hispanic Origin, 1987–2021)

Source: U.S. Census Bureau, Poverty in the United States in 2021, https://www.census.gov/data/tables/2022/demo/income-poverty/p60-277.html, accessed on 5-22-23

In 2021, Americans aged under 18 years experienced the highest poverty level among all age groups at 15.3 percent. Between 1987 and 2021, the percent living in poverty in the under age 18 group had declined by approximately one-fourth across all races and ethnicities.

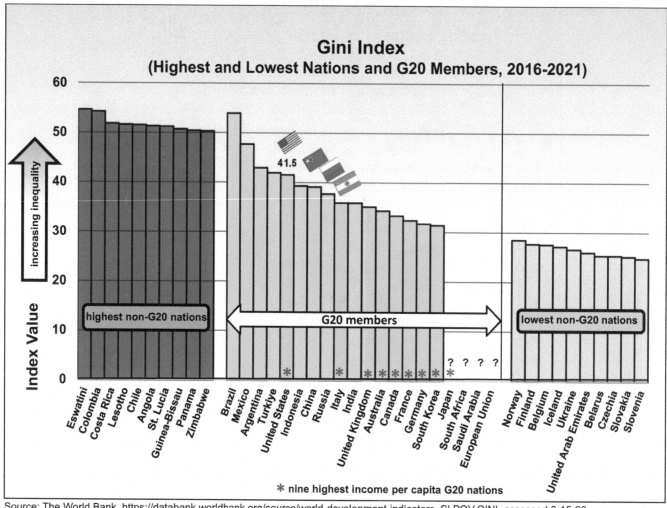

Gini Index
(Highest and Lowest Nations and G20 Members, 2016-2021)

Source: The World Bank, https://databank.worldbank.org/source/world-development-indicators, SI.POV.GINI, accessed 8-15-23, https://data.worldbank.org/summary-terms-of-use

In the time period 2016–2021, inequality in the U.S. as measured by the Gini index ranked fifth within the G20 members and higher than any of the eight principal U.S. partners. The U.S. inequality index of 41.5 points was higher than the levels of fourteen of the G20 nations, including China and Russia. (Data are latest available between 2016 and 2021.)

The Gini index measures the area between the Lorenz curve and a hypothetical line of absolute equality, expressed as a percentage of the maximum area under the line. A Lorenz curve plots the cumulative percentages of total income received against the cumulative number of recipients, starting with the poorest individual. Thus, a Gini index of zero represents perfect equality, while an index of 100 implies perfect inequality.

The Gini index provides a convenient summary measure of the degree of inequality. Data on the distribution of income or consumption come from nationally representative household surveys. Where the original data from the household survey were available, they have been used to calculate the income or consumption shares by quintile. Otherwise, shares have been estimated from the best available grouped data.

The distribution data have been adjusted for household size, providing a more consistent measure of per capita income or consumption.

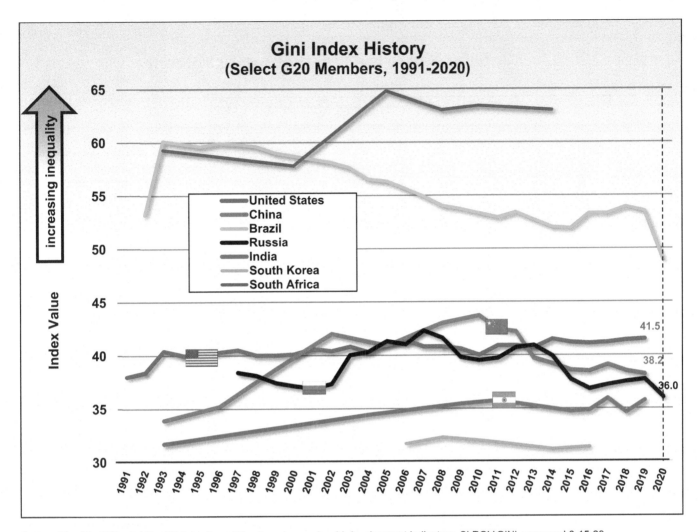

Source: The World Bank, https://databank.worldbank.org/source/world-development-indicators, SI.POV.GINI, accessed 8-15-23, https://data.worldbank.org/summary-terms-of-use

Between 1991 and 2020, inequality in the U.S. as measured by the Gini index had increased by 9 percent, while inequality in China and Russia has declined over the past decade.

The Gini index measures the area between the Lorenz curve and a hypothetical line of absolute equality, expressed as a percentage of the maximum area under the line. A Lorenz curve plots the cumulative percentages of total income received against the cumulative number of recipients, starting with the poorest individual. Therefore, a Gini index of zero represents perfect equality, while an index of 100 implies perfect inequality.

The Gini index provides a convenient summary measure of the degree of inequality. Data on the distribution of income or consumption come from nationally representative household surveys. Where the original data from the household survey were available, they have been used to calculate the income or consumption shares by quintile. Otherwise, shares have been estimated from the best available grouped data.

The distribution data have been adjusted for household size, providing a more consistent measure of per capita income or consumption.

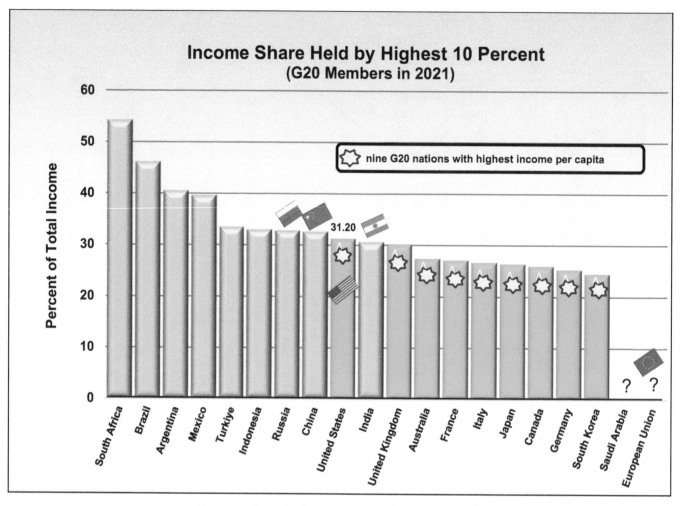

Income Share Held by Highest 10 Percent
(G20 Members in 2021)

nine G20 nations with highest income per capita

31.20

Percent of Total Income

South Africa, Brazil, Argentina, Mexico, Turkiye, Indonesia, Russia, China, United States, India, United Kingdom, Australia, France, Italy, Japan, Canada, Germany, South Korea, Saudi Arabia, European Union

Source: The World Bank, https://databank.worldbank.org/source/world-development-indicators, SI.DST.10TH.10, accessed 8-15-23, https://data.worldbank.org/summary-terms-of-use

In 2021, the income share held by the top 10 percent in the U.S. was 31.2 percent, ranking ninth among G20 members and approximately the same as Russia, China, and India. However, the U.S. ranked highest among the nine highest income per capita G20 nations.

Inequality in the distribution of income is reflected in the share of income or consumption accruing to a portion of the population ranked by income or consumption levels. The portions ranked lowest by personal income receive the smallest shares of total income.

Data on the distribution of income or consumption come from nationally representative household surveys. Where the original data from the household survey were available, they have been used to directly calculate the income or consumption shares by quintile. Otherwise, shares have been estimated from the best available grouped data.

The distribution data have been adjusted for household size, providing a more consistent measure of per capita income or consumption.

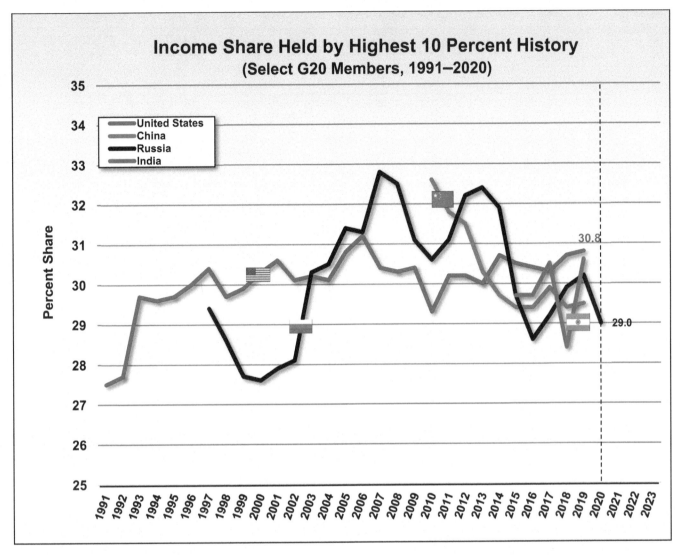

Source: The World Bank, https://databank.worldbank.org/source/world-development-indicators, SI.DST.10TH.10, accessed 8-15-23, https://data.worldbank.org/summary-terms-of-use

In 2020, the income share held by the top 10 percent in the U.S. had reached near the highest level over the previous 30-year period, and was 12 percent higher than in 1991.

Inequality in the distribution of income is reflected in the share of income or consumption accruing to a portion of the population ranked by income or consumption levels. The portions ranked lowest by personal income receive the smallest shares of total income.

Data on the distribution of income or consumption come from nationally representative household surveys. Where the original data from the household survey were available, they have been used to directly calculate the income or consumption shares by quintile. Otherwise, shares have been estimated from the best available grouped data.

The distribution data have been adjusted for household size, providing a more consistent measure of per capita income or consumption.

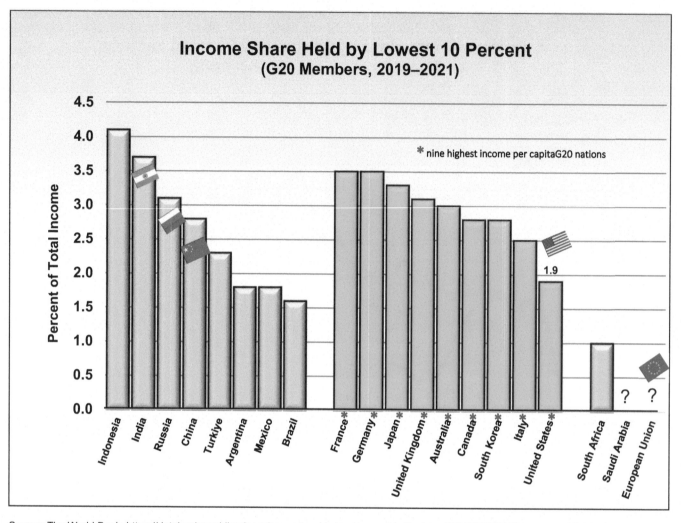

Income Share Held by Lowest 10 Percent
(G20 Members, 2019–2021)

Source: The World Bank, https://databank.worldbank.org/source/world-development-indicators, SI.DST.FRST.10, accessed 8-15-23, https://data.worldbank.org/summary-terms-of-use

In the 2019–21, period, the share of income for the lowest 10 percent in the U.S. was 1.9 percent, placing the U.S. in the bottom among the nine G20 members with the highest income per capita. This share was lower than India's, Russia's, and China's.

Inequality in the distribution of income is reflected in the share of income or consumption accruing to a portion of the population ranked by income or consumption levels. The portions ranked lowest by personal income receive the smallest shares of total income.

Data on the distribution of income or consumption come from nationally representative household surveys. Where the original data from the household survey were available, they have been used to directly calculate the income or consumption shares by quintile. Otherwise, shares have been estimated from the best available grouped data.

The distribution data have been adjusted for household size, providing a more consistent measure of per capita income or consumption. No adjustment has been made for spatial differences in cost of living within countries, because the data needed for such calculations are generally unavailable.

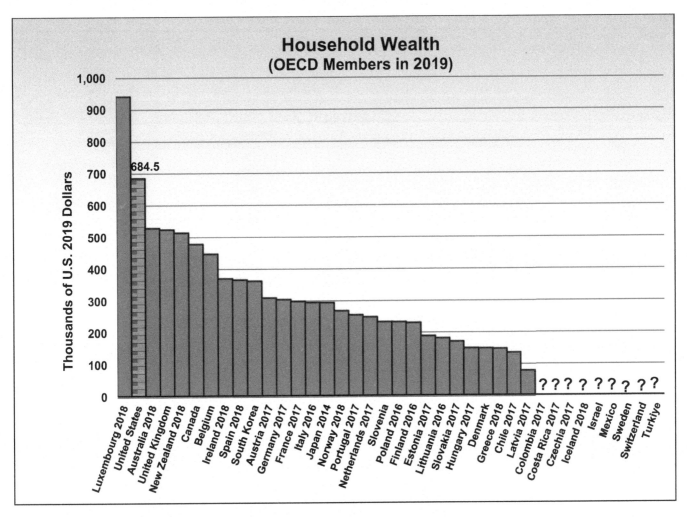

Household Wealth
(OECD Members in 2019)

Sources: OECD, https://stats.oecd.org/Index.aspx?DataSetCode=WEALTH, accessed 5-20-23

In 2019, the U.S. ranked second, after Luxembourg, for highest household wealth among the 29 OECD members for whom data existed. (Note that dates shown as suffix to nation names specify any exceptions to the 2019 date of data.)

Household wealth considers the total wealth: financial and non-financial assets, net of liabilities, held by private households resident in the nation. Non-financial assets include the principal residence, other real estate properties, vehicles, valuables and other non-financial assets (e.g., other consumer durables). It is compiled following the OECD Guidelines for Micro Statistics on Household Wealth (OECD, 2013).

Chapter 12

Inflation and Employment

Overview of Inflation and Employment

In 2022, the consumer price index (CPI) in the U.S. was at 134.2 when the base year 2010, was equal to 100. This level was approximately the same as for one-third of the G20 nations. By contrast, those nations with the highest CPI, South Sudan, Sudan and Zimbabwe, had levels 50 to 200 times greater.

Comparing the CPI growth rate among leading G20 nations, the U.S. and China experienced approximately the same growth rate between 2000 and 2021, increasing by approximately 25 percent per decade. In contrast, both Russia and India have experienced about the same CPI growth since 2006, approximately doubling every decade.

In 2022, during the COVID-19 pandemic, the U.S. inflation rate for consumer prices rose to 8.0 percent, and ranked as the fifth highest among the 17 G20 members with available data. The high U.S. rate was lower than the European Union's level of 9.2 percent and lower than the G20 average of 10.1 percent which included Turkiye's extreme rate of 72.3 percent. After removing Turkiye from the G20 average the remaining average was 6.3 percent. The U.S. inflation rate also ranked below the OECD's 38-member average of 10.8 percent. After removing Turkiye from the OECD average the revised average was 9.1 percent. Japan's inflation rate was 2.5 percent, the lowest of G20 or OECD members.

Between 1980 and 2020, the U.S. experienced very uniform CPI growth over that 40-year period of approximately 17 points per decade. However, between 2021 and 2022, during the COVID-19 pandemic which began in March 2020, that rate jumped to approximately 15 points over that two-year period.

Over the four-decade period between 1982 and 2022, the U.S. consumer experienced an erosion of the purchasing power of the U.S. dollar by approximately two-thirds in the urban areas of the country. Goods and services that were purchased for $1.00 in 1982 cost $3.00 in 2022.

On October 1, 2019, the U.S. unemployment rate was officially at 3.6 percent, the lowest level since 1969. On April 1, 2020—after the World Health Organization (WHO) declared COVID-19 a pandemic on March 11, 2020, which disrupted employment globally—that rate had reached 13.0 percent, the highest level since World War II. By April 1, 2023, total unemployment had recovered to achieve a new low of 3.5 percent.

In 2021, the U.S. labor force participation rate was at 61.7 percent, approximately the same as for the average G20 member. In 1972, the U.S. labor force participation rate was at 79.0 percent, however, between 1973 and 2021, labor force participation rate in the U.S. steadily declined by approximately one-sixth. Between 1986 and 2021, the labor force participation in the U.S declined from 76.3 percent to 61.7 percent, representing a reduction of approximately 21 million workers. During that same period the rate in the European Union participation rate dropped from 70.3 percent to 63.3 percent.

In 2016, the level of job insecurity in the U.S. was approximately the same as for the average OECD member.

~

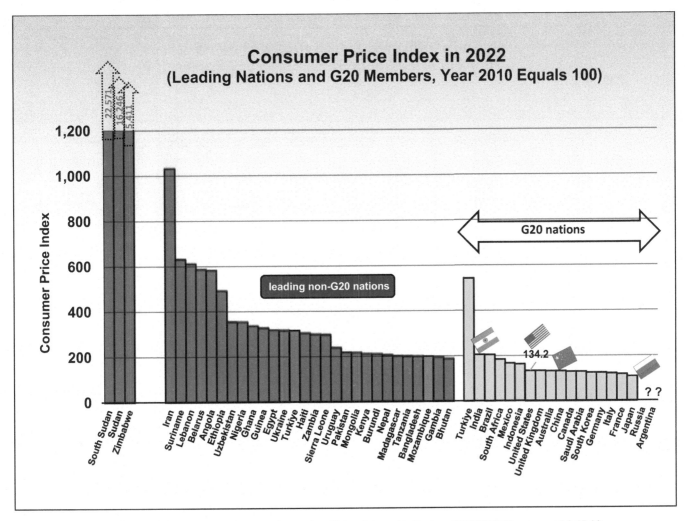

Source: The World Bank, https://databank.worldbank.org/source/world-development-indicators, FP.CPI.TOTL, accessed 8-15-23
https://data.worldbank.org/summary-terms-of-use

In 2022, the consumer price index (CPI) in the U.S. was at 134.2 when the base year of 2010, was equal to 100. This level was 7.5 percent above the average of the other eight highest income per capita G20 nations. By contrast, those nations with the highest CPI, South Sudan, Sudan, and Zimbabwe, had levels 50 to 200 times greater.

Consumer price indexes are constructed explicitly, using surveys of the cost of a defined basket of consumer goods and services. Consumer price indexes should be interpreted with caution. The definition of a household, the basket of goods, and the geographic (urban or rural) and income group coverage of consumer price surveys can vary widely by nation. In addition, weights are derived from household expenditure surveys, which, for budgetary reasons, tend to be conducted infrequently in developing countries, impairing comparability over time. Although useful for measuring consumer price inflation within a country, consumer price indexes are of less value in comparing countries.

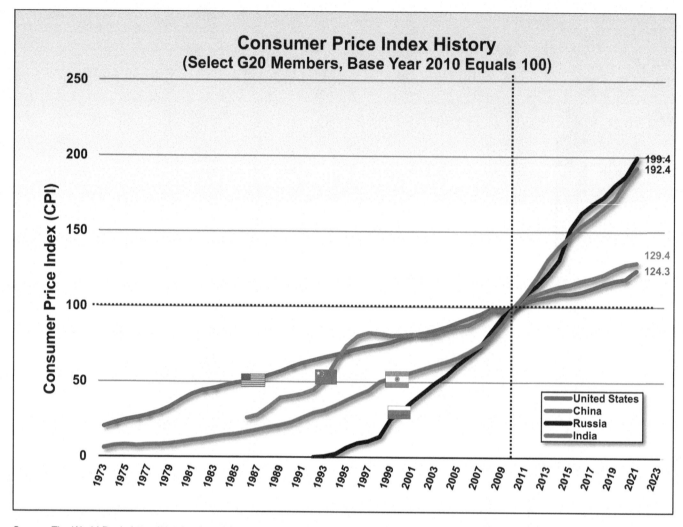

Consumer Price Index History
(Select G20 Members, Base Year 2010 Equals 100)

Source: The World Bank, https://databank.worldbank.org/source/world-development-indicators, FP.CPI.TOTL, accessed 8-15-23, https://data.worldbank.org/summary-terms-of-use

Comparing the CPI growth rate among leading G20 nations, the U.S. and China have been approximately the same between 2000 and 2021, increasing by approximately 25 percent per decade. In contrast, Russia and India have both doubled in just the past decade.

Consumer price indexes are constructed explicitly, using surveys of the cost of a defined basket of consumer goods and services. Consumer price indexes should be interpreted with caution. The definition of a household, the basket of goods, and the geographic (urban or rural) and income group coverage of consumer price surveys can vary widely by country. In addition, weights are derived from household expenditure surveys, which, for budgetary reasons, tend to be conducted infrequently in developing countries, impairing comparability over time. Although useful for measuring consumer price inflation within a country, consumer price indexes are of less value in comparing countries.

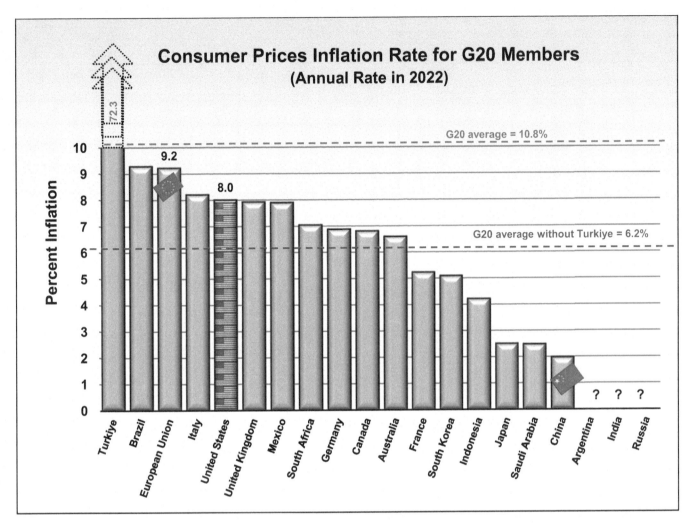

Consumer Prices Inflation Rate for G20 Members
(Annual Rate in 2022)

Source: The World Bank, https://databank.worldbank.org/source/world-development-indicators, FP.CPI.TOTL.ZG, accessed 8-15-23, https://data.worldbank.org/summary-terms-of-use

In 2022, the U.S. inflation rate for consumer prices was at 8.0 percent, and ranked as the fifth highest among the 17 G20 members with available data. The average among all G20 nations was 10.1 percent driven up by Turkiye's extreme rate of 72.3 percent. The G20 average with Turkiye removed from the average was 6.2 percent. The inflation rate in the United States (8.0 percent) was lower than in the European Union (9.2 percent).

Inflation as measured by the consumer price index reflects the annual percentage change in the cost to the average consumer of acquiring a basket of goods and services that may be fixed or changed at specified intervals, such as yearly.

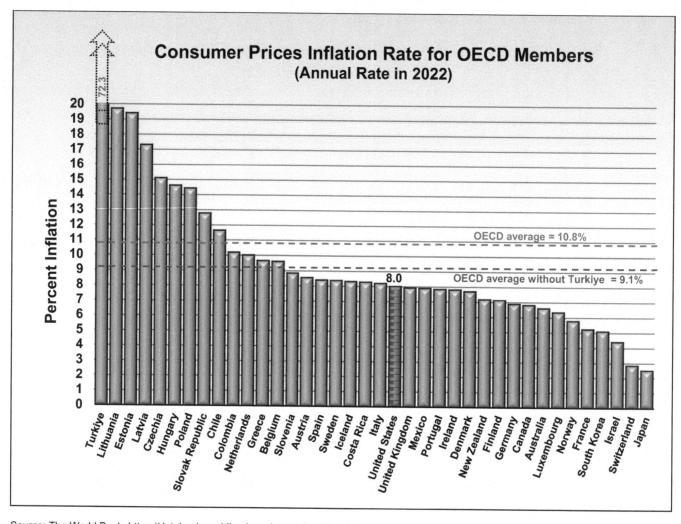

Consumer Prices Inflation Rate for OECD Members
(Annual Rate in 2022)

Source: The World Bank, https://databank.worldbank.org/source/world-development-indicators, FP.CPI.TOTL.ZG, accessed 8-15-23
https://data.worldbank.org/summary-terms-of-use

In 2022, the U.S. inflation rate for consumer prices was at 8.0 percent, and ranked as the 21st among the OECD 38 members and below the OECD average of 10.8 percent. Turkiye's rate was at the extreme level of 72.3 percent. The average with Turkiye excluded was 9.1 percent.

Inflation as measured by the consumer price index reflects the annual percentage change in the cost to the average consumer of acquiring a basket of goods and services that may be fixed or changed at specified intervals, such as yearly.

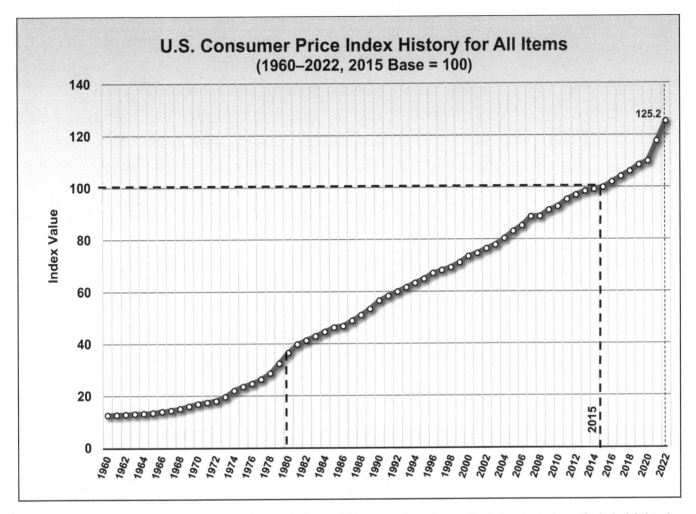

U.S. Consumer Price Index History for All Items
(1960–2022, 2015 Base = 100)

Sources: FRED, Federal Reserve Economic Data, Economic Research Division, Federal Reserve Bank of St. Louis, https://fred.stlouisfed.org/series/USACPIALLMINMEI; Organization for Economic Co-operation and Development, Consumer Price Index: All Items for the United States [USACPIALLMINMEI], retrieved from FRED, Federal Reserve Bank of St. Louis; https://fred.stlouisfed.org/series/USACPIALLMINMEI, September 12, 2023

Between 1980 and 2020, the U.S. experienced very uniform CPI growth over that 40-year period of approximately 17 points per decade. However, between 2021 and 2022, during the COVID-19 pandemic which began in March 2020, that rate jumped to approximately 15 points over that two-year period.

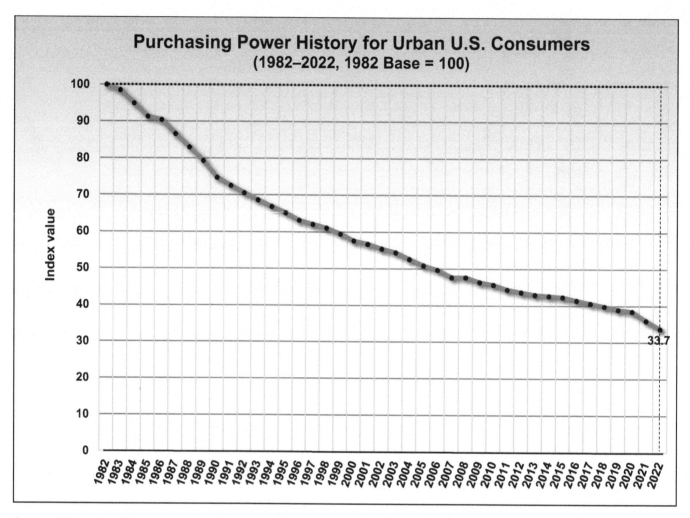

Purchasing Power History for Urban U.S. Consumers
(1982–2022, 1982 Base = 100)

Sources: FRED, Federal Reserve Economic Data, Economic Research Division, Federal Reserve Bank of St. Louis, https://fred.stlouisfed.org/series/FDHBFIN, data accessed 4/23/23. The Bank grants a non-exclusive, limited right and license to display and reproduce the charts and graphs.

Over the four-decade period, between 1982 and 2022, the U.S. experienced an erosion of the purchasing power of the U.S. consumer dollar by approximately two-thirds in the urban areas of the country. Goods and services that were purchased for $1.00 in 1982 cost $3.00 in 2022.

Mortgage Rates History in the U.S.
(1972–2022, 30-Year Fixed Rate)

Source: FRED, Federal Reserve Economic Data, Economic Research Division, Federal Reserve Bank of St. Louis, https://fred.stlouisfed.org/series/FDHBFIN, data accessed 4/23/23. The Bank grants a non-exclusive, limited right and license to display and reproduce the charts and graphs.

Since the peak in mortgage interest rates in 1981, of 16.9 percent, rates declined to a low level of 2.8 percent in 2020, then rose to 7.1 percent by 2022, during the COVID-19 pandemic which was declared in March 2020.

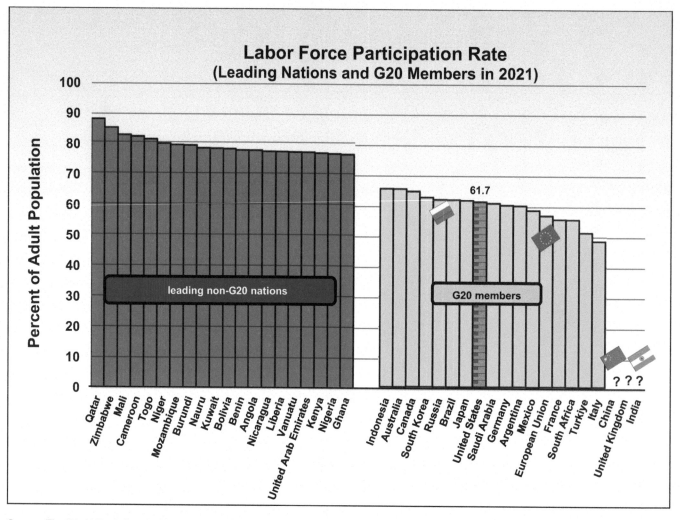

Labor Force Participation Rate
(Leading Nations and G20 Members in 2021)

Source: The World Bank, https://databank.worldbank.org/source/world-development-indicators, SL.TLF.CACT.NE.ZS, accessed 8-15-23, https://data.worldbank.org/summary-terms-of-use

In 2021, the U.S. labor force participation rate was at 61.7 percent, approximately the same as for the average G20 member and eight percent above the E.U.'s.

The labor force is the supply of labor available for producing goods and services in an economy. It includes people who are currently employed and people who are unemployed but seeking work as well as first-time job-seekers. Not everyone who works is included, however. Unpaid workers, family workers, and students are often omitted, and some countries do not count members of the armed forces. Labor force size tends to vary during the year as seasonal workers enter and leave.

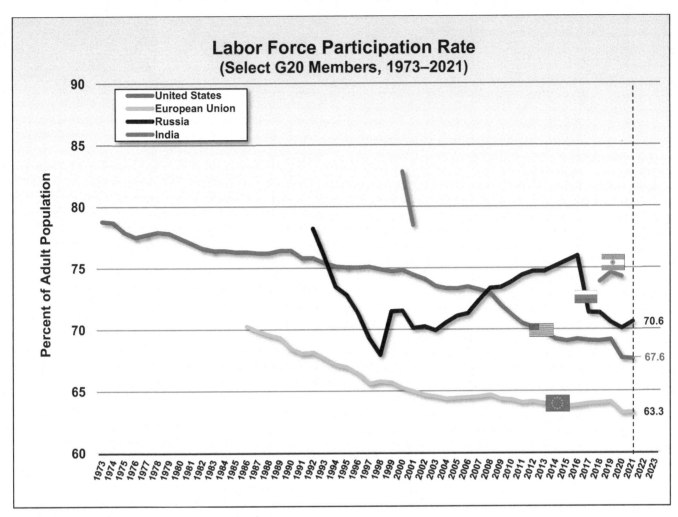

Labor Force Participation Rate
(Select G20 Members, 1973–2021)

Legend:
- United States
- European Union
- Russia
- India

Y-axis: Percent of Adult Population (60 to 90)

X-axis: 1973 to 2023

Values at right: 70.6, 67.6, 63.3

Source: The World Bank, https://databank.worldbank.org/source/world-development-indicators, SL.TLF.CACT.NE.ZS, accessed 8-15-23, https://data.worldbank.org/summary-terms-of-use

Between 1973 and 2021, labor force participation rate in the United States steadily declined by approximately one-sixth.

The labor force is the supply of labor available for producing goods and services in an economy. It includes people who are currently employed and people who are unemployed but seeking work as well as first-time job-seekers. Not everyone who works is included, however. Unpaid workers, family workers, and students are often omitted, and some countries do not count members of the armed forces. Labor force size tends to vary during the year as seasonal workers enter and leave.

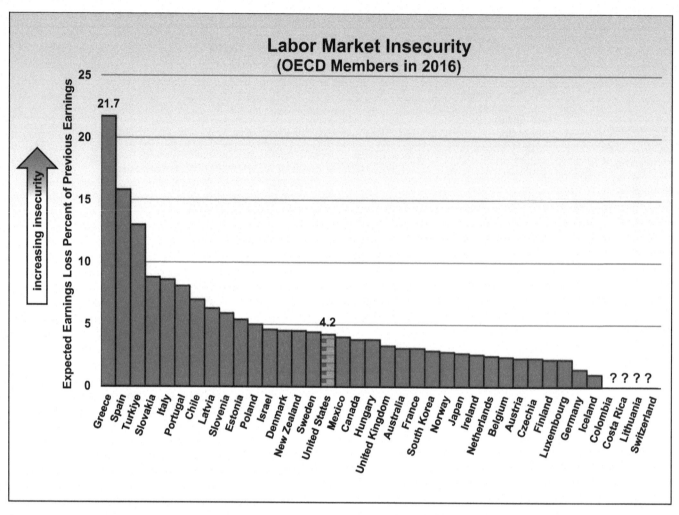

Labor Market Insecurity
(OECD Members in 2016)

Source: OECD Job quality (database), http://dotstat.oecd.org/Index.aspx?DataSetCode=JOBQ, accessed 5.20.23

In 2016, the level of job insecurity in the U.S. was approximately the same as for the average OECD member.

Labor market insecurity is defined in terms of the expected earnings loss, measured as the percentage of the previous earnings, associated with unemployment. This loss depends on the risk of becoming unemployed, the expected duration of unemployment and the degree of mitigation against these losses provided by government transfers to the unemployed (effective insurance).

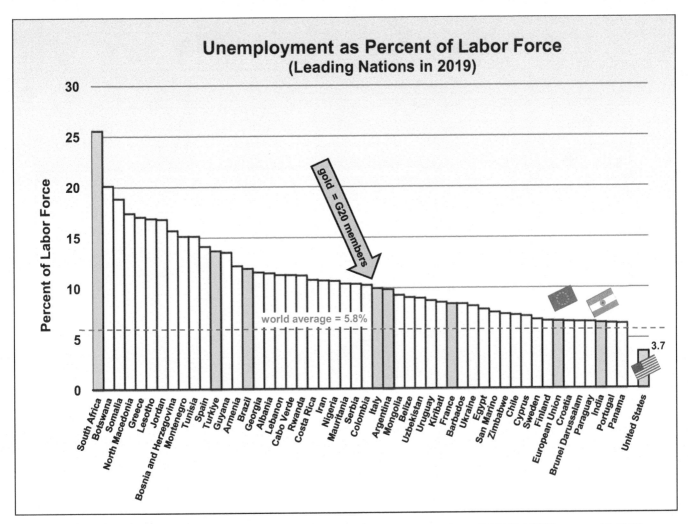

Unemployment as Percent of Labor Force
(Leading Nations in 2019)

gold = G20 members

world average = 5.8%

3.7

Source: The World Bank, https://databank.worldbank.org/source/world-development-indicators, SL.UEM.TOTL.NE.ZS, accessed 8-15-23, https://data.worldbank.org/summary-terms-of-use

In 2019, prior to the COVID-19 pandemic that disrupted employment globally, the U.S. unemployment rate of 3.7 percent was approximately one-third below the world's average rate of 5.8 percent.

The standard definition of unemployed persons is those individuals without work, seeking work in a recent past period, and currently available for work, including people who have lost their jobs or who have voluntarily left work. Persons who did not look for work but have an arrangements for a future job are also counted as unemployed.

Some unemployment is unavoidable. At any time, some workers are temporarily unemployed between jobs as employers look for the right workers and workers search for better jobs. It is the labor force or the economically active portion of the population that serves as the base for this indicator, not the total population.

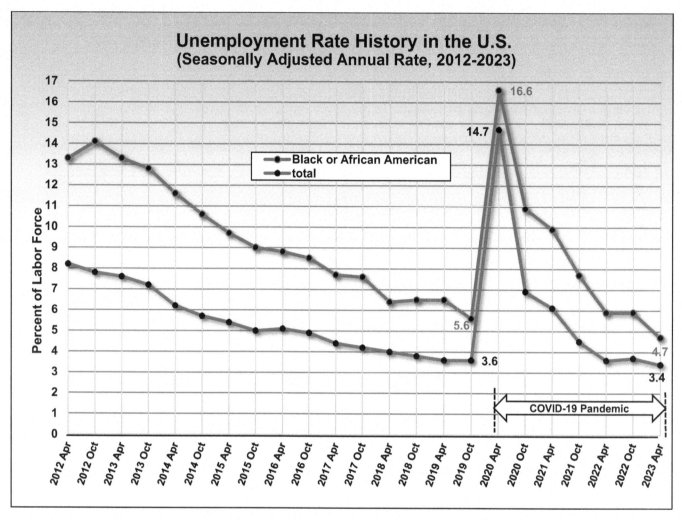

Sources: U.S. Bureau of Labor Statistics, Unemployment Rate [UNRATE], https://beta.bls.gov/dataViewer/view/timeseries/LNS14000006, accessed 9-28-23

On October 1, 2019, U.S. unemployment rate was officially 3.6 percent, the lowest level since 1969. On April 1, 2020, that rate had reached 14.7 percent, the highest level since World War II—after the World Health Organization had declared COVID-19 a pandemic on March 11, 2020, which disrupted employment globally. By April 2023, the unemployment rate in the United States fell to a low of 3.4 percent and also reached a low of 4.7 percent for Black or African Americans.

The U.S. unemployment rate represents the number of unemployed as a percentage of the labor force. Labor force data are restricted to people 16 years of age and older, who currently reside in one of the 50 states or the District of Columbia, who do not reside in institutions (e.g., penal and mental facilities, homes for the aged), and who are not on active duty in the Armed Forces.

The standard definition of unemployed persons is those individuals without work, seeking work in a recent past period, and currently available for work, including people who have lost their jobs or who have voluntarily left work. Persons who did not look for work but have arrangements for a future job are also counted as unemployed.

Chapter 13

Society

Overview of Society

In 2022, the U.S. ranked 18th for happiness, placing it in the top 10 percent of all nations. The happiness scale ranks populations based on their responses to a series of life evaluation questions that have been used for 12 years to compare nations.

The happiness rating result for the U.S. was not too different from the result of a similar survey taken among OECD member populations in 2020. That life satisfaction survey showed on average Americans rated their overall satisfaction with life at 7 of 10 points, where 10 points is best. This level was slightly above the average response among OECD members of 6.7 points.

In 2019, 88 percent of Americans self-reported that their health was "Good." The U.S. ranked second` among the OECD members, behind Canada with 89 percent for the best self-reported health. On average, only 68 percent of OECD members rated their health as "Good."

In another survey in 2020, among OECD member populations, 78 percent of Americans felt safe walking alone at night in the city or area where they live. This was comparable to the average response of 74 percent among OECD members.

OECD members have democratic forms of government, however, comparing voter turnout among countries is fundamentally difficult due to the structural differences in government institutions and different election cycles. Voter turnout data among OECD members in the 2014–2021 time period, show that on average 69 percent of eligible voters actually voted. The U.S. turnout in the 2016 election for president was 65 percent. According to the U.S. Census Bureau the 2020 U.S. presidential election had the highest voter turnout of the 21st century, with 66.8 percent of citizens 18 years and older voting in the election. These data come from surveying the civilian noninstitutionalized population in the U.S. In the U.S. 2022 midterm elections, 46 percent of eligible voters actually voted.

In 2016, the U.S. led all the G20 nations and most Western nations for the highest adult obesity rate at 36 percent—ranking tenth place in the world, and in 2019, the U.S. experienced the highest age-standardized death rate from cardiovascular disease among any of the principal U.S. partners.

In 2020, 28.5 percent of U.S. males smoked tobacco, which was below the world's average of 38 percent and below levels for France, Japan, and South Korea. France also experienced an 8 percent higher rate of age-standardized death rate due to lung cancer than the U.S., however, despite the higher smoking rates in Japan and South Korea their death rates due to lung cancer were approximately 25 percent lower the U.S. rate.

During the period 2000–2021, the U.S. reached a peak incarceration level of 2.3 million prisoners in 2008. Subsequently, the number of prisoners declined 27 percent while only Russia of the leading G20 members also experienced a decline in that same timeframe. The U.S. number of incarcerated people in 2021 was 1.69 million, still the highest level in the world and about the same number as China, but with a U.S. population approximately one-fourth that of China's. The U.S. also ranked fourth in the world for the rate of incarceration per 100,000 population which was also the highest rate among G20 nations. U.S. Incarceration levels include populations of federal and state prisons, and local jails.

In 2020, the U.S. ranked 15th among the G20 members in taxes levied by the central government measured as percent of GDP. The U.S. level of 9.9 percent was approximately one-half the rate of the average E.U. nation.

Since mortgage interest rates peaked in 1981, at 16.9 percent, rates in the U.S. had been on a downward trajectory until reaching its lowest level of 2.8 percent in 2020, then rose to 7.1 percent in 2022 during the COVID-19 pandemic which began in March 2020.

Over the period 1963–2005, the annual number of new single-family homes sold in the U.S. increased by approximately threefold, reaching a peak of 1,242,000 units in 2005. By 2010, that level had plummeted by three-fourths to 326,000 units, the lowest level since 1963. Subsequently, sales recovered to 871,000 units in 2020, but declined to 622,000 units after March 2022, during the COVID-19 pandemic.

In 2021, according to a study published by the World Bank, only two-thirds of the G20 nations demonstrate a positive respect for the rule of law. The U.S. was ranked approximately average of the highest income per capita G20 nations (principal U.S. partners).

In 2021, the World Bank published the result of an analysis that rated the level of political instability and violence among nations. Of the 19 member nations in the G20, half scored above average, whereas the U.S. was rated near zero, the lowest of any high income per capita G20 nation. Political Stability and Absence of Violence/Terrorism measures perceptions of the likelihood of political instability and/or politically motivated violence, including terrorism.

~

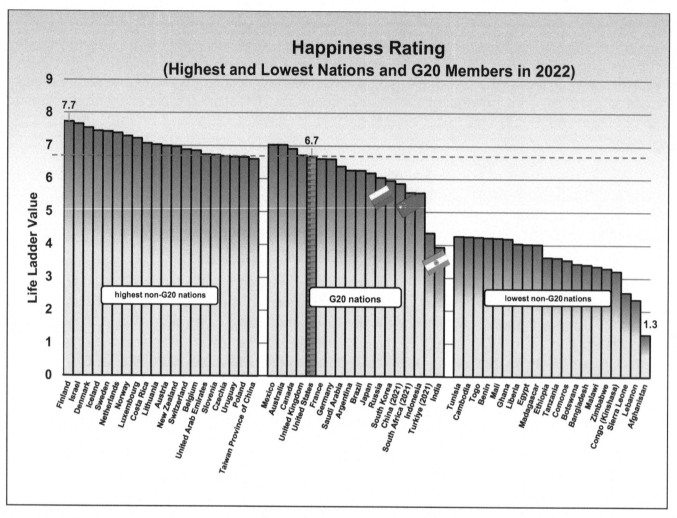

Happiness Rating
(Highest and Lowest Nations and G20 Members in 2022)

Source: Helliwell, J. F., Layard, R., Sachs, J. D., De Neve, J.-E., Aknin, L. B., & Wang, S. (Eds.). (2022). World Happiness Report 2022. New York: Sustainable Development Solutions Network, https://worldhappiness.report/, accessed 7-1-23

In 2022, the U.S. ranked sixth place among the G20 nations on the happiness scale and 15th in the world. Nordic countries and Israel ranked the highest while African and Middle Eastern countries rated lowest.

Note that data for China, South Africa and Turkiye are from 2021, the latest available, as indicated adjacent to the country name.

Life evaluations from the Gallup World Poll provide the basis for the annual happiness rankings. They are based on answers to the main life evaluation question. The Cantril ladder asks respondents to think of a ladder, with the best possible life for them being a ten and the worst possible life being a zero. They are then asked to rate their own current lives on that zero-to-ten scale. The rankings are from nationally representative samples over three years. We use observed data on the six variables and estimates of their associations with life evaluations to explain the variation across countries. They include GDP per capita, social support, healthy life expectancy, freedom, generosity, and corruption. Our happiness rankings are not based on any index of these six factors. The scores are instead based on individuals' own assessments of their lives, in particular, their answers to the single-item Cantril ladder life-evaluation question, much as epidemiologists estimate the extent to which life expectancy is affected by factors such as smoking, exercise, and diet.

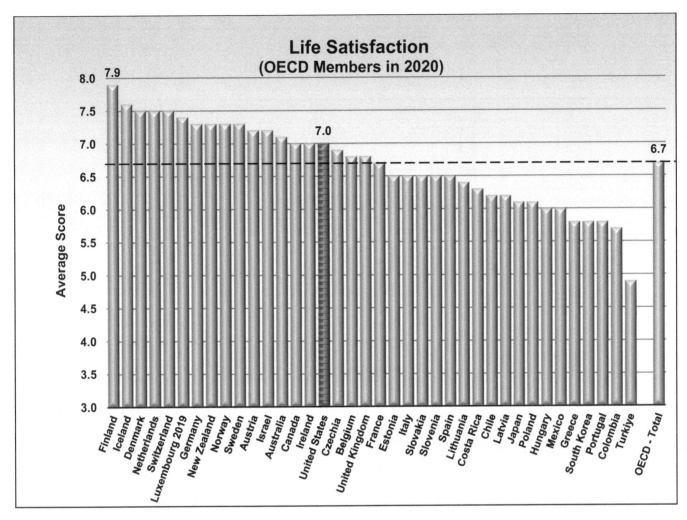

Source: OECD Better Life Index, https://stats.oecd.org/index.aspx?lang=en, accessed 5-20-23

In 2020, a survey among OECD member populations showed that on average Americans rated their overall satisfaction with life at seven of ten points, where ten points is best. This is slightly better than the average response among OECD members of 6.7 points.

Life satisfaction measures how people evaluate their life as a whole rather than their current feelings. When asked to rate their general satisfaction with life on a scale from zero-to-ten, people on average across the OECD gave it a 6.7. Life satisfaction is not evenly shared across the OECD however. Some countries—Colombia, Greece, Korea, Portugal, and Turkiye—have a relatively low level of overall life satisfaction, with average scores below six. In contrast, scores reached 7.5 or above in Denmark, Finland, Iceland, the Netherlands and Switzerland.

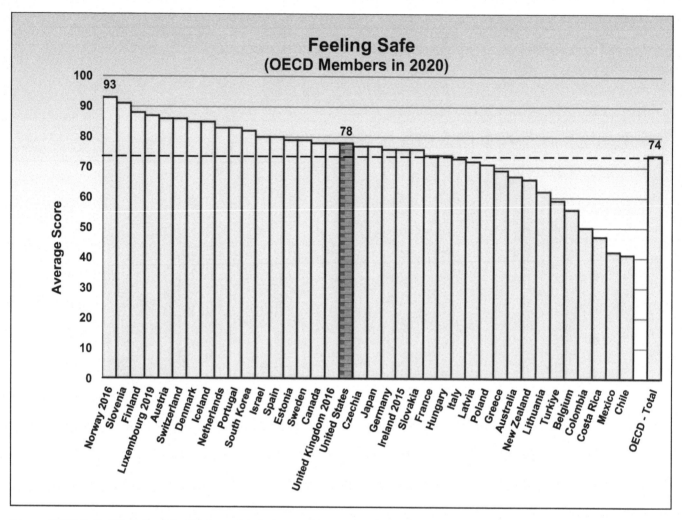

Feeling Safe
(OECD Members in 2020)

Source: OECD Better Life Index, https://stats.oecd.org/index.aspx?lang=en, accessed 5-20-23

In 2020, a survey among OECD member populations showed that 78 percent of Americans felt safe walking alone at night in the city or area where they live. That compared near the average response among OECD members of 74 percent. (Note that data for some countries are from surveys taken prior to 2020, as indicated by a date as suffix to the country name.)

The indicator is based on the question: "Do you feel safe walking alone at night in the city or area where you live?" and it shows people declaring they feel safe. According to recent data, about 74 percent of people in OECD countries say they feel safe walking alone at night. There are major differences, however, between countries. While 85 percent or more of people in Austria, Denmark, Finland, Iceland, Luxembourg, Norway, Slovenia, and Switzerland say they feel safe, the level in Brazil, Chile, Colombia, Costa Rica and Mexico is just below 50 percent, and below 40 percent in South Africa.

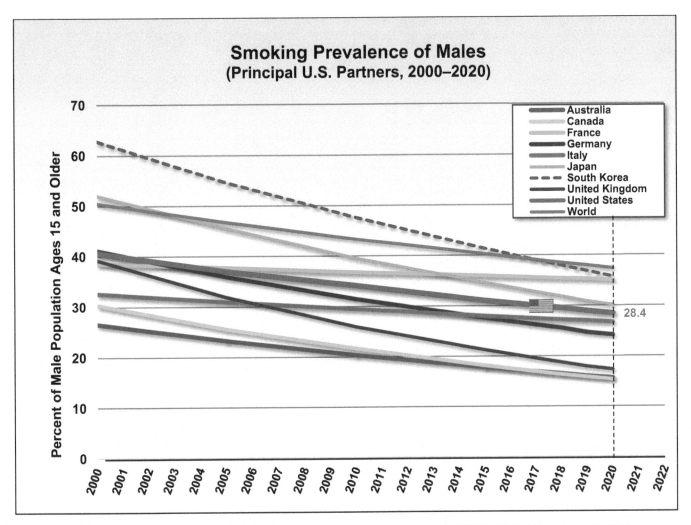

Smoking Prevalence of Males
(Principal U.S. Partners, 2000–2020)

Source: The World Bank, https://databank.worldbank.org/source/world-development-indicators, SH.PRV.SMOK.MA, accessed 8-24-23, https://data.worldbank.org/summary-terms-of-use

In 2020, 28.4 percent of American men smoked tobacco products, a reduction of 40 percent since 2000. This compared with the world's average in 2020, of 37 percent and was lower than three of the principal U.S. partners: France, Japan, and South Korea.

This graph shows the percentage of the male population ages 15 years and over who currently use any tobacco product (smoked and/or smokeless tobacco) on a daily or non-daily basis. Tobacco products include cigarettes, pipes, cigars, cigarillos, waterpipes (hookah, shisha), bidis, kretek, heated tobacco products, and all forms of smokeless (oral and nasal) tobacco. Tobacco products exclude e-cigarettes (which do not contain tobacco), "e-cigars," e-hookahs," JUUL and "e-pipes." The rates are age-standardized to the WHO Standard Population.

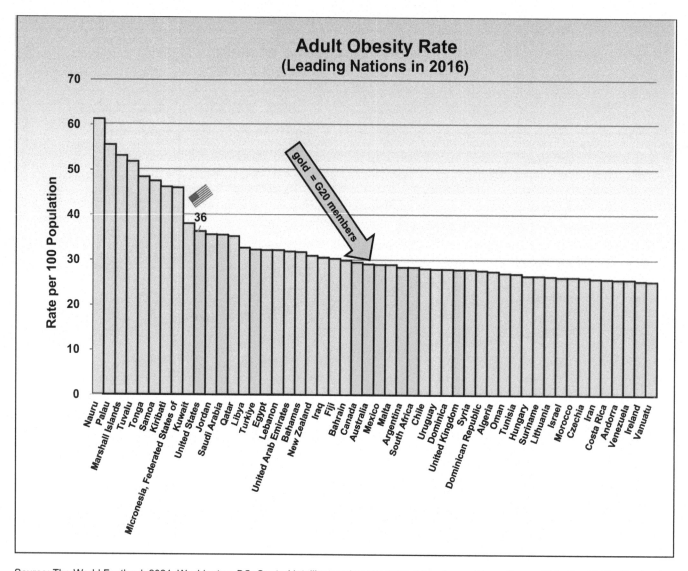

Adult Obesity Rate
(Leading Nations in 2016)

gold = G20 members

Source: The World Factbook 2021. Washington, DC: Central Intelligence Agency, 2021, https://www.cia.gov/the-world-factbook/, The Factbook is in the public domain.

In 2016, the U.S. led the G20 nations and all Western nations with the highest adult obesity rate of 36 percent, and ranked in tenth place in the world.

Adult obesity prevalence rate gives the percent of a country's population considered to be obese. Obesity is defined as an adult having a Body Mass Index (BMI) greater to or equal to 30.0. BMI is calculated by taking a person's weight in kg and dividing it by the person's squared height in meters.

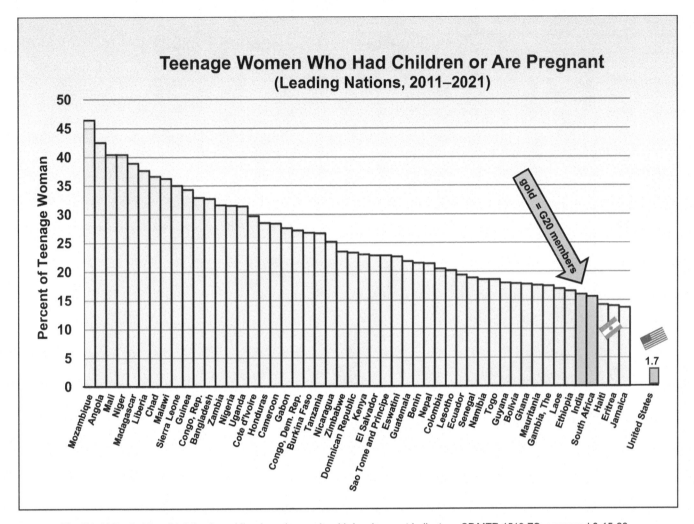

Teenage Women Who Had Children or Are Pregnant
(Leading Nations, 2011–2021)

gold = G20 members

Sources: The World Bank, https://databank.worldbank.org/source/world-development-indicators, SP.MTR.1519.ZS, accessed 8-15-23, https://data.worldbank.org/summary-terms-of-use, https://www.cdc.gov/teenpregnancy/about/index.htm

The data are for 2011–2021, the latest information available. There were 25 nations where at least 20 percent of teenage women were pregnant or already had children. Although there were no U.S. data included in this World Bank survey, the CDC reported that the U.S. teen birth rate was substantially higher than in other Western industrialized nations. In 2019, the CDC published the U.S. birth rate as 16.7 per 1,000 women aged 15–19 years.

Teenage mothers are the percentage of women aged 15–19 years who already have children or are currently pregnant. Having a child during the teenage years limits girls' opportunities for better education, jobs, and income. Pregnancy is more likely to be unintended during the teenage years, and births are more likely to be premature and are associated with greater risks of complications during delivery and of death. In many countries maternal mortality is a leading cause of death among women of reproductive age, although most of those deaths are preventable. Infants of adolescent mothers are also more likely to have low birth weight, which can have a long-term impact on their health and development. Complications from pregnancy and childbirth are the leading cause of death among girls aged 15–19 years in many low and middle-income countries.

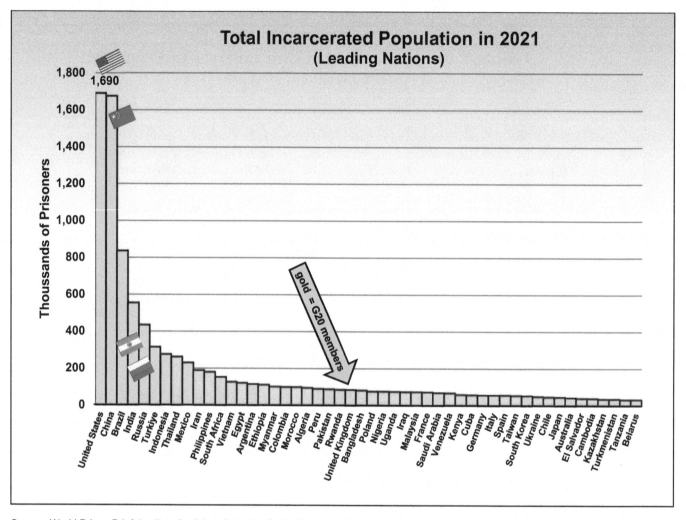

Total Incarcerated Population in 2021
(Leading Nations)

gold = G20 members

Thoussands of Prisoners (y-axis)

1,690 (United States)

Source: World Prison Brief, Institute for Crime & Justice Policy Research, https://www.prisonstudies.org/world-prison-brief-data, data accessed 5-21-23

In 2021, the U.S. led the world for having the largest number of incarcerated persons, at 1.69 million, approximately the same number as China.

The World Prison Brief (WPB) is a unique database that provides free access to information about prison systems throughout the world. Country information is updated on a monthly basis, using data largely derived from governmental or other official sources.

In the U.S. in 2021, according to the U.S. Bureau of Justice Statistics: 636,300 in local jails as of 6/30/21, 959,300 in state prisons as of 12/31/21, 171,600 in federal prisons as of 12/31/21. In addition, there are prisoners in the Indian Country jails (2,040 in 2021).

In 2019, 23.3 percent of all prisoners in the U.S. were pre-trial/remand prisoners and 10.2 percent of all prisoners in the U.S. were female.

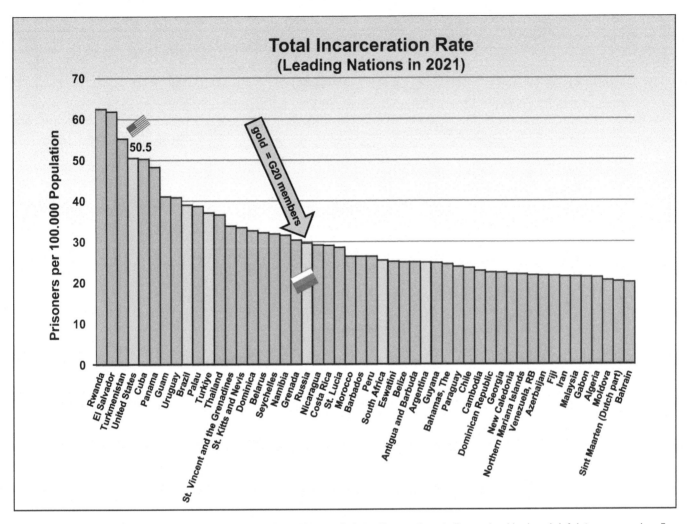

Total Incarceration Rate
(Leading Nations in 2021)

Source: World Prison Brief, Institute for Crime & Justice Policy Research, https://www.prisonstudies.org/world-prison-brief-data, accessed on 5-21-23

In 2021, the U.S. ranked fourth in the world for incarceration rate per 100,000 population and ranked in first place for incarceration rate among G20 nations.

The World Prison Brief (WPB) is a unique database that provides free access to information about prison systems throughout the world. Country information is updated on a monthly basis, using data largely derived from governmental or other official sources.

The rate in the U.S. is based on an estimated national population of 332.70 million at the end of 2021 (U.S. Census Bureau).

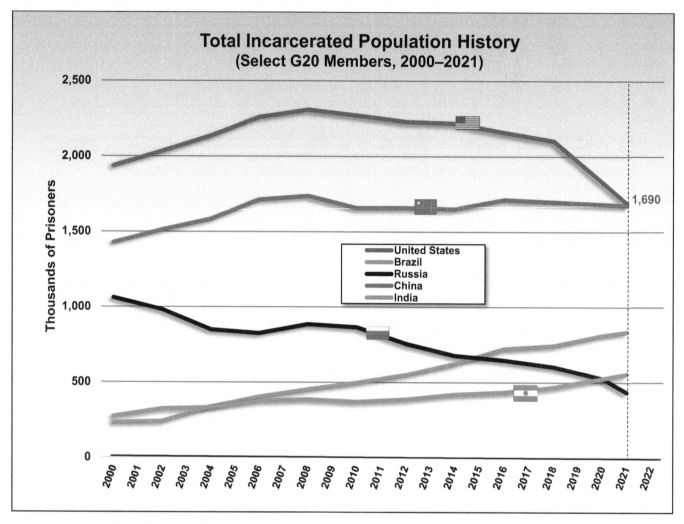

Source: World Prison Brief, Institute for Crime & Justice Policy Research, https://www.prisonstudies.org/world-prison-brief-data, accessed 5-21-23

During the period 2000–2021, the U.S. reached a peak incarceration level of 2.3 million prisoners in 2008. Subsequently, the number of prisoners declined 27 percent to 1.69 million in 2021. Of the leading G20 members only Russia has seen a decline in the same timeframe.

The World Prison Brief (WPB) is a unique database that provides free access to information about prison systems throughout the world. Country information is updated on a monthly basis, using data largely derived from governmental or other official sources.

In 2019, 23.3 percent of all prisoners in the U.S. were pre-trial/remand prisoners and 10.2 percent of all prisoners in the U.S. were female.

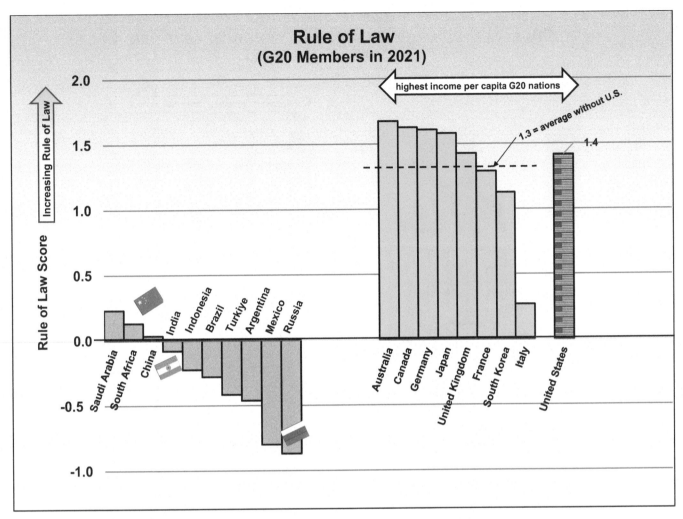

Source: The World Bank, https://databank.worldbank.org/source/world-development-indicators, SG.GEN.PARL.ZS, https://data.worldbank.org/summary-terms-of-use, accessed 7-9-23

In 2021, according to a study published by the World Bank, only two-thirds of the G20 nations experienced a positive respect for the rule of law. The U.S. was ranked approximately average among the highest income per capita G20 nations.

Rule of Law captures perceptions of the extent to which agents have confidence in and abide by the rules of society, and in particular the quality of contract enforcement, property rights, the police, and the courts, as well as the likelihood of crime and violence. Estimate gives the country's score on the aggregate indicator, in units of a standard normal distribution, i.e., ranging from approximately -2.5 to 2.5. The Worldwide Governance Indicators (WGI) are a research dataset summarizing the views on the quality of governance provided by a large number of enterprise, citizen and expert survey respondents in industrial and developing countries. These data are gathered from a number of survey institutes, think tanks, non-governmental organizations, international organizations, and private sector firms. The WGI do not reflect the official views of the Natural Resource Governance Institute, the Brookings Institution, the World Bank, its Executive Directors, or the countries they represent. The WGI are not used by the World Bank Group to allocate resources.

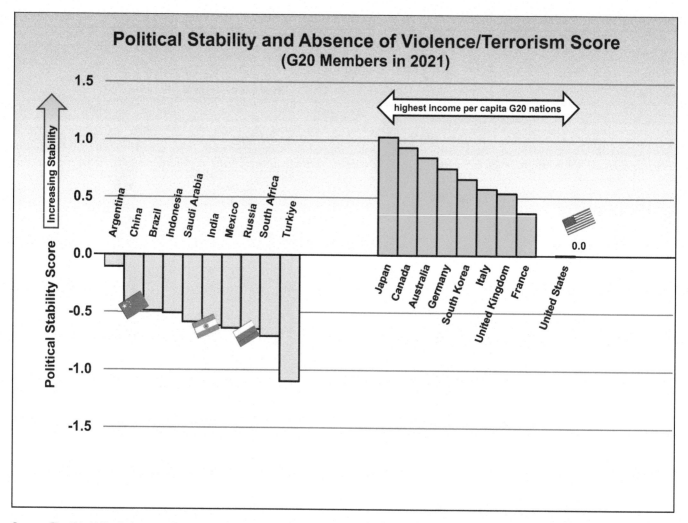

Source: The World Bank, https://databank.worldbank.org/source/world-development-indicators, PV.EST, https://data.worldbank.org/summary-terms-of-use, accessed 7-9-23

In 2021, the World Bank published the result of an analysis that rated the level of political instability and violence among nations. Of the 19 member nations of the G20, half scored above average, whereas the U.S. was rated near zero, the lowest of any of the high income-per-capita G20 nations.

Political Stability and Absence of Violence/Terrorism measures perceptions of the likelihood of political instability and/or politically motivated violence, including terrorism. Estimate gives the country's score on the aggregate indicator, in units of a standard normal distribution, i.e., ranging from approximately –2.5 to 2.5.

The Worldwide Governance Indicators (WGI) are a research dataset summarizing the views on the quality of governance provided by a large number of enterprise, citizen and expert survey respondents in industrial and developing countries. These data are gathered from a number of survey institutes, think tanks, non-governmental organizations, international organizations, and private sector firms. The WGI do not reflect the official views of the Natural Resource Governance Institute, the Brookings Institution, the World Bank, its Executive Directors, or the countries they represent. The WGI are not used by the World Bank Group to allocate resources.

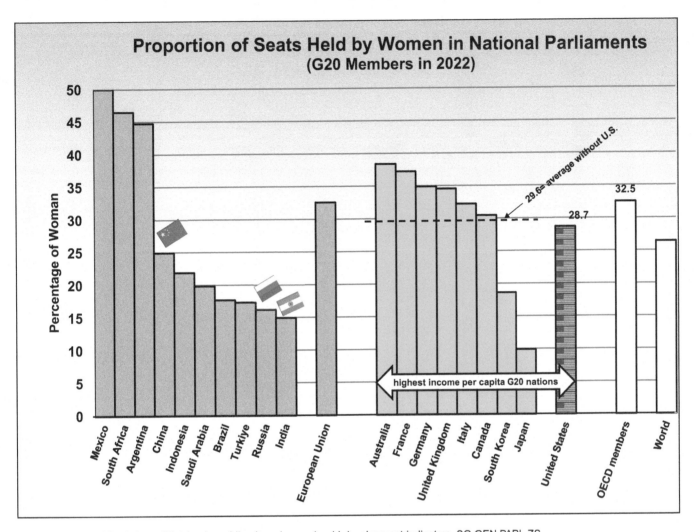

Proportion of Seats Held by Women in National Parliaments
(G20 Members in 2022)

Source: The World Bank, https://databank.worldbank.org/source/world-development-indicators, SG.GEN.PARL.ZS, https://data.worldbank.org/summary-terms-of-use, accessed 7-9-23

In 2022, women held 29 percent of the legislative seats in the U.S. congress, which was about 8 percent below the average of the other high income per capita G20 nations.

Women in parliaments are the percentage of parliamentary seats in a single or lower chamber held by women. The proportion of seats held by women in national parliaments is the number of seats held by women members in single or lower chambers of national parliaments, expressed as a percentage of all occupied seats; it is derived by dividing the total number of seats occupied by women by the total number of seats in parliament. National parliaments can be bicameral or unicameral. This indicator covers the single chamber in unicameral parliaments and the lower chamber in bicameral parliaments. It does not cover the upper chamber of bicameral parliaments. Seats are usually won by members in general parliamentary elections. Seats may also be filled by nomination, appointment, indirect election, rotation of members and by election. Seats refer to the number of parliamentary mandates, or the number of members of parliament.

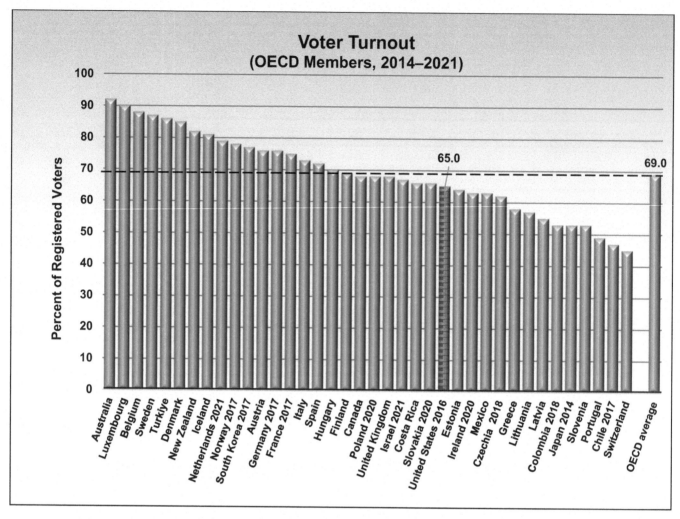

Voter Turnout
(OECD Members, 2014–2021)

Sources: OECD Better Life Index, https://stats.oecd.org/index.aspx?lang=en, accessed 5-20-23, U.S. Census bureau, https://www.census.gov/newsroom/press-releases/2021/2020-presidential-election-voting-and-registration-tables-now-available.html

Comparing voter turnout among countries is fundamentally difficult due to the different forms of government and different election cycles. The data presented are among OECD members voting in the 2014–2021 time period. The specific year for each nation was based on data availability and election cycle differences among nations, however most data are from 2020. Data from surveys taken in other years are indicated by the year listed as a suffix to the country name.

Voter turnout for OECD members averaged 69 percent of eligible voters, while the U.S. turnout in the 2016 election for president was 65 percent. According to the U.S. Census Bureau the 2020 U.S. presidential election had the highest voter turnout of the 21st century, with 66.8 percent of citizens 18 years and older voting in the election. These data come from surveying the civilian noninstitutionalized population in the U.S.

Voter turnout is defined as the ratio between the number of individuals that cast a ballot during an election (whether this vote is valid or not) to the population registered to vote. As institutional features of voting systems vary a lot across countries and across types of elections, the indicator refers to the elections (parliamentary or presidential) that have attracted the largest number of voters in each country. Voter turnout is defined as the percentage of the registered population that voted during an election.

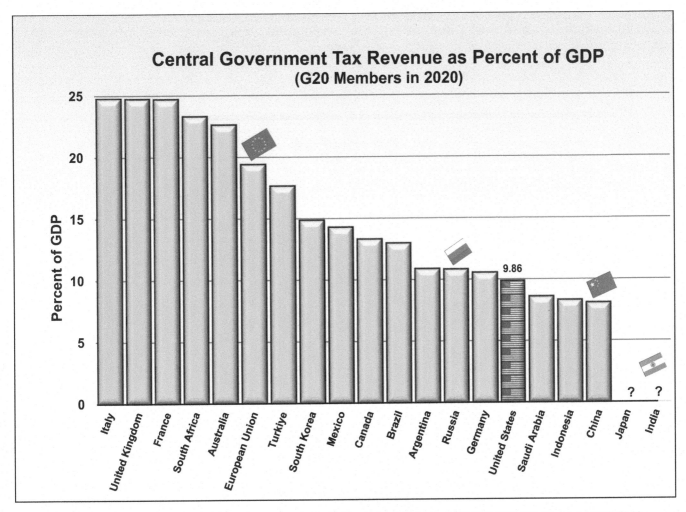

Central Government Tax Revenue as Percent of GDP
(G20 Members in 2020)

Source: The World Bank, https://databank.worldbank.org/source/world-development-indicators, GC.TAX.TOTL.GD.ZS, accessed 8-15-23, https://data.worldbank.org/summary-terms-of-use

In 2020, the U.S. ranked 15th among the G20 members in taxes levied by the central government measured as percent of GDP. That level was approximately one-half the rate of the average E.U. nation.

Tax revenue refers to compulsory transfers to the central government for public purposes. Certain compulsory transfers such as fines, penalties, and most social security contributions are excluded. Refunds and corrections of erroneously collected tax revenue are treated as negative revenue. The International Monetary Fund (IMF)'s Government Finance Statistics Manual 2014, harmonized with the 2008 SNA, recommends an accrual accounting method, focusing on all economic events affecting assets, liabilities, revenues, and expenses, not just those represented by cash transactions. It accounts for all changes in stocks, so stock data at the end of an accounting period equal stock data at the beginning of the period plus flows over the period. The 1986 manual considered only debt stocks.

Chapter 14

Education

Overview of Education

In 2018, prior to the COVID-19 pandemic that disrupted international travel, the U.S. hosted approximately 1.1 million international college students. They accounted for approximately 5.5 percent of all tertiary students in the U.S. that year. The U.S. was the world's leading destination for tertiary students studying abroad. That number had declined 14 percent to 948,000 for the semester beginning in 2021, while the COVID-19 pandemic still persisted. In 2021, China was the nation of origin for 35 percent of the international students attending college in the U.S., the most from any country. Together, students from China plus India made up 52.5 percent of all international college students in the U.S.

The top 12 destinations for international tertiary students in the world were all G20 nations.

In 2020, the U.S. ranked seventh in the world for percent of aged 25 years and older with educational attainment of master's degree or higher and was in first place in the world for percent of aged 25 years and older with educational attainment of doctoral degree or higher.

In 2021, approximately one-third of adult females in India were illiterate. Many of the countries with the lowest literacy rate for women were located in Africa, with Chad having the lowest literacy rate of 18 percent. Approximately one-of-five women in one-quarter of the world's 193 nations were illiterate. Although the U.S. was not included in this world survey, according to the Barbara Bush Foundation for Family Literacy: "130 million Americans—54 percent of adults between the ages of 16 and 74 years old—lack proficiency in literacy, essentially reading below the equivalent of a sixth-grade level" (see barbarabush.org).

In 2017, the U.S. ranked in the bottom third for number of years of education for OECD members. The U.S. averaged 17 years compared with 20 years for the top tier countries: Australia, Finland, and Sweden.

In 2018, the U.S. spent $14,439 per elementary and secondary student for education (expressed in 2020 U.S. dollars), the fourth-highest level among 36 OECD members reporting data, and 34 percent above the average OECD expenditure. For postsecondary students the U.S. spent $35,080 per student (expressed in 2020 U.S. dollars), the second-highest level among 37 OECD members reporting data, and approximately double the average OECD expenditures.

In 2020, expenditure on education per capita in the U.S. was 2.2 times the OECD average and 3.1 times more than the E.U.'s average, however, mathematical literacy scores for U.S. 15-year-old boys and girls were below average. For science literacy they scored in the second-highest quartile and for reading the boys were in the top quartile while girls were in the second-highest quartile. These results were inconsistent with the extremely high expenditure per capita for education in the U.S.

Low literacy proficiencies by U.S. children were also apparent in the assessments made by the National Center for Education Statistics (NCES). This organization is the primary statistical agency of the U.S. Department of Education. NCES has a Congressional mandate to collect, collate, analyze, and report complete statistics on the condition of American education; conduct and publish reports; and review and report on education activities internationally.

In 2022, NCES conducted assessments of reading and mathematics for age nine students to examine student achievement during the COVID-19 pandemic. Average scores for age nine students in 2022 declined five points in reading and seven points in mathematics compared to 2020. This was the largest average score decline in reading since 1990, and the first ever score decline in mathematics. Assessments were also conducted for 13-year-old students from October to December of the 2022/23 school year. The average scores for 13-year-olds declined four points in reading and nine points in mathematics compared to the previous assessment administered during the 2019/20 school year. Compared to a decade ago, the average scores declined seven points in reading and 14 points in mathematics.

~

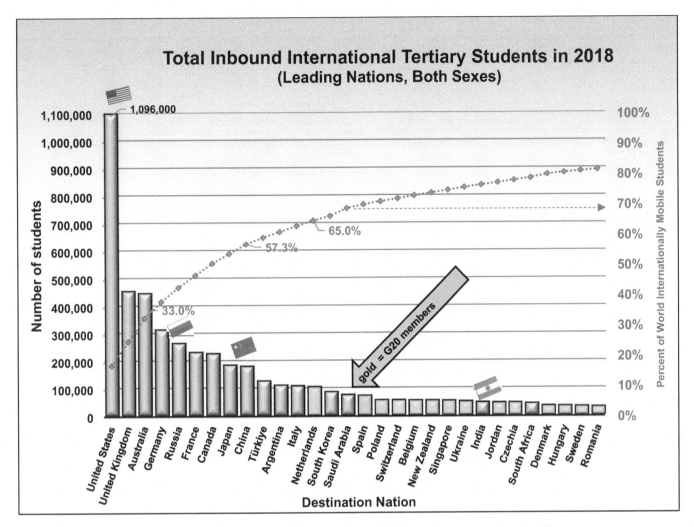

Total Inbound International Tertiary Students in 2018
(Leading Nations, Both Sexes)

Source: Institute of International Education, iie.org, https://opendoorsdata.org/annual-release/international-students/, https://studyabroad.state.gov/value-study-abroad/study-abroad-data, accessed 6/26/23,

In 2018, prior to the COVID-19 pandemic that disrupted international travel, the U.S. was the world's leader for destination of tertiary students studying abroad. The top 12 destinations for international tertiary students were all G20 nations. In 2021, the number of students inbound to the U.S. had declined to 948,000, while the COVID-19 pandemic continued.

Established in 1919, Institute of International Education (IIE) is a global not-for-profit that creates and implements international education programs, conducts research, and provides life-changing opportunities for students and scholars worldwide.

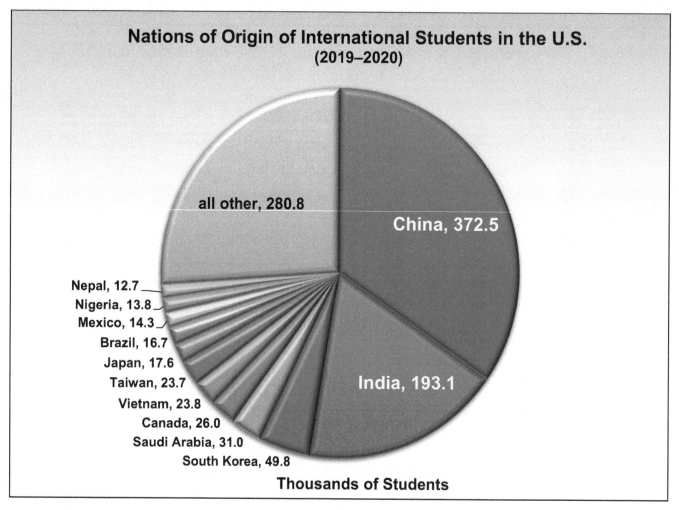

Nations of Origin of International Students in the U.S.
(2019–2020)

all other, 280.8

China, 372.5

India, 193.1

Nepal, 12.7
Nigeria, 13.8
Mexico, 14.3
Brazil, 16.7
Japan, 17.6
Taiwan, 23.7
Vietnam, 23.8
Canada, 26.0
Saudi Arabia, 31.0
South Korea, 49.8

Thousands of Students

Sources: Institute of International Education. (2022). "Leading Places of Origin of International Students, 2000/01 - 2021/22" Open Doors Report, https://opendoorsdata.org/ accessed on 5-1-23

In 2019–2020, prior to the COVID-19 pandemic, the U.S. hosted 1,075,496 international tertiary students which accounted for 5.5 percent of all U.S. tertiary students. Of all international students the largest nation of origin was China, accounting for 35 percent of all those hosted in the U.S. Together, students from China plus India made up 52.5 percent of all international tertiary students in the U.S.

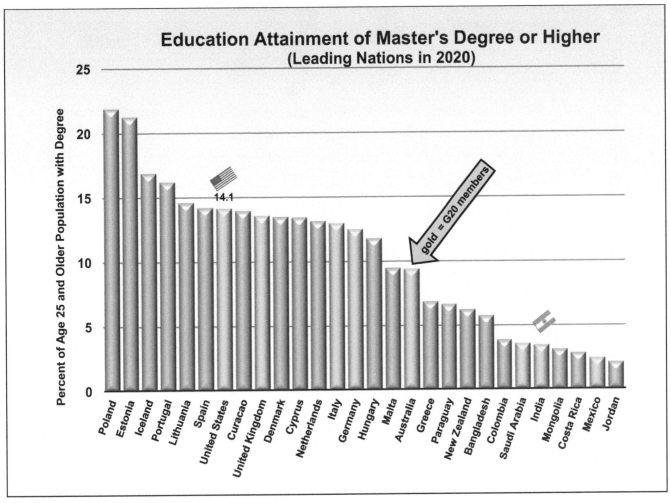

Education Attainment of Master's Degree or Higher
(Leading Nations in 2020)

Source: The World Bank, https://databank.worldbank.org/source/world-development-indicators, SE.TER.CUAT.MS.MA.ZS, accessed 8-15-23, https://data.worldbank.org/summary-terms-of-use

In 2020, the U.S. ranked seventh in the world for percent of age 25 and older with educational attainment of master's degree or higher.

The percent is calculated by dividing the number of population aged 25 years and older who attained or completed master's or equivalent by the total population of the same age-group and multiplying by 100.

Data are collected by the UNESCO Institute for Statistics mainly from national population census, household survey, and labor force survey. All the data are mapped to the International Standard Classification of Education (ISCED) to ensure the comparability of education programs at the international level. The current version was formally adopted by UNESCO member states in 2011.

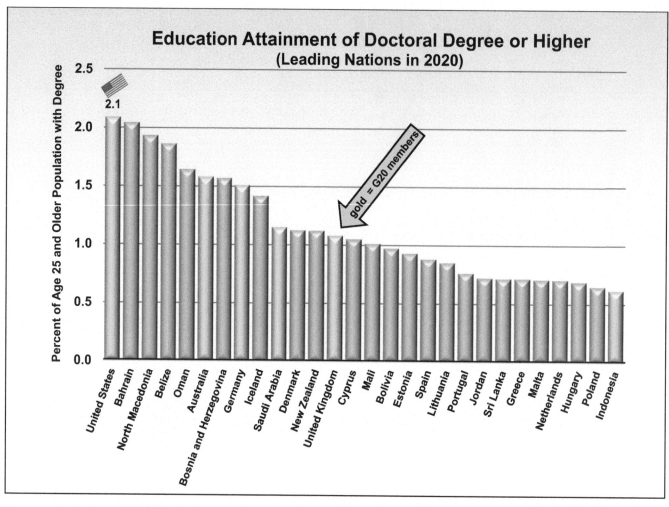

Education Attainment of Doctoral Degree or Higher
(Leading Nations in 2020)

Source: The World Bank, https://databank.worldbank.org/source/world-development-indicators, SE.TER.CUAT.DO.FE.ZS, accessed 8-15-23, https://data.worldbank.org/summary-terms-of-use

In 2020, the U.S. ranked first in the world for percent of aged 25 years and older with educational attainment of doctoral degree or higher.

The percent is calculated by dividing the number of population ages 25 and older who attained or completed doctoral or equivalent by the total population of the same age-group and multiplying by 100.

Data are collected by the UNESCO Institute for Statistics mainly from national population census, household survey, and labor force survey. All the data are mapped to the International Standard Classification of Education (ISCED) to ensure the comparability of education programs at the international level. The current version was formally adopted by UNESCO member states in 2011.

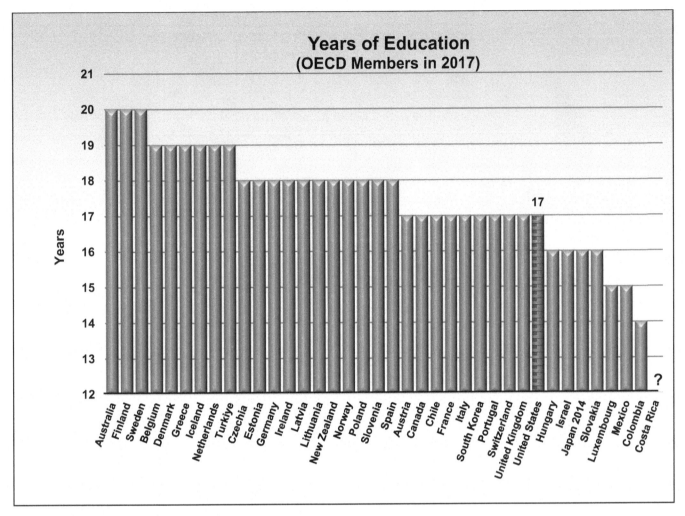

Source: OECD Education at a Glance. https://stats.oecd.org/index.aspx?lang=en accessed 5-20-23

In 2017, the U.S. ranked in the bottom third for years of education for OECD members. The U.S. averaged 17 years compared with 20 years for the top tier countries: Australia, Finland, and Sweden.

Data in this chart refer to 2017, except for Japan (2014). This indicator is the average duration of education in which a child aged five years can expect to enroll during his/her lifetime until the age of 39. It is calculated under the current enrollment conditions by adding the net enrollment rates for each single year of age from the age of five onwards.

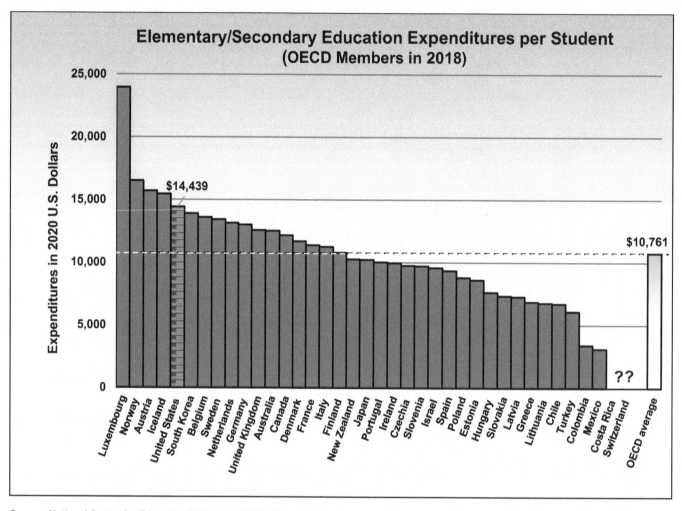

Elementary/Secondary Education Expenditures per Student
(OECD Members in 2018)

Source: National Center for Education Statistics. (2022). Education Expenditures by Country. *Condition of Education*. U.S. Department of Education, Institute of Education Sciences. Accessed on 4-1-23, from https://nces.ed.gov/programs/coe/indicator/cmd, https://nces.ed.gov/programs/coe/indicator/cmd/education-expenditures-by-country.

In 2018, the U.S. spent $14,439 per elementary and secondary student for education (expressed in 2020 U.S. dollars), the fourth-highest level among 36 OECD members reporting data, and 34 percent above the average OECD expenditure.

This indicator uses material from the Organization for Economic Cooperation and Development (OECD) to compare countries' expenditures on education using two measures: expenditures on public and private education institutions per full-time-equivalent (FTE) student and total government and private expenditures on education institutions as a percentage of gross domestic product (GDP).

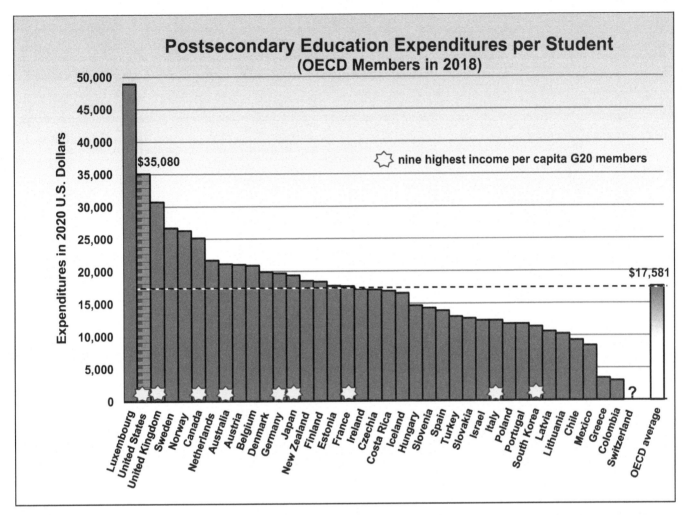

Postsecondary Education Expenditures per Student
(OECD Members in 2018)

Sources: National Center for Education Statistics. (2022). Education Expenditures by Country. *Condition of Education*. U.S. Department of Education, Institute of Education Sciences. Accessed on 4-1-23, from https://nces.ed.gov/programs/coe/indicator/cmd, https://nces.ed.gov/programs/coe/indicator/cmd/education-expenditures-by-country.

In 2018, the U.S. spent $35,080 per postsecondary student for education (expressed in 2020 U.S. dollars), the second highest among the 37 OECD members reporting data, approximately double the average OECD expenditure. The U.S. expended 1.64 times the $21,367 average expenditure per student of the nine highest income per capita G20 members.

This indicator uses material from the Organization for Economic Cooperation and Development (OECD) to compare countries' expenditures on education using two measures: expenditures on public and private education institutions per full-time-equivalent (FTE) student and total government and private expenditures on education institutions as a percentage of gross domestic product (GDP). The OECD is an organization of 38 countries that collects and publishes an array of data on its member countries.

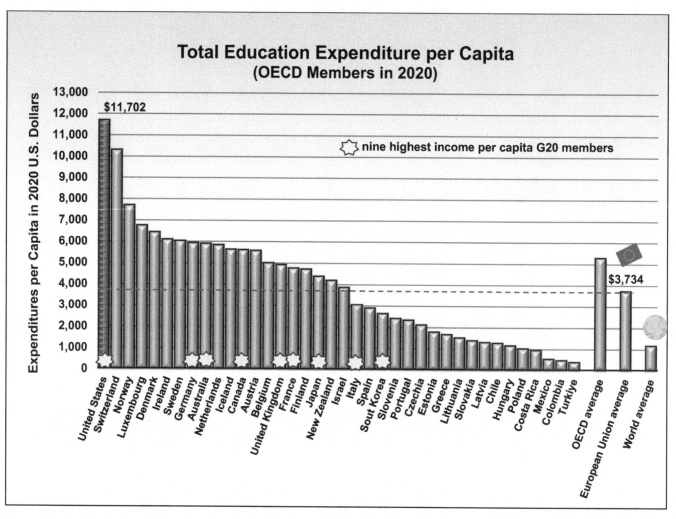

Total Education Expenditure per Capita
(OECD Members in 2020)

Source: The World Bank, https://databank.worldbank.org/source/world-development-indicators SH.XPD.CHEX.PC.CD, accessed 8-15-23, https://data.worldbank.org/summary-terms-of-use, http://apps.who.int/nha/database

In 2020, the U.S. expenditures on education per capita were 2.2 times the OECD average expenditures per capita and 3.1 times more than the European Union's average. However, mathematical literacy scores for U.S. 15-year-old boys and girls were below average. Compared with the nine G20 nations with the highest income per capita, averaging $5,437 per capita expenditures for education, the U.S. spent 2.2 times as much.

Estimates of current health expenditures include healthcare goods and services consumed during each year.

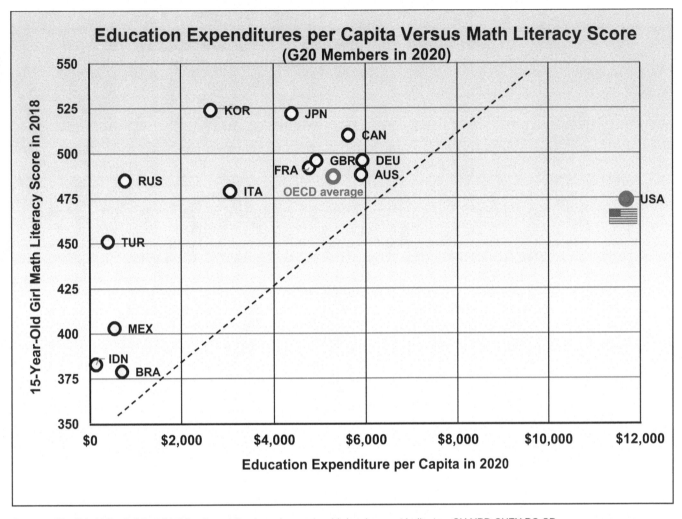

Sources: The World Bank, https://databank.worldbank.org/source/world-development-indicators SH.XPD.CHEX.PC.CD, https://data.worldbank.org/summary-terms-of-use, and OECD (2023), Mathematics performance (PISA) (indicator). doi: 10.1787/04711c74-en (Accessed on 20 May 2023) https://data.oecd.org/pisa/mathematics-performance-pisa.htm

In 2018, the U.S. expenditures on education were more than double the OECD average, however, despite these high expenditures math literacy scores for U.S. 15-year-old boys and girls were below average. This data plot for girls illustrates the U.S. is an extreme outlier.

Country Codes

Argentina*	ARG
Australia	AUS
Brazil	BRA
Canada	CAN
China*	CHN
France	FRA
Germany	DEU
India*	IND
Indonesia	IDN
Italy	ITA
Japan	JPN
South Korea	KOR
Mexico	MEX
Russia	RUS
Saudi Arabia*	SAU
South Africa*	ZAF
Turkiye	TUR
United Kingdom	GBR
United States	USA

*Test scores not available

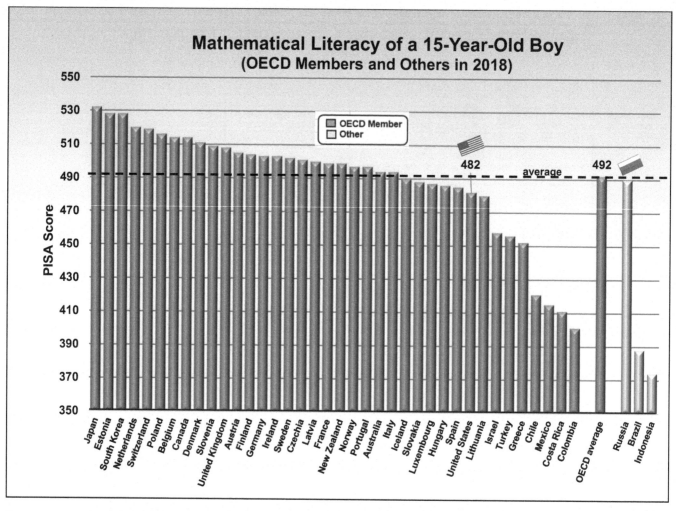

Mathematical Literacy of a 15-Year-Old Boy
(OECD Members and Others in 2018)

Source: OECD (2023), Mathematics performance (PISA) (indicator). doi: 10.1787/04711c74-en (Accessed on 20 May 2023)
https://data.oecd.org/pisa/mathematics-performance-pisa.htm

In 2018, the U.S. ranked 29th out of 38 OECD member nations in mathematical literacy for 15-year-old boys.

Mathematical performance, for PISA (Program for International Student Assessment), measures the mathematical literacy of a 15-year-old to formulate, employ and interpret mathematics in a variety of contexts to describe, predict and explain phenomena, recognizing the role that mathematics plays in the world. The mean score is the measure. A mathematically literate student recognizes the role that mathematics plays in the world in order to make well-founded judgments and decisions needed by constructive, engaged and reflective citizens. PISA is the OECD's Program for International Student Assessment. PISA measures 15-year-olds' ability to use their reading, mathematics and science knowledge and skills to meet real-life challenges.

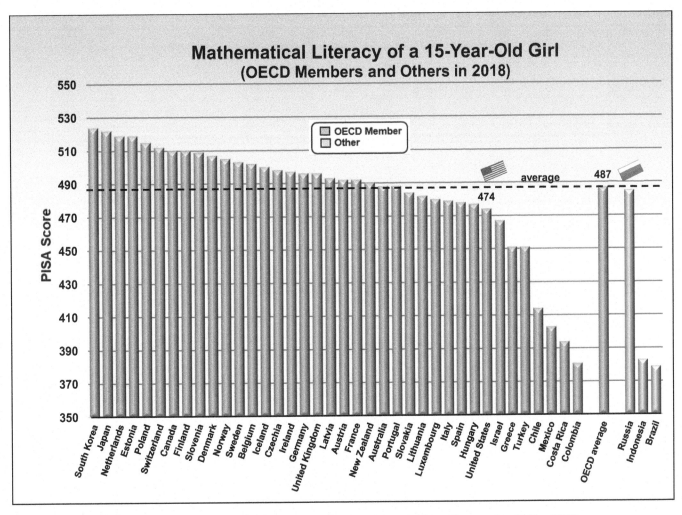

Mathematical Literacy of a 15-Year-Old Girl
(OECD Members and Others in 2018)

Source: OECD (2023), Mathematics performance (PISA) (indicator). doi: 10.1787/04711c74-en (Accessed on 20 May 2023)
https://data.oecd.org/pisa/mathematics-performance-pisa.htm

In 2018, the U.S. ranked 30th out of 38 OECD member nations in mathematical literacy for 15-year-old girls.

Mathematical performance, for PISA (Program for International Student Assessment), measures the mathematical literacy of a 15-year-old to formulate, employ and interpret mathematics in a variety of contexts to describe, predict and explain phenomena, recognizing the role that mathematics plays in the world. The mean score is the measure. A mathematically literate student recognizes the role that mathematics plays in the world in order to make well-founded judgments and decisions needed by constructive, engaged and reflective citizens. PISA is the OECD's Program for International Student Assessment. PISA measures 15-year-olds' ability to use their reading, mathematics, and science knowledge and skills to meet real-life challenges.

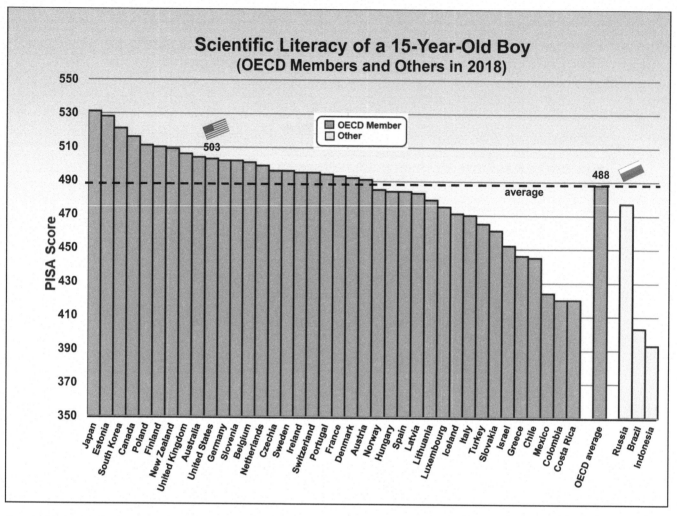

Source: OECD (2023), Science performance (PISA) (indicator). doi: 10.1787/91952204-en (Accessed on 20 May 2023),
https://data.oecd.org/pisa/science-performance-pisa.htm

In 2018, the U.S. ranked tenth out of 38 OECD member nations in scientific literacy for 15-year-old boys.

Scientific performance, for PISA (Program for International Student Assessment), measures the scientific literacy of 15-year-olds in the use of scientific knowledge to identify questions, acquire new knowledge, explain scientific phenomena, and draw evidence-based conclusions about science-related issues. The mean score is the measure. PISA is the OECD's Program for International Student Assessment. PISA measures 15-year-olds' ability to use their reading, mathematics and science knowledge and skills to meet real-life challenges.

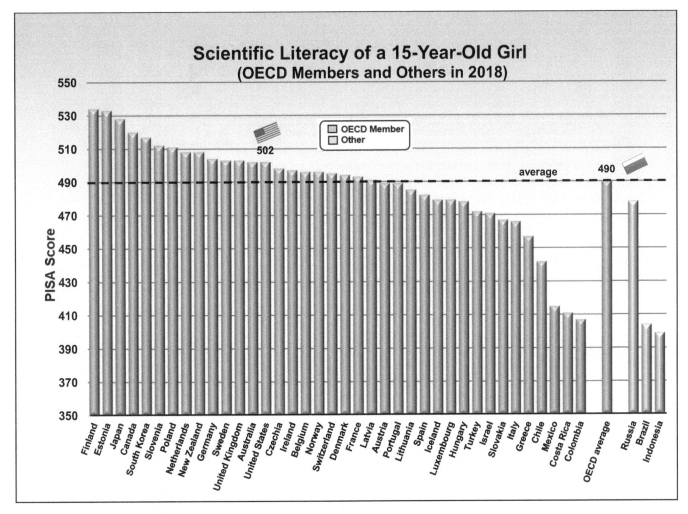

Source: OECD (2023), Science performance (PISA) (indicator). doi: 10.1787/91952204-en (Accessed on 20 May 2023),
https://data.oecd.org/pisa/science-performance-pisa.htm

In 2018, the U.S. ranked 14th out of 38 OECD member nations in scientific literacy for 15-year-old girls.

Scientific performance, for PISA (Program for International Student Assessment), measures the scientific literacy of 15-year-olds in the use of scientific knowledge to identify questions, acquire new knowledge, explain scientific phenomena, and draw evidence-based conclusions about science-related issues. The mean score is the measure. PISA is the OECD's Program for International Student Assessment. PISA measures 15-year-olds' ability to use their reading, mathematics and science knowledge and skills to meet real-life challenges.

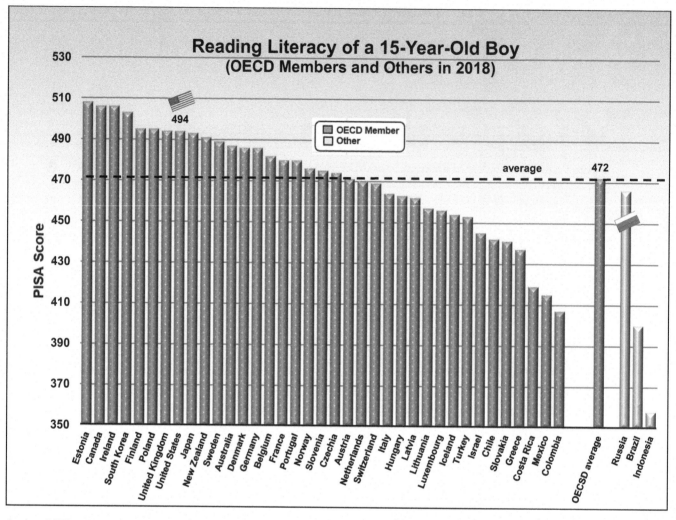

Reading Literacy of a 15-Year-Old Boy
(OECD Members and Others in 2018)

Source: OECD (2023), Reading performance (PISA) doi: 10.1787/79913c69-en (Accessed on 20 May 2023) https://data.oecd.org/pisa/reading-performance-pisa.htm

In 2018, the U.S. ranked eighth of 38 OECD member nations in reading literacy for 15-year-old boys.

Reading performance, for PISA (Program for International Student Assessment), measures the capacity to understand, use and reflect on written texts in order to achieve goals, develop knowledge and potential, and participate in society. The mean score is the measure. PISA is the OECD's Program for International Student Assessment. PISA measures 15-year-olds' ability to use their reading, mathematics and science knowledge and skills to meet real-life challenges.

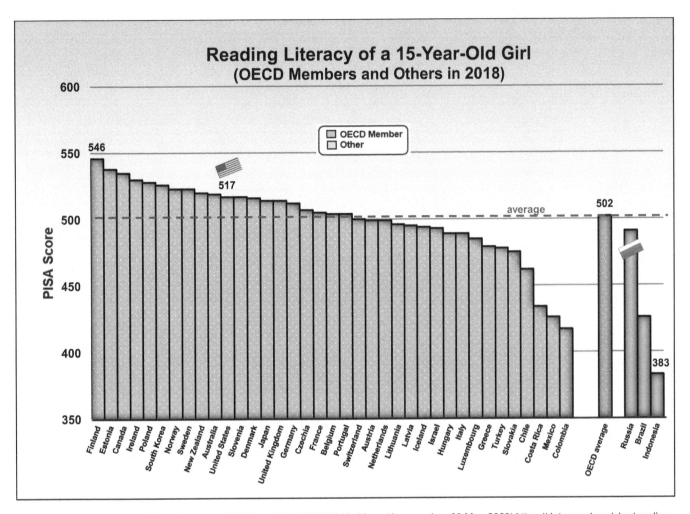

Source: OECD (2023), Reading performance (PISA) doi: 10.1787/79913c69-en (Accessed on 20 May 2023) https://data.oecd.org/pisa/reading-performance-pisa.htm

In 2018, the U.S. ranked 11th out of 38 OECD member nations in reading literacy for 15-year-old girls.

Reading performance, for PISA (Program for International Student Assessment), measures the capacity to understand, use and reflect on written texts in order to achieve goals, develop knowledge and potential, and participate in society. The mean score is the measure. PISA is the OECD's Program for International Student Assessment. PISA measures 15-year-olds' ability to use their reading, mathematics and science knowledge and skills to meet real-life challenges.

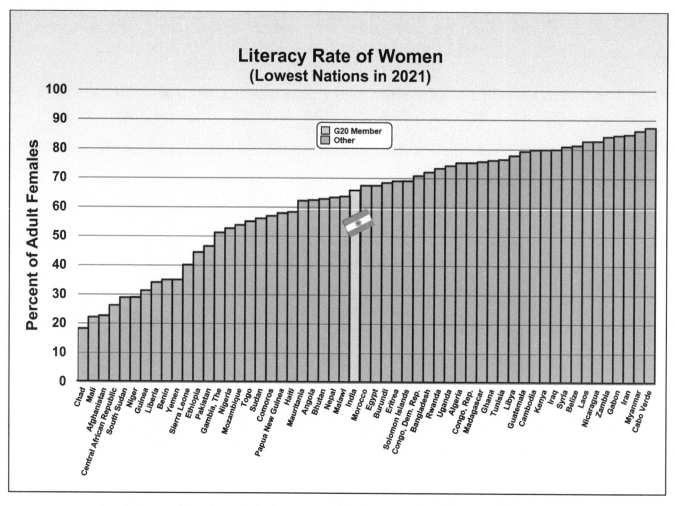

Literacy Rate of Women
(Lowest Nations in 2021)

Percent of Adult Females

Legend: G20 Member / Other

Countries (left to right): Chad, Mali, Afghanistan, Central African Republic, South Sudan, Niger, Guinea, Liberia, Benin, Yemen, Sierra Leone, Ethiopia, Pakistan, Gambia, The, Nigeria, Mozambique, Togo, Sudan, Comoros, Papua New Guinea, Haiti, Mauritania, Angola, Bhutan, Nepal, Malawi, India, Morocco, Egypt, Burundi, Eritrea, Solomon Islands, Congo, Dem. Rep., Bangladesh, Rwanda, Uganda, Algeria, Congo, Rep., Madagascar, Ghana, Tunisia, Libya, Guatemala, Cambodia, Kenya, Iraq, Syria, Belize, Laos, Nicaragua, Zambia, Gabon, Iran, Myanmar, Cabo Verde

Source: The World Bank, https://databank.worldbank.org/source/world-development-indicators, SE.ADT.LITR.FE.ZS, accessed 8-15-23, https://data.worldbank.org/summary-terms-of-use

In 2021, approximately one-third of adult females in India were illiterate. Many of the countries with the lowest literacy rate for women were located in Africa, with Chad having the lowest rate of 18 percent. Although the U.S. was not included in this World Bank survey, however, according to the Barbara Bush Foundation for Family Literacy: "*130 million Americans—54 percent of adults between the ages of 16 and 74 years old—lack proficiency in literacy, essentially reading below the equivalent of a sixth-grade level*" (see barbarabush.org).

Literacy statistics for most countries cover the population ages 15 and older, but some include younger ages or are confined to age ranges that tend to inflate literacy rates. The youth literacy rate for ages 15–24 reflects recent progress in education. It measures the accumulated outcomes of primary education over the previous ten years or so by indicating the proportion of the population who have passed through the primary education system and acquired basic literacy and numeracy skills. Generally, literacy also encompasses numeracy, the ability to make simple arithmetic calculations.

Data on literacy are compiled by the UNESCO Institute for Statistics based on national censuses and household surveys and, for countries without recent literacy data, using the Global Age-Specific Literacy Projection Model (GALP). For detailed information, see www.uis.unesco.org.

Chapter 15

Energy

Overview of Energy

In the period 1980–2005, the U.S. energy production shortfall had reached its highest level in 2005, requiring approximately 30 percent of energy consumed to be imported. Between 2005 and 2021, the shortfall began to decline, and by 2021, it was essentially eliminated. However, the U.S continued to import energy to offset U.S. energy production that is exported. Technically, the U.S. has achieved energy independence. While the U.S. dependency on imports was declining China's dependency has increased from seven percent in 2005, to 18 percent in 2021.

Most of this increase in production of oil and gas in the U.S. was achieved through extraction of shale oil and use of fracking. According to the U.S. Energy Information Administration (EIA) in 2022, about 2.84 billion barrels (or about 7.79 million barrels per day) of crude oil were produced directly from tight-oil resources in the U.S. Tight-oil refers to oil produced from petroleum-bearing formations with low permeability that must be hydraulically fractured to produce oil at commercial rates. Shale oil is a subset of tight oil. Tight-oil was equal to about 66% of total U.S. crude oil production in 2022.

Even though hydraulic fracturing has been in use for more than six decades, it has only recently been used to produce a significant portion of crude oil in the U.S. This technique, often used in combination with horizontal drilling, has allowed the U.S. to increase its oil production faster than at any time in its history. Hydraulic fracturing involves forcing a liquid (primarily water) under high pressure from a wellbore against a rock formation until it fractures. The fracture lengthens as the high-pressure liquid in the wellbore flows into the formation. This injected liquid contains a proppant, or small, solid particles (usually sand or a man-made granular solid of similar size) that fills the expanding fracture. When the injection is stopped and the high pressure is reduced, the formation attempts to settle back into its original configuration, but the proppant keeps the fracture open. This allows hydrocarbons such as crude oil and natural gas to flow from the rock formation back to the wellbore and then to the surface.

In the same period between 2005 and 2021, while the U.S. was eliminating its energy shortfall the energy shortfall for China and India increased while Russia's surplus increased.

In 2021, the U.S consumed 16.2 percent of the world's energy while China consumed 27.4 percent. U.S. energy consumption consisted of almost one-fourth (22.4 percent) renewable—including nuclear power, and 10.6 percent of U.S. energy consumption was coal. China's consumption was 15 percent renewable—including nuclear power, and 58.3 percent coal.

In 2019, on a per capita basis, the U.S. ranked 11th in the world for total energy consumed, ranked second among G20 members, and first among OECD members. Canada consumed the most energy per capita of both the G20 and the OECD members. That year the U.S. was the second largest emitter of carbon dioxide, accounting for 15 percent of the world's total, behind China, which emitted 30 percent. Collectively, the G20 nations were responsible for 78 percent of the world's carbon dioxide emissions.

In 2020, the U.S. ranked 13th out of 18 G20 members reporting, for percent of energy consumed that was renewable. The leading G20 member was Brazil at 47.5 percent, followed by India where approximately one-third of their energy consumed was renewable. U.S. renewable energy (excluding nuclear) was 10.4 percent of U.S. consumption.

Energy surplus is the energy produced less the energy consumed. In 2005, the U.S. experienced its largest energy deficit for the period 1980–2021, of approximately 31 quadrillion BTUs, which was 39 percent as large as the European Union's (E.U.) deficit that year. In 2021, the U.S. deficit was eliminated while the E.U. deficit has been reduced to approximately half its peak but a deficit of 37 quadrillion BTUs remained. China's deficit in 2021 was 81 percent as large as the E.U.'s.

Between 1992 and 2021 Russia more than doubled its energy surplus. According to the U.S. Energy Information Agency *"revenues from oil and natural gas accounted for 45 percent of Russia's federal budget in 2021."*

In 2021 the U.S.:

- was the world's leader in production of oil and petroleum liquids, accounting for 20 percent of world's production. Saudi Arabia and Russia were tied for second place, both at approximately 11 percent of the world's production. U.S. production of oil and petroleum liquids was approximately equivalent to the production of Saudi Arabia and Russia combined. Saudi Arabia, Russia, Canada, and China together accounted for 53 percent of the world's production.

- was also the leading producer of natural gas, accounting for 23.7 percent of the world's total, followed by Russia at 17.6 percent. The U.S. was also the world's leader in consumption of oil and petroleum liquids and natural gas. The U.S., along with China, India, Russia, and Japan, accounted for 49 percent of the world's oil and petroleum consumption that year. That year the U.S. was also the leading consumer of natural gas, accounting for 21.1 percent of the world's total.

- produced approximately 7 percent of the world's coal. China was the leader of coal production, producing 54 percent of the total world's supply which is approximately the amount they consumed. The U.S. consumed approximately 10 percent of the amount of coal as China.

- was the second-highest emitter in the world of carbon dioxide, behind China. Together, the U.S. and China accounted for 45 percent of the world's carbon dioxide emitted that year.

- held reserves of crude oil ranked in tenth place in the world and amounted to only 3 percent of the estimated total world's reserves. The U.S. ranked in fourth place for the largest natural gas reserves, behind Russia, Iran, and Qatar that together have six times as much natural gas reserves as the U.S.

~

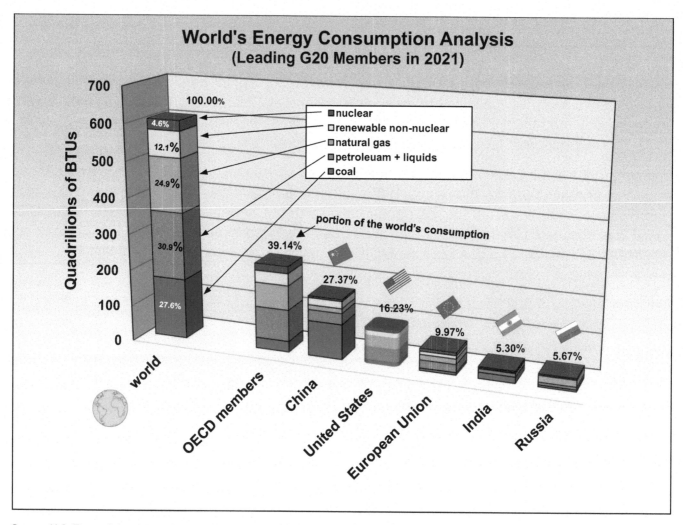

Source: U.S. Energy Information Administration (EIA), https://www.eia.gov/international/data/world/petroleum-and-other-liquids/annual-crude-and-lease-condensate-reserves?pd=5&p=00000000000000000000008&u=0&f=A&v=mapbubble&a=-&i=none&vo=value&&t=C&g=0000000000000000000000000000000000000000000000001&l=249-ruvvvvvvfvtvnvv1vrvvvvfvvvvvvfvvvou20evvvvvvvvvvvnvvvs0008&s=315532800000&e=1609459200000, accessed on 5-22-23

In 2021, the U.S consumed 16.2 percent of the world's energy of which 22.4 percent was renewable—including nuclear power, and 10.6 percent was coal. In contrast, China consumed 27.4 percent of the world's energy of which 15 percent was renewable—including nuclear power, and 58.3 percent was coal. Renewable energy plus nuclear energy accounted for 16.7 percent of all the world's energy consumed.

Total energy consumption includes the consumption of petroleum, dry natural gas, coal, net nuclear, hydroelectric, and non-hydroelectric renewable electricity. Total energy consumption for each nation also includes net electricity imports (electricity imports – electricity exports) and net coke imports (coke imports – coke exports). Electricity net imports are included because the net electricity consumption by energy type data, noted above, are really net electricity generation data that have not been adjusted to include electricity imports and exclude electricity exports.

Total energy consumption for the U.S. also includes the consumption of biomass, geothermal, and solar energy not used for electricity generation.

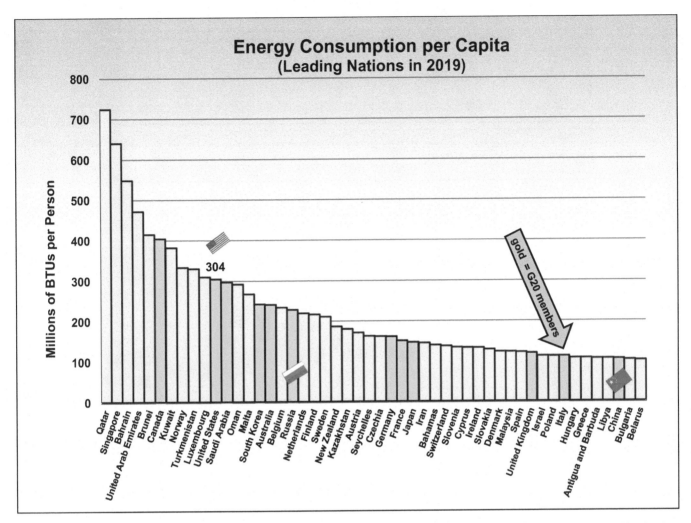

Energy Consumption per Capita
(Leading Nations in 2019)

Y-axis: Millions of BTUs per Person

304

gold = G20 members

Countries (left to right): Qatar, Singapore, Bahrain, United Arab Emirates, Brunei, Canada, Kuwait, Norway, Turkmenistan, Luxembourg, United States, Saudi Arabia, Oman, Malta, South Korea, Australia, Belgium, Russia, Netherlands, Finland, Sweden, New Zealand, Kazakhstan, Austria, Seychelles, Czechia, Germany, France, Japan, Iran, Bahamas, Switzerland, Slovenia, Cyprus, Ireland, Slovakia, Denmark, Malaysia, Spain, United Kingdom, Israel, Poland, Italy, Hungary, Greece, Antigua and Barbuda, Libya, China, Bulgaria, Belarus

Source: The World Factbook 2021. Washington, DC: Central Intelligence Agency, 2021, https://www.cia.gov/the-world-factbook/, The Factbook is in the public domain.

In 2019, on a per capita basis, the U.S. ranked 11th in the world for total energy consumed, ranked second among G20 members, and ranked first among OECD members. Canada was ranked first for both the G20 and the OECD.

Energy consumption per capita measures the total amount of consumed energy divided by a country's population, reported in BTU per person.

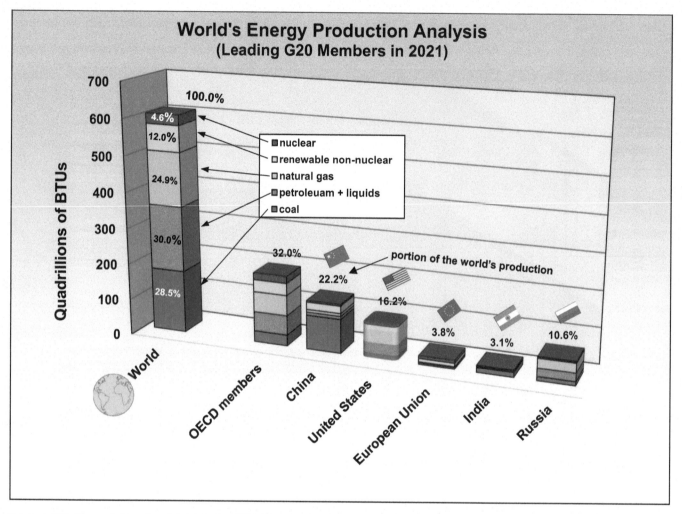

World's Energy Production Analysis
(Leading G20 Members in 2021)

Sources: U.S. Energy Information Administration (EIA), https://www.eia.gov/international/data/world/petroleum-and-other-liquids/annual-crude-and-lease-condensate-reserves?pd=5&p=00000000000000000000008&u=0&f=A&v=mapbubble&a=-&i=none&vo=value&&t=C&g=0000000000000000000000000000000000000000000000001&l=249-ruvvvvvfvtvnvv1vrvvvvfvvvvvvfvvvou20evvvvvvvvvvvvnvvvs0008&s=315532800000&e=1609459200000, accessed on 5-22-23

In 2021, the U.S. produced 16.2 percent of the world's energy, approximately equivalent to the amount that the U.S. consumed. Since the U.S. is an exporter of energy there were still energy imports required to meet domestic demand. Technically the U.S. achieved energy independence.

Total energy production includes the production of petroleum (crude oil and natural gas plant liquids), dry natural gas, and coal. It also includes net generation of nuclear, hydroelectric, and non-hydroelectric renewable electricity.

Total energy production for the U.S. also includes the production of biomass, geothermal, and solar energy not used for electricity generation.

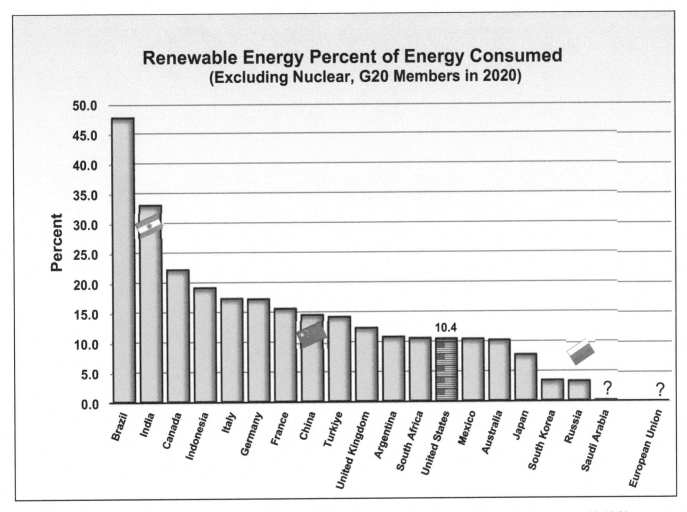

Renewable Energy Percent of Energy Consumed
(Excluding Nuclear, G20 Members in 2020)

Source: The World Bank, https://databank.worldbank.org/source/world-development-indicators, EG.FEC.RNEW.ZS, accessed 8-15-23, https://data.worldbank.org/summary-terms-of-use

In 2020, the U.S. ranked 13th out of 18 G20 nations reporting, for percent of energy consumed that was renewable, excluding nuclear power. The leading G20 member was Brazil at 47.5 percent. U.S. renewable energy was only 10.4 percent of total energy consumption in the United States. China's portion of total energy consumed that was renewable was 39 percent greater than was the U.S.

Renewable energy consumption is the share of renewable energy in total final energy consumption, excluding nuclear energy.

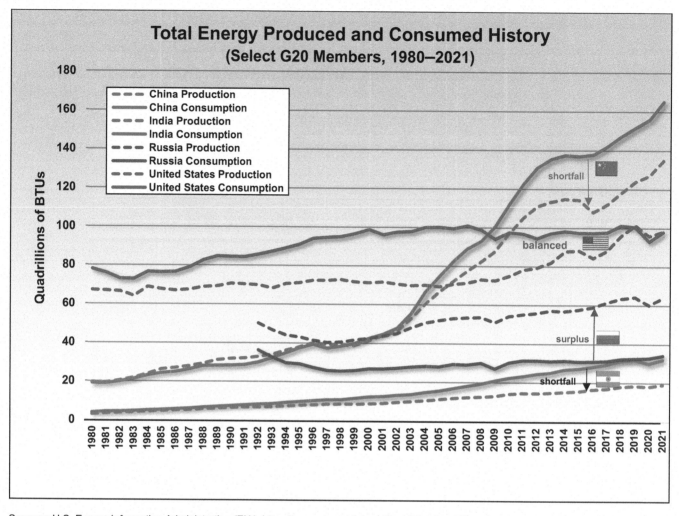

Total Energy Produced and Consumed History
(Select G20 Members, 1980–2021)

Sources: U.S. Energy Information Administration (EIA), https://www.eia.gov/international/data/world/petroleum-and-other-liquids/annual-crude-and-lease-condensate-reserves?pd=5&p=000000000000000000000008&u=0&f=A&v=mapbubble&a=-&i=none&vo=value&&t=C&g=00000000000000000000000000000000000000000000000001&l=249-ruvvvvvfvtvnvv1vrvvvvfvvvvvvvfvvvou20evvvvvvvvvvvvnvvvs0008&s=315532800000&e=1609459200000, accessed on 5-22-23

In 2005, U.S. energy production shortfall (consumption – production) had grown to its highest level since 1980. Subsequently, between 2005 and 2021, the shortfall declined due primarily to increased production and by 2021, the shortfall had been essentially eliminated. However, the U.S continued to import energy to offset U.S. production that is exported. Over the same period, between 2005 and 2021, China's and India's energy shortfalls continually increased as did Russia's energy surplus.

Total energy production for the U.S. also includes the production of biomass, geothermal, and solar energy not used for electricity generation. Total energy consumption includes the consumption of petroleum, dry natural gas, coal, net nuclear, hydroelectric, and non-hydroelectric renewable electricity. Total energy consumption for each country also includes net electricity imports (electricity imports – electricity exports) and net coke imports (coke imports – coke exports).

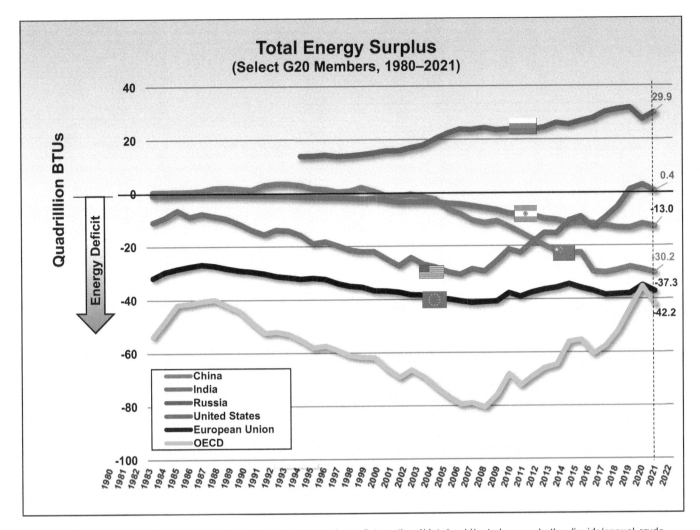

Total Energy Surplus
(Select G20 Members, 1980–2021)

Source: U.S. Energy Information Administration (EIA), https://www.eia.gov/international/data/world/petroleum-and-other-liquids/annual-crude-and-lease-condensate-reserves?pd=5&p=00000000000000000000008&u=0&f=A&v=mapbubble&a=-&i=none&vo=value&&t=C&g=00000000000000000000000000000000000000000000000001&l=249-ruvvvvvfvtvnvv1vrvvvvfvvvvvvfvvvou20evvvvvvvvvvvvnvvvs0008&s=315532800000&e=1609459200000, accessed on 5-22-23

Energy surplus is the energy produced less the energy consumed. In 2005, the U.S. experienced its largest energy deficit for the period 1980–2021, of approximately 31 quadrillion BTUs, which was 39 percent as large as the E.U.'s deficit that year. Since then, the U.S. has essentially eliminated its deficit while the E.U.'s has been reduced by approximately 50 percent.

Total energy production includes the production of petroleum (crude oil and natural gas plant liquids), dry natural gas, and coal. It also includes net generation of nuclear, hydroelectric, and non-hydroelectric renewable electricity. Total energy production for the U.S. also includes the production of biomass, geothermal, and solar energy not used for electricity generation.

Total energy consumption includes the consumption of petroleum, dry natural gas, coal, net nuclear, hydroelectric, and non-hydroelectric renewable electricity. Total energy consumption for each country also includes net electricity imports (electricity imports – electricity exports) and net coke imports (coke imports – coke exports).

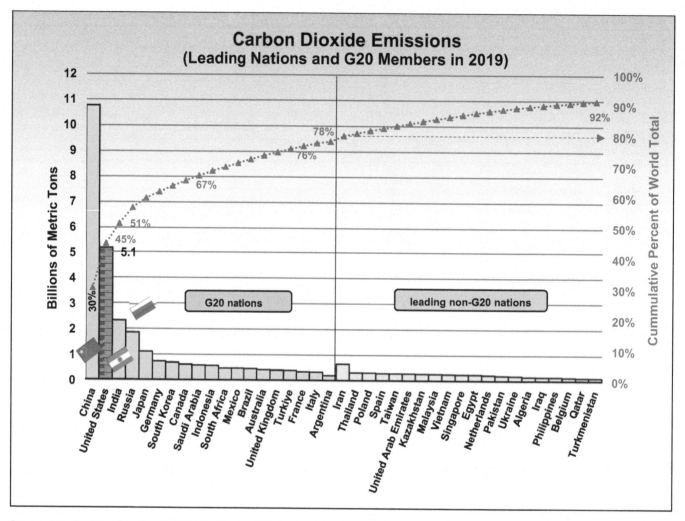

Source: CIA, The World Factbook 2021. Washington, DC: Central Intelligence Agency, 2021, https://www.cia.gov/the-world-factbook/, The Factbook is in the public domain.

In 2019, the U.S was the second-largest emitter of carbon dioxide, accounting for 15 percent of the world's total, behind China who emitted 30 percent of the world's total. Collectively, the G20 nations are responsible for 78 percent of the world's carbon dioxide emissions.

Carbon dioxide emissions from consumption of energy is the total amount of carbon dioxide, measured in metric tons, released by burning fossil fuels in the process of producing and consuming energy.

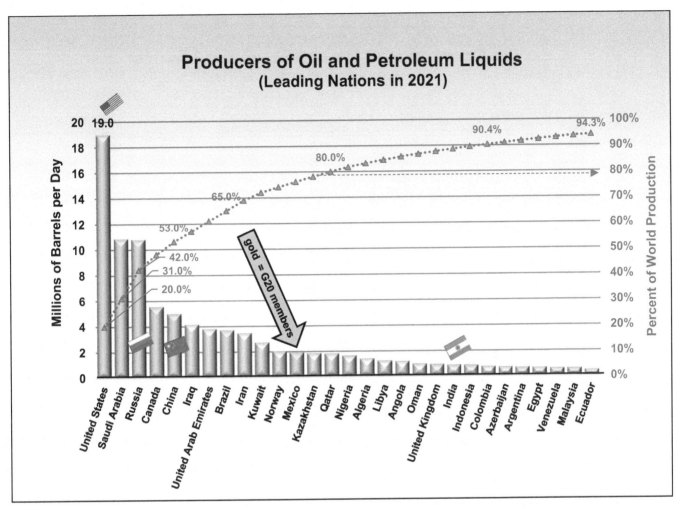

Source: U.S. Energy Information Administration (EIA), https://www.eia.gov/tools/faqs/faq.php?id=709&t=6, accessed on 5-22-23

In 2021, the U.S. was the world's leader in production of oil and petroleum liquids, accounting for 20 percent of world's production. Saudi Arabia and Russia were tied for second place, both at approximately 11 percent of the world's production. Therefore, U.S production of oil and petroleum liquids in 2021 was approximately equivalent to the production of Saudi Arabia and Russia combined. Altogether, the U.S., Saudi Arabia, Russia, Canada, and China accounted for 53 percent of the world's production.

Petroleum supply includes the production of crude oil (including lease condensate), natural gas plant liquids, and other liquids, and it also includes refinery processing gain for volume (TBPD) only. Other Liquids includes biodiesel, ethanol, liquids produced from coal, gas, and oil shale, Orimulsion, blending components, and other hydrocarbons.

Crude Oil data for Canada include Alberta oil sands production. Negative refinery processing gain data values indicate the reported volumetric output is lower than reported inputs.

The Liquefied Petroleum Gases category includes propane and butane blends. Pentanes plus are included under LPG for the U.S. and Canada.

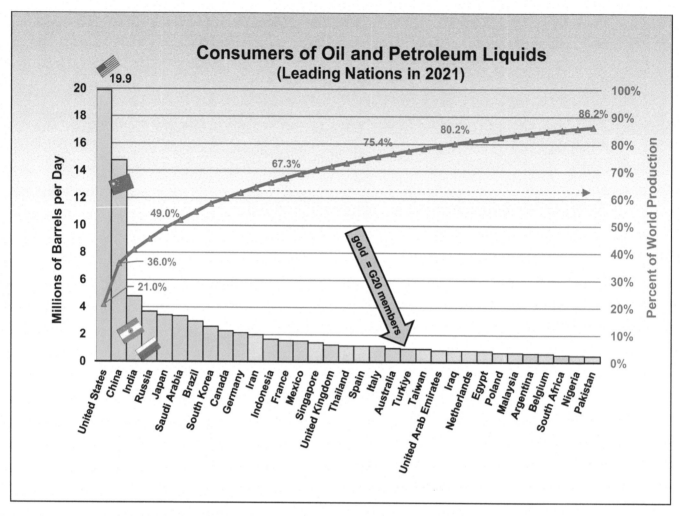

Source: U.S. Energy Information Administration (EIA), https://www.eia.gov/tools/faqs/faq.php?id=709&t=6, accessed on 5-22-23

In 2021, the U.S. was the world's leader in consumption of oil and petroleum liquids. The U.S., along with China, India, Russia, and Japan, accounted for 49 percent of the world's consumption that year.

Petroleum and other liquids consumption includes all domestic use and international bunkering of refined products, refinery fuel, and where available, direct combustion of crude oil and refinery by-products. Other products include asphalt, petroleum coke, aviation gasoline, lubricants, ethane, naphtha, paraffin wax, petrochemical feedstocks, unfinished oils, white spirits, and direct use of crude oil.

The Liquefied Petroleum Gases category includes propane and butane blends. Pentanes plus are included under LPG for the U.S. and Canada.

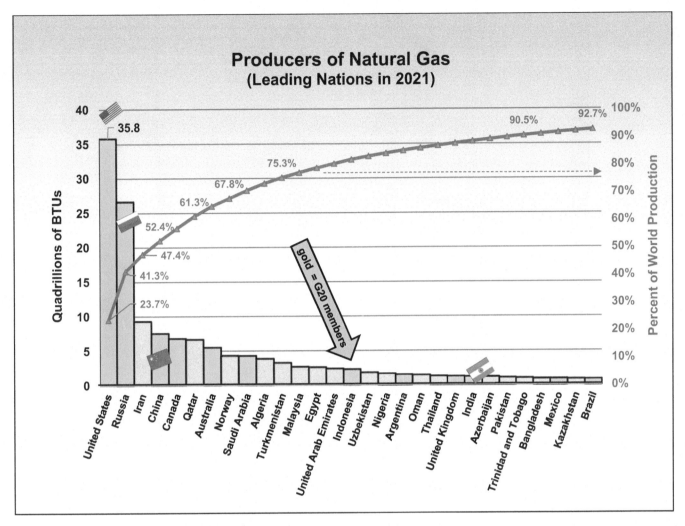

Producers of Natural Gas
(Leading Nations in 2021)

gold = G20 members

Sources: U.S. Energy Information Administration (EIA),
https://www.eia.gov/international/rankings/country/USA?pa=291&u=2&f=A&v=none&y=01 percent2F01 percent2F2021, accessed on 5-22-23

In 2021, the U.S. was the leading producer of natural gas, accounting for 23.7 percent of the world's total production, followed by Russia at 17.6 percent.

To ensure comparability of data across countries, natural gas production numbers exclude non-hydrocarbon gases for all countries.

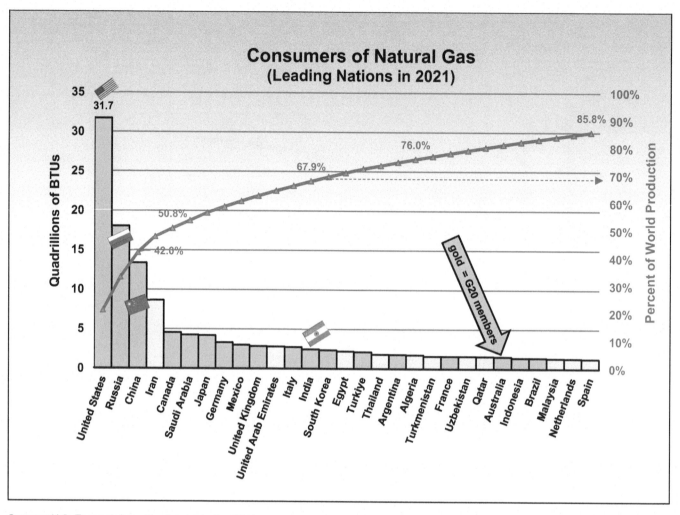

Sources: U.S. Energy Information Administration (EIA),
https://www.eia.gov/international/rankings/country/USA?pa=291&u=2&f=A&v=none&y=01 percent2F01 percent2F2021, accessed on 5-22-23

In 2021, the U.S. was also the leading consumer of natural gas, accounting for 21.1 percent of the world's total consumption of natural gas.

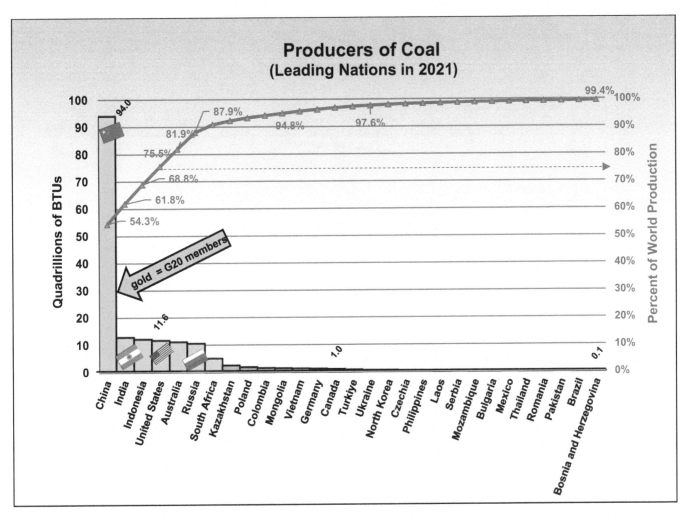

Producers of Coal
(Leading Nations in 2021)

Source: U.S. Energy Information Administration (EIA), https://www.eia.gov/international/rankings/country/CHN?pid=4411&aid=1&f=A&y=01 percent2F01 percent2F2021&u=0&v=none&pa=286, accessed on 5-22-23

In 2021, the U.S. produced approximately 7 percent of the world's coal. China was the leading producer at 54 percent of the total world's coal supply.

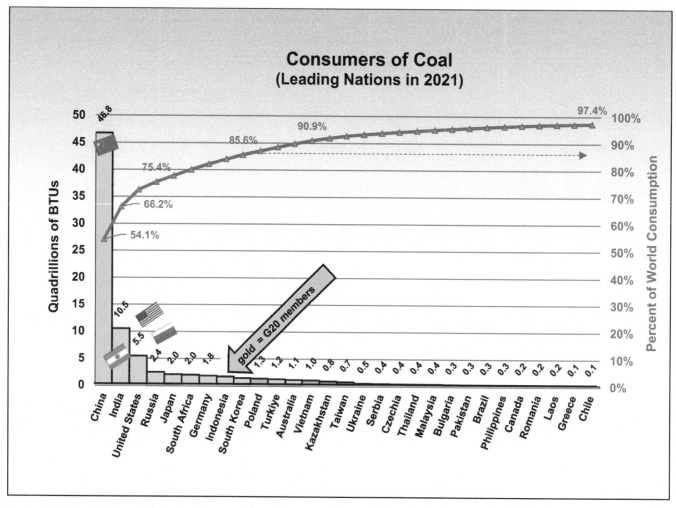

Consumers of Coal
(Leading Nations in 2021)

Source: U.S. Energy Information Administration (EIA), https://www.eia.gov/international/rankings/country/CHN?pid=4411&aid=1&f=A&y=01 percent2F01 percent2F2021&u=0&v=none&pa=286, accessed on 5-22-23

In 2021, China was the world's leader in consumption of coal, accounting for 54 percent of the world's total which amounted to approximately all they produced. U.S. consumption was approximately one-tenth of China's.

Coal consumption represents coal used domestically. Consumption accounts for coal used in the transformation sector, energy sector, and industrial sector. It also includes distribution losses. Note that metallurgical coal refers to pulverized coal consumed in making steel. Bituminous coal is a fuel used in steam-electric power generation, and substantial quantities are also used for heat and power applications in manufacturing.

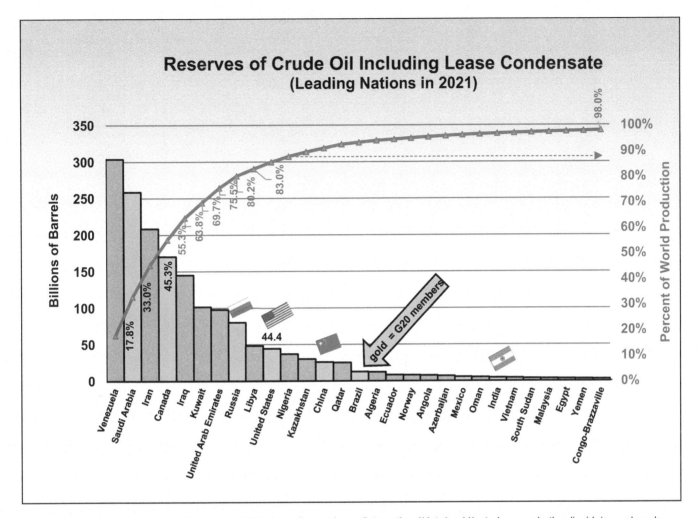

Source: U.S. Energy Information Administration (EIA), https://www.eia.gov/international/data/world/petroleum-and-other-liquids/annual-crude-and-lease-condensate-reserves?pd=5&p=0000000000000000000008&u=0&f=A&v=mapbubble&a=-&i=none&vo=value&&t=C&g=00000000000000000000000000000000000000000000000001&l=249-ruvvvvvfvtvnvv1vrvvvvfvvvvvvfvvvou20evvvvvvvvvvvnvvvs0008&s=315532800000&e=1609459200000, accessed on 5-22-23

In 2021, U.S. reserves of crude oil ranked in tenth place and amounted to only 3 percent of the estimated total world's reserves of oil.

Proved reserves of crude oil (including lease condensate) are the estimated quantities of all liquids defined as crude oil that geological and engineering data demonstrate with reasonable certainty to be recoverable in future years from reservoirs under existing economic and operating conditions.

Data for the U.S. are from the U.S. Energy Information Administration and are as of December 31, of the previous full year. Data for other countries are from the *Oil & Gas Journal* and are as of January 1 of current year.

Reserve estimates for crude oil are very difficult to develop. As a convenience to the public, EIA provides these crude oil reserve estimates from other sources, but it does not certify these data. Please carefully note the sources of the data when using and citing estimates of crude oil reserves.

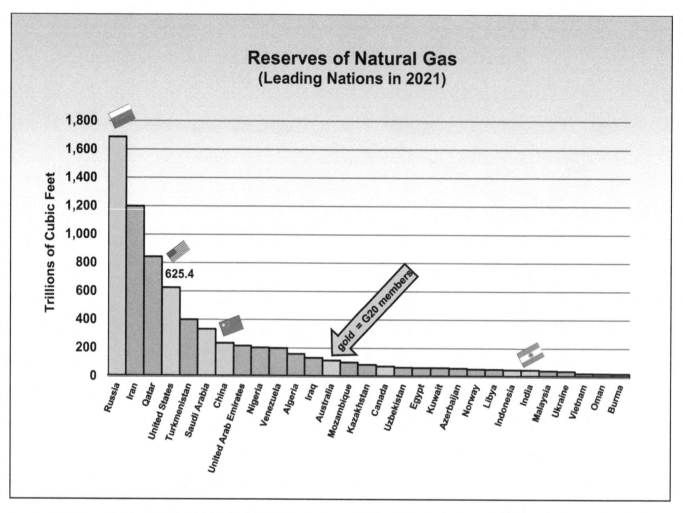

Reserves of Natural Gas
(Leading Nations in 2021)

Sources: U.S. Energy Information Administration (EIA), https://www.eia.gov/international/data/world/petroleum-and-other-liquids/annual-crude-and-lease-condensate-reserves?pd=5&p=00000000000000000000008&u=0&f=A&v=mapbubble&a=-&i=none&vo=value&&t=C&g=0000000000000000000000000000000000000000000000000001&l=249-ruvvvvvfvtvnvv1vrvvvvfvvvvvvvfvvvou20evvvvvvvvvvvvnvvvs0008&s=315532800000&e=1609459200000, accessed on 5-22-23

In 2021, the U.S. ranked fourth for the largest natural gas reserves, behind Russia, Iran, and Qatar that together have six times as much reserves as the U.S.

Proved reserves of natural gas are the estimated quantities that analysis of geological and engineering data demonstrate with reasonable certainty to be recoverable in future years from reservoirs under existing economic and operating conditions.

Data for the United States are from the U.S. Energy Information Administration and are as of December 31 of the previous full year. Data for other countries are from the *Oil & Gas Journal* and are as of January 1 of current year.

Reserve estimates for natural gas are very difficult to develop. As a convenience to the public, EIA provides these natural gas reserve estimates from other sources, but it does not certify these data. Please carefully note the sources of the data when using and citing estimates of natural gas reserves. Data for Kuwait and for Saudi Arabia each include one-half of the reserves in the Neutral Zone. Similar allocations may exist for areas with joint production agreements.

193 United Nations Members, March 2024

International Memberships: (1) = G20 member (2) = OECD member   (3) = NATO member

Freedom House Assessment: | Free | | Not Free | | *Partly Free* |

Afghanistan	Dominica	Libya	San Marino
Albania (3)	Dominican Republic	Liechtenstein	São Tomé and Principe
Algeria	Ecuador	Lithuania (2) (3)	Saudi Arabia (1)
Andorra	Egypt	Luxembourg (3)	Senegal
Angola	El Salvador	Madagascar	Serbia
Antigua and Barbuda	Equatorial Guinea	Malawi	Seychelles
Argentina (1)	Eritrea	Malaysia	Sierra Leone
Armenia	Estonia (2) (3)	Maldives	Singapore
Australia (1) (2)	Eswatini	Mali	Slovakia (2) (3)
Austria (2)	Ethiopia	Malta	Slovenia (2) (3)
Azerbaijan	Fiji	Marshall Islands	Solomon Islands
Bahamas	Finland (2) (3)	Mauritania	Somalia
Bahrain	France (1) (2) (3)	Mauritius	South Africa (1)
Bangladesh	Gabon	Mexico (1) (2)	South Korea (1) (2)
Barbados	Gambia	Micronesia	South Sudan
Belarus	Georgia	Moldova	Spain (2) (3)
Belgium (2) (3)	Germany (1) (2) (3)	Monaco	Sri Lanka
Belize	Ghana	Mongolia	St. Kitts and Nevis
Benin	Greece (2) (3)	Montenegro (3)	St. Lucia
Bhutan	Grenada	Morocco	St. Vincent and the Grenadines
Bolivia	Guatemala	Mozambique	Sudan
Bosnia and Herzegovina	Guinea	Myanmar	Suriname
Botswana	Guinea-Bissau	Namibia	Sweden (2) (3)
Brazil (1)	Guyana	Nauru	Switzerland (2)
Brunei	Haiti	Nepal	Syria
Bulgaria (3)	Honduras	Netherlands (2) (3)	Tajikistan
Burkina Faso	Hungary (2) (3)	New Zealand (2)	Tanzania
Burundi	Iceland (2) (3)	Nicaragua	Thailand
Cabo Verde	India (1)	Niger	Timor-Leste
Cambodia	Indonesia (1)	Nigeria	Togo
Cameroon	Iran	North Korea	Tonga
Canada (1) (2) (3)	Iraq	North Macedonia (3)	Trinidad and Tobago
Central African Republic	Ireland (2)	Norway (2) (3)	Tunisia
Chad	Israel (2)	Oman	Turkiye (1) (2) (3)
Chile (2)	Italy (1) (2) (3)	Pakistan	Turkmenistan
China (1)	Jamaica	Palau	Tuvalu
Colombia (2)	Japan (1) (2)	Panama	Uganda
Comoros	Jordan	Papua New Guinea	Ukraine
Congo (Brazzaville)	Kazakhstan	Paraguay	United Arab Emirates
Congo (Kinshasa)	Kenya	Peru	United Kingdom (1) (2) (3)
Costa Rica (2)	Kiribati	Philippines	United States (1) (2) (3)
Cote d'Ivoire	Kuwait	Poland (2) (3)	Uruguay
Croatia (3)	Kyrgyzstan	Portugal (2) (3)	Uzbekistan
Cuba	Laos	Qatar	Vanuatu
Cyprus	Latvia (2) (3)	Romania (3)	Venezuela
Czechia (2) (3)	Lebanon	Russia (1)	Vietnam
Denmark (2) (3)	Lesotho	Rwanda	Yemen
Djibouti	Liberia	Samoa	Zambia
			Zimbabwe

Source: Freedom House, https://freedomhouse.org/countries/freedom-world/scores, accessed on 10-10-23

Appendix I: U.N. Members (continued)

U.N. Resolution Vote on February 23, 2023, for Russia to withdraw from Ukraine:

In Favor	**Against**	*Abstained*	Did Not Vote

Afghanistan	Dominica	Libya	San Marino
Albania	Dominican Republic	Liechtenstein	São Tomé and Principe
Algeria	Ecuador	Lithuania	Saudi Arabia
Andorra	Egypt	Luxembourg	Senegal
Angola	**El Salvador**	Madagascar	Serbia
Antigua and Barbuda	Equatorial Guinea	Malawi	Seychelles
Argentina	Eritrea	Malaysia	Sierra Leone
Armenia	Estonia	Maldives	Singapore
Australia	Eswatini	**Mali**	Slovakia
Austria	**Ethiopia**	Malta	Slovenia
Azerbaijan	Fiji	Marshall Islands	Solomon Islands
Bahamas	Finland	Mauritania	Somalia
Bahrain	France	Mauritius	**South Africa**
Bangladesh	**Gabon**	Mexico	South Korea
Barbados	Gambia	Micronesia	South Sudan
Belarus	Georgia	Moldova	Spain
Belgium	Germany	Monaco	**Sri Lanka**
Belize	Ghana	**Mongolia**	St. Kitts and Nevis
Benin	Greece	Montenegro	St. Lucia
Bhutan	Grenada	Morocco	St. Vincent and the Grenadines
Bolivia	Guatemala	**Mozambique**	**Sudan**
Bosnia and Herzegovina	**Guinea**	Myanmar	Suriname
Botswana	Guinea-Bissau	**Namibia**	Sweden
Brazil	Guyana	Nauru	Switzerland
Brunei	Haiti	Nepal	**Syria**
Bulgaria	Honduras	Netherlands	**Tajikistan**
Burkina Faso	Hungary	New Zealand	Tanzania
Burundi	Iceland	**Nicaragua**	Thailand
Cabo Verde	**India**	Niger	Timor-Leste
Cambodia	Indonesia	Nigeria	**Togo**
Cameroon	**Iran**	**North Korea**	Tonga
Canada	Iraq	North Macedonia	Trinidad and Tobago
Central African Republic	Ireland	Norway	Tunisia
Chad	Israel	Oman	Turkiye
Chile	Italy	**Pakistan**	Turkmenistan
China	Jamaica	Palau	Tuvalu
Colombia	Japan	Panama	**Uganda**
Comoros	Jordan	Papua New Guinea	Ukraine
Congo (Brazzaville)	**Kazakhstan**	Paraguay	United Arab Emirates
Congo (Kinshasa)	Kenya	Peru	United Kingdom
Costa Rica	Kiribati	Philippines	United States
Cote d'Ivoire	Kuwait	Poland	Uruguay
Croatia	**Kyrgyzstan**	Portugal	**Uzbekistan**
Cuba	**Laos**	Qatar	Vanuatu
Cyprus	Latvia	Romania	Venezuela
Czechia	Lebanon	**Russia**	**Vietnam**
Denmark	Lesotho	Rwanda	Yemen
Djibouti	Liberia	Samoa	Zambia
			Zimbabwe

Appendix I: U.N. Members (continued)

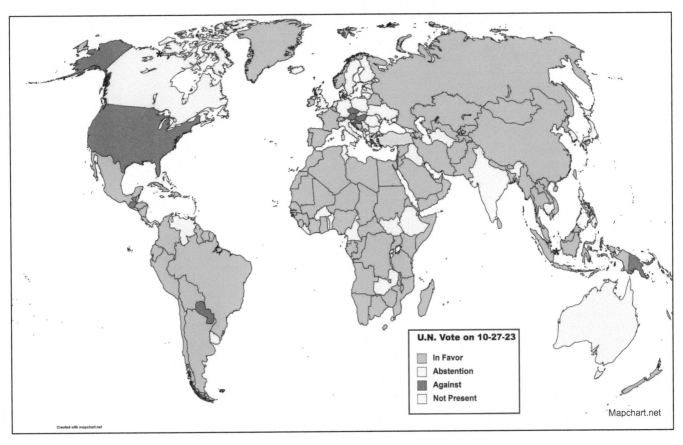

Source: United Nations, https://news.un.org/en/story/2023/10/1142932

World Map Showing U.N. Resolution Vote on October 27, 2023
(for Humanitarian Truce in Gaza)

Israel and Hamas were at war after the Palestinian militant group (Hamas) launched surprise cross-border raids from Gaza into Israel on October 7, 2023, killing more than 1,200 civilians and taking hundreds of hostages. Subsequently, the U.N. Security Council voted on multiple occasions for cessation of hostilities to enable humanitarian aid to reach the Palestinian civilians, however, as of February 2024, these resolutions were vetoed by the U.S.—the only permanent member of the Security Council to do so.

Also, on October 27th, the U.N. General Assembly held a vote calling for an "*immediate, durable and sustained humanitarian truce leading to a cessation of hostilities.*" Of the 179 General Assembly members that participated in the vote only 14 nations—including the U.S—voted "Against" the resolution. None of the eight principal U.S. partners voted "Against" the resolution.

U.N. Vote on October 27, 2023, for "*Humanitarian Truce*" in Gaza Crisis

General Assembly Vote: | In Favor | **Against** | Abstained | *Not Present*

Afghanistan	Dominica	Libya	San Marino
Albania	Dominican Republic	Liechtenstein	São Tomé and Principe
Algeria	Ecuador	**Lithuania**	Saudi Arabia
Andorra	Egypt	Luxembourg	Senegal
Angola	El Salvador	Madagascar	**Serbia**
Antigua and Barbuda	Equatorial Guinea	**Malawi**	*Seychelles*
Argentina	Eritrea	Malaysia	Sierra Leone
Armenia	**Estonia**	Maldives	Singapore
Australia	*Eswatini*	Mali	**Slovakia**
Austria	**Ethiopia**	Malta	Slovenia
Azerbaijan	**Fiji**	**Marshall Islands**	Solomon Islands
Bahamas	**Finland**	Mauritania	Somalia
Bahrain	France	Mauritius	South Africa
Bangladesh	Gabon	Mexico	**South Korea**
Barbados	Gambia	**Micronesia**	**South Sudan**
Belarus	**Georgia**	**Moldova**	Spain
Belgium	**Germany**	**Monaco**	Sri Lanka
Belize	Ghana	Mongolia	St. Kitts and Nevis
Benin	**Greece**	Montenegro	St. Lucia
Bhutan	Grenada	Morocco	St. Vincent and the Grenadines
Bolivia	**Guatemala**	Mozambique	Sudan
Bosnia and Herzegovina	Guinea	Myanmar	Suriname
Botswana	Guinea-Bissau	Namibia	**Sweden**
Brazil	Guyana	**Nauru**	Switzerland
Brunei	**Haiti**	Nepal	Syria
Bulgaria	Honduras	**Netherlands**	Tajikistan
Burkina Faso	**Hungary**	New Zealand	Tanzania
Burundi	**Iceland**	Nicaragua	Thailand
Cabo Verde	**India**	Niger	Timor-Leste
Cambodia	Indonesia	Nigeria	*Togo*
Cameroon	Iran	North Korea	**Tonga**
Canada	**Iraq**	**North Macedonia**	Trinidad and Tobago
Central African Republic	Ireland	Norway	**Tunisia**
Chad	**Israel**	Oman	Turkiye
Chile	**Italy**	Pakistan	*Turkmenistan*
China	*Jamaica*	**Palau**	**Tuvalu**
Colombia	**Japan**	**Panama**	Uganda
Comoros	Jordan	**Papua New Guinea**	**Ukraine**
Congo (Brazzaville)	Kazakhstan	**Paraguay**	United Arab Emirates
Congo (Kinshasa)	Kenya	**Peru**	**United Kingdom**
Costa Rica	**Kiribati**	**Philippines**	United States
Cote d'Ivoire	Kuwait	Poland	**Uruguay**
Croatia	Kyrgyzstan	Portugal	Uzbekistan
Cuba	Laos	Qatar	**Vanuatu**
Cyprus	**Latvia**	**Romania**	*Venezuela*
Czechia	Lebanon	Russia	Vietnam
Denmark	Lesotho	*Rwanda*	Yemen
Djibouti	*Liberia*	*Samoa*	**Zambia**
			Zimbabwe

Source: United Nations, https://news.un.org/en/story/2023/10/1142932

G20*** Members' Portion of World

(19 nations plus the European Union)

G20 members account for 86 percent of global GDP, 62 percent of the world's population, 61 percent of the world's land area, and 76 percent of world trade. Three members have poverty levels above the world's average, and five have a GDP per capita below the world's average.

G20 Members' Percent of World in 2021

	GDP	Population	Surface Area	Trade
Reference page #	*page 137*	*page 29*	*page 21*	*page 169*
Argentina	0.50%	0.58%	2.06%	0.29%
Australia§	1.61%	0.33%	5.75%	1.13%
Brazil	1.67%	2.72%	6.32%	1.16%
Canada§*	2.06%	0.48%	7.34%	2.24%
China	18.37%	17.90%	7.13%	12.18%
France§*	3.06%	0.86%	0.41%	3.30%
Germany§*	4.41%	1.05%	0.27%	6.93%
India	3.29%	17.84%	2.44%	2.64%
Indonesia	1.23%	3.47%	1.42%	0.88%
Italy§*	2.18%	0.75%	0.22%	2.43%
Japan§	5.12%	1.59%	0.28%	3.38%
Mexico§	1.32%	1.61%	1.46%	1.95%
Russia	1.84%	1.82%	12.70%	1.70%
Saudi Arabia	0.86%	0.46%	1.60%	0.90%
South Africa	0.43%	0.75%	0.91%	0.43%
South Korea§	1.88%	0.66%	0.07%	2.67%
Turkiye§*	0.85%	1.07%	0.58%	1.06%
United Kingdom§*	3.24%	0.85%	0.18%	3.25%
United States§*	24.15%	4.21%	7.30%	10.89%
European Union**	17.80%	5.68%	3.16%	29.22%
Total Percent**	86.23%	62.02%	60.70%	76.14%

** *The European Union membership includes Germany, France and Italy that are also individually G20 members as shown above. The total percentages shown do not double count these countries.*

Source: The World Bank, https://databank.worldbank.org/source/world-development-indicators, NY.GDP.MKTP.CD, https://data.worldbank.org/summary-terms-of-use

* also NATO member   § also OECD member

*** In September 2023, the G20 turned into the G21 when the African Union (AU) became a permanent member which marked the first expansion of the group since its formation as a group of 20 major economies in 1999. The AU is a continental body consisting of the 55 member states that make up the nations of the African continent. It was officially launched in 2002, as a successor to the Organization of African Unity (OAU).

<u>G20 Members' Population Wealth in 2021</u>

		GDP per Capita	% Below Poverty Level
	Reference page #	*page 147*	*page 226*
	Argentina	$10,600	14.1%
3	**Australia**	$60,400	1.0%
2	**Brazil**	$7,500	18.7%
3	**Canada**	$52,000	1.0%
	China	$12,600	24.7%
3	**France**	$43,700	0.2%
3	**Germany**	$51,200	0.2%
1, 2	**India**	$2,300	83.8%
1, 2	**Indonesia**	$4,300	60.1%
3	**Italy**	$35,700	3.1%
3	**Japan**	$39,300	1.4%
2	**Mexico**	$10,100	32.5%
	Russia	$12,200	4.1%
	Saudi Arabia	$23,200	?
1, 2	**South Africa**	$7,100	61.6%
3	**South Korea**	$35,000	1.5%
2	**Turkiye**	$9,700	12.4%
3	**United Kingdom**	$46,500	0.8%
3	**United States**	$70,200	2.0%
	European Union average	$38,400	
	World average	$12,200	46.9%

Source: The World Bank, https://databank.worldbank.org/source/world-development-indicators, NY.GDP.MKTP.CD, https://data.worldbank.org/summary-terms-of-use

three members with poverty levels above the world's average:
(1) India, Indonesia and South Africa

six members with GDP per capita below the world's average:
(2) Brazil, India, Indonesia, Mexico, South Africa, and Turkiye

nine members among the world's top 27 GDP-per-capita nations:
(3) Australia, Canada, France, Germany, Italy, Japan, South Korea, the U.K., and the U.S

38 OECD Members, March 2024

Organization for Economic Cooperation and Development (OECD)
Members' percent of world's GDP in 2021

Australia*	1.61%	Japan*	5.12%
Austria	0.50%	Latvia	0.04%
Belgium	0.62%	Lithuania	0.07%
Canada*	2.06%	Luxembourg	0.09%
Chile	0.33%	Mexico	1.32%
Colombia	0.33%	Netherlands	1.05%
Costa Rica	0.07%	New Zealand	0.26%
Czechia	0.29%	Norway	0.50%
Denmark	0.41%	Poland	0.70%
Estonia	0.04%	Portugal	0.26%
Finland	0.31%	Slovakia	0.12%
France*	3.06%	Slovenia	0.06%
Germany*	4.41%	South Korea*	1.88%
Greece	0.22%	Spain	1.48%
Hungary	0.19%	Sweden	0.66%
Iceland	0.03%	Switzerland	0.83%
Ireland	0.52%	Turkiye*	0.85%
Israel	0.51%	United Kingdom*	3.24%
Italy*	2.18%	United States*	24.15%

Source: The World Bank, https://databank.worldbank.org/source/world-development-indicators, NY.GDP.MKTP.CD, https://data.worldbank.org/summary-terms-of-use

* also G20 member

In 2021, the 38 OECD members accounted for 60.4 percent of the world's GDP.

32 NATO Members, March 2024

32 NATO Members

Member	Military Personnel	Member	Military Personnel
Albania	6,800	Lithuania*	21,000
Belgium*	26,000	Luxembourg*	900
Bulgaria	25,000	Montenegro	1,600
Canada*¥	72,000	Netherlands*	41,000
Croatia	15,000	North Macedonia	7,200
Czechia	26,000	Norway*	20,000
Denmark*	17,000	Poland*	123,000
Estonia*	6,300	Portugal*	30,000
Finland*	27,000	Romania	69,000
France*¥	208,000	Slovakia*	13,000
Germany*¥	184,000	Slovenia*	6,800
Greece*	105,000	Spain*	121,000
Hungary*	20,000	Sweden*	24,000
Iceland*	0	Turkiye*¥ United	435,000
Italy*¥	179,000	Kingdom*¥	144,000
Latvia*	6,400	United States*¥	1,338,000

Total Military Personnel = 3,319,000 in 2021

Source: The World Bank, https://databank.worldbank.org/source/world-development-indicators, MS.MIL.TOTL.P1, accessed 8-15-23, https://data.worldbank.org/summary-terms-of-use

* also OECD member   ¥ also G20 member

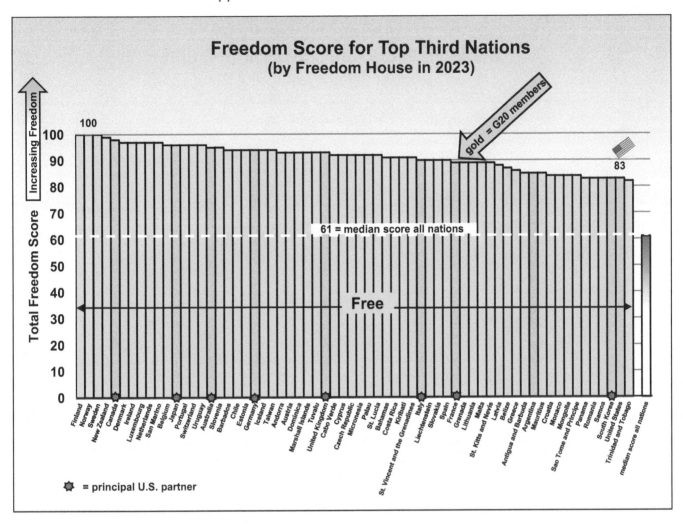

Freedom Score for Top Third Nations
(by Freedom House in 2023)

Source: Freedom House, https://freedomhouse.org/countries/freedom-world/scores, accessed on 5-1-23 with permission

In 2023, Freedom House rated 82 sovereign nations as "Free":

Andorra	Dominica	Luxembourg	Slovakia
Antigua and Barbuda	Ecuador	Malta	Slovenia
Argentina	Estonia	Marshall Islands	Solomon Islands
Australia ✪	Finland	Mauritius Micronesia	South Africa
Austria	France ✪	Monaco	South Korea ✪
Bahamas	Germany ✪	Mongolia	Spain
Barbados	Ghana	Namibia	St. Kitts and Nevis
Belgium	Greece	Nauru	St. Lucia
Belize	Grenada	Netherlands	St. Vincent and the Grenadines
Botswana	Guyana	New Zealand Norway	Suriname
Brazil	Iceland	Palau	Sweden
Bulgaria	Ireland	Panama	Switzerland
Cabo Verde	Israel	Poland	Timor-Leste
Canada ✪	Italy ✪	Portugal	Tonga
Chile	Jamaica	Romania	Trinidad and Tobago
Colombia	Japan ✪	Samoa	Tuvalu
Costa Rica	Kiribati	San Marino	United Kingdom ✪
Croatia	Latvia	São Tomé and Principe	United States
Cyprus	Lesotho	Seychelles	Uruguay
Czech Republic	Liechtenstein		Vanuatu
Denmark	Lithuania		

Appendix V: Freedom House Scores (continued)

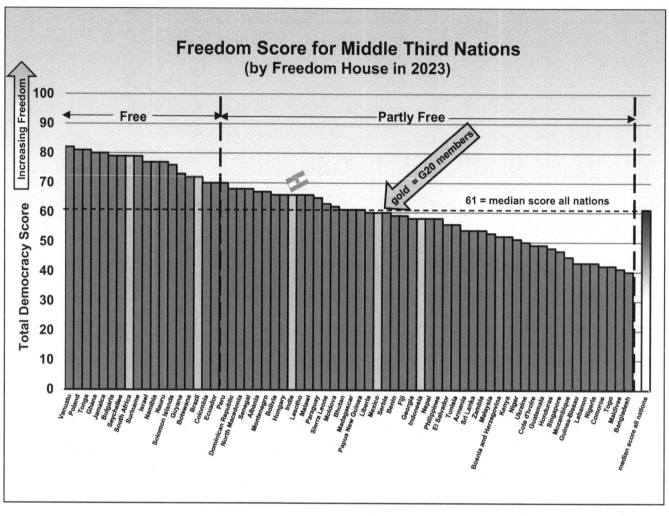

Source: Freedom House, https://freedomhouse.org/countries/freedom-world/scores, accessed on 5-1-23 with permission

In 2023, Freedom House rated 52 sovereign nations as "Partly Free":

Albania	Guatemala	Maldives	Paraguay
Armenia	Guinea-Bissau	Mauritania	Peru
Bangladesh	Honduras	Mexico	Philippines
Benin	Hungary	Moldova	Senegal
Bhutan	India	Montenegro	Serbia
Bolivia	Indonesia	Morocco	Sierra Leone
Bosnia and Herzegovina	Kenya	Mozambique	Singapore
Comoros	Kuwait	Nepal	Sri Lanka
Cote d'Ivoire	Lebanon	Niger	Tanzania
Dominican Republic	Liberia	Nigeria	Togo
El Salvador	Madagascar	North Macedonia	Tunisia
Fiji	Malawi	Pakistan	Ukraine
Georgia	Malaysia	Papua New Guinea	Zambia

Appendix V: Freedom House Scores (continued)

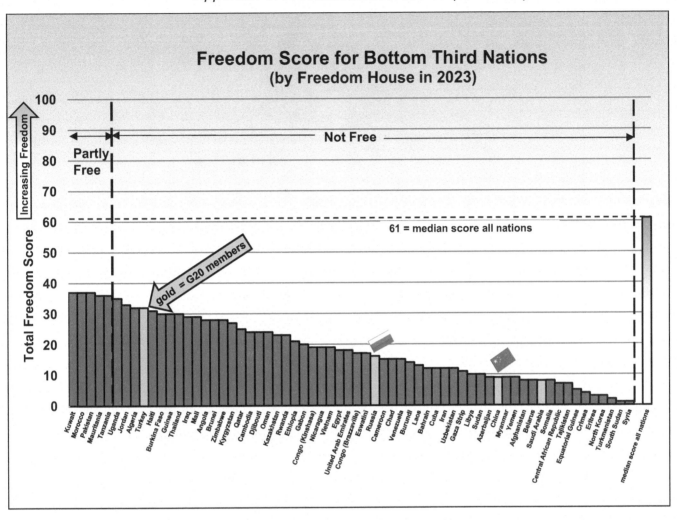

Freedom Score for Bottom Third Nations
(by Freedom House in 2023)

In 2023, Freedom House rated 59 sovereign nations as "Not Free":

Afghanistan	Congo (Kinshasa)	Jordan	South Sudan
Algeria	Crimea	Kazakhstan	Sudan
Angola	Cuba	Kyrgyzstan	Syria
Azerbaijan	Djibouti	Laos	Tajikistan
Bahrain	Egypt	Libya	Thailand
Belarus	Equatorial Guinea	Mali	Turkey
Brunei	Eritrea	Myanmar	Turkmenistan
Burkina Faso	Eswatini	Nicaragua	Uganda
Burundi	Ethiopia	North Korea	United Arab Emirates
Cambodia	Gabon	Oman	Uzbekistan
Cameroon	Gaza Strip	Qatar	Venezuela
Central African Republic	Guinea	Russia	Vietnam
Chad	Haiti	Rwanda	Yemen
China	Iran	Saudi Arabia	Zimbabwe
Congo (Brazzaville)	Iraq	Somalia	

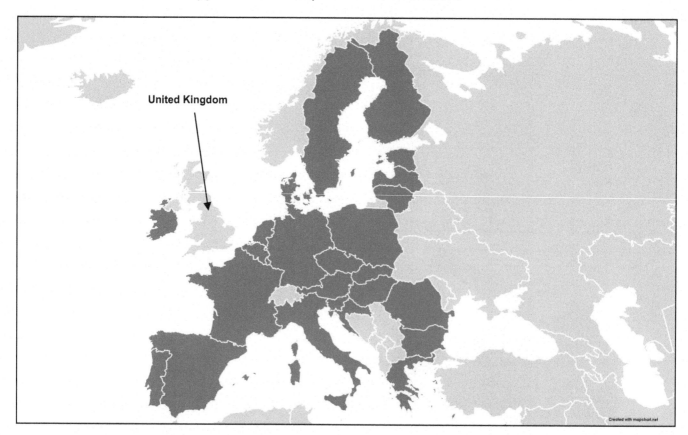

Map Showing European Union (E.U.) Members in March 2024

Source: European Union, https://www.europarl.europa.eu/meps/en/home

In March 2024, the E.U. consisted of 27 of the 45 European countries. (In 2020, the United Kingdom withdrew from the E.U.) In 2021, the GDP for the E.U. was 73.3% as large as the U.S. GDP. The security of E.U. and NATO are inter-connected; 23 E.U. member states were also NATO members in 2023. The aims of the E.U. within its borders are: promote peace, its values and the well-being of its citizens, offer freedom, security and justice without internal borders, while also taking appropriate measures at its external borders to regulate asylum and immigration and prevent and combat crime.

European Union (E.U.) Members

Austria	Ireland
Belgium	Italy*
Bulgaria	Latvia
Croatia	Lithuania
Cyprus	Luxembourg
Czechia	Malta
Denmark	Netherlands
Estonia	Poland
Finland	Portugal
France*	Romania
Germany*	Slovakia
Greece	Slovenia
Hungary	Spain
	Sweden

* the E.U., France, Germany, and Italy are members of the G20

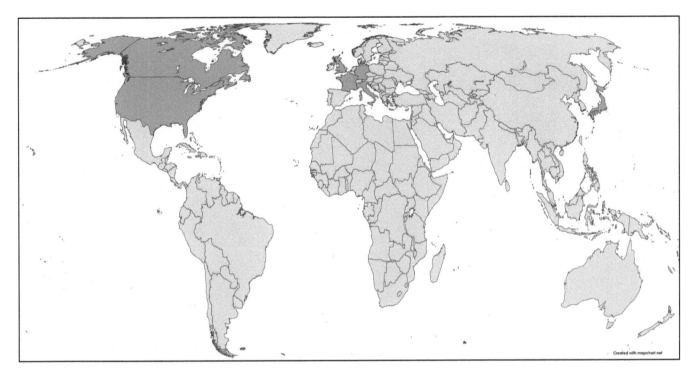

World Map Showing G7 Members in March 2024

The G7 is an informal grouping of advanced non-communist powers, formed in 1975, to coordinate global economic policy and address other transnational issues. During World War II, these same Group of Seven (G7) nations were actually either an Ally nation or an Axis nation. Canada was not an Ally but supported the Allies during the World War II.

In 1998, Russia was invited to join the group creating the G8. However, in March 2014, the G7 suspended Russia's membership in the group, due to Russia's annexation of Crimea. All G7 members are also members of the G20 and the Organization for Economic Cooperation and Development (OECD). With the exception of Japan all G7 members are members of NATO. Japan has a bilateral defense agreement with the U.S. These seven nations plus Australia and South Korea are principal U.S. partners.

G7 Member's Percent of World in 2021

	GDP	Population	Surface Area	Exports
Canada	2.06%	0.48%	7.34%	2.21%
France	3.06%	0.86%	0.41%	3.47%
Germany	4.41%	1.05%	0.27%	7.23%
Italy	2.18%	0.75%	0.22%	2.51%
Japan	5.12%	1.59%	0.28%	3.59%
United Kingdom	3.24%	0.85%	0.18%	3.87%
United States	24.15%	4.21%	7.30%	10.11%
total	44.24%	9.80%	16.00%	32.98%

Source: The World Bank, https://databank.worldbank.org/source/world-development-indicators, AG.SRF.TOTL.K2, https://data.worldbank.org/summary-terms-of-use

---

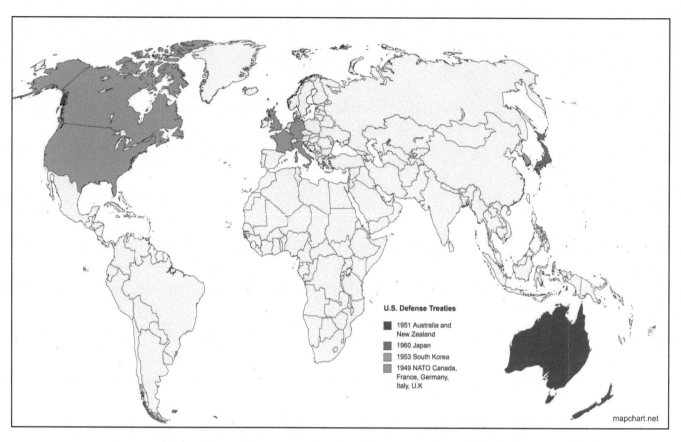

Eight Principal U.S. Partners in March 2024

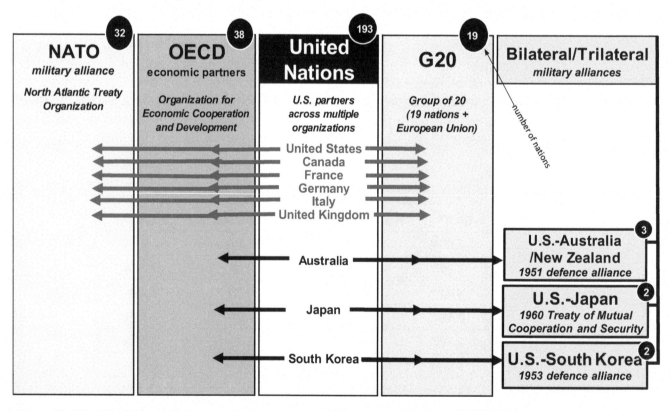

Source: The World Bank, https://databank.worldbank.org/source/world-development-indicators, AG.SRF.TOTL.K2, accessed September 1, 2023 https://data.worldbank.org/summary-terms-of-use

Appendix VIII: Principal U.S. Partners (continued)

<u>Eight Principal U.S. Partners</u>

In March 2024 there were eight nations that had a unique relationship with the U.S. Together, with the U.S., they are the only nations that met the following five conditions:

1. Economic partner with the U.S. as OECD member
2. Defense partner with the U.S. as member of NATO or with Bilateral agreement
3. Voted "In Favor" of the U.N. resolution that Russia withdraw from Ukraine
4. Classified as "Free" by Freedom House
5. One of the top nine G20 members based on income per capita

These nations are:

Australia, Canada, France, Germany, Italy, Japan, South Korea, and the U.K.

> (Note that Turkiye satisfied the first three conditions, however, Turkiye was classified as "Not Free" by Freedom House, and Turkiye's national income per capita of $10,700 was 60 percent below the G20 average.)

Seven of these nations made up the G7 (group of seven—see page 319). In addition to the G7 nations Australia and South Korea also meet all five conditions and combined with the G7 are considered the principal U.S. partners.

In 2021, these eight nations had a combined population of 522 million and accounted for 23.6 percent of the world's GDP. When combined with the U.S. these nine "Free" nations accounted for 47.7 percent of the world's GDP while their combined population constituted 10.8 percent of the world's total population. Collectively they exported 37.4 percent of all goods and services in the world. The average gross national income per capita for all nine nations in 2021 was $44,000.

In 2021, the average life expectancy for newborn males among these eight principal U.S. partners was 6.6 years greater than those born in the U.S. and 5.8 years greater for female newborns.

Military Assessment of Principal U.S. Partners

Source: Central Intelligence Agency (CIA), World Factbook, 2022-2023

Australia

Australia has been part of the Australia, New Zealand, and U.S. Security (ANZUS) Treaty since 1951; Australia is also a member of the Five Powers Defense Arrangements (FPDA), a series of mutual assistance agreements reached in 1971, embracing Australia, Malaysia, New Zealand, Singapore, and the U.K.; the FPDA commits the members to consult with one another in the event or threat of an armed attack on any of the members and to mutually decide what measures should be taken, jointly or separately; there is no specific obligation to intervene militarily.

Australia has a long-standing military relationship with the U.S.; Australian and U.S. forces first fought together in France in 1918, at the Battle of Hamel, and have fought together in every major U.S. conflict since; Australia and the U.S. signed an agreement in 2014, that allowed for closer bilateral defense and security cooperation, including annual rotations of U.S. Marines and enhanced rotations of U.S. Air Force aircraft to Australia; Australian military forces train often with U.S. forces; Australia has Major Non-NATO Ally (MNNA) status with the U.S., a designation under U.S. law that provides foreign partners with certain benefits in the areas of defense trade and security cooperation.

Australia also has long-standing defense and security ties to the U.K., including a Defense and Security Cooperation Treaty signed in 2013; in 2020, Australia and the U.K. signed a memorandum of understanding to cooperate on the building of a next generation of frigates for their respective navies; the Australia-U.K. Ministerial Consultations (AUKMIN) is their premier bilateral forum on foreign policy, defense, and security issues

in 2021, Australia, the U.K., and the U.S. announced an enhanced trilateral security partnership called "AUKUS" which would build on existing bilateral ties, including deeper integration of defense and security-related science, technology, industrial bases, and supply chains, as well as deeper cooperation on a range of defense and security capabilities; the first initiative under AUKUS was a commitment to support Australia in acquiring conventionally armed nuclear-powered submarines for the Royal Australian Navy.

The ADF is an experienced and professional force equipped with modern weapons; its missions include protecting Australia's borders and maritime interests, responding to domestic natural disasters, and deploying overseas for humanitarian, peacekeeping, and other security-related missions; it trains regularly and participates in international exercises; the Army's principal combat forces include a divisional headquarters with three mechanized brigades and a special operations command; the Navy operates over 40 surface craft and submarines, including 11 destroyers and frigates, two landing helicopter dock (LHD) amphibious assault ships, and six attack-type submarines; the RAF has an air combat group with more than 140 modern combat aircraft, as well as transport and surveillance air groups (2023).

Canada

The Canadian Armed Forces (CAF) are a professional volunteer force responsible for external security; the CAF's core missions include detecting, deterring, and defending against threats to or attacks on Canada; the military also provides assistance to civil authorities and law enforcement as needed for such missions as counterterrorism, search and rescue, and responding to natural disasters or other major emergencies; it regularly participates in bilateral and multinational training exercises with a variety of partners, including NATO (Canada is one of the original members) and the U.S.; the CAF also contributes to international peacekeeping, stability, humanitarian, combat, and capacity building operations with the U.N., NATO, and other security partners.

The Canadian Joint Operations Command (CJOC) plans, directs, and leads most CAF operations in Canada, North America, and around the world; it has six standing regional Joint Task Force (JTF) headquarters across Canada, as well as other JTFs deployed overseas; the CJOC is assisted by air, ground, and naval components; the Canadian Army is the land component of the CAF and its largest element; it has four divisional headquarters (plus one under the CJOC), three Regular Force combined arms mechanized brigade groups, and ten brigade groups in the Reserve Force; the Navy's principal warships are 12 frigates and four attack submarines, which are supported by six Arctic/offshore patrol ships and 12 coastal defense vessels; the Air Force has over 400 fixed-wing aircraft and helicopters, including about 100 U.S.-made F/A-18 multirole fighters; Canada has ordered more than 80 U.S.-made F-35 stealth multirole fighter aircraft which the Air Force expects to start receiving in 2026; the CAF also has a separate Special Operations Forces Command with a special operations regiment and a joint task force, plus air, incident response, and training units.

Canada is part of the North American Aerospace Defense Command (NORAD; established 1958); NORAD is a Canada-U.S. binational military command responsible for monitoring and defending North American airspace; traditionally, a Canadian Armed Forces officer has served as the deputy commander of NORAD; Canada's defense relationship with the U.S. extends back to the Ogdensburg Declaration of 1940, when the two countries formally agreed on military cooperation, including the establishment of the Permanent Joint Board on Defense (PJBD), which continues to be the highest-level bilateral defense forum between Canada and the U.S.

France

France was one of the original 12 countries to sign the North Atlantic Treaty (also known as the Washington Treaty), which created NATO in 1949; in 1966, President Charles de Gaulle decided to withdraw France from NATO's integrated military structure, reflecting his desire for greater military independence, particularly vis-à-vis the U.S., and the refusal to integrate France's nuclear deterrent or accept any form of control over its armed forces; it did, however, sign agreements with NATO setting out procedures in the event of Soviet aggression. Beginning with the fall of the Berlin Wall in 1989, France distanced itself from the 1966 decision and has regularly contributed troops to NATO's military operations, being one of the largest troop-contributing states; in 2009, it officially announced its decision to fully participate in NATO structures. In 2010, France and the U.K signed a declaration on defense and security cooperation that included greater military interoperability and a Combined Joint Expeditionary Force (CJEF), a deployable, combined Anglo-French military force for use in a wide range of crisis scenarios, up to and including high-intensity combat operations; the CJEF has no standing forces, but would be available at short notice for French-U.K. bilateral, NATO, E.U., U.N., or other operations; combined training exercises began in 2011; as of 2020, the CJEF was assessed as having full operating capacity with the ability to rapidly deploy over 10,000 personnel capable of high-intensity operations, peacekeeping, disaster relief, and humanitarian assistance.

The French Foreign Legion, established in 1831, is a military force that is open to foreign recruits willing to serve in the French military for service in France and abroad; the Foreign Legion is an integrated part of the French Army and is comprised of approximately 8,000 personnel; its combat units are a mix of armored cavalry and airborne, light, mechanized, and motorized infantry regiments (2023).

Appendix VIII: Principal U.S. Partners (continued)

Germany

The Federal Republic of Germany joined NATO in May 1955; with the reunification of Germany in October 1990, the states of the former German Democratic Republic joined the Federal Republic of Germany in its membership of NATO.

The German Army has incorporated a joint Franco-German mechanized infantry brigade since 1989, a Dutch airmobile infantry brigade since 2014, and a Dutch mechanized infantry brigade since 2016; in addition, the German Navy's Sea Battalion (includes marine infantry, naval divers, reconnaissance, and security forces) has worked closely with the Dutch Marine Corps since 2016, including as a binational amphibious landing group (2023).

Italy

Italy is a member of NATO and was one of the original 12 countries to sign the North Atlantic Treaty (also known as the Washington Treaty) in 1949.

Italy is an active participant in E.U., NATO, U.N., and other multinational military, security, and humanitarian operations abroad; as of 2022, it hosted the headquarters for the E.U.'s Mediterranean naval operations force (EUNAVFOR-MED) in Rome and the U.S. Navy's sixth Fleet in Naples; Italy was admitted to the U.N. in 1955, and in 1960, participated in its first U.N. peacekeeping mission, the U.N. Operation in Congo (ONUC); since 1960, it has committed more than 60,000 troops to U.N. missions; since 2006, Italy has hosted a training center in Vicenza for police personnel destined for peacekeeping missions (2023).

Japan

Japan was disarmed after its defeat in World War II; shortly after the Korean War began in 1950, U.S. occupation forces in Japan created a 75,000-member lightly armed force called the National Police Reserve; the Japan Self-Defense Force (JSDF) was founded in 1954.

Japan's alliance with the U.S. (signed in 1951) is one of the cornerstones of the nation's security, as well as a large part of the U.S. security role in Asia; approximately 55,000 U.S. troops and other military assets, including aircraft and naval ships, are stationed in Japan and have exclusive use of more than 80 bases and facilities; in exchange for their use, the U.S. guarantees Japan's security; the Japanese government provides about $2 billion per year to offset the cost of stationing U.S. forces in Japan; in addition, it pays compensation to localities hosting U.S. troops, rent for bases, and costs for new facilities to support the U.S. presence; Japan also has Major Non-NATO Ally (MNNA) status with the U.S., a designation under U.S. law that provides foreign partners with certain benefits in the areas of defense trade and security cooperation (2023).

South Korea

The South Korean military is a professional and well-equipped force that trains regularly, including bilateral and multinational exercises; the military is primarily focused on the threat from North Korea but also deploys abroad for multinational missions, including peacekeeping and other security operations.

South Korea's primary defense partner is the U.S., and the 1953, U.S.-South Korea Mutual Defense Treaty is a cornerstone of South Korea's security; the Treaty committed the U.S. to provide assistance in the event of an attack, particularly from North Korea; in addition, the Treaty gave the U.S. permission to station land, air, and sea forces in and about the territory of South Korea as determined by mutual agreement; the U.S. maintains approximately 28,000 military personnel in the country and conducts bilateral exercises with the South Korean military; South Korea has Major Non-NATO Ally (MNNA) status with the U.S., a designation under U.S. law that provides foreign partners with certain benefits in the areas of defense trade and security cooperation; the South Korean military has assisted the U.S. in conflicts in Afghanistan (5,000 troops; 2001–2014), Iraq (20,000 troops; 2003–2008), and Vietnam (325,000 troops; 1964–1973).

South Korea has been engaged with NATO through dialogue and security cooperation since 2005, and is considered by NATO to be a global partner; in 2022, South Korea established its Mission to NATO to further institutionalize its cooperative relationship; it has participated in NATO-led missions and exercises, including leading an integrated civilian-military reconstruction team in Afghanistan as part of the NATO-led International Security Assistance Force, 2010–2013; it has also cooperated with NATO in countering the threat of piracy in the Gulf of Aden by providing naval vessels as escorts.

United Kingdom (U.K.)

The U.K. is a member of NATO and was one of the original 12 countries to sign the North Atlantic Treaty (also known as the Washington Treaty) in 1949; the U.K. is also a member of the Five Power Defense Arrangements (FPDA), a series of mutual assistance agreements reached in 1971, embracing Australia, Malaysia, New Zealand, Singapore, and the U.K.; the FPDA commits the members to consult with one another in the event or threat of an armed attack on any of the members and to mutually decide what measures should be taken, jointly or separately; there is no specific obligation to intervene militarily.

in 2010, France and the U.K. signed a declaration on defense and security cooperation that included greater military interoperability and a Combined Joint Expeditionary Force (CJEF), a deployable, combined Anglo-French military force for use in a wide range of crisis scenarios, up to and including high-intensity combat operations; the CJEF has no standing forces but would be available at short notice for U.K.-French bilateral, NATO, E.U., U.N., or other operations; combined training exercises began in 2011; as of 2020, the CJEF was assessed as having full operating capacity with the ability to rapidly deploy over 10,000 personnel capable of high-intensity operations, peacekeeping, disaster relief, and humanitarian assistance.

in 2014, the U.K. led the formation of the Joint Expeditionary Force (JEF), a pool of high-readiness military forces from Baltic and Scandinavian countries able to respond to a wide range of contingencies both in peacetime and in times of crisis or conflict; its principal geographic area of interest is the High North, North Atlantic, and Baltic Sea regions, where the JEF can complement national capabilities or NATO's deterrence posture, although it is designed to be flexible and prepared to respond to humanitarian crises further afield; the JEF consists of ten countries (Denmark, Estonia, Finland, Iceland, Latvia, Lithuania, the Netherlands, Norway, Sweden, and the U.K.) and was declared operational in 2018; most of the forces in the pool are British, and the U.K. provides the most rapidly deployable units as well as the command and control elements.

Appendix IX: BRICS Members

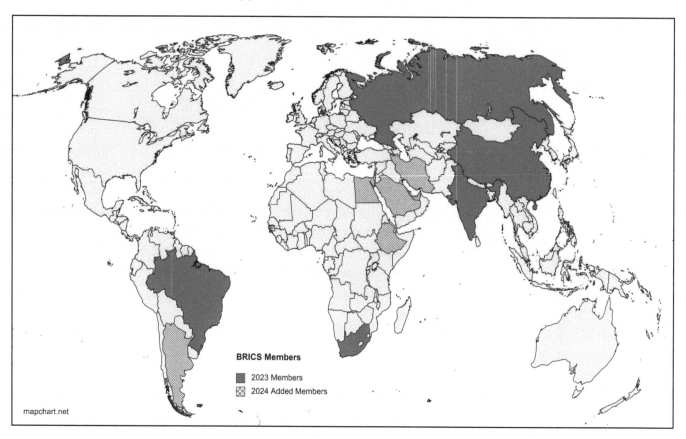

BRICS (Brazil, Russia, India, China, and South Africa)

The BRICS forum is an independent international organization encouraging commercial, political, and cultural cooperation among the BRICS nations. In 2023, the organization consisted of:

  Brazil, Russia, India, China and South Africa.

The original formation (BRIC) in 2006, did not include South Africa, which joined in 2010.

In February 2023, of these five nations only Brazil voted "In Favor" of the U.N. resolution for Russia to withdraw from Ukraine. India, China and South Africa abstained from voting and Russia voted "Against" (of course).

On August 24, 2023 six additional nations were formally invited to become members of BRICS, as of January 1, 2024, they are:

  Argentina, Egypt, Ethiopia, Iran, Saudi Arabia and the United Arab Emirates.

Appendix X: APEC Members

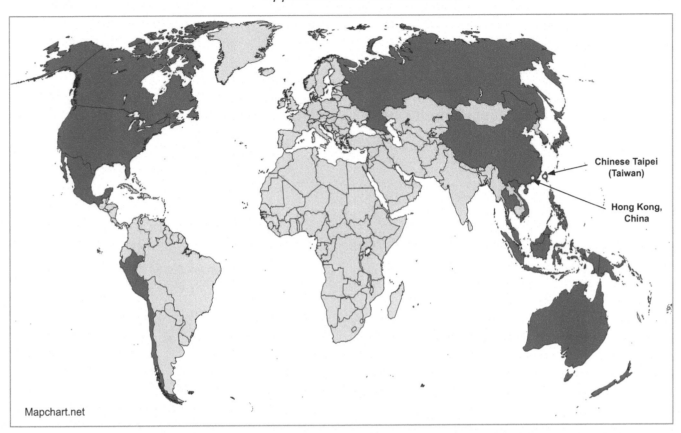

Mapchart.net

APEC (Asia-Pacific Economic Cooperation) Economies in 2024

The Asia-Pacific Economic Cooperation (APEC) is a regional economic forum established in 1989 to leverage the growing interdependence of the Asia-Pacific region. In 2024, 21 economies were members including Hong Kong and Chinese Taipei (Taiwan)—despite both not being recognized by the United Nations as sovereign nations. On November 15, 2023, Joe Biden, the President of the U.S., and China's President Xi Jinping used this as an opportunity to reopen face-to-face dialogue on many issues.

Members in 2024:

Australia	Mexico
Brunei Darussalam	New Zealand
Canada	Papua New Guinea
Chile	Peru
China	Philippines
Hong Kong, China	Russia
Indonesia	Singapore
Japan	Chinese Taipei (Taiwan)
South Korea	Thailand
Malaysia	United States
	Viet Nam

Resources

The primary data sources used to create the charts in this book are:

Resource	Website Address
Centers for Disease Control and Prevention (CDC)	www.cdc.gov/
Central Intelligence Agency (CIA)	www.cia.gov/
Congressional Report Service	crsreports.congress.gov/
Defense Security Cooperation Agency	www.dsca.mil/
Energy Information Administration (EIA)	www.eia.gov/
Federal Elections Commission	www.FEC.gov/
Federal Reserve Economic Data (FRED)	www.fred.stlouisfed.org
Foreign assistance	foreignassistance.gov
Freedom House	freedomhouse.org/
Happiness	worldhappiness.report/
Institute for Health Metrics Evaluation	www.healthdata.org/
Institute of International Education	opendoorsdata.org/
National Center for Education Statistics	nces.ed.gov/
National Highway Traffic Administration (NHTSA)	www.nhtsa.gov/
North Atlantic Treaty Organization (NATO)	www.nato.int/
Organization for Economic Cooperation and Development (OECD)	www.oecd.org/
Our World in Data	ourworldindata.org/
Stockholm International Peace Research Institute (SIPRI)	www.sipri.org/
U.S. Bureau of Economic Analysis (BEA)	www.bea.gov/
U.S. Census Bureau	www2.census.gov/
U.S. Department of State	www.state.gov
U.S. Geological Survey (USGS)	www.usgs.gov/
U.S. Treasury Department	www.fiscaldata.treasury.gov/
United Nations (U.N.)	news.un.org/
White House	https://www.whitehouse.gov/
World Bank	www.databank.worldbank.org/
World Health Organization (WHO)	www.who.int/
World Prison Brief	www.prisonstudies.org/

Index